I0763113

DALLAS

Other books by Carolyn Brown

The Historic Fort Worth Stockyards with text by J'Nell Pate

Architecture That Speaks: S. C. P. Vosper and Ten Remarkable Buildings at Texas A&M with text by Nancy T. McCoy and David G. Woodcock

Dallas Fair Park: Art Deco Forever

The Painted Tombs of Swift

Caddo: Visions of a Southern Cypress Lake with text by Thad Sitton

Dallas: Portrait of a City

Crafting Traditions: The Architecture of Mark Lemmon

Dallas: Where Dreams Come True

Dynamic Dallas

Dallas: World Class Texas (coauthor)

Houston: Simply Spectacular

Dallas: Shining Star of Texas (coauthor)

Aswan and Abu Simbel (photographs)

Upper Egypt (photographs)

DALLAS

A TEXAS STAR

Carolyn Brown

with essays by Dallas leaders

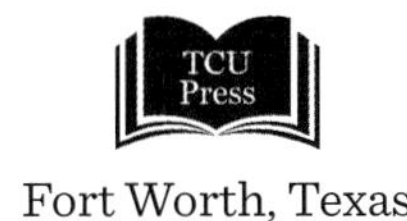

Fort Worth, Texas

Library of Congress Control Number: 2022938428

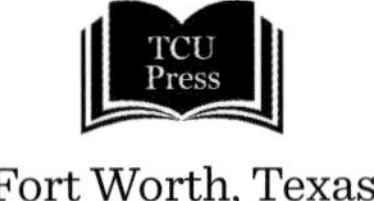

Fort Worth, Texas

TCU Box 298300
Fort Worth, Texas 76129
To order books: 1.800.826.8911

Design by Bill Brammer

Dallas: A Texas Star is dedicated
to all Dallas residents and visitors.

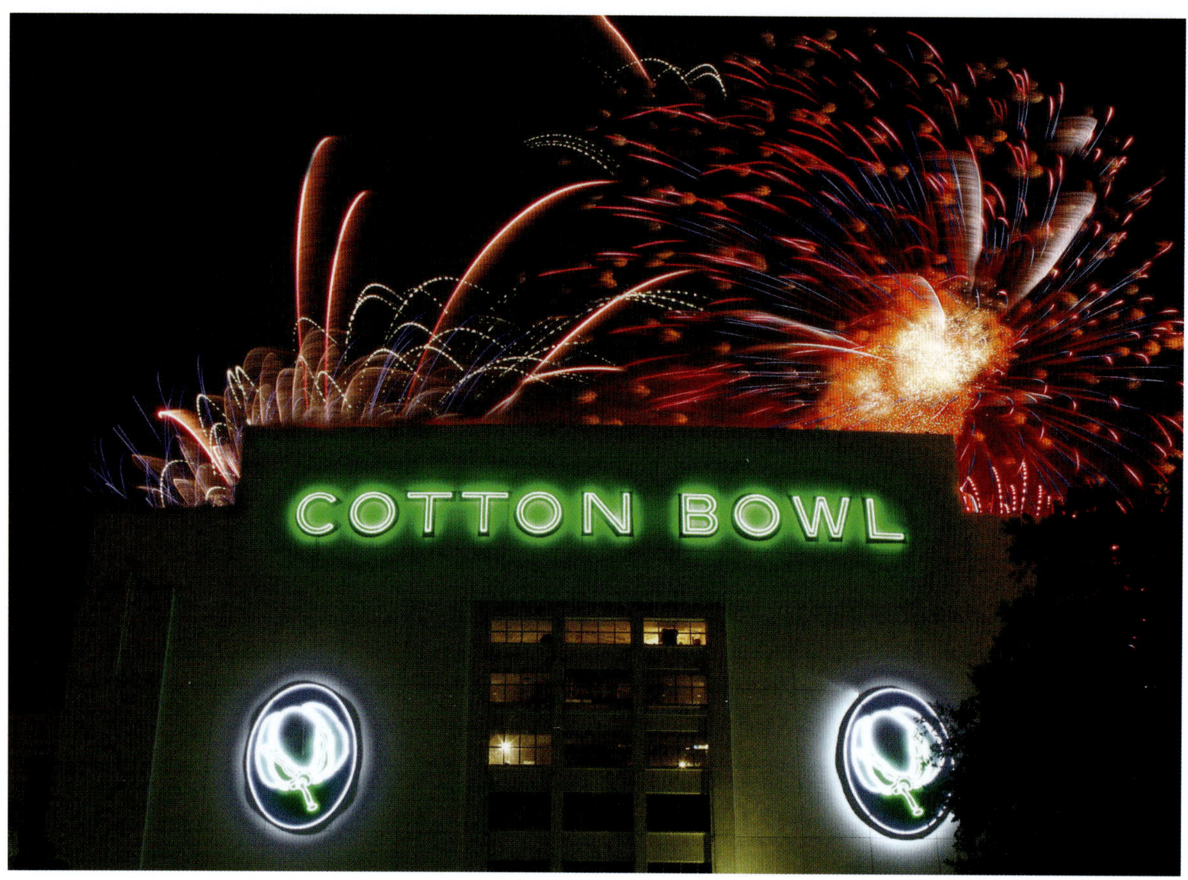

Above
The Cotton Bowl Stadium at Fair Park opened in 1930 as a 46,000-seat venue. It is the historic landmark for the annual showdown football game between the University of Texas and the University of Oklahoma, but in 2009 the annual Cotton Bowl Classic was moved to AT&T Stadium in Arlington. Fair Park Fourth features fireworks, hands-on activities, and live music every July 4.

Contents

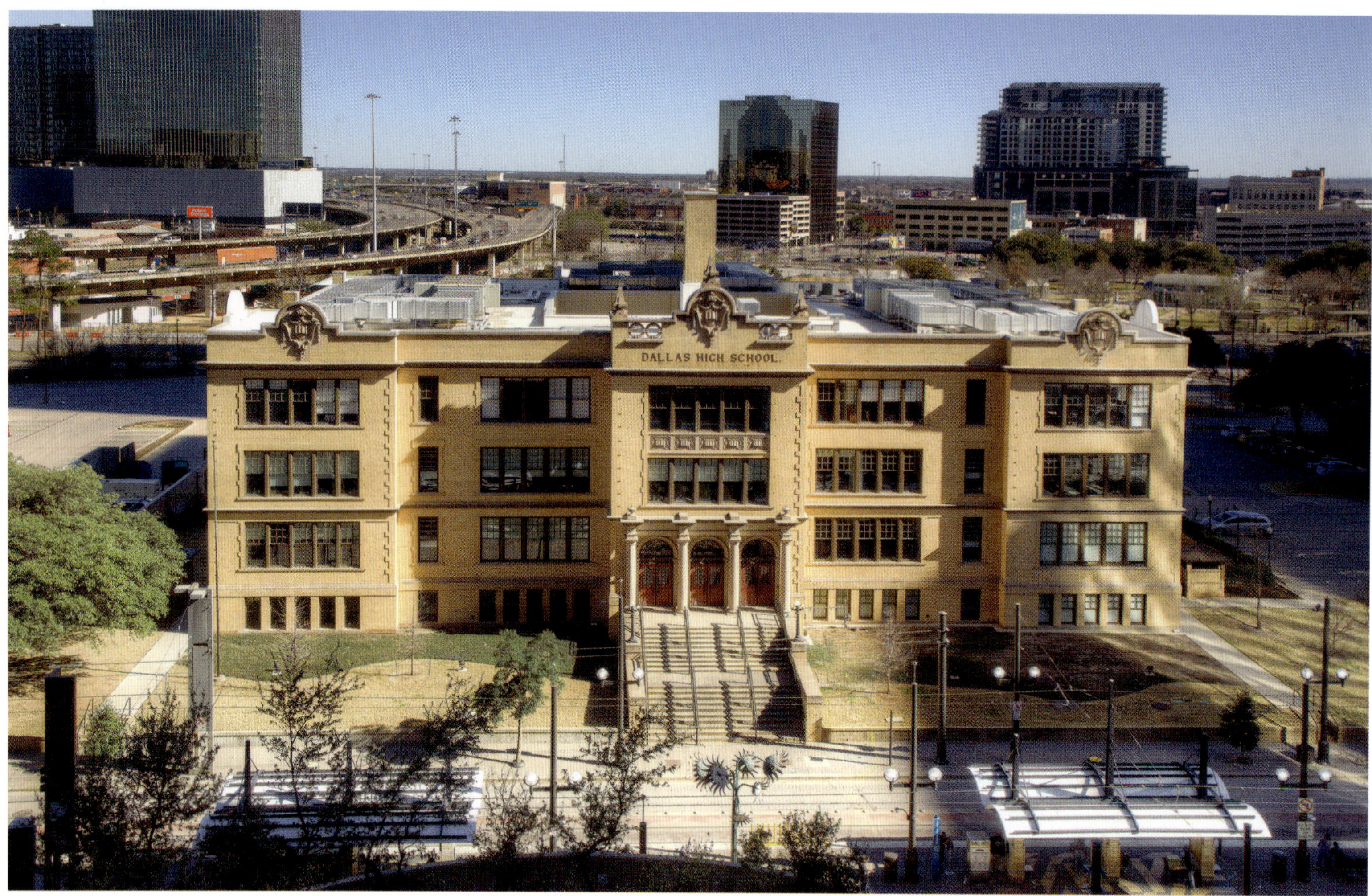

Above
View of the old Dallas High School.

Foreword

Dallas is a city of lucid dreamers.

By that, I mean the people of Dallas have always been willing to change the narrative of their city in the pursuit of lofty goals and aspirations.

After all, this city has no real reason to exist. We lack a navigable river or port. We are not located along a coastline. Our natural resources pale in comparison to those of other cities.

But through our ingenuity, our skills, and our determination, the people of Dallas have built a great city over many generations. And we are constantly building—and rebuilding—for our future.

Dallas today boasts an amazing arts and culture scene, a dynamic economy that serves as the engine for the fourth-largest region in the country, and a talented and diverse population. In fact, about 25 percent of people who live in Dallas were born in another country.

I was born and raised in Dallas. What makes that fact remarkable is that I am one of only three mayors of Dallas to be born in this city's 165-year history. That is because Dallas has long been a city that encourages renewal and attracts people from all over the country and the world. It is also a city that provides people with new opportunities to shape their lives.

Dallas is not perfect, of course. No city is. But there is something for everyone here. It is simply an exciting place to be. The glamour, the grit, the contradictions, the tension, the ambition, the drive, the history, the community spirit, the victories, and the tragedies—it's all part of a uniquely American story that is still being written every day.

I love Dallas. I hope, as you look through this book, you will understand why. Because no matter who you are—no matter if you were born here or if you got here as quickly as you could—Dallas is home, and no matter how it changes, who comes and goes, and how our dreams shift over time, it always will be.

Eric Johnson

Eric Johnson is the sixtieth mayor of Dallas, Texas, elected in June 2019. Prior to becoming mayor, Johnson served as a member of the Texas House of Representatives, where he represented the City of Dallas from April 2010 to June 2019. During his tenure in the Texas legislature, Johnson served on twenty prominent legislative committees, including Appropriations, Ways and Means, Higher Education, and Natural Resources. He also served as chairman of the Dallas Area Legislative Delegation. In addition to his service as mayor of Dallas, Johnson is an attorney and partner with the international law firm of Locke Lord.

Preface

Dallas from the Inside Out

Dallas has come a long way from its beginning nearly 170 years ago as the Three Forks trading post on the Trinity River, run by the city's founder, John Bryan. It's now one of the greatest cities in the world: sophisticated, vibrant, and friendly, it's an architectural, shopping, and medical mecca rich with successful businesses, nationally respected arts and museums, high fashion, higher education, entertainment, parks, and big-league sports teams. And it just won't stop. One learns about something new or renovated in Dallas every day—and it's got more buildings designed by Pritzker Prize-winning architects than any other place in the world.

I've been privileged to live in Dallas and photograph it for five decades, and doing so has led to more than my share of special moments. There was the thrill of standing center stage to photograph a priceless chandelier, and having my own cart and driver on the campus of one of the country's finest universities. Or of driving through parking garages looking for a high view—and sometimes being chased away by security because I had no permission. It was visiting deep, wild Africa, but with a PhD guide and a golf cart while discovering the city's own savanna at the Dallas Zoo, complete with wandering giraffes, elephants, zebras, ostriches, guinea hens, and deer.

Gear on my back, I climbed the ladder eighty-four feet inside the Parry Avenue Gate Pylon to photograph the new fountains on the Esplanade at Fair Park. With special access I climbed up another ladder five stories and through a hatch to reach the top of the Hall of State for the opposite view, toward the city: white fountains on the reflecting pool, as Dallas glowed beyond.

They won't let me on top of the buildings at Fair Park anymore, but the State Fair folks helped me photograph the new Big Tex by providing an agreeable man named Teddy and his lift. I couldn't compete with Big Tex, but fairgoers got two shows that afternoon.

Little-known sides of Dallas were revealed when I visited the Buddhist Temple and the Coptic Church as well as the Holocaust Museum, the Sixth Floor Museum, the Great Trinity Forest, and the Audubon Center; I became a tourist in my own city.

These memories, all documented with photographs, will live as long as I breathe—they represent what I love most in life. It has been a perfect way to spend my days in our splendid city.

Carolyn Brown

Introduction

Where Dreams Come True

John Neely Bryan stood on the bluff above the river. The sun was low and red, and the November wind was cool on his face. To the west the two streams became one, and the plains beyond were dotted with trees. No living thing moved within his sight. Only the water flowed slowly to the east, and it ran smooth and clear.

"Mi a ka—wash tay," *he said, and turned to the Cherokee chief called Indian Ned. "Here is the place we heard speak of, old friend. The Land of the Three Forks—"*

"Yes, I remember."

"It is a good place. We will return here to settle."

Bryan's gray pony, Neshoba, breathed noisily behind them. The Indian's sorrel raised her head and whinnied, and the brown-and-white bear dog yawned.

Bryan shouldered his rifle, a faint smile playing on his lips.

Behind them a twig cracked. Bryan turned.

Six Cherokee stood not thirty feet away. At their head was their chief Jesse Chisholm . . .

That's the beginning of the city of Dallas, not a Larry McMurtry Western. And almost every detail is true—Indian Ned, Neshoba, even the bear-hunting dog (named Tubby, after *tubbee*, a Choctaw word meaning "killer"). Jesse Chisholm, for whom the Chisholm Trail is named, was a good friend of Bryan's—fifteen years later Chisholm would provide sanctuary for Bryan after he shot a man who had insulted his wife.

The Three Forks area of Texas was Indian country long before Bryan came on the scene. Native Americans had fished its waters and hunted its deer, bear, and bison for at least forty thousand years. An ancient Indian village existed on today's Tenison Municipal Golf Course in present-day East Dallas. A "kill-site" for bison, used by Indians as long as five hundred years ago, was located on the eastern side of White Rock Lake, along with an extensive campsite at the lake's spillway. Most of these early residents were Caddo Indians, who settled along waterways in the Oklahoma-Arkansas-Texas triangle.

But there were no permanent residents of the area in early November of 1841 when Bryan left Holland Coffee's Trading Post on the Red River and ambled about one hundred miles down an Indian trail that is now Preston Road. He was an educated man, having attended college and studied law in his native Tennessee. He was also an experienced backwoodsman who spoke seven Indian dialects and had many Indian friends. By the time he returned to Three Forks, the old Indian chief Ned had died. But Bryan brought two horses, a dog, and five other frontiersmen who stayed long enough to help erect a shelter and then lit out for greener pastures. And he brought a dream.

It was not by chance that he decided on that particular spot on the river, which was known even then as the Trinity. He knew it had the shallowest and best natural ford for many miles. He was also confident that the Trinity would prove navigable. His goal was to found a settlement, and he believed that these natural assets could one day make it a major trading center.

Bryan and his friends set up camp—a ramshackle hut of poles, brush, and mud—on a bluff overlooking the river, just about where Main Street goes under the Triple Underpass in Dallas today. (The river was diverted a mile west in 1928.) Soon he began a primitive trading post; his first customers were the peaceful Caddo Indians. Then he staked a claim to the 640 acres that were lawfully his. The Republic of Texas was then a young nation eager to attract new homesteaders to north Texas. It established a national road (beginning in Bastrop, below Austin, and running north to the Red River), and protected it with eight forts and fifteen Ranger companies. In addition, the promotional efforts of the Peters Colony, a Texas-approved company that sold land in this virgin wilderness, attracted many pioneers from the western states of Kentucky, Illinois, Tennessee, and Missouri. As the settlers arrived, Bryan surveyed and platted his township and began selling lots to them (newlyweds got one free). Within a year there were several families in the small town that Bryan dubbed "Dallas," probably after Commodore Alexander James Dallas, a well-known naval hero of the War of 1812.

Soon Bryan was also operating a ferry across the Trinity. For several years the little hamlet had more visitors than permanent residents. But European emigrants, including many well-educated Swiss, Belgian, and French people involved in the idealistic but ill-fated La Réunion utopian colony to the west, soon joined the town. They helped lay the foundations for many of Dallas's important cultural institutions.

The life of Dallas's colorful founder reads like several Louis L'Amour novels rolled into one. When Bryan wasn't tending to the full-time job of making his young town work, he served as a go-between for Sam Houston, then president of Texas, in peace negotiations with the Indians. He took off (with every other man in town except one) for the California gold rush; he returned, unsuccessful, a year later. He served for years as a captain in the Texas Rangers, chasing outlaws and renegades. And, at the ripe old age of fifty, he enlisted in the Texas cavalry to fight in the Civil War.

In 1852 Bryan sold his holdings in Dallas to Alexander Cockrell, a close friend and businessman, for seven thousand dollars. Bryan's personal life spiraled downward from there—assisted by good friend John Barleycorn. He died in 1877 in the State Lunatic Asylum in Austin, six months after he was admitted for "intemperance." No one knows where he is buried.

Bryan's dream of Dallas as a great port city, and thus a center of trade, never materialized. A local entrepreneur built a flatboat in 1852, loaded it with cotton bales, and started downstream bound for Houston. Four months later he had only gone seventy miles. Then the river became too low, and the cotton was shipped to its destination by wagon. In 1868 the only steamboat to make the journey up the unpredictable Trinity from Galveston took a year and four days—an unacceptable delivery time, even before Federal Express began offering next-day service. But when some Dallas businessmen formed the Trinity River Navigation Company in 1892 and their steamship the *Harvey* arrived the next year, the celebration was even bigger than the one that had greeted the railroad two decades earlier. The *Harvey* operated as a pleasure boat over the next five years, running day trips to McCommas Bluff. By 1898, the boat was sold. But hardheaded dreamers continued to sink money into Trinity improvement, and it's only been over the last sixty years that the idea of a navigable river has faded away.

Bryan's successor as Dallas's #1 citizen, Alexander Cockrell, was a man of boundless energy. Within a few years he had built a sawmill, a general store, and a sturdy bridge over the Trinity that brought a steady flow of travelers and nearby settlers. Dallas was growing, and Cockrell was its chief architect. But he was shot to death in 1858 (the town marshal emptied eight bullets into his abdomen in a dispute over money). He left a thirty-eight-year-old wife and mother of four, Sarah Horton Cockrell. She quickly assumed control of her husband's assets and became the town's leading entrepreneur, often listing men as the heads of her businesses in those pre-suffragist days. For fourteen years she owned the ferry once owned by Bryan; developed three of the town's finest hotels; led the fight to get the first iron bridge built over the Trinity; was the dominant partner in the first flour mill; and owned a considerable amount of downtown property. She was Dallas's first great businesswoman, and its first millionaire. When she died in 1892, Dallas was the most populous city in Texas. The city directory listed her occupation as "capitalist."

How did a town that had no viable outlet to the sea, no mineral resources, little fertile land, and poor access become the signature city of Texas? Because its farsighted, determined citizens wanted it that way—and then made it happen. Like this:

• In 1850 they won two close elections that made Dallas a permanent county seat—mainly due to Bryan's offer to donate land for a courthouse square. As the area's center of government, Dallas gained considerable status.

• In 1872 the city offered five thousand dollars, 115 acres of land, and a free right-of-way to the north-south Houston and Texas Central Railway (H&TC). The offer brought the first railroad in the state steaming through Dallas. A year later, they got the state legislature to require that the transcontinental Texas and Pacific Railway (T&P) cross the H&TC "within one mile" of Browder Springs—the source of Dallas's water. Not satisfied with having the T&P merely nearby, the townspeople went further. They voted 192-0 to offer the T&P $100,000 and a right-of-way, bringing the railroad right through downtown. The railroads made Dallas a key distribution center for the entire Southwest, and helped develop the wealth of cotton and grain resources found in the blackland prairies surrounding it.

• In 1912 the townspeople lobbied to bring a Federal Reserve Bank to Dallas. Though competing with several larger cities, they won, establishing Dallas as a secure financial center.

• In 1936 they went after another big prize—the Texas Centennial Exposition. Their by now well-honed powers of persuasion (plus an offer of ten million dollars, 242 acres of land, and many buildings, museums, and other cultural facilities) made them winners again. Over the next two years, thirteen million visitors and the millions of dollars of revenue they generated virtually pulled the city out of the Depression. And Dallas became the major city in Texas—though it hadn't even existed a hundred years earlier.

Today Dallas continues to reflect its "make it happen" history. A recent report named it the number-one city for small businesses, encouraged in no small part by its continuing revival of historic neighborhoods. Dallas is a mecca for entrepreneurs, speculators, developers, and hucksters—in short, for every kind of dreamer alive. Those who have seen their dreams come true include Roger Horchow, the mail-order mogul; Stanley Marcus and family, retailers par excellence; Bette Graham, inventor of Liquid Paper; Kenneth Cooper, the aerobics pioneer; Robert Crandall, the American Airlines steersman; Ebby Halliday, one of the most successful realtors in America; H. L. Hunt, the gambling oilman who at one time was called "the world's richest man"; his son, Lamar Hunt, the founder of the American Football League and the Super Bowl; Mary Kay Ash, the cosmetics queen; J. M. Haggar, the world's largest manufacturer of dress slacks; Trammell Crow, the nation's most successful real estate developer; and of course H. Ross Perot, the former IBM salesman turned millionaire and presidential candidate. And don't forget Barney, the world's most popular dinosaur, who lives in Dallas when he's not on the road entertaining his millions of pre-MTV fans.

Big D has come a long way from the single shack of poles and mud built by John Neely Bryan. Now the ninth-largest city in the nation, Dallas is known for its upscale department stores and malls. It has more shopping centers and more retail space per capita than any other US city, and the Dallas Market Center is the world's largest wholesale merchandise mart. As longtime Texas historian A. C. Greene pointed out, "Dallas has always been a city with its excuse for being that 'you can get it there'"—and you still can, at some of the best malls in the country, and smaller malls and other upscale shopping centers. Loaded with every kind of retail outlet imaginable, they celebrate the city's patron saints of shopping, the Sanger brothers. Lehman and Philip Sanger arrived in Dallas with the railroads after the Civil War and revolutionized mercantile marketing in the Southwest. Their influence is still felt; Herbert Marcus worked for them, and Roger Horchow worked for Neiman Marcus.

You can certainly get sports here, too. Dallas is a sports-mad city in every way. The city boasts competitive big-league teams in every major sport: the Mavericks (basketball), the Stars (hockey), and the nearby Texas Rangers (baseball) and FC Dallas (soccer). The best-known local pro team is the Dallas Cowboys, who play their home games in state-of-the-art AT&T Stadium in Arlington, thirty minutes from downtown

Dallas. Winners of five Super Bowls and perennial contenders, the Cowboys have been called "America's Team" for decades, and own a national fan base second to none. It seems that most Dallas residents eagerly watch games, compete in them, or work out in some low- or high-impact fashion. (They look good doing it, too.)

And Dallas continues to welcome new businesses with open arms. In fact, the Dallas-Fort Worth area is one of the country's fastest-growing job markets. The city's financial dependence on oil production and petroleum-based products has decreased in recent years as the local economy has embraced a number of other industries, including aviation and aerospace, meatpacking, defense, banking, fashion, technology, and advertising. Nineteen Fortune 500 companies headquarter here, and more are on their way. Dallas emerged from the 2008 recession as a stronger, and more diverse, city.

That's diversity with a big D. Dallas has many faces, and they are all open and inviting. Dallas is exactly what it appears to be—a city that rewards hard work and confidence, a city that congratulates ambition and success.

And Dallas knows how to celebrate that success. The city knows how to have a good time, with plenty of places to do it. The funky neighborhood of Deep Ellum, just east of downtown, is a Soho-like combination of artists' lofts, hip nightclubs, and hipper shops and art galleries; it's one of the first destinations on the list of any visitors who want to see the city's sights. Deep Ellum began as a black "freedmen's town" built after the Civil War, and the thriving neighborhood was later home to musicians such as Blind Lemon Jefferson, Leadbelly (Huddie Ledbetter), and a host of others; it fell into disuse following the building of Central Expressway in the early 1950s. Four decades ago, a new generation of musicians, artists, and gallery owners began to reclaim it. Its considerable popularity now almost threatens to subvert the fresh independence that defines its allure.

Dallas's nightlife rivals that of the greatest world cities. Nightclubbers are drawn to the many watering holes along lower Greenville Avenue, which runs north from just above downtown; until a couple of decades or so ago the stretch north of Mockingbird Lane was home to bigger and louder nightspots, but many of those have disappeared. Just across Central Expressway at Mockingbird lies Southern Methodist University, the city's center of higher learning since it was founded in 1910. Restaurant Row, in far northwest Dallas, is a conglomeration of large, upscale chain restaurants and clubs whose neon signs and size make this strip a little Las Vegas. These areas and others—Uptown (McKinney Avenue and the surrounding area just north of downtown); Addison's Belt Line Road, in far North Dallas; Cedar Springs and Lemmon Avenues in Oak Lawn; Trinity Groves, west of downtown just across the Margaret Hunt Hill Bridge, with its large collection of restaurants and shops; and Bishop Arts, in Oak Cliff, the alt-edged area with some of the best eateries and shops in town—give Dallas a diversity in cuisine, music, arts, and entertainment equaled in few other cities.

Balancing the conspicuous consumption and nightlife of Dallas is a strong religious spirit. New York's borough of Brooklyn was called "the City of Churches" in the nineteenth century, but Dallas rivals that reputation today with its 1,300 churches and temples. (It's been known as the "Buckle of the Bible Belt" for quite some time.) Religion here is a pervasive presence. Billboards advertise competing churches, and prayer invocations are given before many large, public gatherings. Big D is home to the largest Episcopalian, Presbyterian, and Southern Baptist congregations in the country; two of the top ten best-attended Methodist churches are here. Though the city is largely Protestant, a wide variety of religions flourish here, in large Catholic and Jewish congregations as well as in smaller but growing immigrant groups of Buddhist, Muslim, Bahá'í, and many others. There is even a lovely Hare Krishna temple in East Dallas whose income is supplemented by the excellent vegetarian restaurant next door.

The self-congratulatory style of Dallas can inspire jealous rages in many Texans outside the city. But they put these aside when it's time for the State Fair of Texas. It began as a popular county fair in 1859, and became the official State Fair of Texas in 1886. At the turn of the century the fair's site, Fair Park, was open year-round. Like a sprawling Coney Island, Fair Park boasted a Scenic Railway, Amusement Row (today's Midway), and irresistible entertainments like Shoot the Chutes and the Tickler. But it was not until the Texas Centennial Exposition of 1936 that today's fabulous collection of art deco buildings and the Cotton Bowl were constructed at the park. Though many of its attractions are open all year, Fair Park draws its largest crowds when the State Fair is held annually in October. The fair's famous symbol, Big Tex, has greeted fairgoers since 1952. He's a larger-than-life cowboy who wears size seventy boots and a seventy-five-gallon hat.

What, if anything, do other major cities have that Dallas doesn't have? Let's see now:

• Mountains—There's nothing resembling mountains near Dallas. That's why we keep Colorado open twenty-four hours a day—especially during skiing season.

• Coastline/Beach—Two lovely lakes lie within the city limits (White Rock and the smaller Bachman) and a brace of them surround the city (almost every one built by the Army Corps of Engineers). Dallas has no ocean coast nearby, so if the lakes aren't enough, there's always one of the area's massive waterparks.

• Winter—Does Dallas have winter? Technically, yes. Effectively, no. If winter's so great, how do you account for all the snowbirds from points north? They talk about leaves turning red—until their skin turns blue.

• "Great" Earthquakes, Famines, Fires, Floods, Blackouts, Hurricanes, Riots, and Other Disasters—Historic moments we can do without, thank you. A large fire burned most of the Dallas business district in 1860, but the city's population was only about five hundred then. The fire had a positive effect: It forced residents to begin building with more fire-resistant materials, and in no time the town was stronger than ever. There was a serious flood in 1908 which resulted in five deaths and $2.5 million in property damage, but "Great" doesn't apply.

Dallas is a young city, just over a century and a half old. Like many other large American cities, it struggles with crime, unemployment, transportation, housing, education, and growth—challenges that must be addressed. But Dallas's traditions of farsighted planning and bold initiative have helped the city triumph over any number of problems. The failure of the Trinity as a navigable river was an early blow, but it forced Dallas citizens to look to the railroads to satisfy their access needs. The flood of 1908 resulted in the adoption of the 1911 Kessler Plan, which moved the river a mile west. The downtown fire of 1860 and the tragic assassination of President Kennedy a century later also tested the city's mettle. These and many other moments of crisis have, in the end, made Dallas stronger and better. The city's great-hearted people, both civic leaders and private citizens, will do the same in the future. Dallas will undoubtedly meet the challenges of the future with equal courage and aplomb. And Dallas will continue to be a place where dreamers can make something of themselves—a place where dreams come true.

James Donovan

James Donovan is a literary agent and the author of several books, including three acclaimed bestsellers about American history: A Terrible Glory, The Blood of Heroes, *and* Shoot for the Moon. *He lives in Dallas, Texas.*

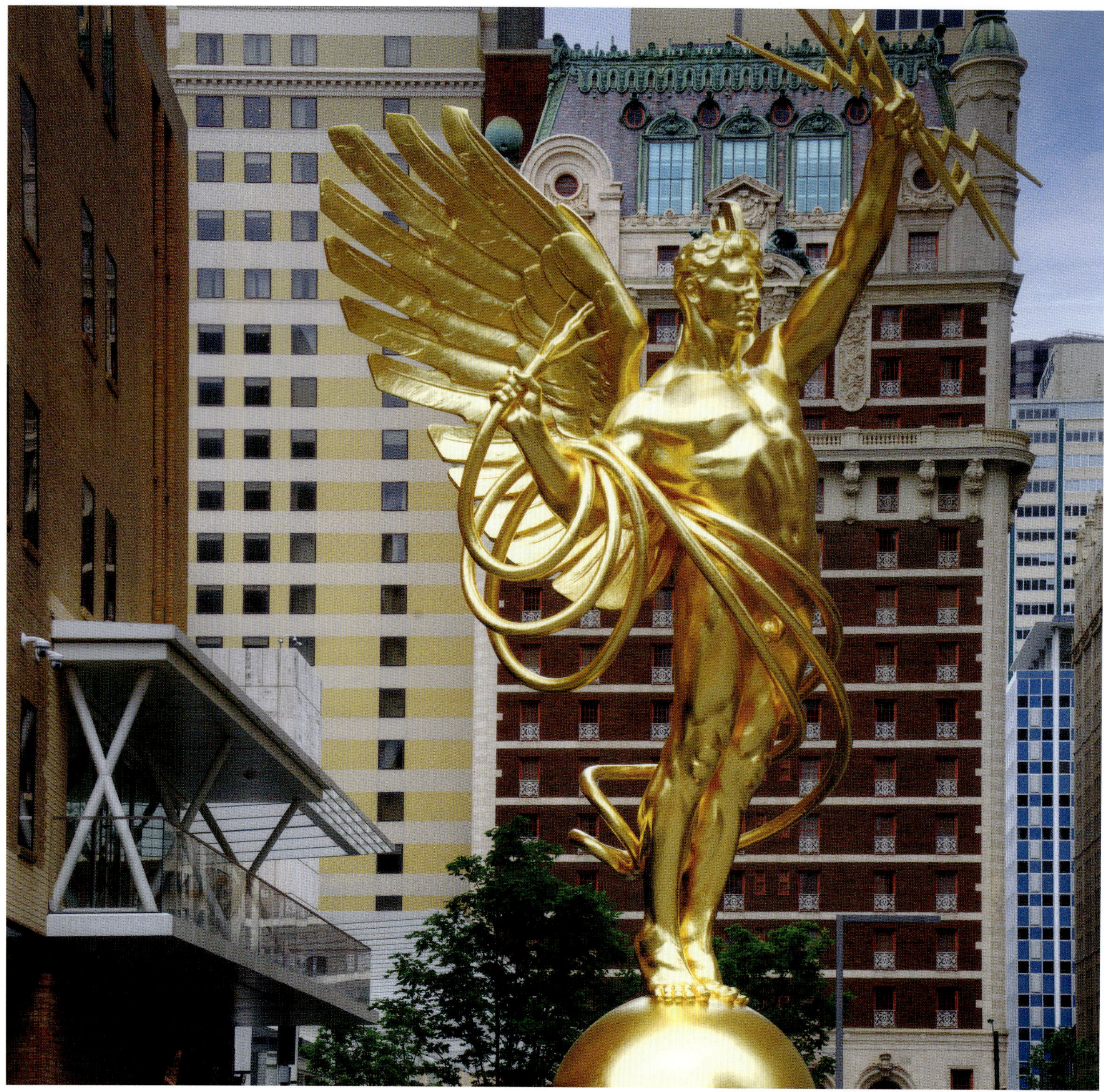

Build

Anne Chow is the chief executive officer of AT&T Business—the first woman to hold this position and the first woman of color CEO in AT&T's history. She's responsible for a $35B operating unit which serves nearly 2.5 million business customers around the world, providing them with communications solutions to manage and transform their businesses.

Opposite
Standing twenty-four feet tall, the Golden Boy greets visitors to the AT&T Discovery District in downtown Dallas. This bronze statue is covered in 23.75-carat gold leaf and anchors a hi-tech park with a giant media wall for livestreamed sports and entertainment, as well as green lawn, fountains, and food.

To build is to establish, develop, and grow. Building can be done both figuratively and literally, as is clearly the case when it comes to Dallas.

Development and growth is palpable in virtually all facets of the city. It is evident in the telltale signs of constant construction. It is felt in the hustle and bustle of both new and established neighborhoods. And it is proven in its quantitative rise on numerous "top cities" lists.

Having arrived to the metroplex less than a decade ago, my tenure in the area pales in comparison to many. My path to present-day Dallas held little glamour and fanfare. Like countless businesspeople, my journey involved a corporate relocation coupled with hopes for personal and professional growth. Hailing from the East Coast and having traveled to numerous cities around the country and world, I've experienced metropolises of all kinds. But from the beginning, this city felt different. My commute provides both day and evening views of Reunion Tower, Bank of America Plaza, Fountain Place, Perot Museum, Dealey Plaza, Margaret Hunt Hill Bridge, the "Eye," and more. The juxtaposition of retro and contemporary, of harmony and dissonance, of history and the future is evident in the dynamic evolution of Dallas. Whether you reflect on the rise of the Arts District, the ever-eclectic expanding Design District, or the emergence of the AT&T Discovery District, there is no question that a key motivator for building is the creation of new connections. These connections beckon us to develop a deeper understanding and appreciation of diverse cultures, including their art, to engage in more vibrant and visible experiences—often enabled by technology—and most importantly, to provide an opportunity for all to strengthen our relationships with companies, organizations, and each other. Connection serves as the foundation for increasing commerce, expanding prosperity, and thriving communities. It is the power of human connection that sustains us, fuels us, shapes who we are, enables our aspirations, and helps us realize our fullest potential. In the words of Walt Disney, "You can dream, create, design, and build the most wonderful place in the world. But it requires people to make the dream a reality." At the core of Dallas's love to build is the enduring commitment to its people—past, present, and future.

Anne Chow

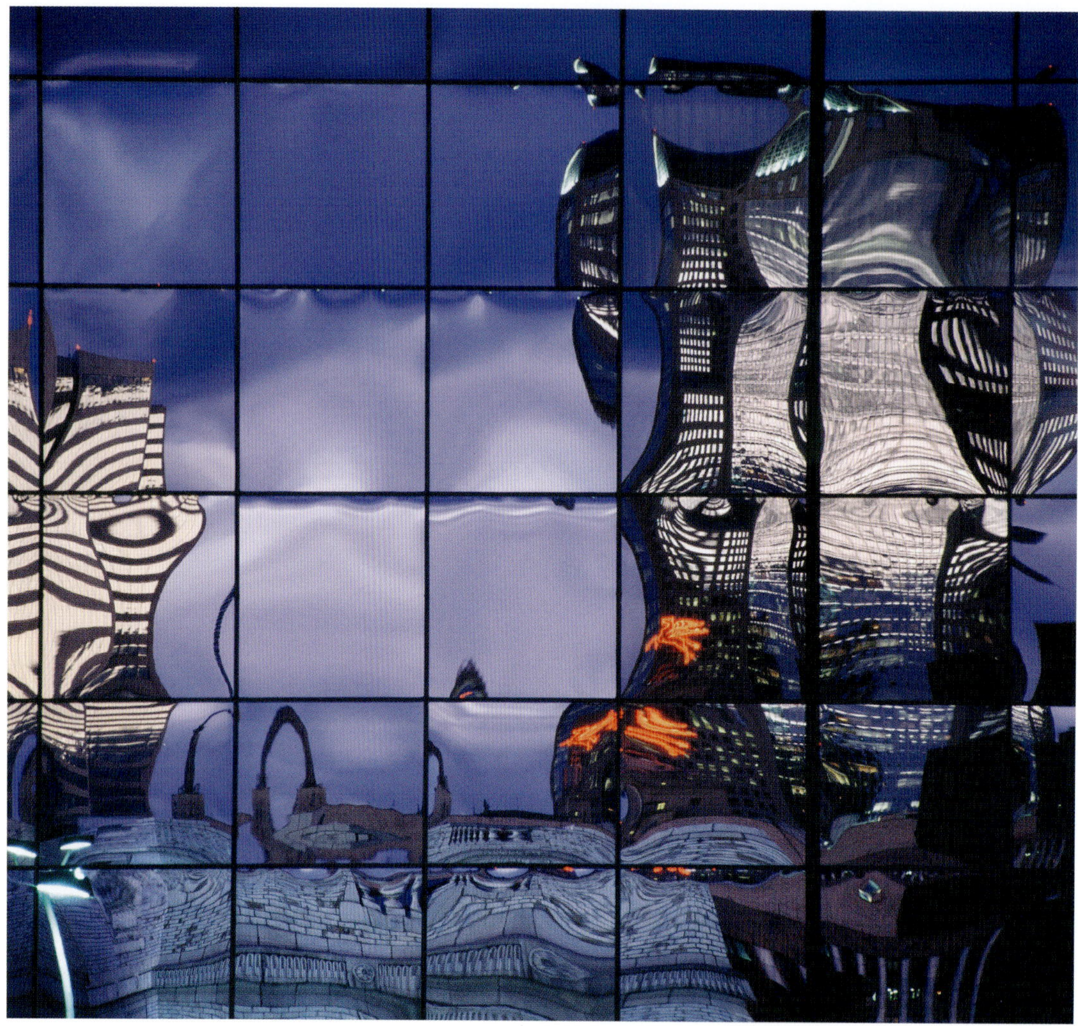

Above
Reflections on Reunion Tower's glass façade reveal the city in abstract.

Opposite
View of Dallas from the Woodall Rodgers Freeway.

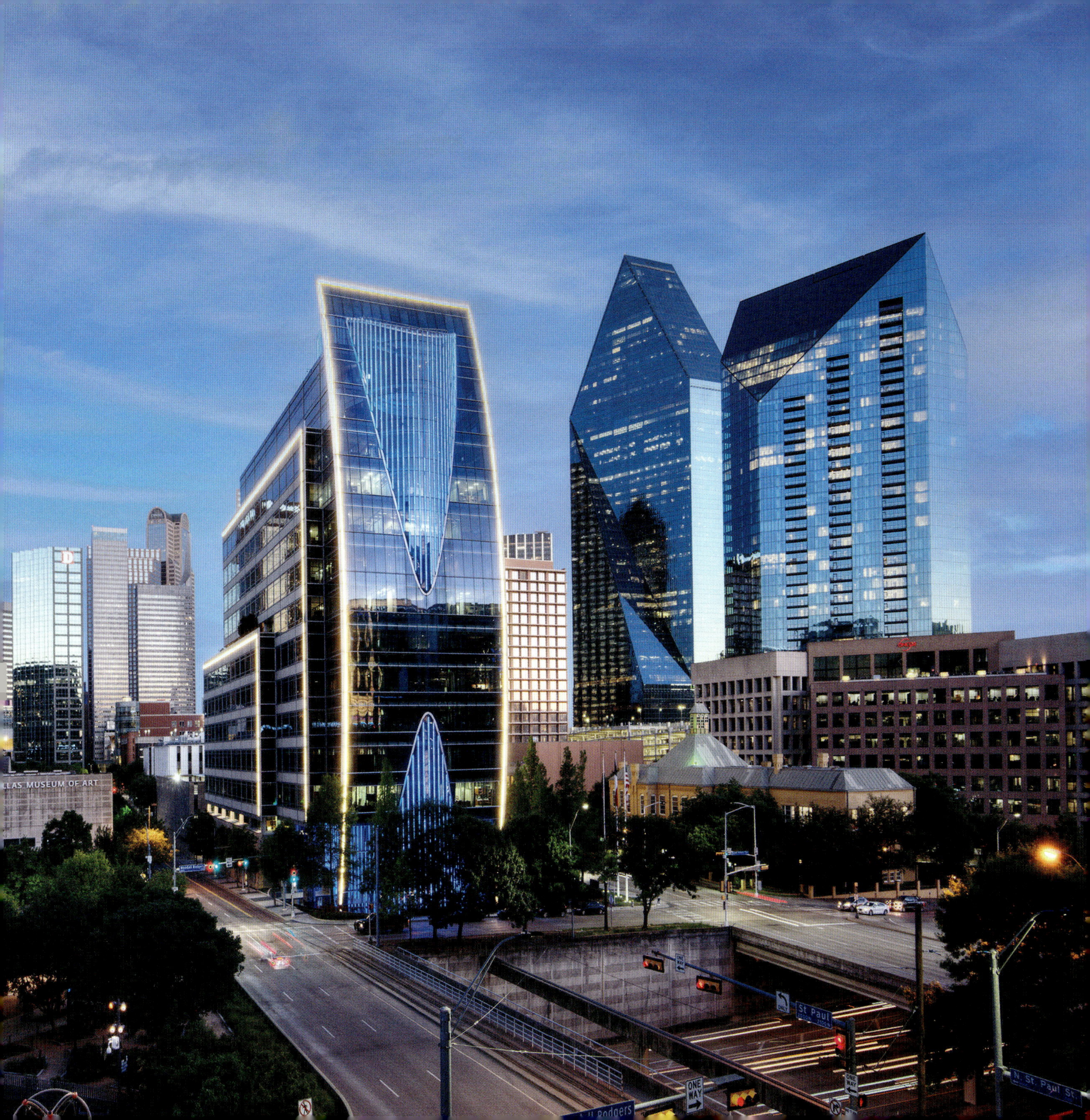
LLAS MUSEUM OF ART
St Paul
ONE WAY
N. St Paul St

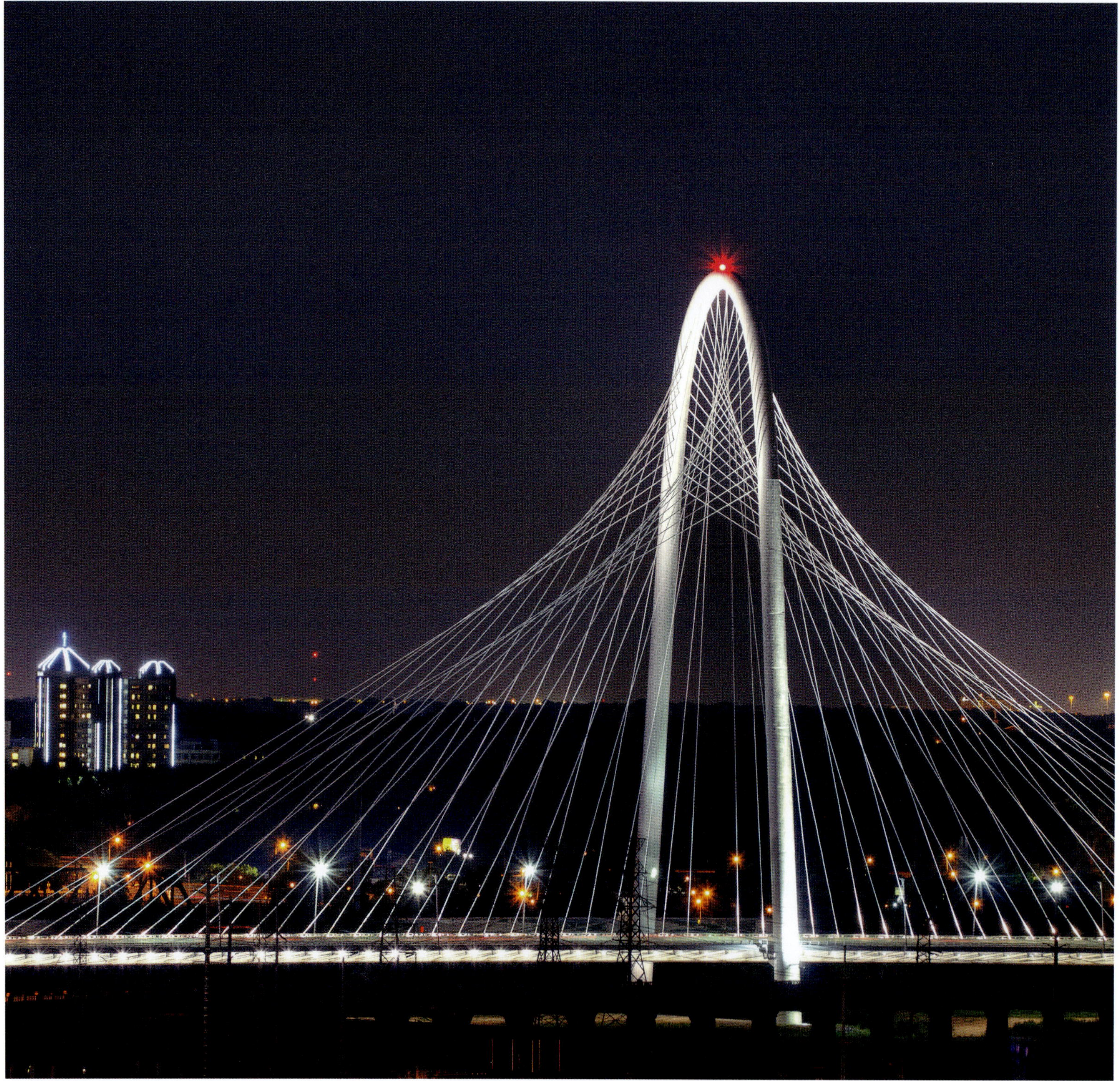

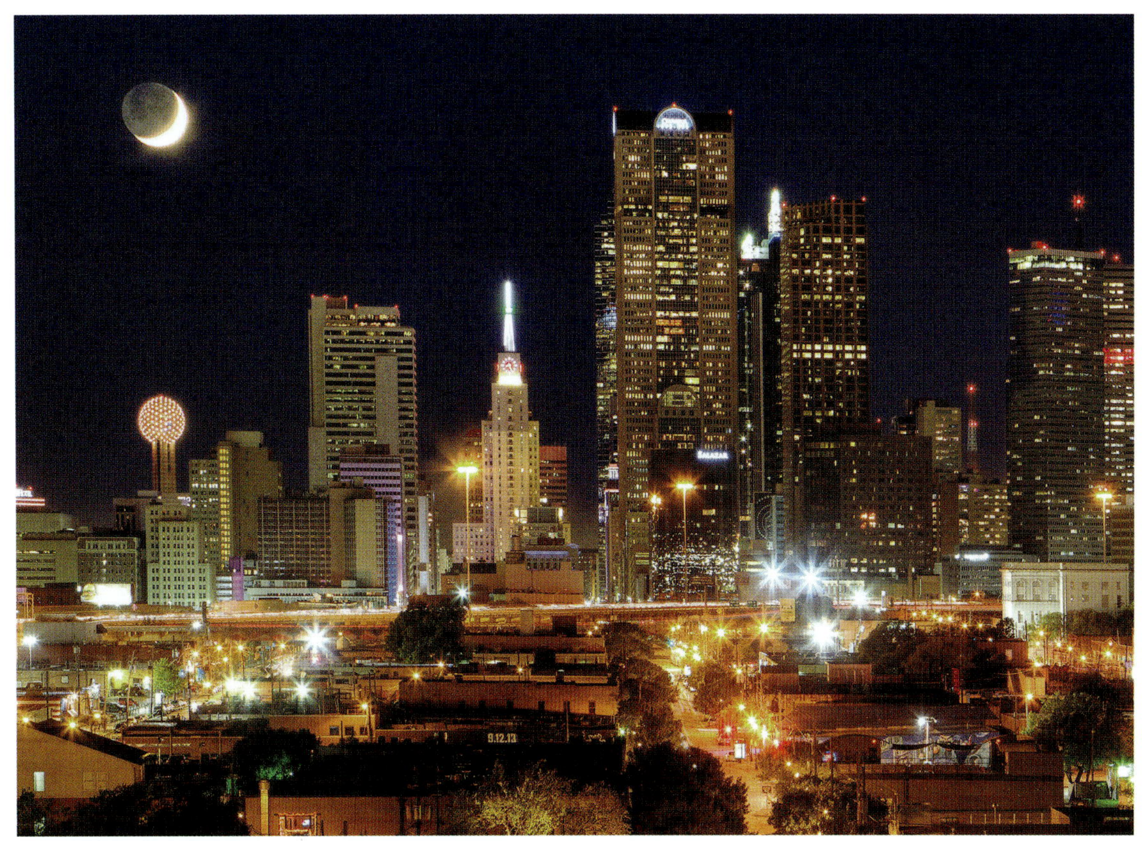

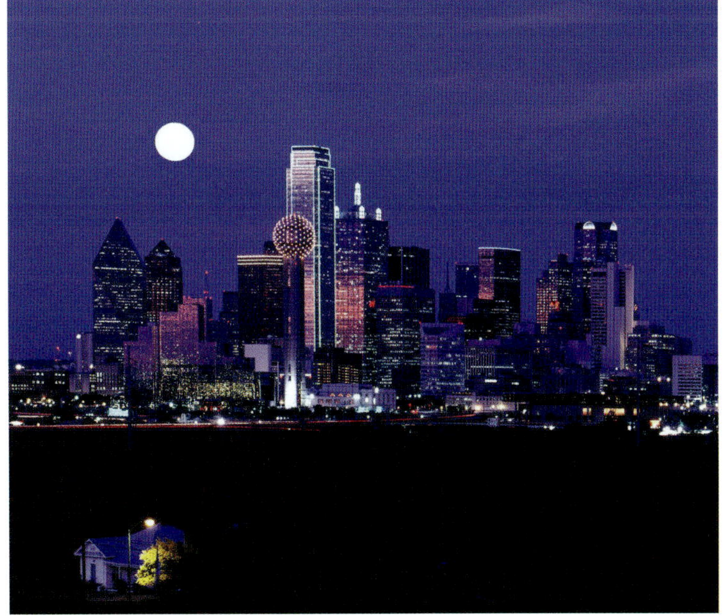

Above
Viewed from Deep Ellum, the city under a crescent moon.

Left
A full moon glows over the Dallas skyline at dusk.

Opposite
The dramatic, white parabolic curve of the Margaret Hunt Hill Bridge adds to the Dallas skyline. In the background, Oak Cliff's Methodist Hospital rises above the horizon.

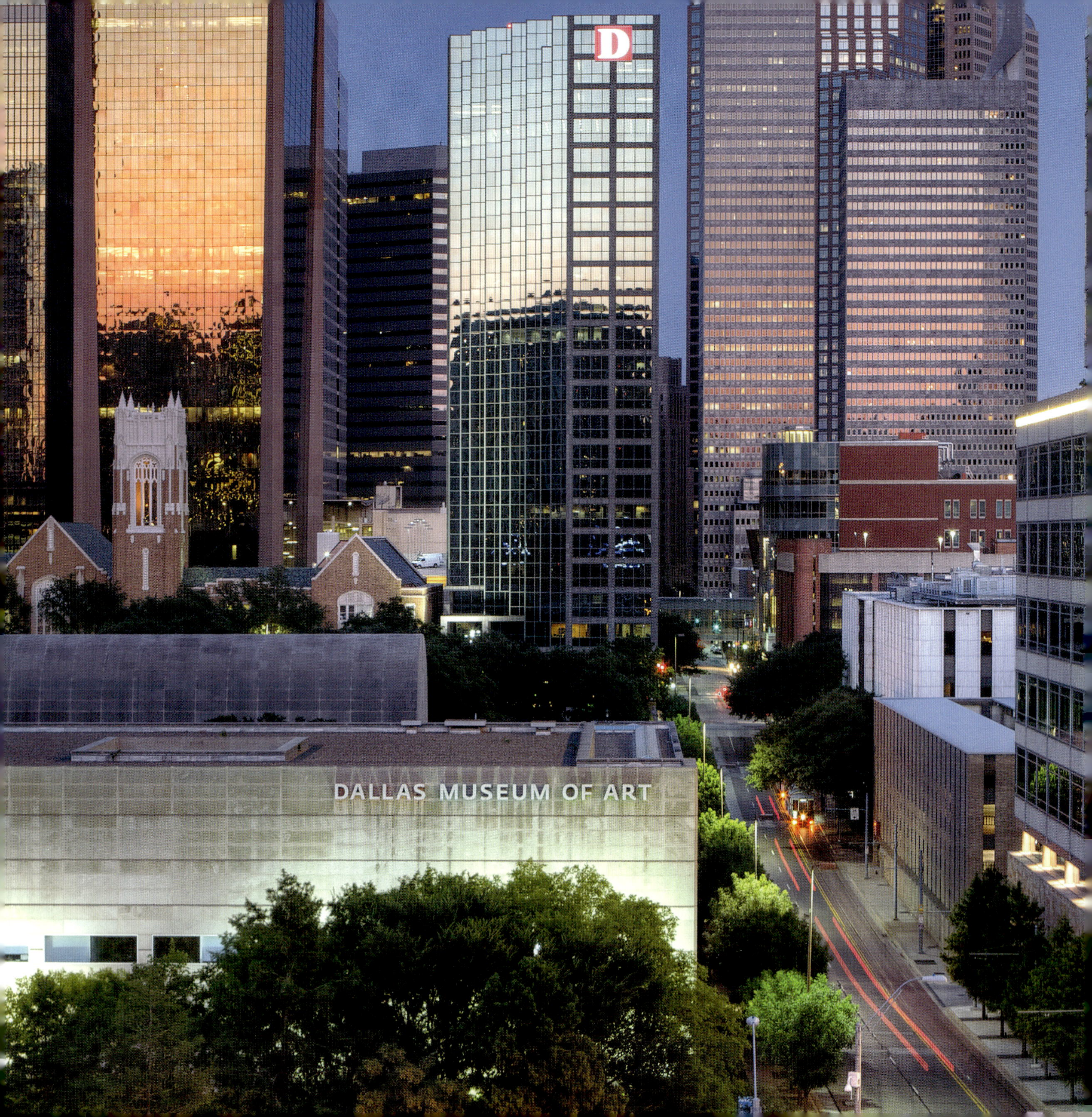
D
DALLAS MUSEUM OF ART

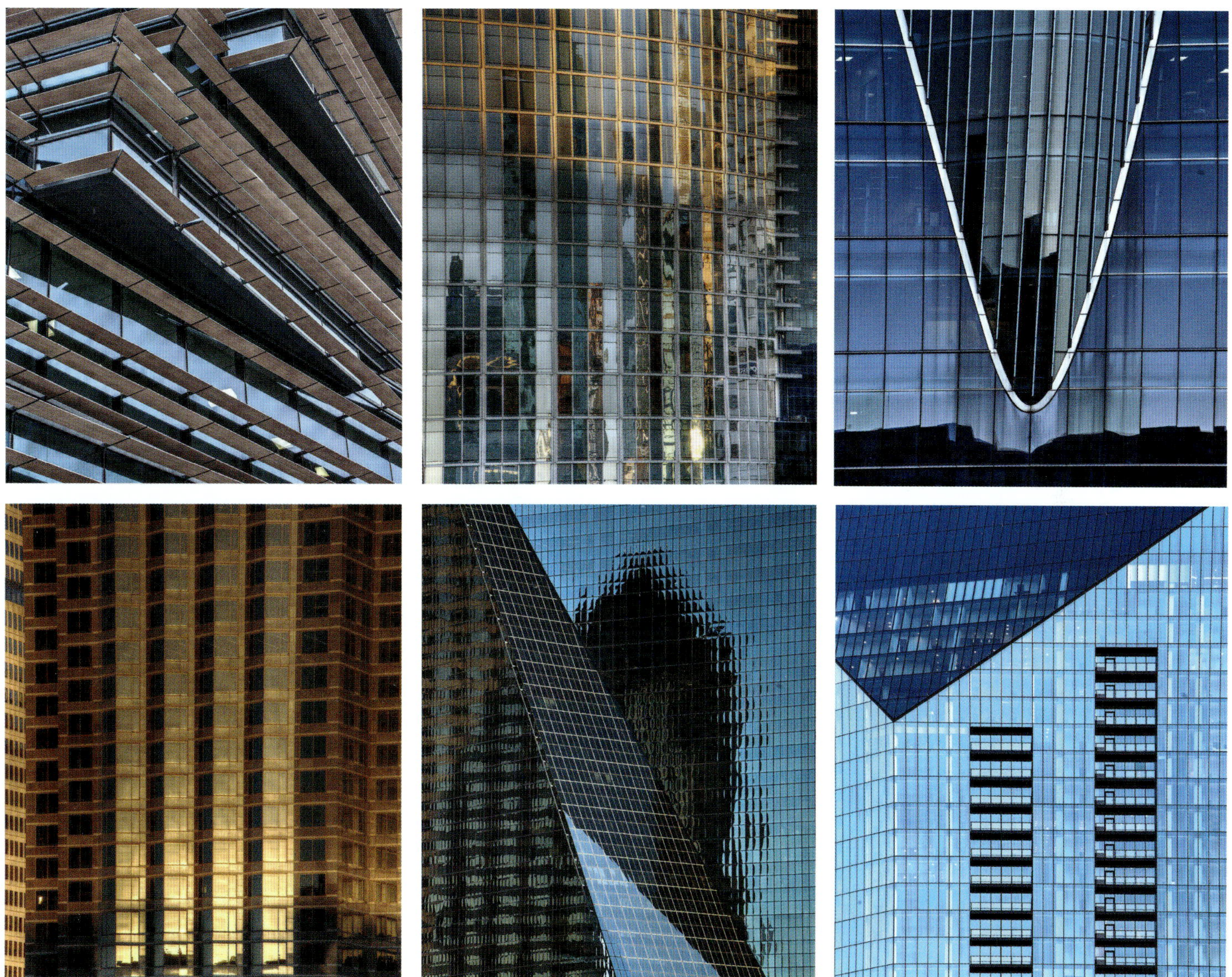

Above
Façade details of some of the city's most dramatic buildings.

Opposite
The Dallas Museum of Art, designed by Edward Larrabee Barnes, was the first cultural institution to be built in the Dallas Arts District.

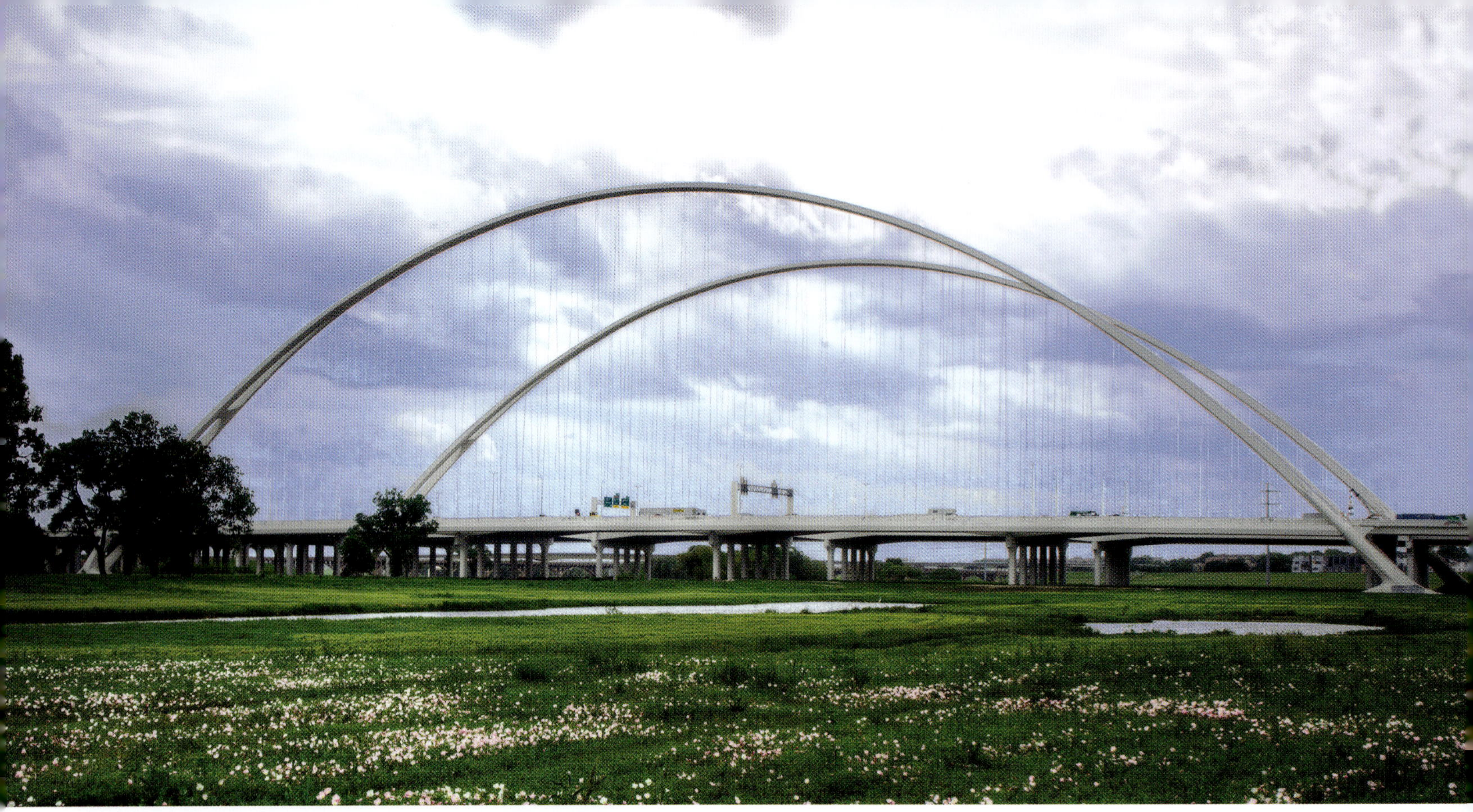

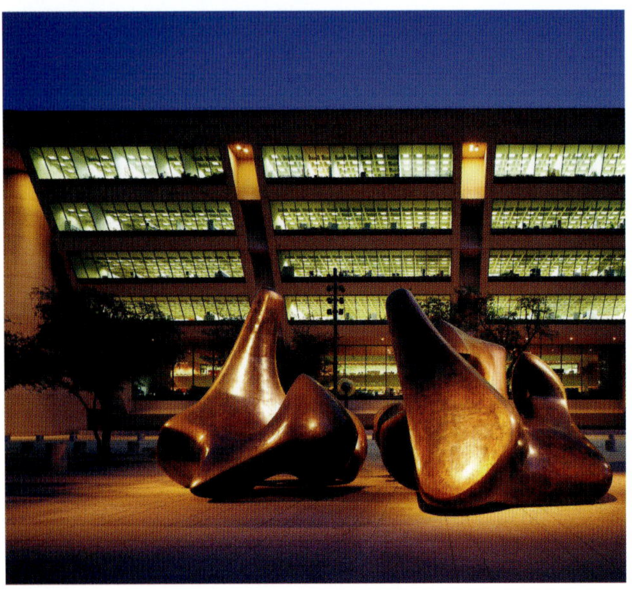

Above
The Margaret McDermott Bridge, partially designed by the Spanish architect Santiago Calatrava, spans the Trinity River floodplain.

Left
Dallas City Hall, designed by I. M. Pei, opened in 1978. In the foreground is the monumental bronze sculpture, *The Dallas Piece*, created by the British artist Henry Moore expressly for City Hall Plaza.

Right
Reunion Tower was named in remembrance of La Réunion, a French utopian community which was established in West Dallas in 1855. The tower's revolving geodesic dome enchants with its nightly light shows.

Below
A building located in Deep Ellum with a mural by artist Daniel Barojas.

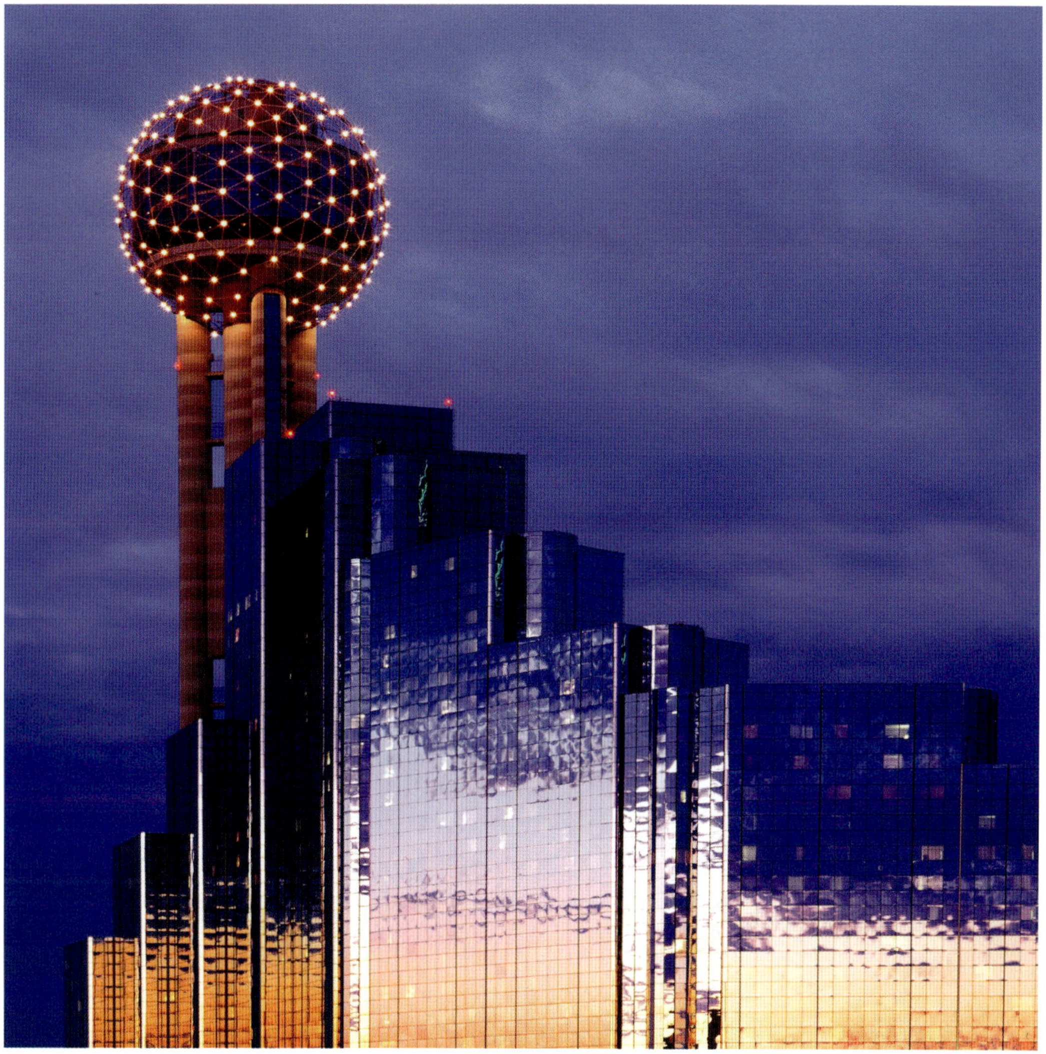

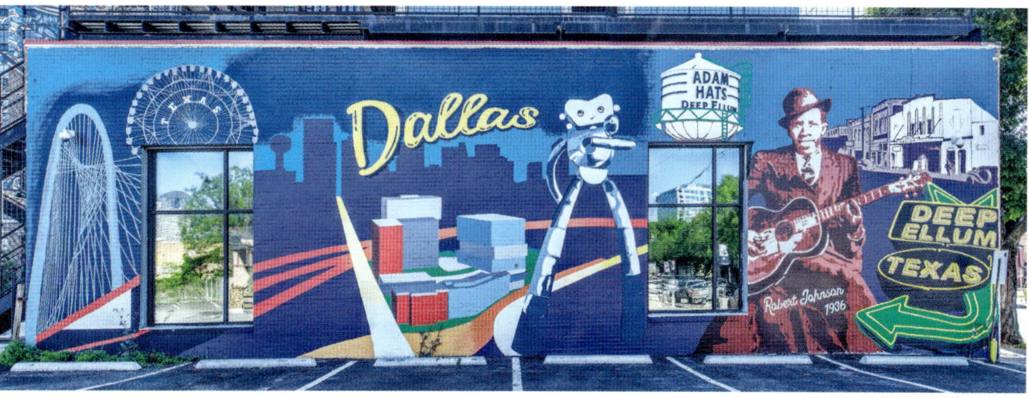

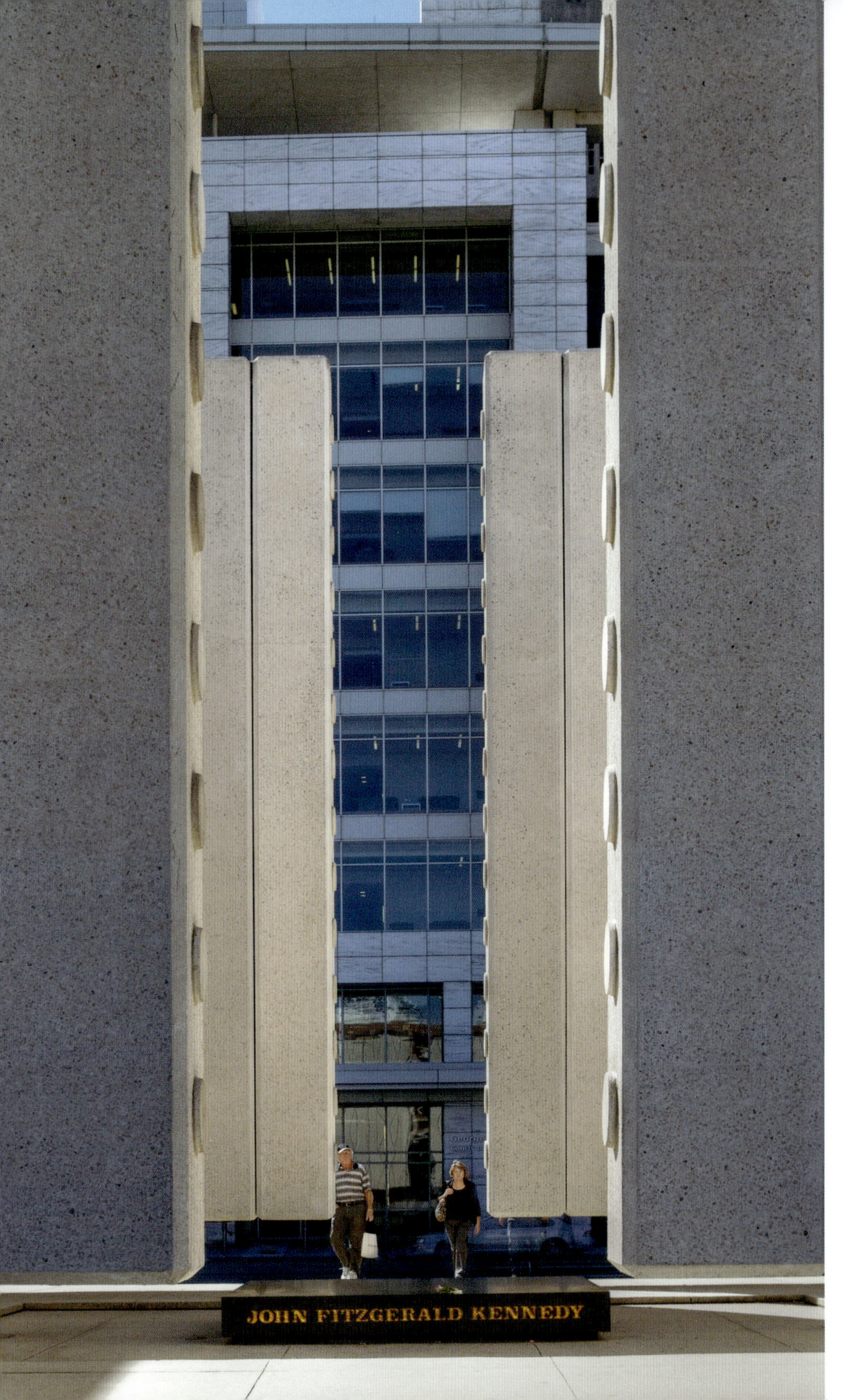

Left
The Kennedy Memorial was dedicated in 1970. After years of debate over what would be an appropriate commemoration, the city chose a simple cenotaph (monument built to someone buried elsewhere) designed by famed architect Philip Johnson.

Opposite
Created in the 1930s as a ceremonial entrance into downtown Dallas, the Triple Underpass took a tragic place in history when President John F. Kennedy was assassinated in Dallas on November 22, 1963.

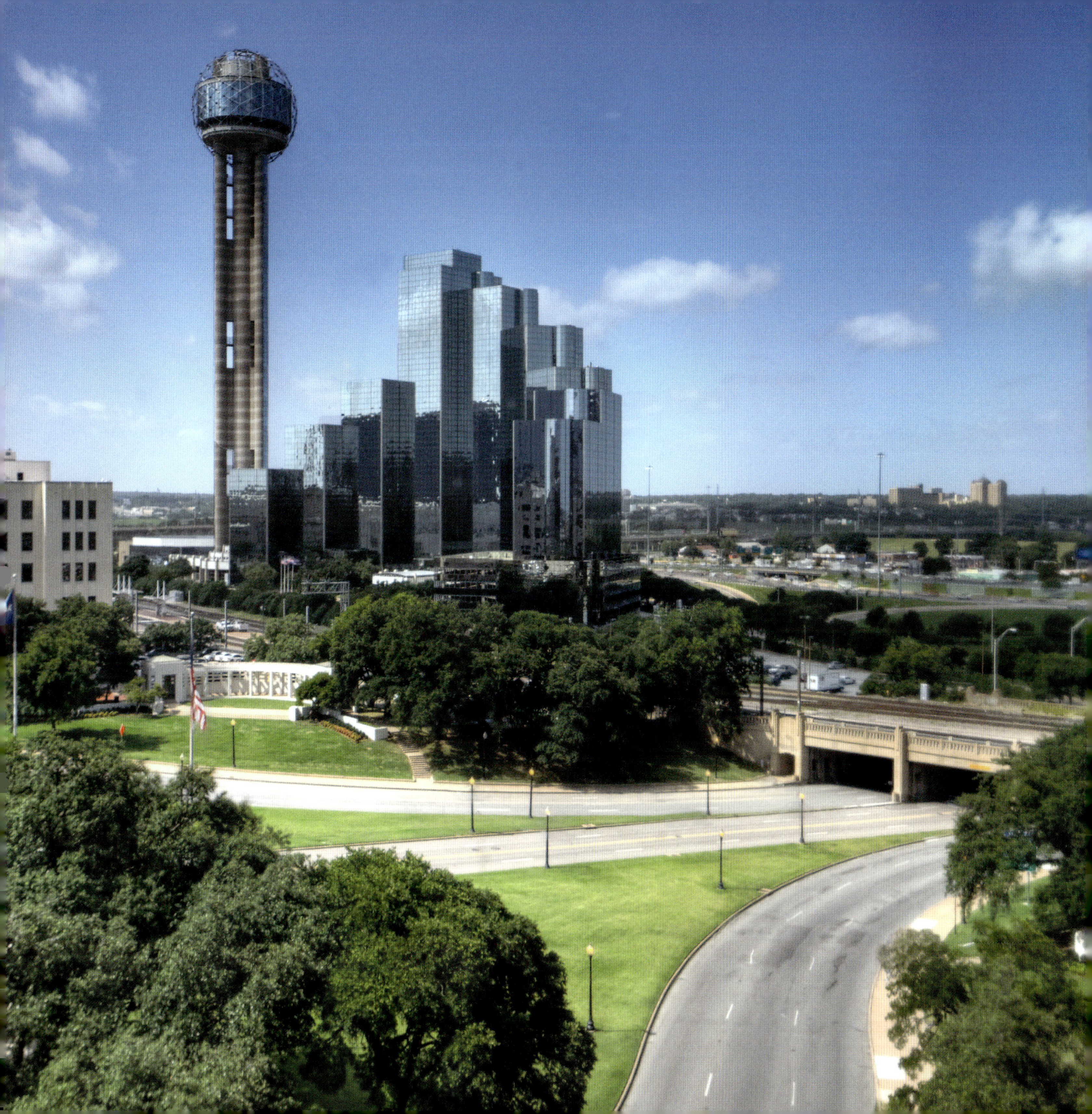

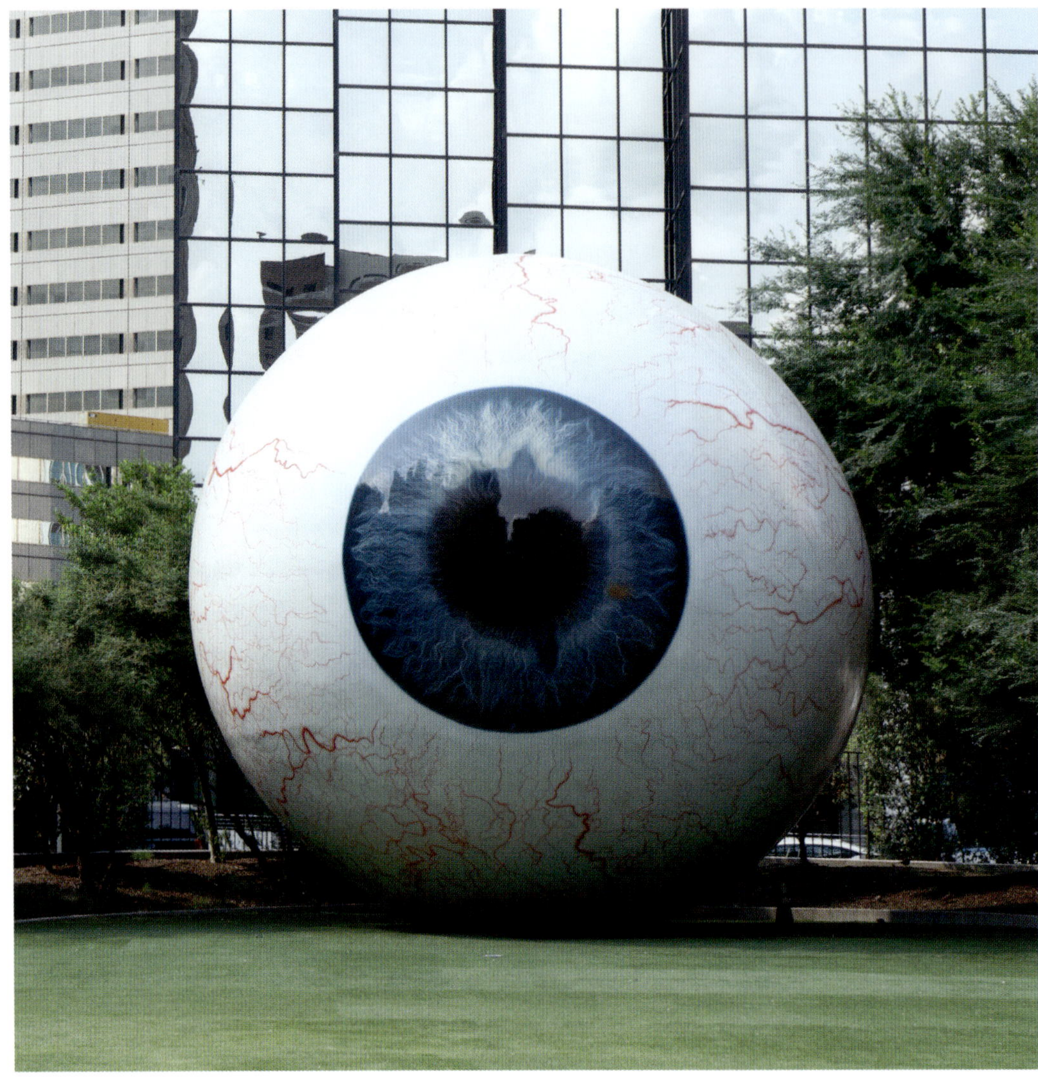

Above
On Main Street in downtown Dallas, a thirty-foot eyeball by Chicago artist Tony Tasset rests on a verdant lawn.

Opposite
Completed in 2018, the Rolex Building anchors the master-planned nineteen-block Harwood District in Uptown. It was designed by the famed Japanese architect Kengo Kuma.

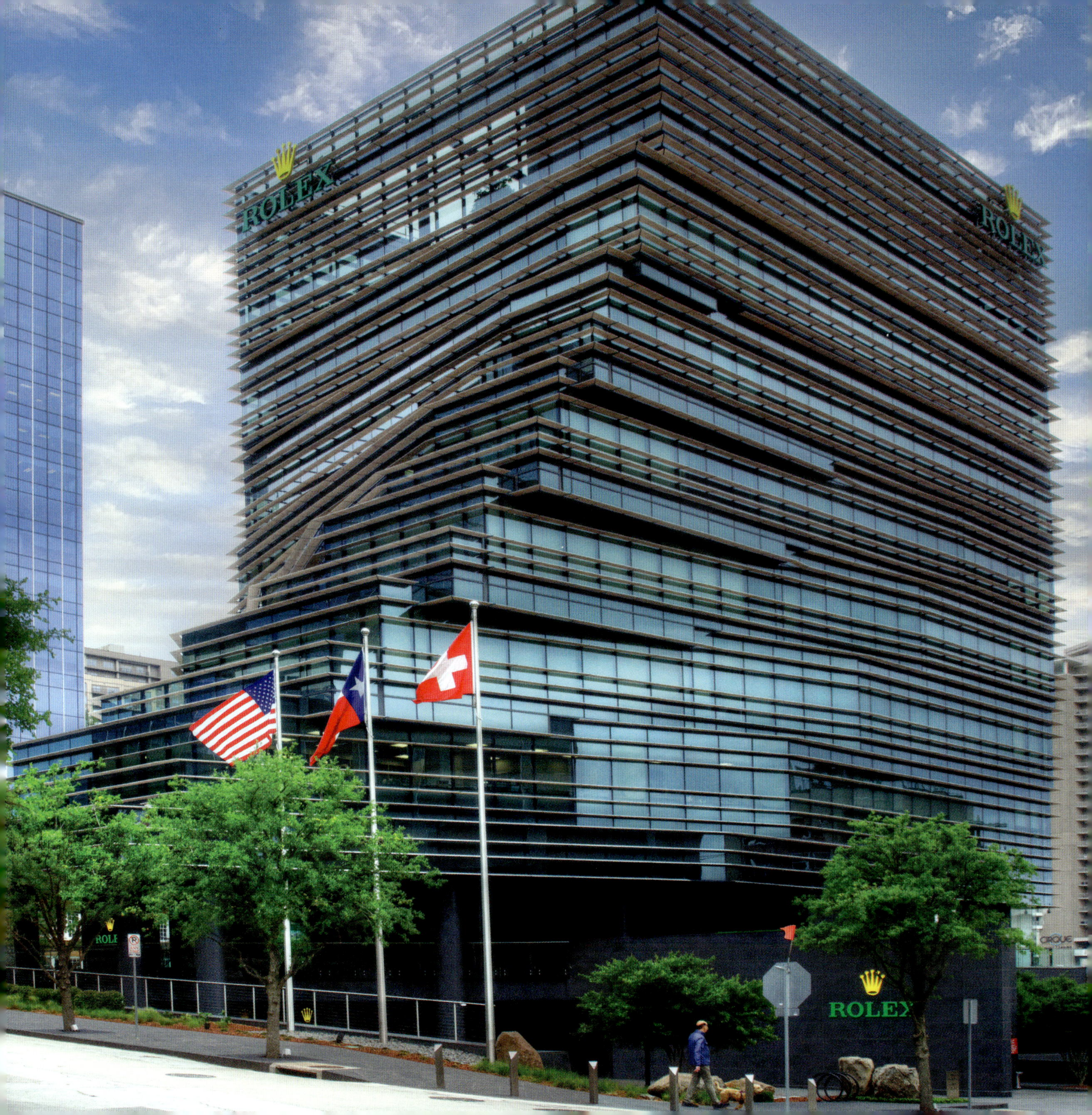
ROLEX
ROLEX
ROLEX

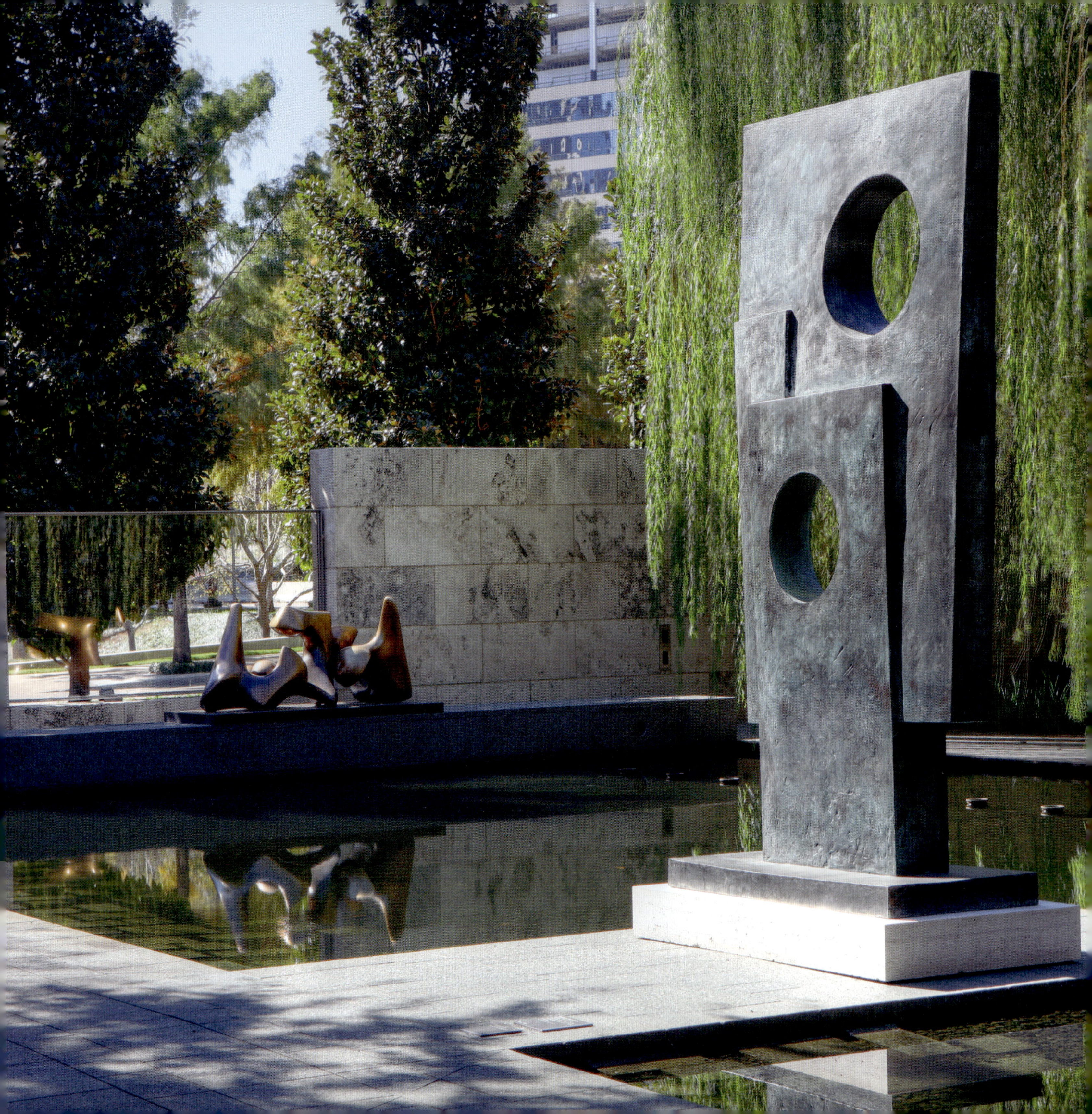

Create

Jeremy Strick has been director of the Nasher Sculpture Center since 2009, burnishing the modern and contemporary sculpture museum's international profile. As director, Strick has organized ambitious exhibitions of sculpture, launched innovative new programming initiatives, and, in 2015, created the Nasher Prize, an international juried award dedicated exclusively to contemporary sculpture.

Opposite
A reflecting pool is in the garden of the Nasher Sculpture Center. In the foreground, *Square with Two Circles* (1963) by British sculptor Barbara Hepworth; in the background, Henry Moore's *Working Model for Three Piece No. 3: Vertebrae* (1968).

I visited Dallas for the first time in 1986 to meet with Raymond and Patsy Nasher and begin work on an exhibition of their sculpture collection for the National Gallery of Art. I stopped by two cultural landmarks: the newly relocated Dallas Museum of Art, in its Edward Larrabee Barnes-designed building, and the Nasher family's unprecedented "shopping museum," NorthPark Center.

Thirty-five years later, I'm fortunate to make Dallas my home. The city has grown much bigger, and along with that expansion, the city's museums and art galleries have grown in size and number. The DMA expanded again, claiming stature among America's most impressive encyclopedic museums. NorthPark expanded, too. Twice. A new building was erected for the Meadows Museum that today houses the most significant collection of Spanish art outside of Spain, and the Dallas Contemporary is now housed in a thirty-seven-thousand-square-foot industrial building in the Design District, expanding its mission to include exhibitions of work by national and international artists.

Back in 1986, the Museum of African-American Life and Culture was housed in the Zale Library of Bishop College (now the campus of Paul Quinn College), moving in 1993 to a new purpose-built locale in Fair Park under a new name: the African American Museum.

In 1986, the Crow Museum of Asian Art didn't exist. That changed in 1998, when Trammell and Margaret Crow opened a permanent home for their collection at the foot of the Trammell Crow Center. Today the Crow Museum plans to expand into a new building on the campus of the University of Texas Dallas, designed by Pritzker Prize-winning architect Thom Mayne.

And, of course, there's the museum that brought me back to Dallas, thirty-three years after my initial visit: the Nasher Sculpture Center. Designed by the premier museum architect of our time, Pritzker Prize winner Renzo Piano, with a garden designed by one of the most lauded landscape architects working today, Peter Walker, the Nasher provides an extraordinary home for the collection that I first discovered in 1986. Still home to the Nasher collection, the museum provides an incomparable setting for temporary exhibitions, educational programs, and community events. Every day, walking into the skylit spaces of the Nasher, seeing the amazing works gathered within its travertine walls, I feel a small rush of joy, a sensation of peace and good fortune.

Jeremy Strick

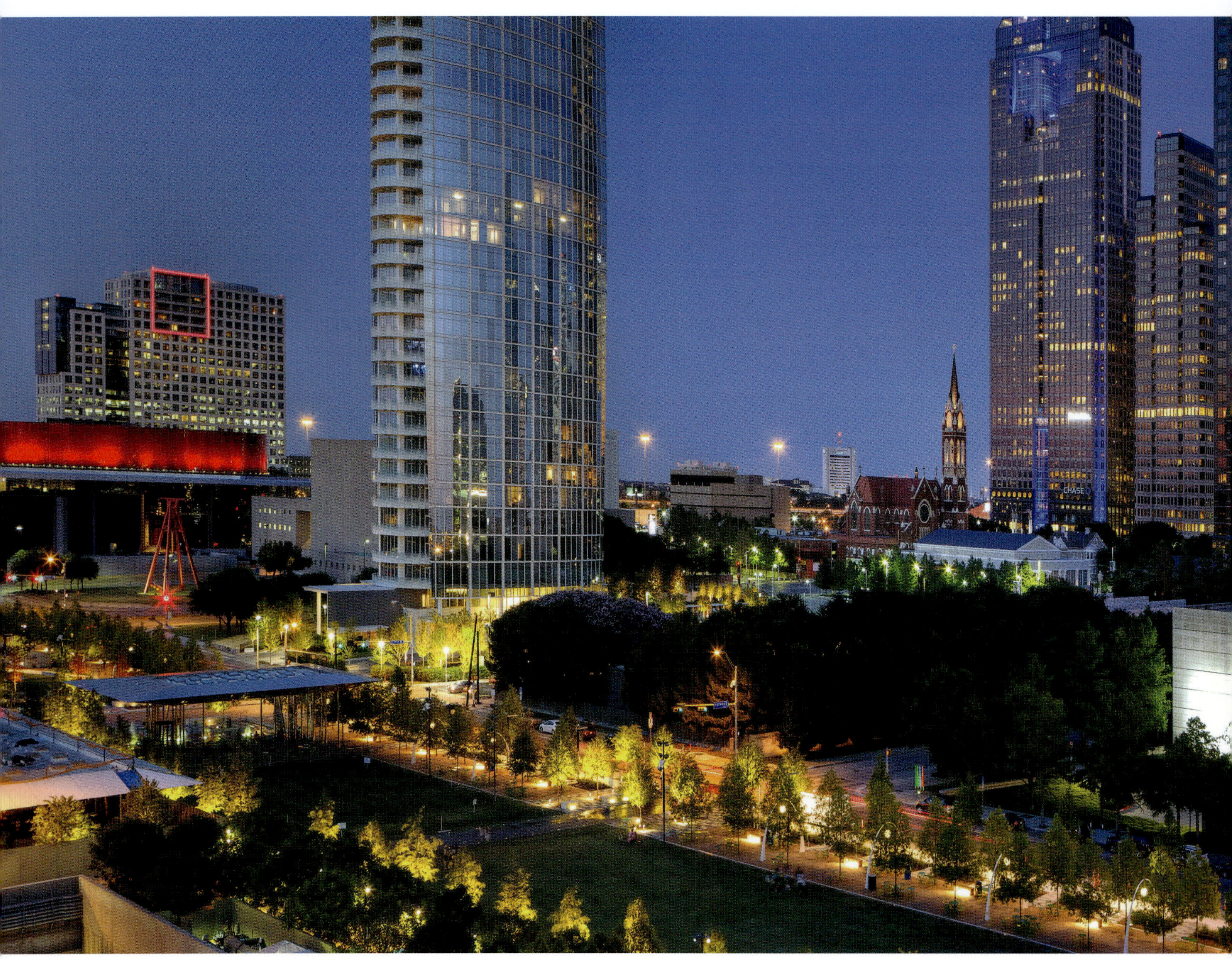

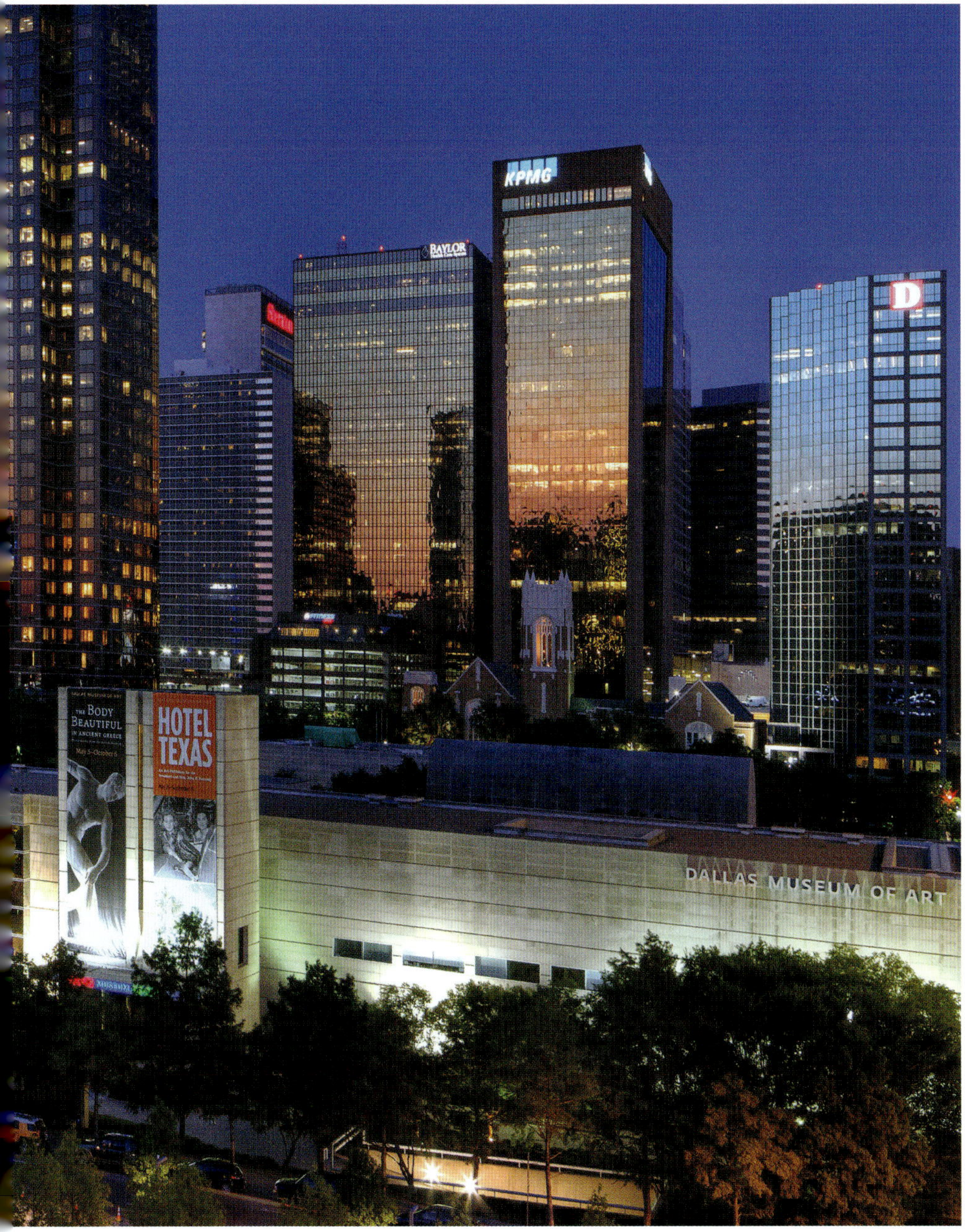

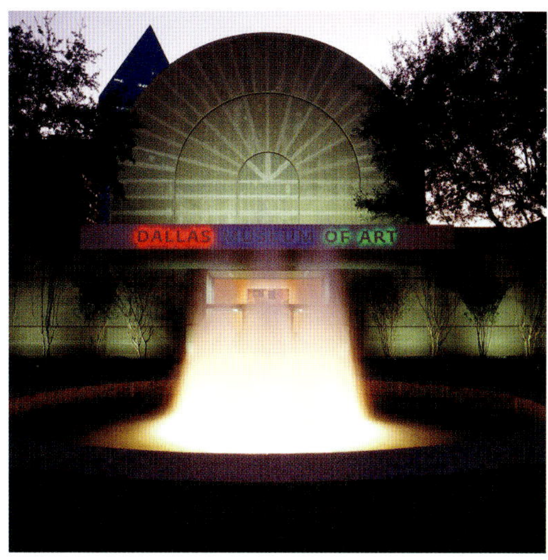

Above
The Flora Street entrance of the Dallas Museum of Art in the Arts District.

Left
The sixty-eight-acre Dallas Arts District is in the foreground. Developed over a period of three decades, it was inaugurated in 1984 with the opening of a new Dallas Museum of Art.

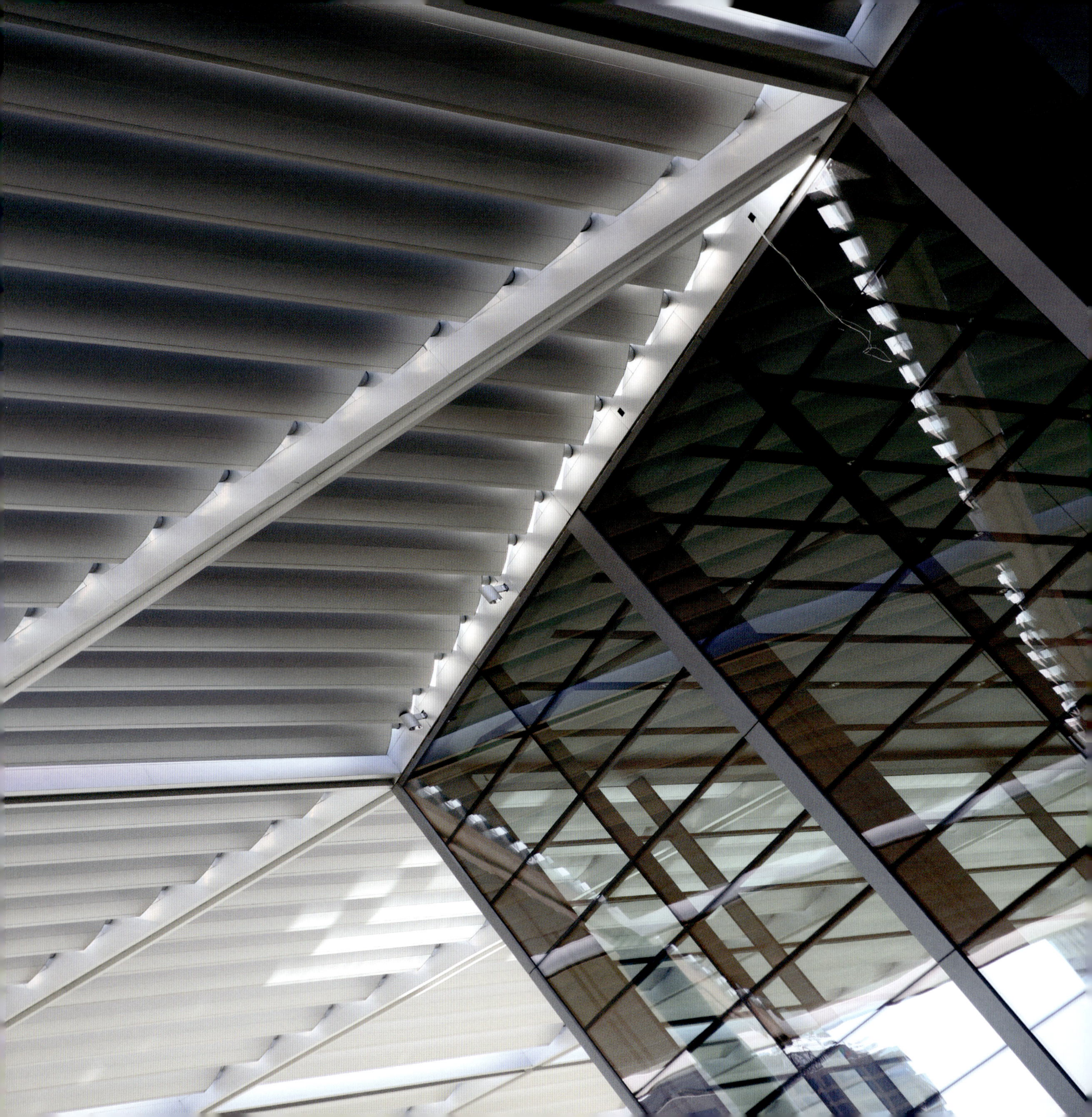

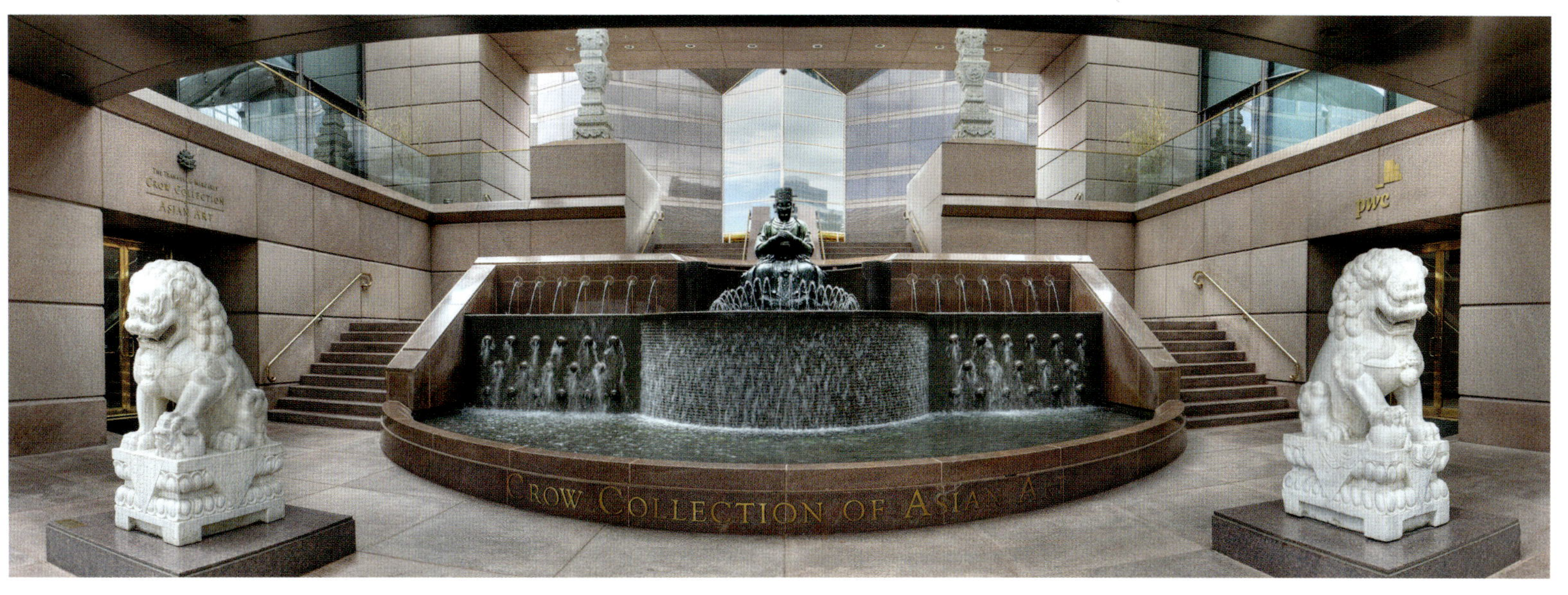

Opposite
Architectural detail of the Winspear Opera House.

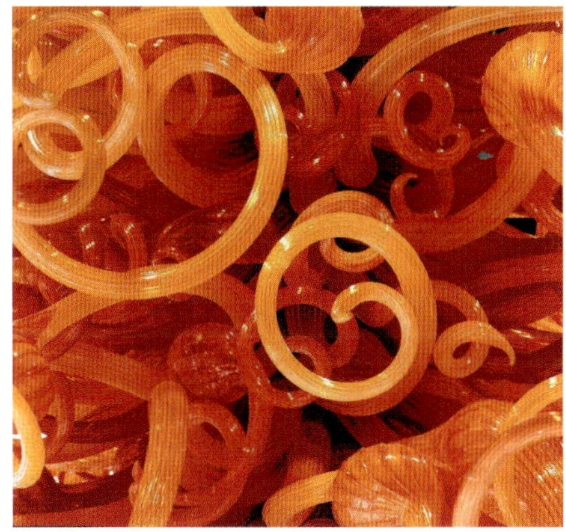

Above (top)
A bronze Buddha resides over the Flora Street courtyard at the Crow Museum of Asian Art at the University of Texas at Dallas, a museum dedicated to the arts of China, Japan, India, and Southeast Asia.

Above
A close-up image of the sixteen-foot Chihuly sculpture is located in the atrium of the Seay Biomedical Building at UT Southwestern. More than one thousand pieces of handblown glass were shipped from the artist's Seattle studio and assembled on site.

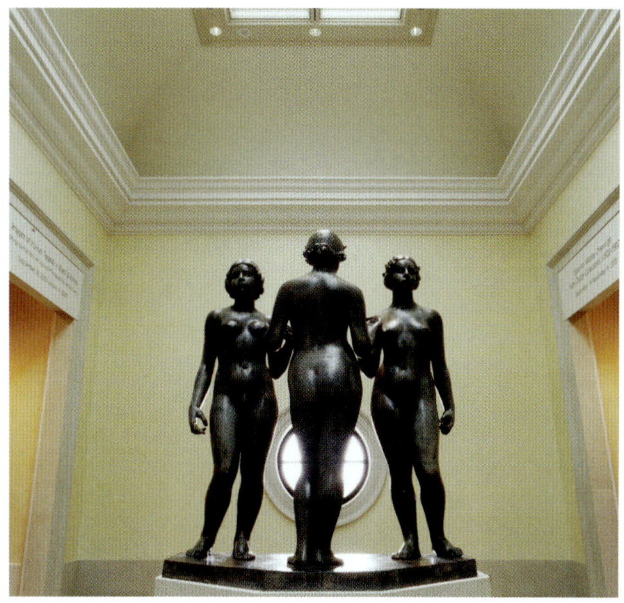

Above
The Three Nymphs, cast in 1939 by Aristide Maillol, grace the Meadows Museum on the Southern Methodist University campus.

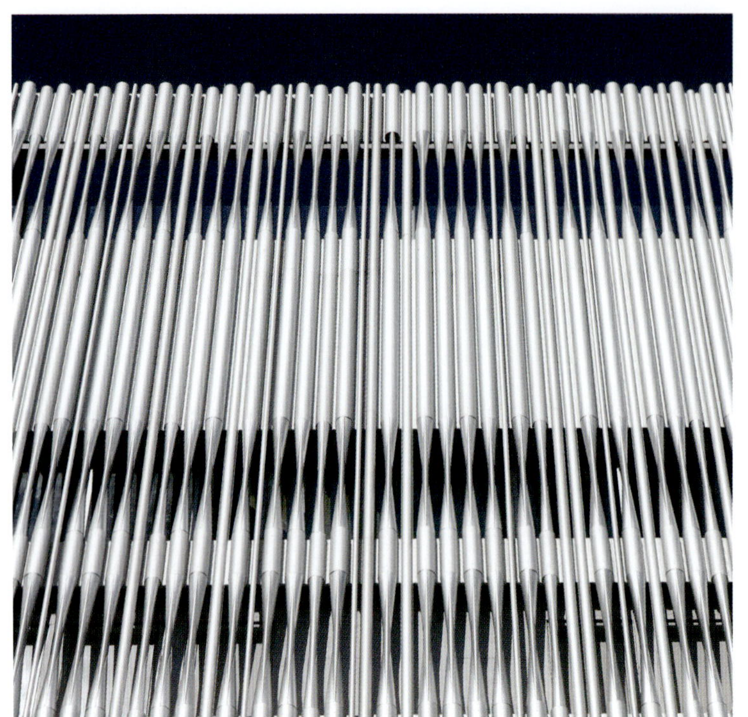

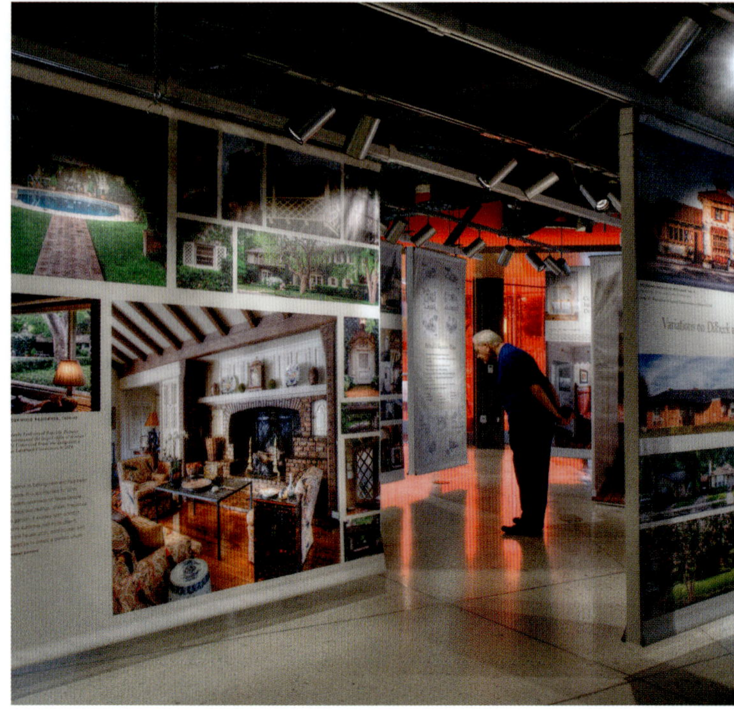

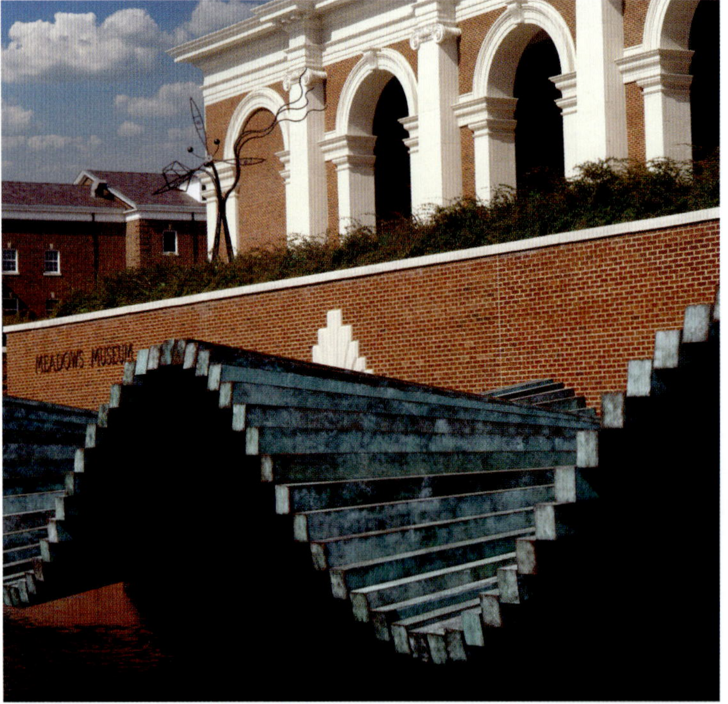

Above (left)
Shimmering metal walls of the Dee and Charles Wyly Theatre.

Above
The ADEX exhibition space at St. Paul and Pacific features architectural exhibits. This particular exhibit honors Charles Stevens Dilbeck, one of Dallas's distinctive residential architects.

Left
SMU's Meadows Museum features *The Wave*, a moving sculpture by Santiago Calatrava, created especially for the plaza in front of the museum.

Opposite
Dale Chihuly's glass creations drape the wall-sized window of the atrium at the Dallas Museum of Art.

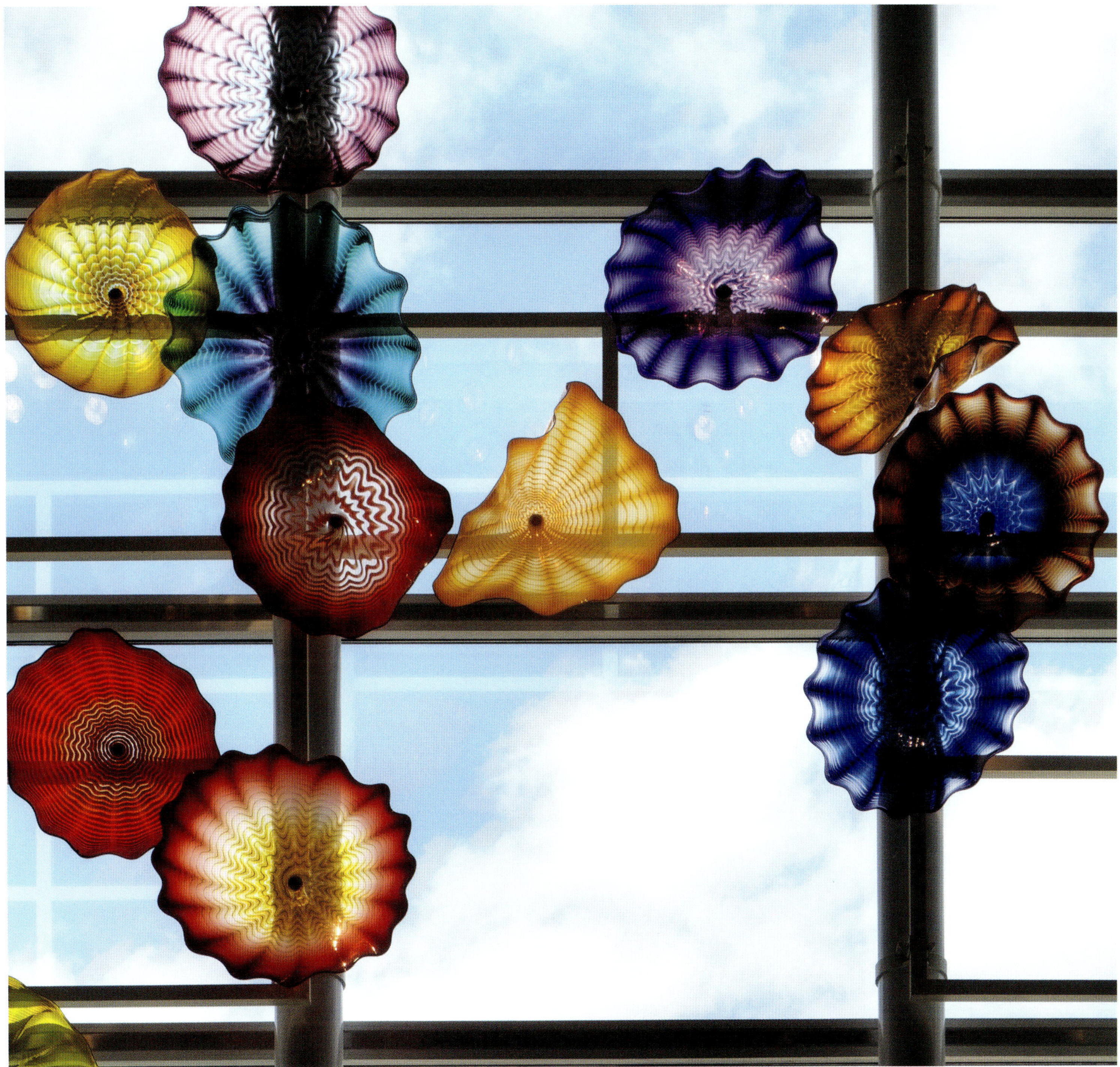

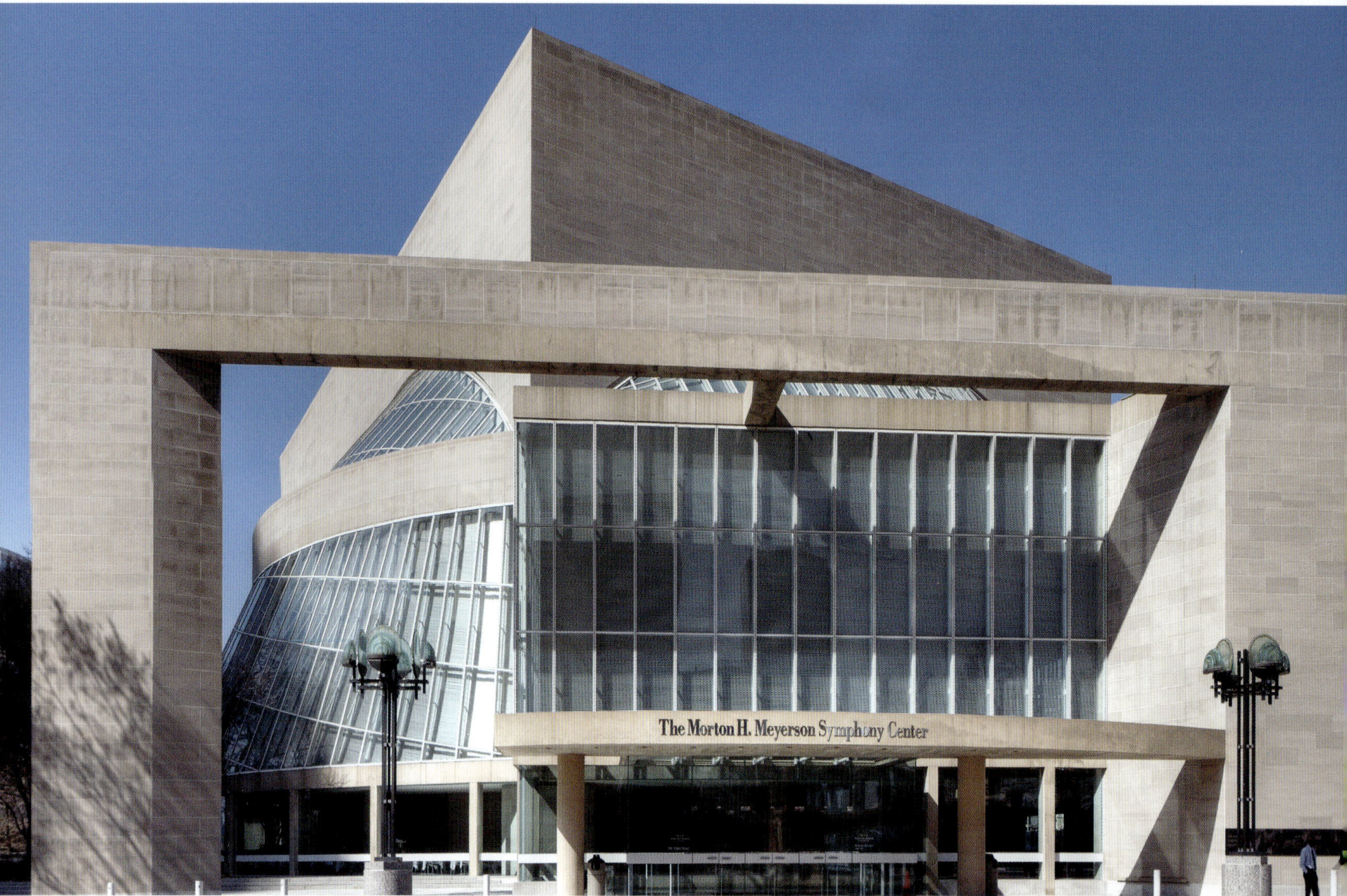

Above
The Morton H. Meyerson Symphony Center, designed by I. M. Pei, opened in 1989 as the first performing arts facility in the Arts District.

Opposite
Architect Renzo Piano collaborated with landscape architect Peter Walker to design the 2.4-acre garden at the Nasher Sculpture Center in the Arts District.

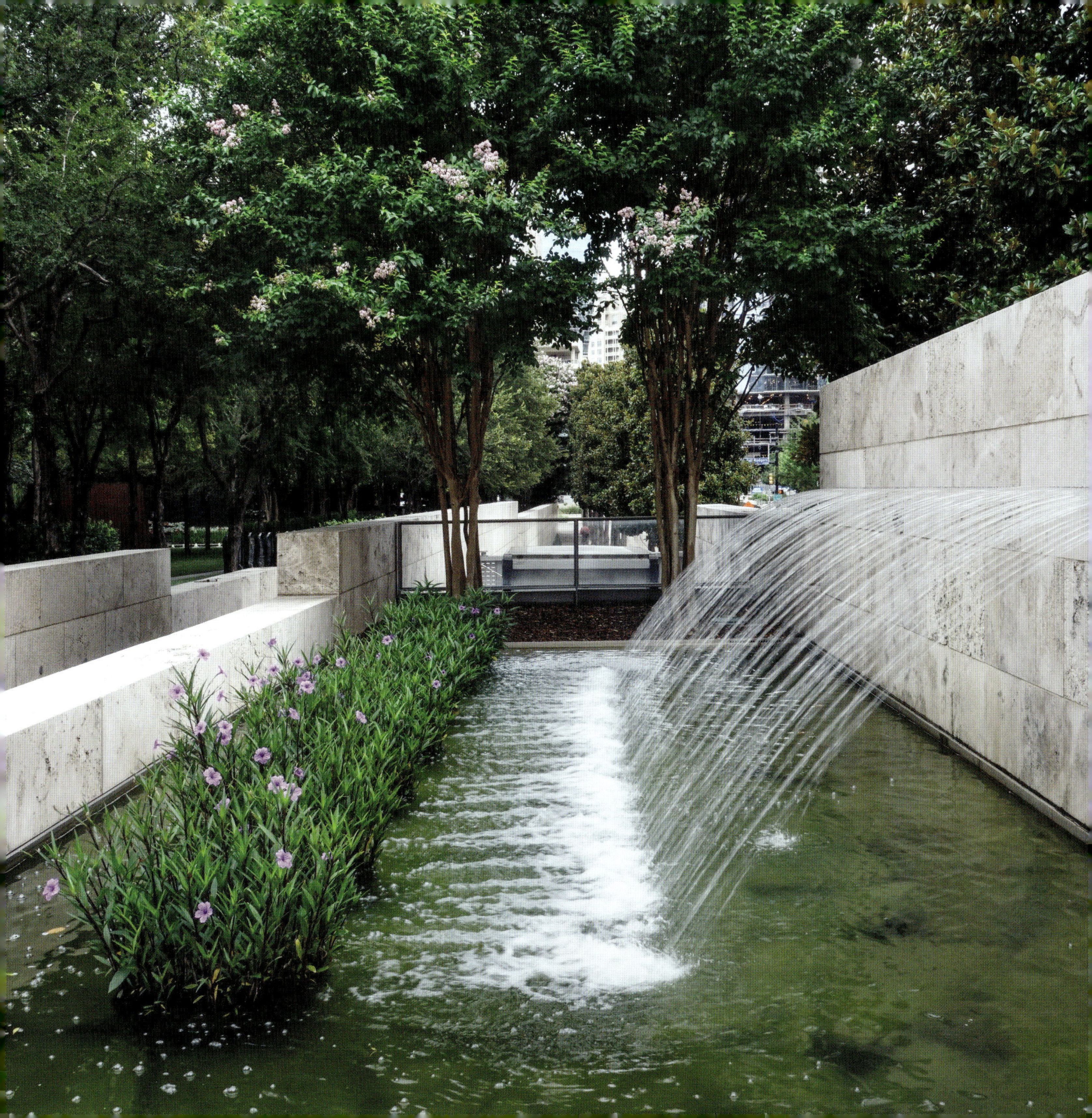

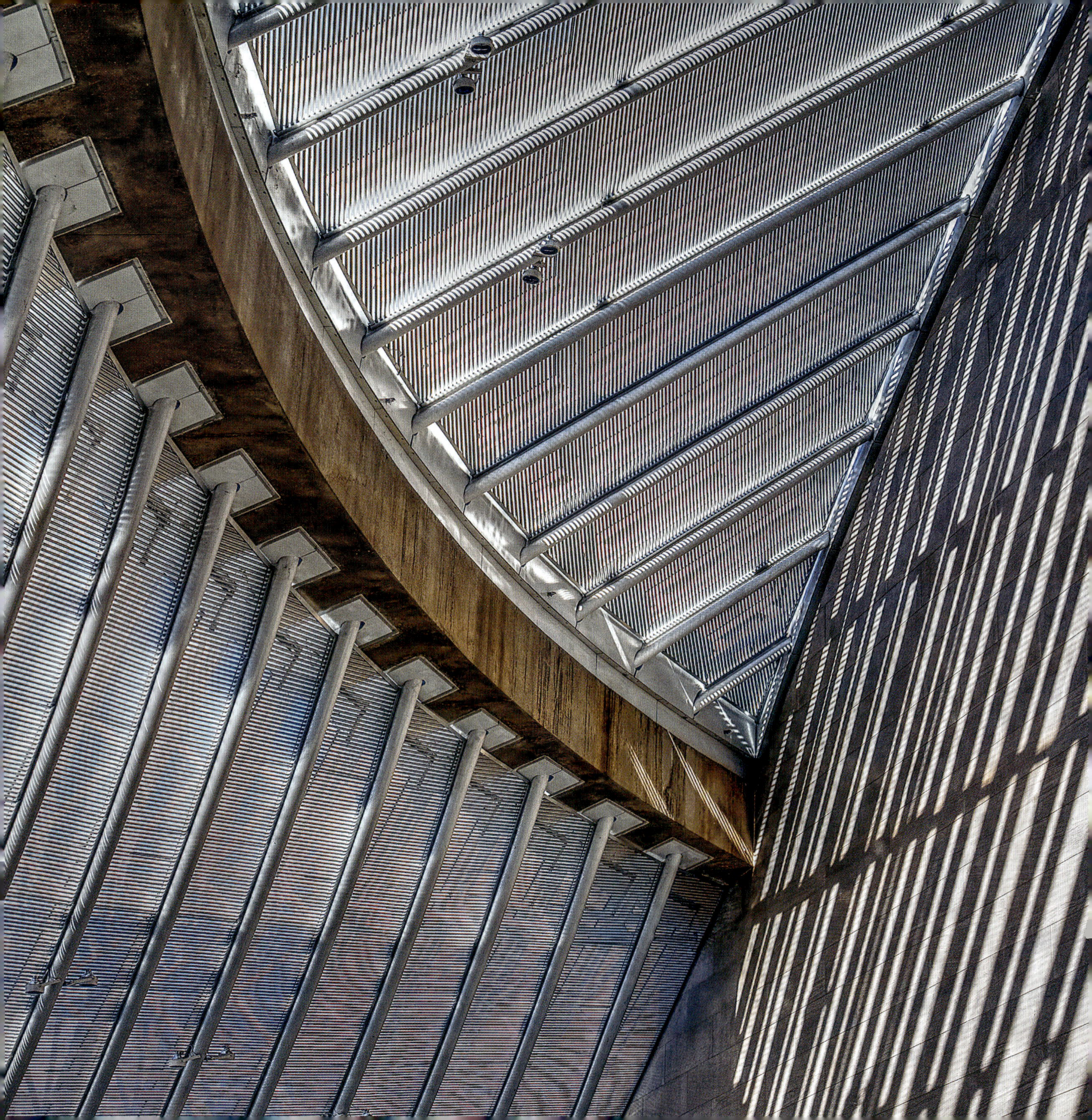

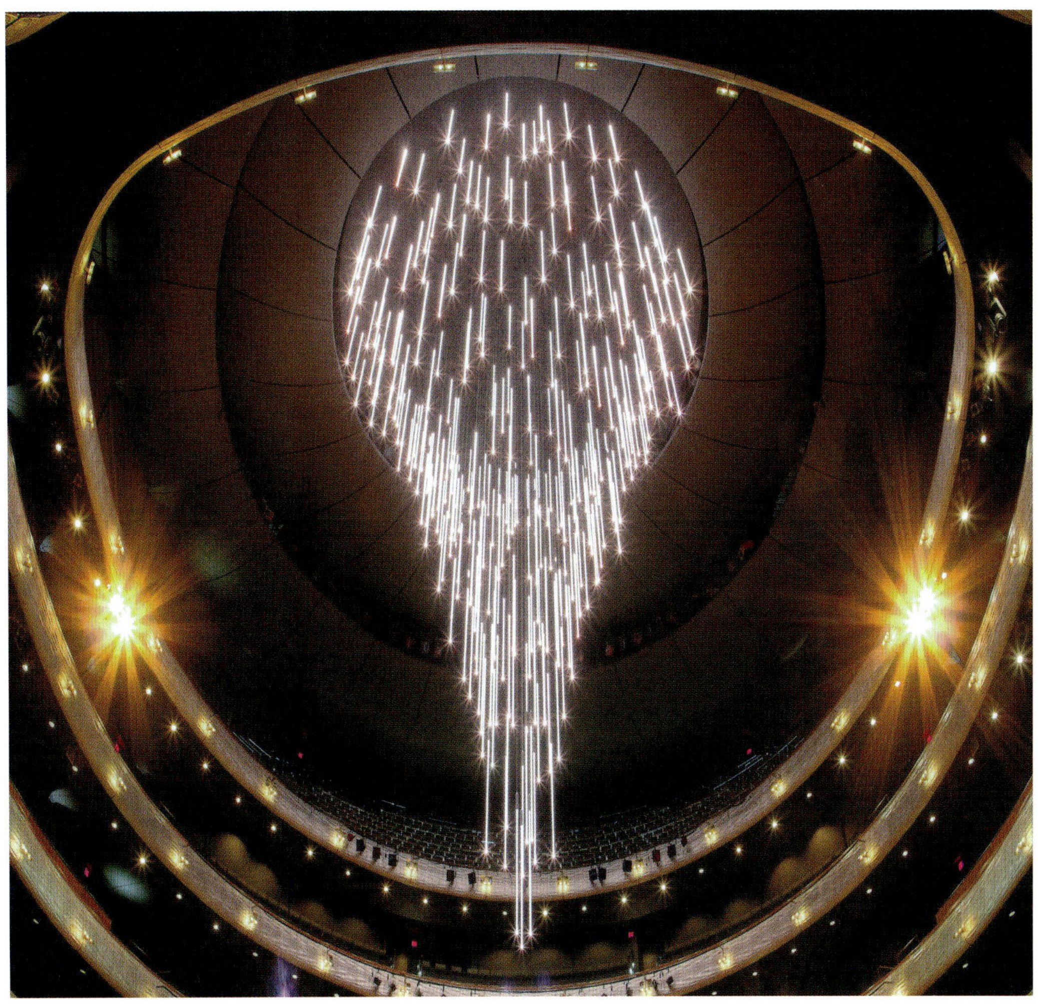

Above
Accompanied by a Philip Glass composition, the Moody chandelier at the Winspear Opera House ascends into the ceiling before each performance, after which its lights become stars in a night sky.

Opposite
The lobby of I. M. Pei's Morton H. Meyerson Symphony Center has a dramatic glass ceiling.

Following Pages
The red drum cylinder and louvered exterior trellis of the Bill and Margot Winspear Opera House was designed by Pritzker Prize-winning architect Lord Norman Foster.

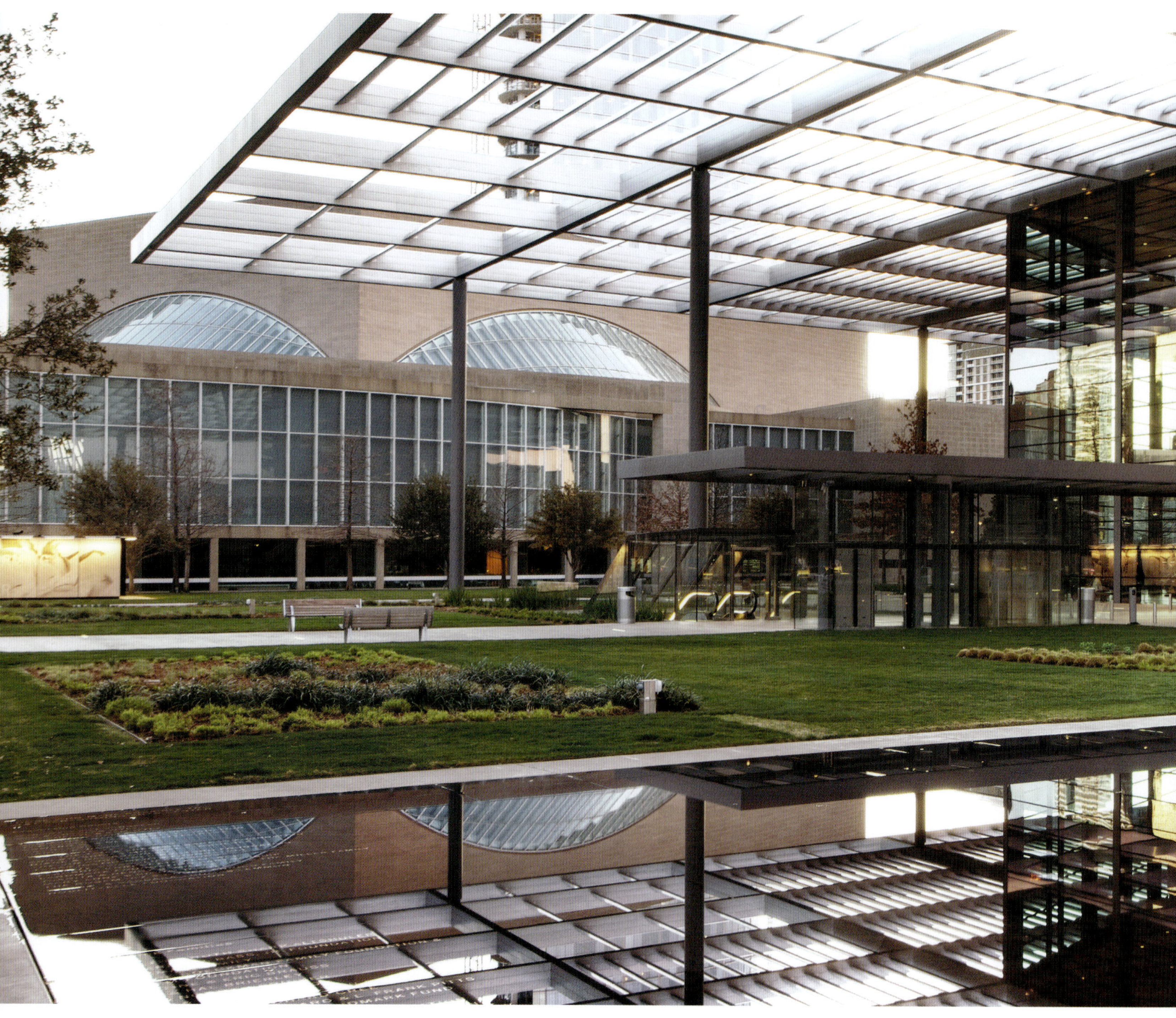

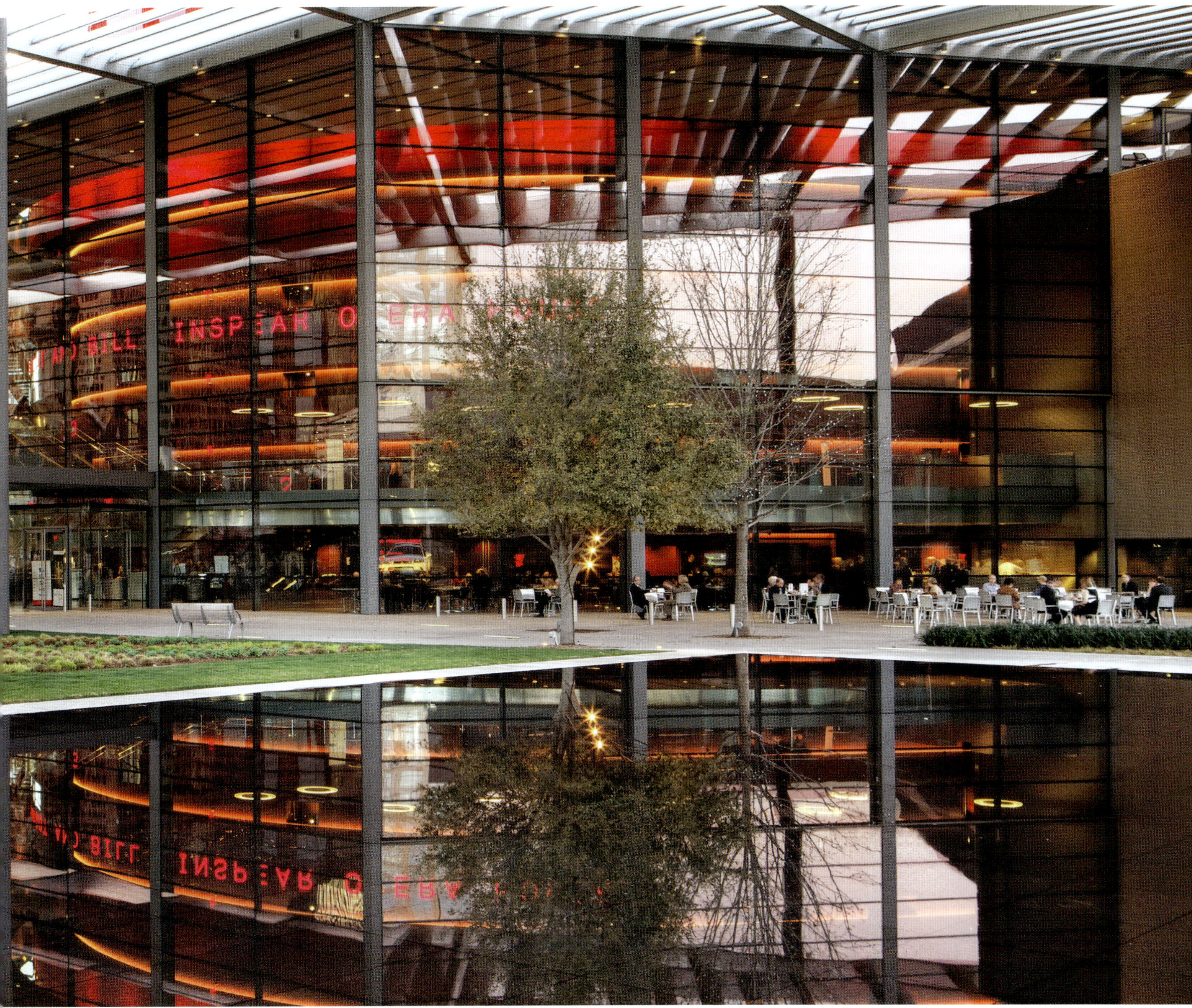

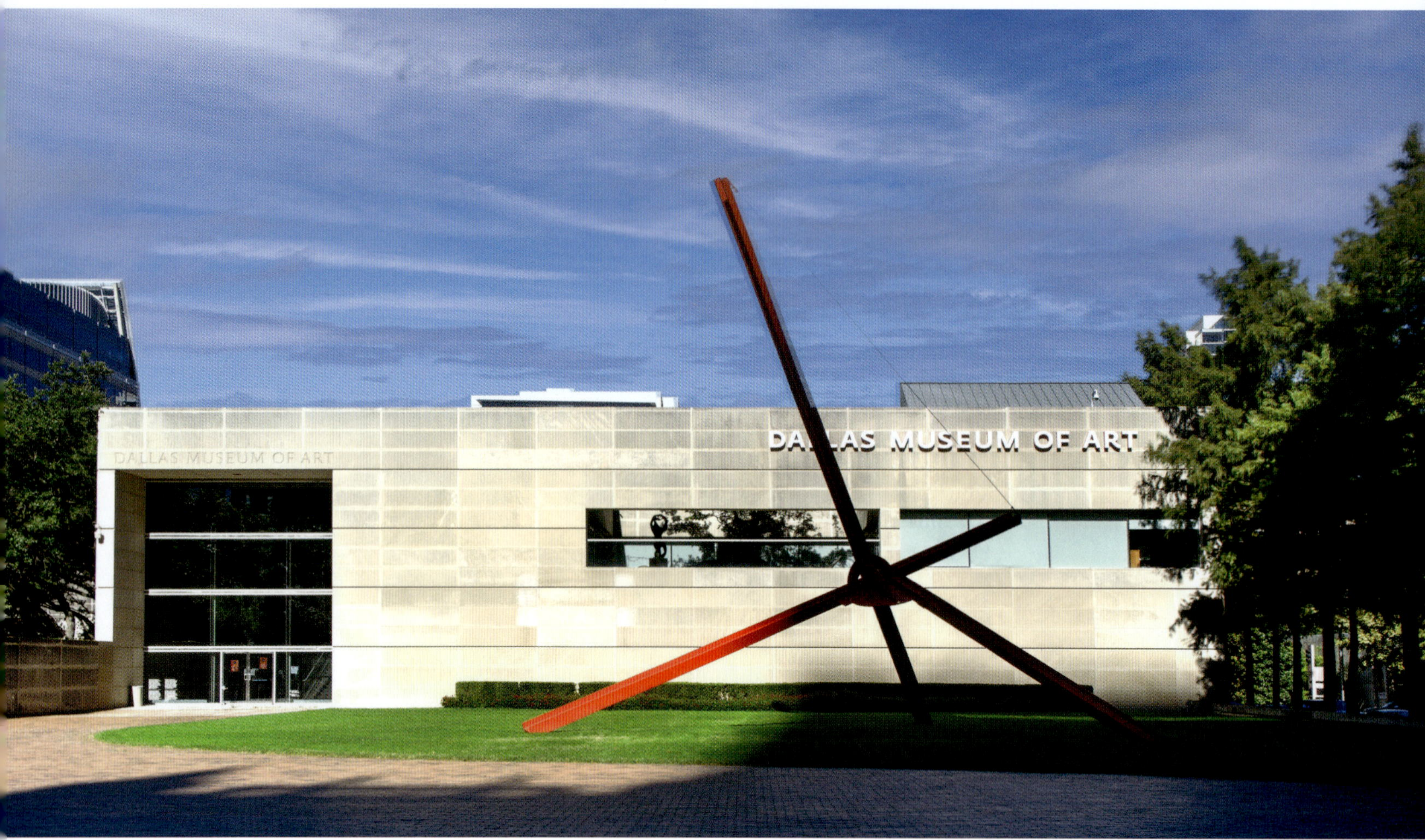

Above
Mark di Suvero's *Ave* stands on the Ross Avenue Plaza at the Dallas Museum of Art.

Opposite
The Dee and Charles Wyly Theatre was designed by Pritzker-winning architect Rem Koolhaas in collaboration with Joshua Prince-Ramus. It opened in 2009 as the home of the Dallas Theater Center. In the foreground, names of donors are etched into the bottom of a shallow reflecting pool.

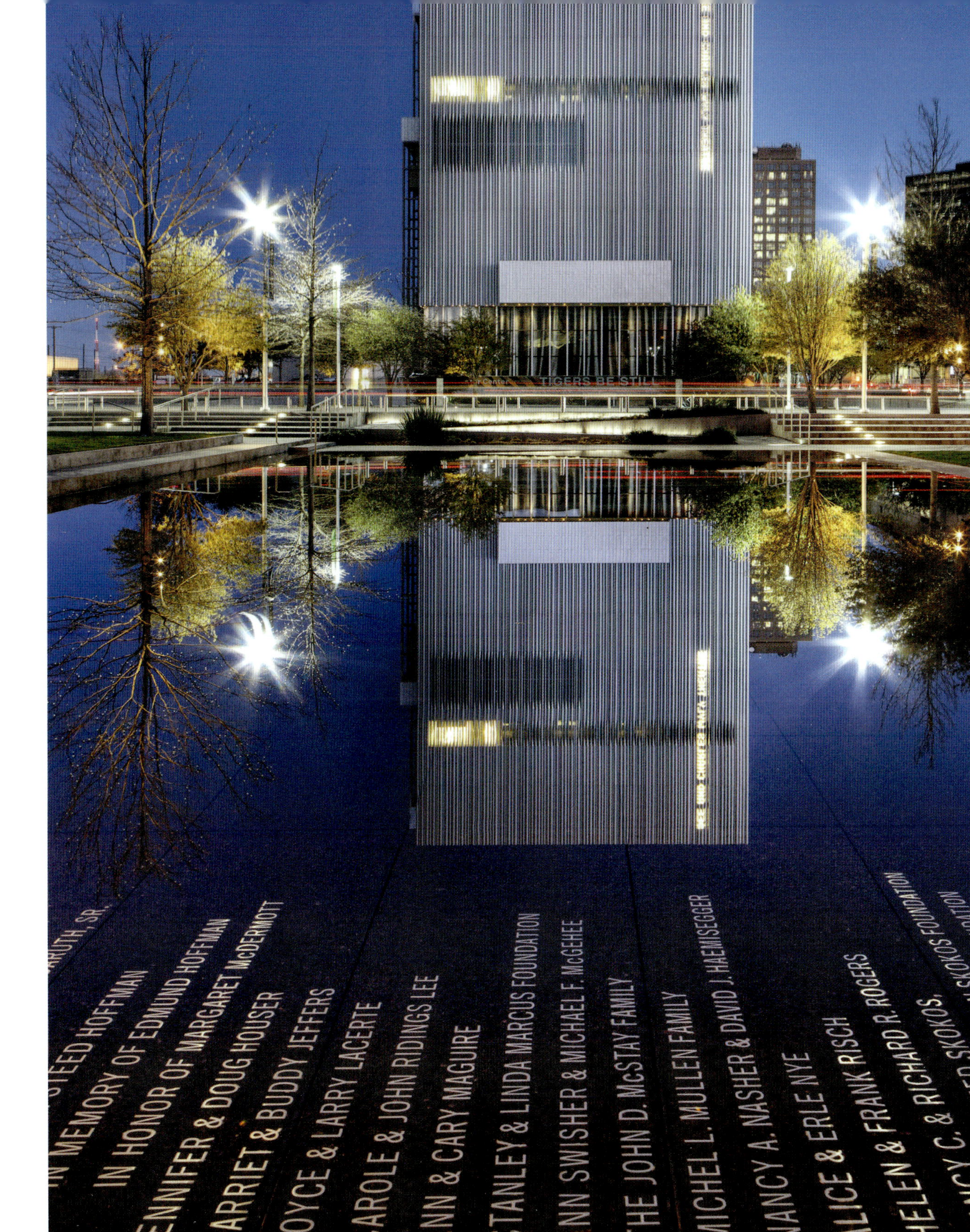
TIGERS BE STILL
STEED HOFFMAN
N MEMORY OF EDMUND HOFFMAN
IN HONOR OF MARGARET McDERMOTT
ENNIFER & DOUG HOUSER
ARRIET & BUDDY JEFFERS
OYCE & LARRY LACERTE
AROLE & JOHN RIDINGS LEE
NN & CARY MAGUIRE
TANLEY & LINDA MARCUS FOUNDATION
NN SWISHER & MICHAEL F. McGEHEE
HE JOHN D. McSTAY FAMILY
MICHEL L. MULLEN FAMILY
ANCY A. NASHER & DAVID J. HAEMISEGGER
ANCY & ERLE NYE
ALICE & FRANK RISCH
HELEN & FRANK R. RICHARD R. ROGERS
ANCY C. & RICHOKOS,
TED SKOKOS FOUNDATION

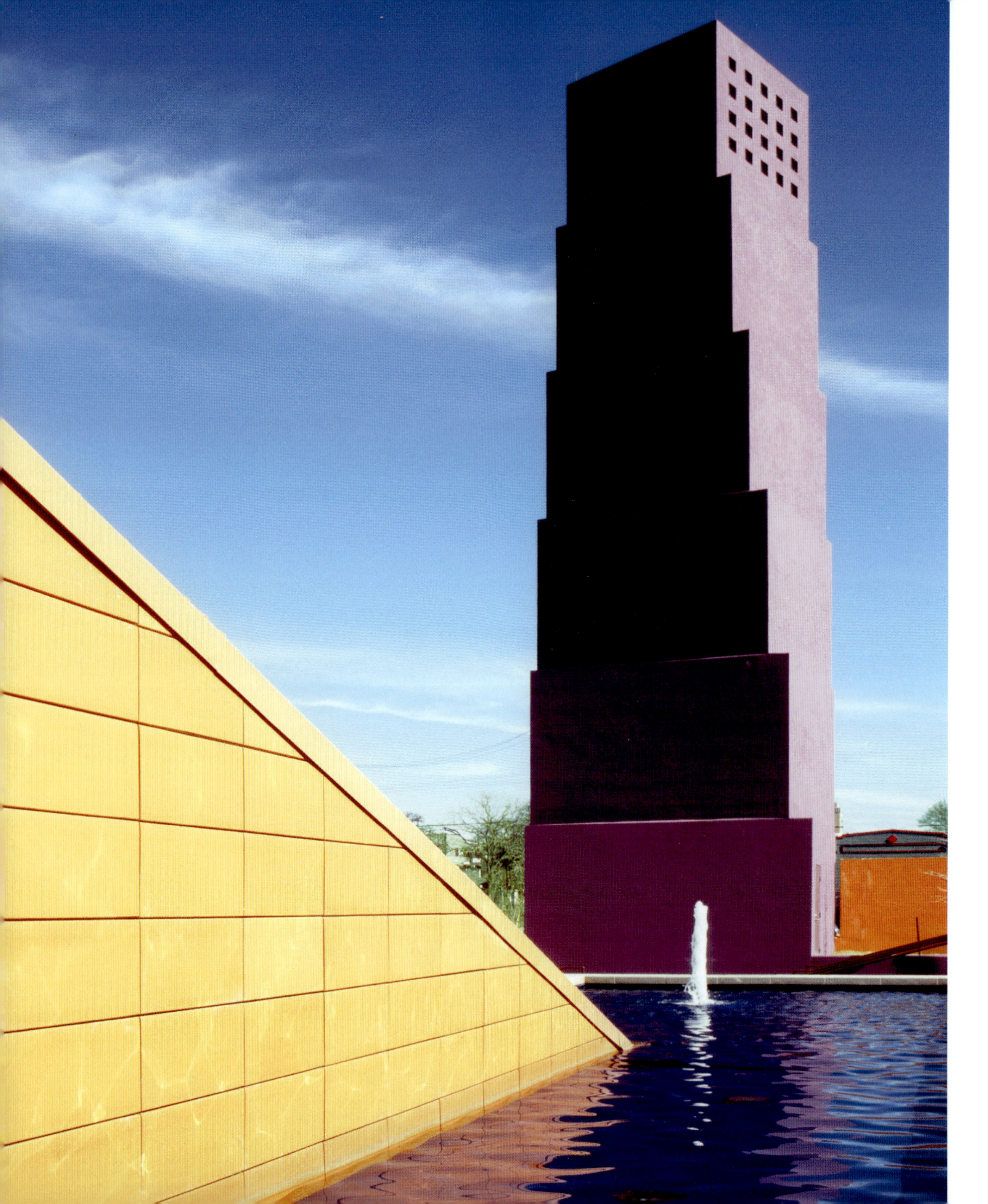

Enrich

Veletta Forsythe Lill, the former member of the Dallas City Council (1997–2005) and longtime community advocate, has played multiple roles in the development of the cultural and physical city. At the end of 2012, she retired as executive director of the Dallas Arts District (2008–2012), responsible for joint marketing and operations of one of the nation's largest cultural districts. She has served on numerous nonprofit boards, from the Dallas Center for Architecture (currently ADEX) to a Texas Advisor to the National Trust for Historic Preservation. Her past work in historic preservation, urban planning, and the arts has been honored at the local, state, and national level.

Opposite
The Latino Cultural Center was designed by Mexican architects Ricardo and Victor Legorreta using bold geometric forms and bright colors. It opened in 2006 and includes a theater, art galleries, and a plaza for outdoor events.

What makes a city unique? How is a city reflected at a macro level and a micro level? The macro level reflecting the grandest of gestures of a city. The micro level reflecting the more local, street-level keepsakes and beliefs of a city. What do we eat? What does the local artist create? What do we as a people define as important? Our city's interests have been defined over time and kept in jewel boxes throughout our community.

We do not, however, view them as stagnant—we see them as dynamic. They are at once historic and contemporary. In these places locals gather and tourists visit to gaze upon our reflections and ponder our future. They *enrich* us by telling our stories to new generations—keeping alive our memories. New works are created and enjoyed. They enrich our visitors through display and interpretation and discussion. Our stories can represent our highest aspirations and they can reflect some of our darkest moments. But they are stories we want to tell to reflect the way we see ourselves—through our lens.

Veletta Forsythe Lill

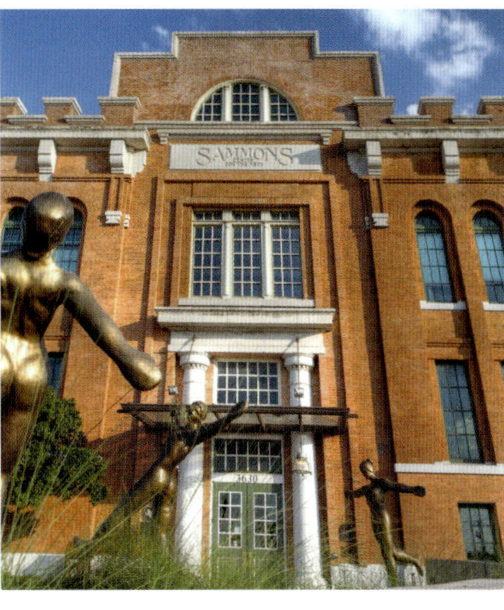

Above
The Sammons Art Center once housed the Turtle Creek Pump Station—the only source of drinking water for the city until 1930. Declared an historic landmark, the building was renovated in 1981to provide nineteen thousand square feet of multiuse space for performing arts organizations.

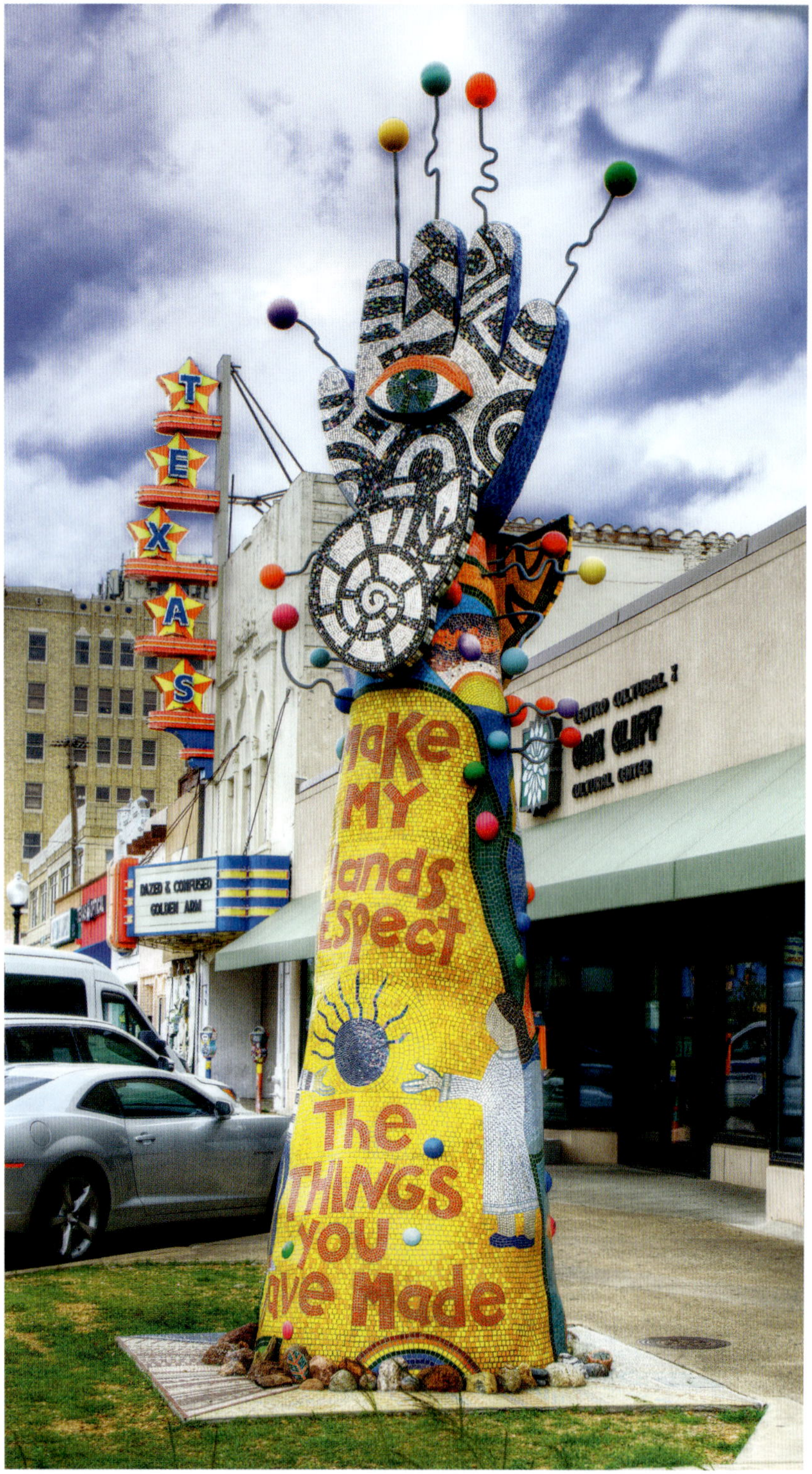

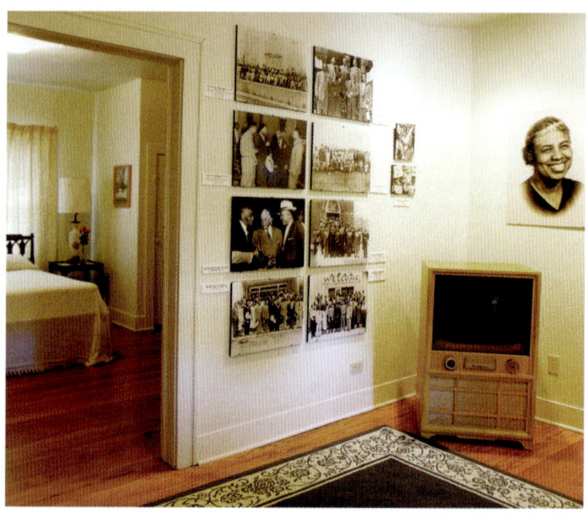

Above
The Juanita J. Craft House in South Dallas documents the inspiring career of its longtime resident who worked as a seamstress, became a civil rights leader, and was elected a member of the Dallas City Council.

Left
The Oak Cliff Cultural Center, located on Jefferson Boulevard next to the historic Texas Theatre, includes an art gallery and multipurpose studios.

Opposite
A visitor enters the Dallas World Aquarium by passing through the Shark Tunnel and soon finds herself in an enchanting world of marine life, reptiles, and amphibians. Ecosystems of rain forests and other habitats have been re-created in this West End attraction.

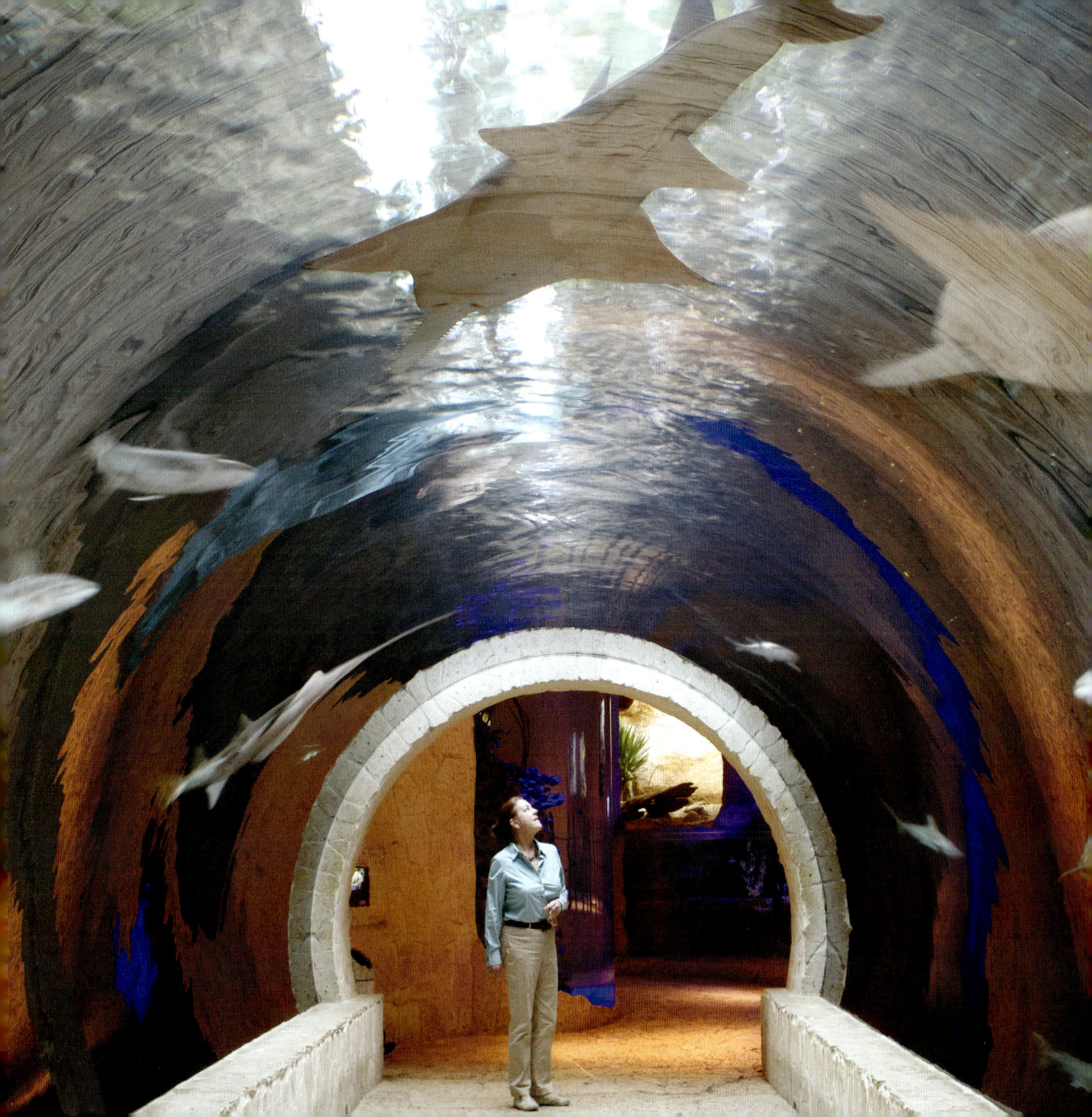

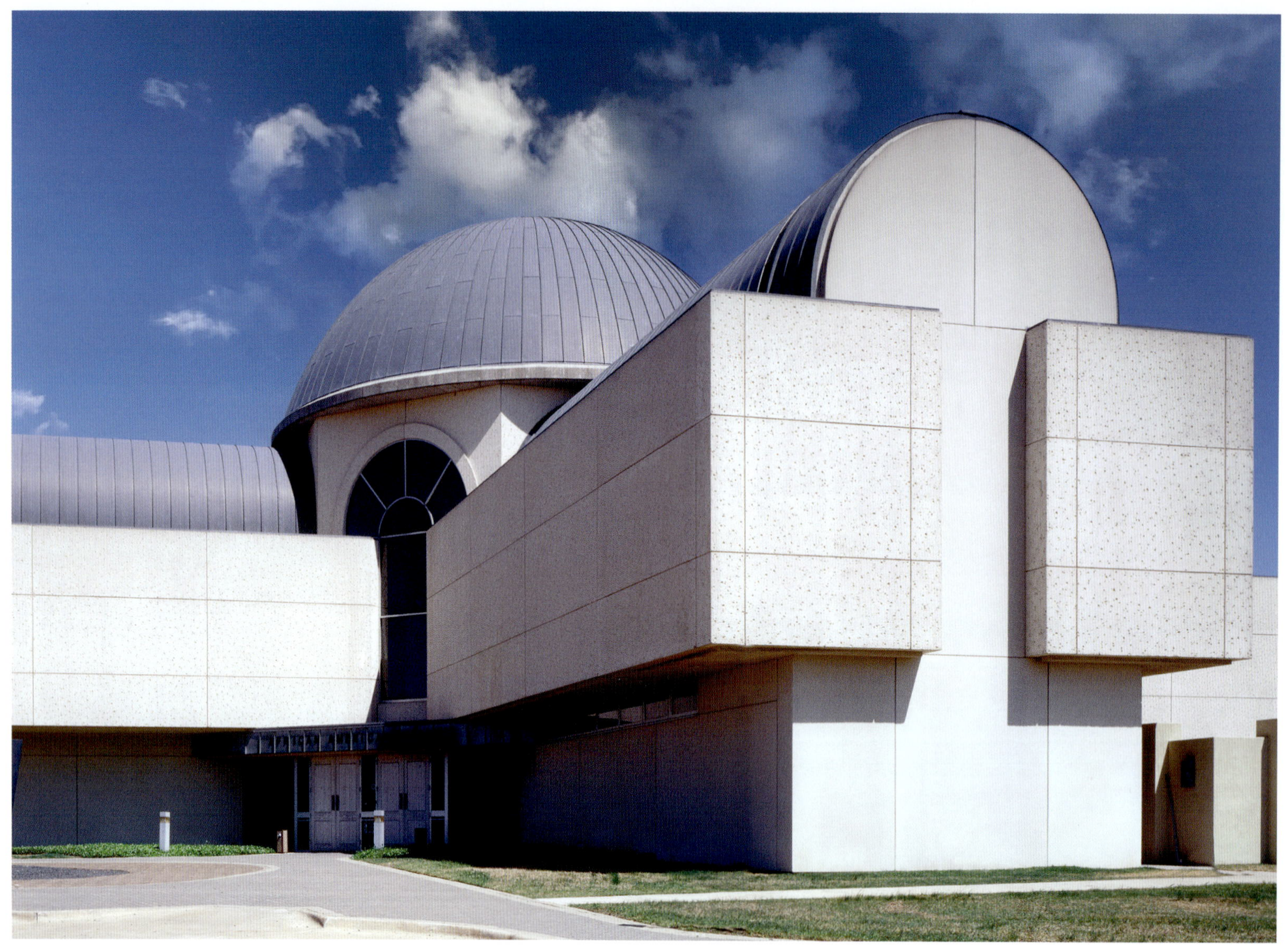

Above
The African American Museum at Fair Park, designed by Arthur J. Rogers in the shape of a traditional African cross, houses the largest African American folk art collection in the United States.

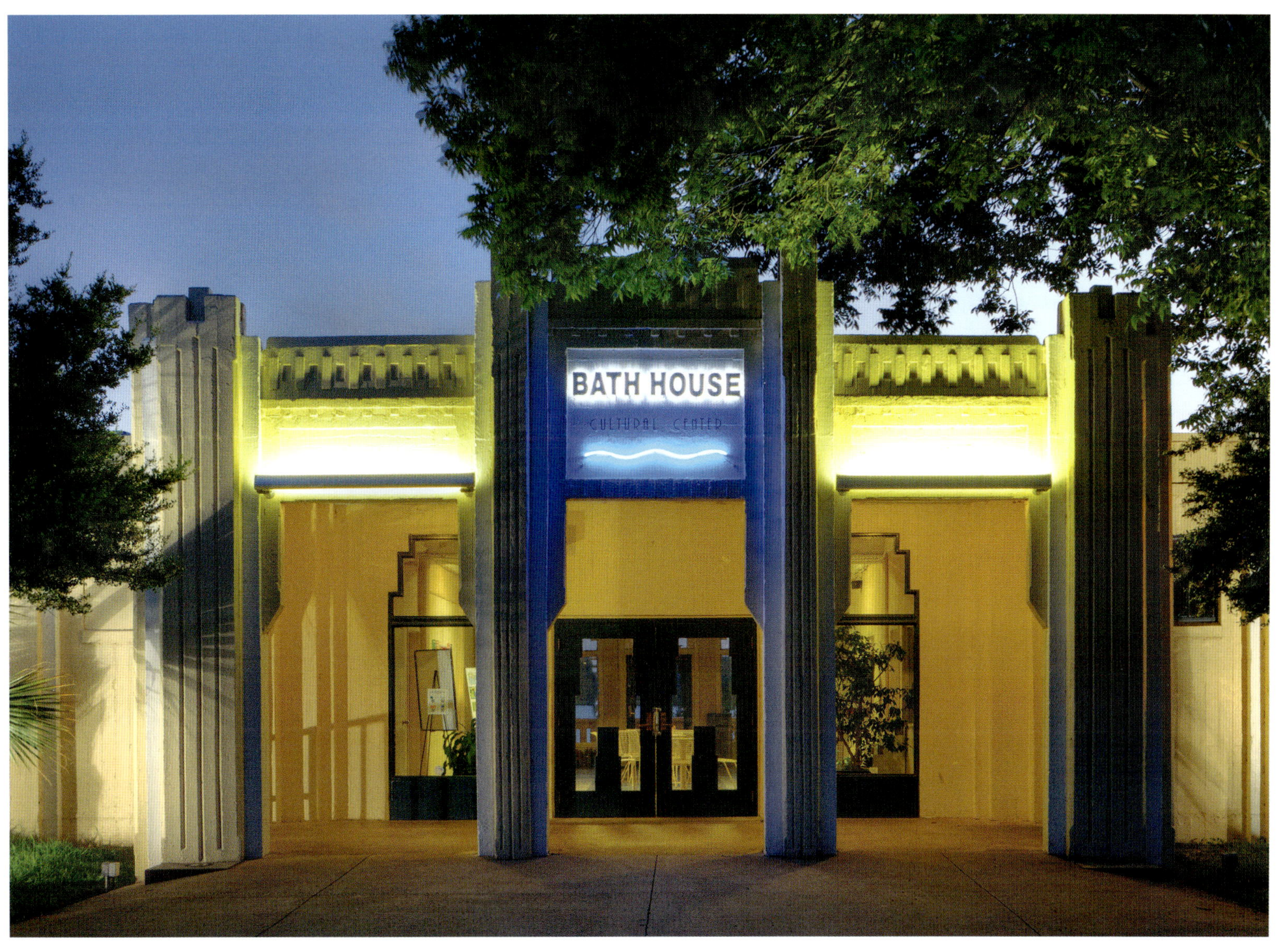

Above
The Bath House Cultural Center stands on the shores of White Rock Lake and provides venues for both visual and performing artists. Constructed in 1930, the Art Deco building was renovated in 1981.

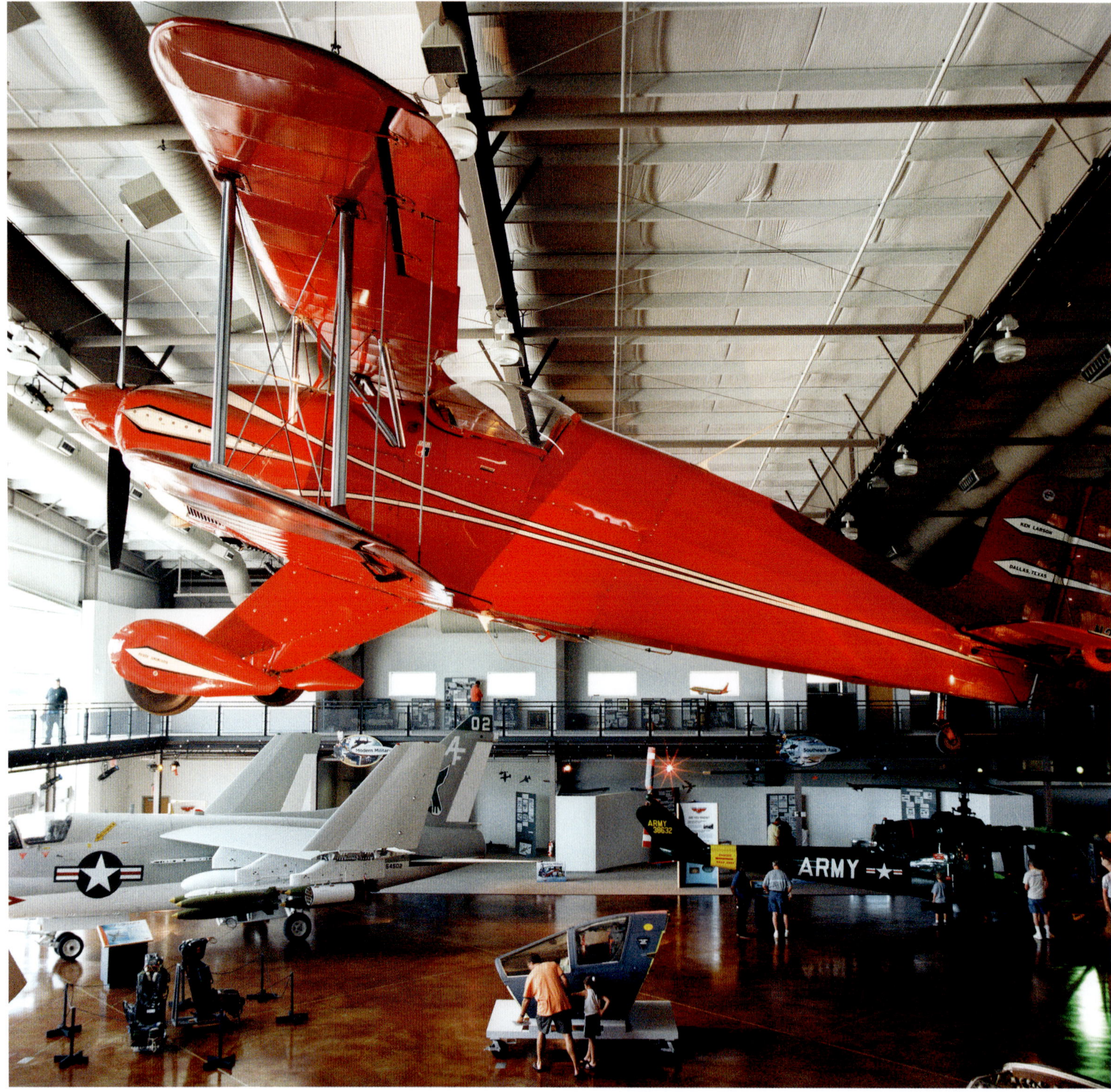
KEN LARSON
DALLAS, TEXAS
02
ARMY
38632
ARMY
Southeast Asia

Right
Night view of the Farmers' Market. Established in 1941 on the edge of the downtown business district as sheds for local farmers, the market is now a modern retail space for crafts and restaurants as well as fresh produce.

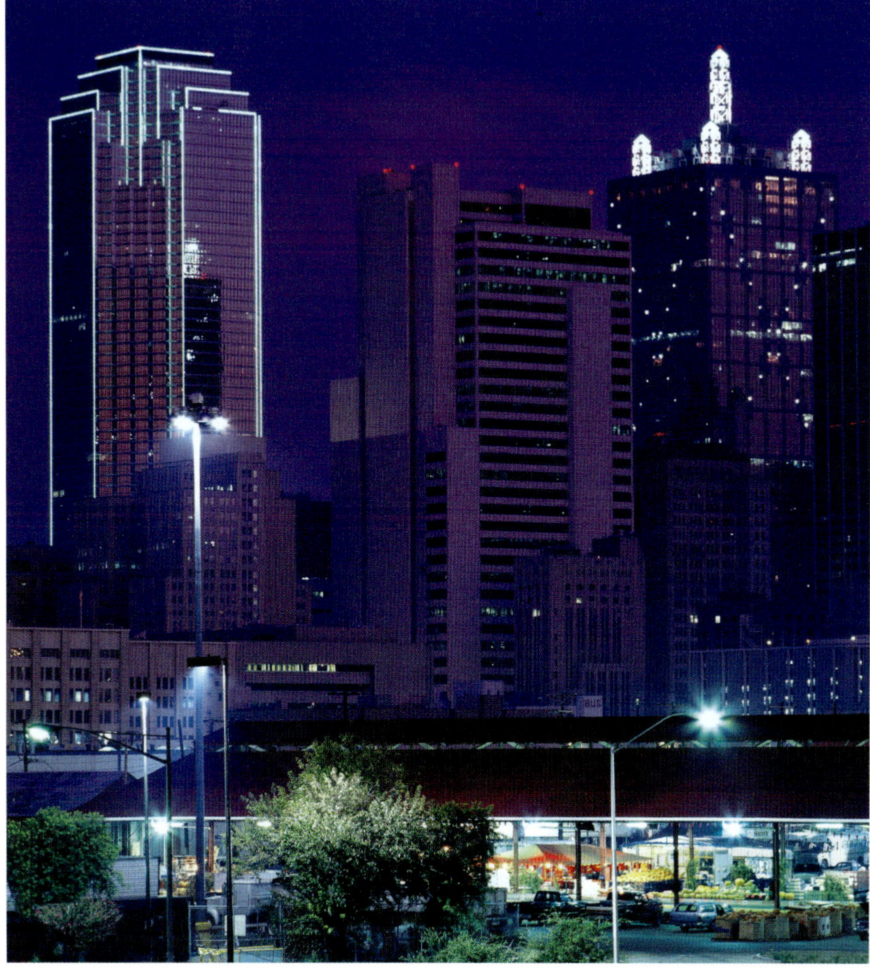

Right
The Dallas Holocaust and Human Rights Museum was established in 1984 by Holocaust survivors in Dallas to preserve the memory of what can happen when prejudice, hatred, and indifference rule. The museum, located in the West End Historic District, opened to the public in 2018.

Opposite
More than two hundred WWII aircraft hang from the ceiling at the Frontiers of Flight Museum near Love Field. The museum documents the history of flight from the Wright Brothers at Kitty Hawk to Neil Armstrong's walk on the moon.

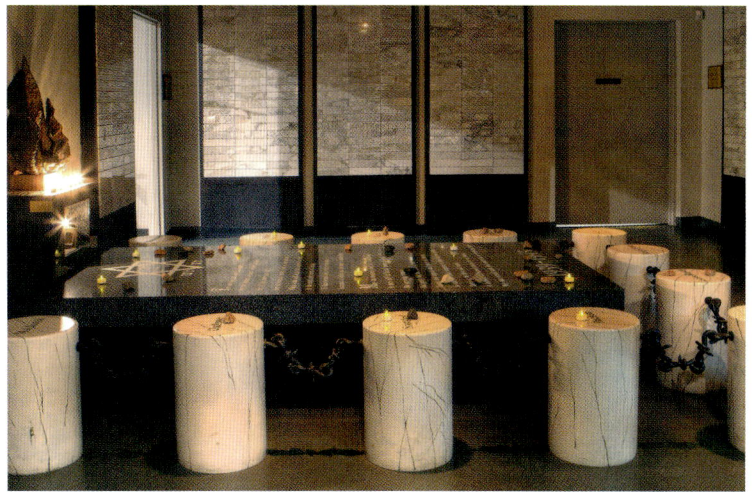

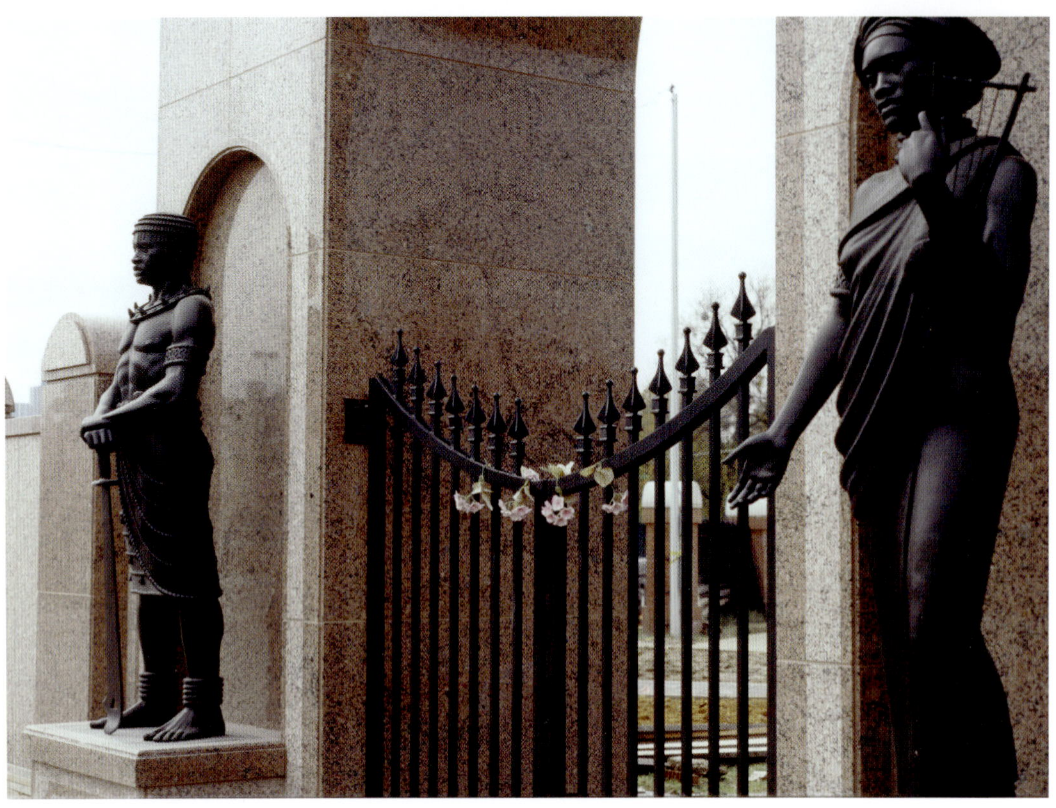

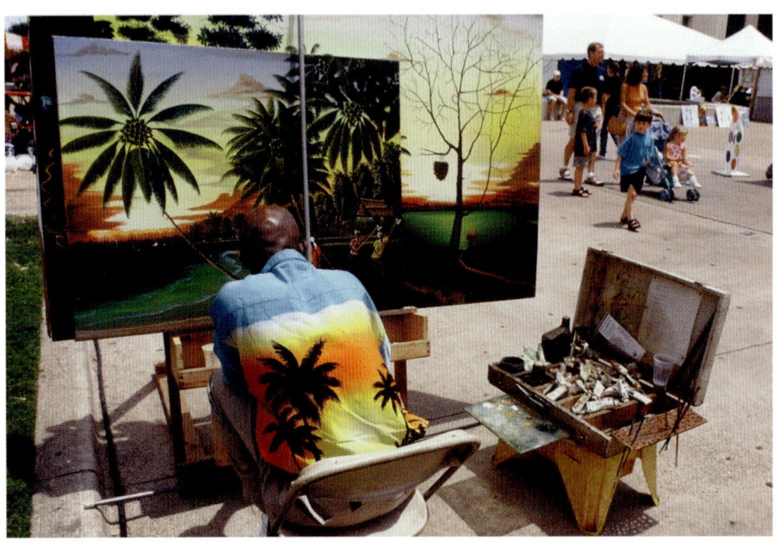

Above
The Freedmen's Cemetery was a burial ground for freed African American slaves after the Civil War. Established as a Memorial by the City of Dallas in 1990, its granite entry is flanked by David S. Newton sculptures.

Left
An artist at work during one of Dallas's many street festivals.

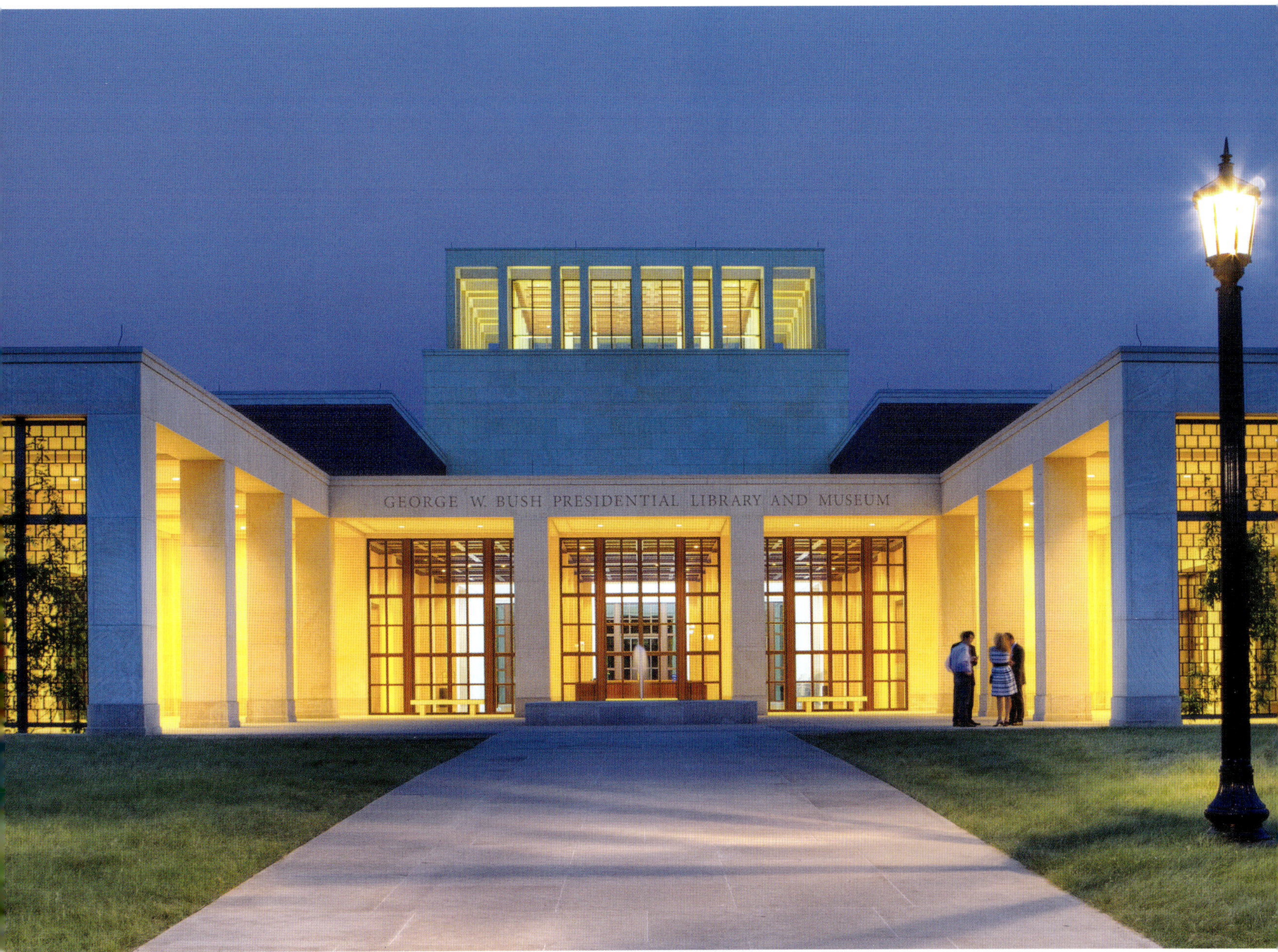

Above
The George W. Bush Presidential Library and Museum, designed by architect Robert A. M. Stern, opened in May 2013 on grounds near the SMU campus.

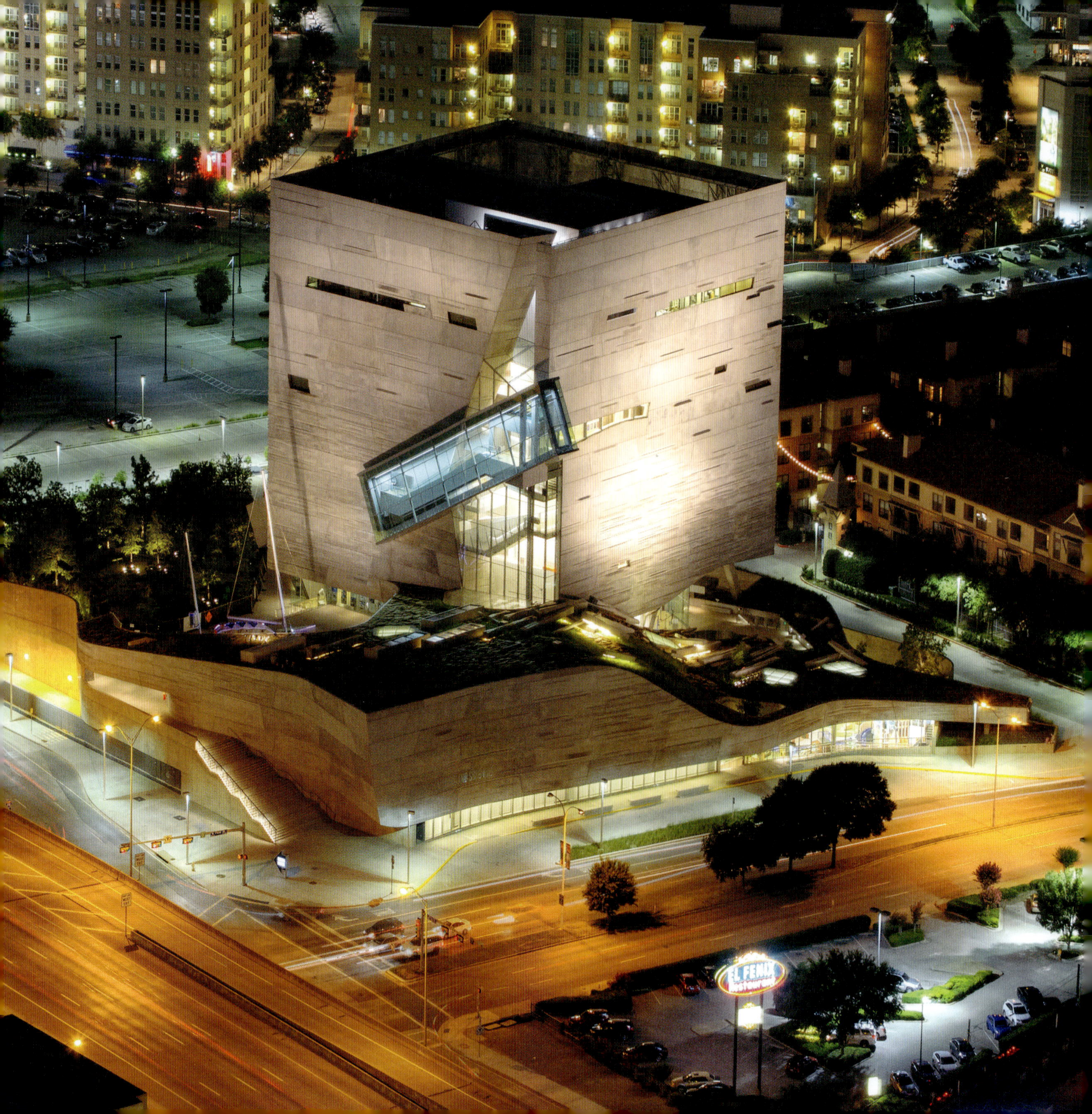
EL FENIX

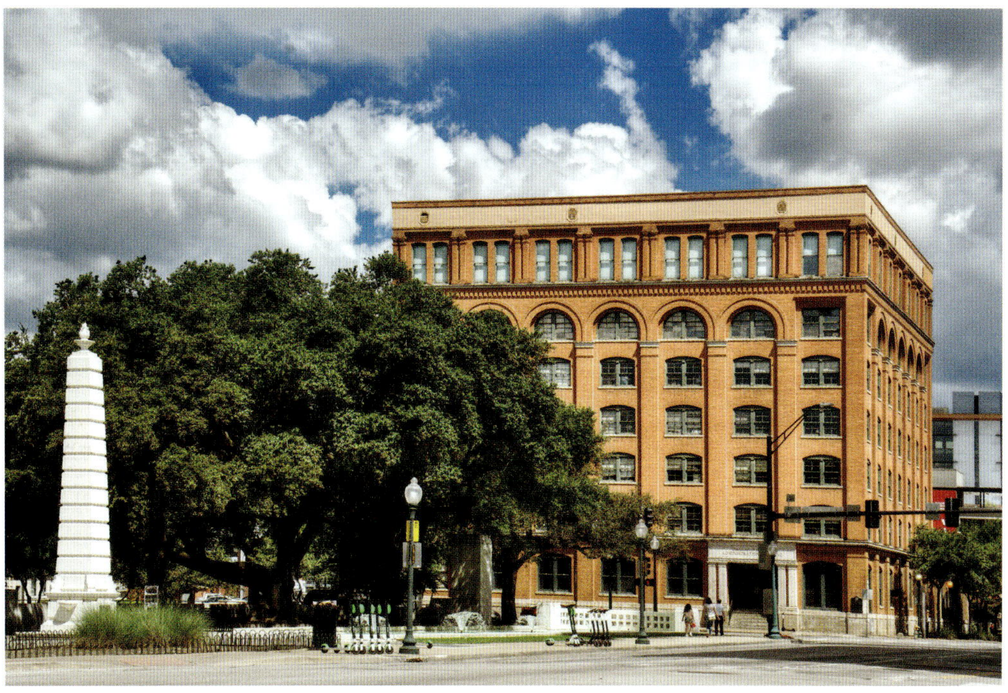

Right
The Sixth Floor Museum at Dealey Plaza examines the life, death, and legacy of President John F. Kennedy. The museum occupies the sixth floor of the former Texas School Book Depository, where Lee Harvey Oswald fired the shots that killed the president on November 22, 1963.

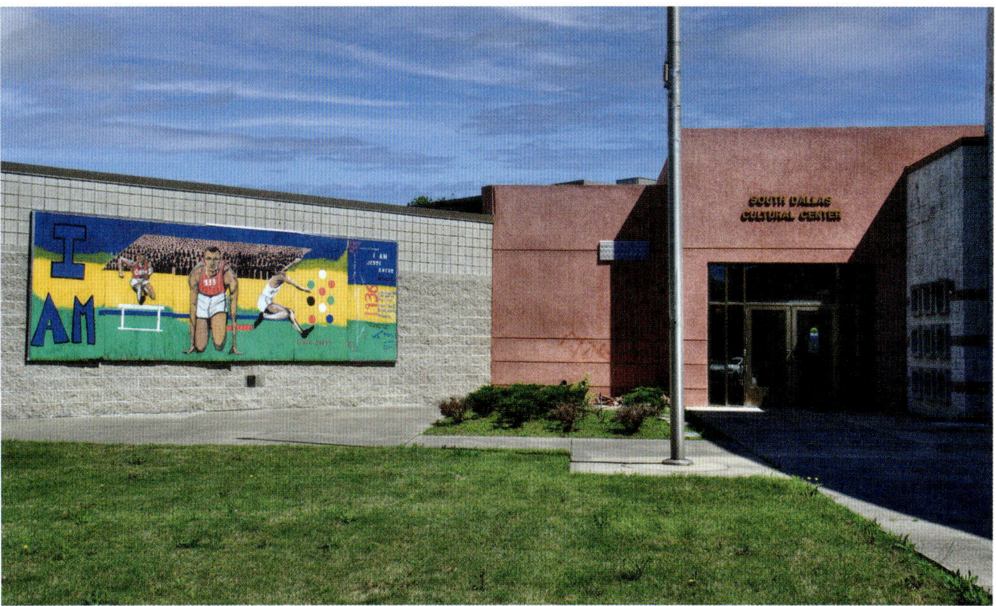

Right
The South Dallas Cultural Center near Fair Park celebrates the African contribution to the culture of Dallas. The center houses a theater, an art gallery, and space for weekly classes in diverse mediums.

Opposite
The Perot Museum of Nature and Science, designed by Pritzker Prize-winning architect Thom Mayne, features a striking exterior glass casing for its fifty-four-foot-long escalator.

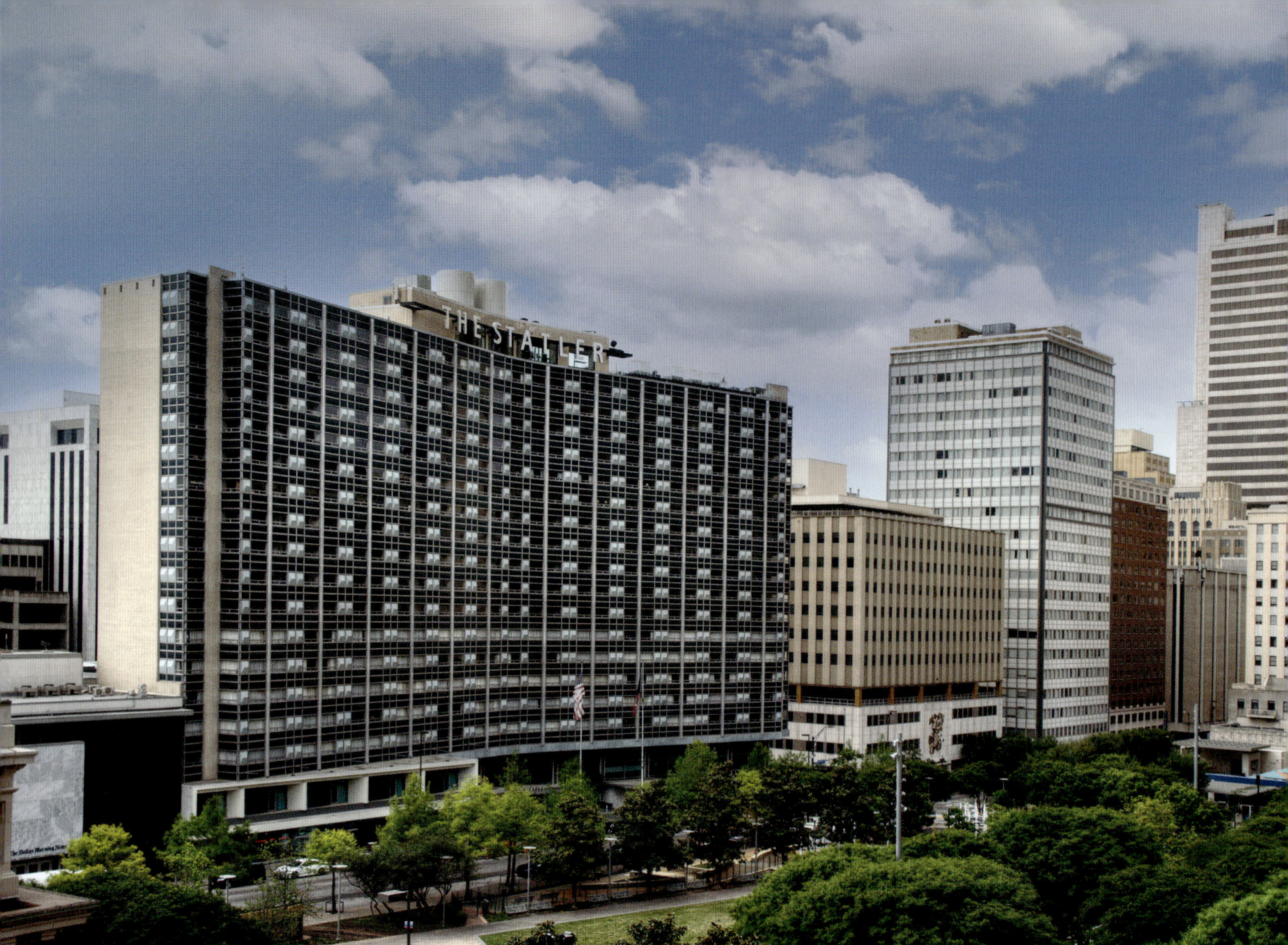

Above
The Statler Hilton Hotel, designed by architect William B. Tabler, was completed in 1956 at a cost of $16 million. The newly renovated hotel accommodates 159 guest rooms on the first five floors and 219 apartments on the upper eleven floors. It overlooks Main Street Gardens, a public park that opened in 1999.

Preserve

David Preziosi, FAICP, served as the executive director of Preservation Dallas, an organization dedicated to the preservation of Dallas's historic places, from 2012 to 2022 and is currently the executive director of the Texas Historical Foundation. David has a great passion for historic preservation and has worked in the field of preservation planning his more than twenty-five-year career, during which he has received numerous accolades for his work. He has worked in both the government and nonprofit sectors, starting his career in Mississippi and returning to Texas in 2012 to lead Preservation Dallas.

Why should we preserve historic places? The answer is simple: our historic places are our visual connection to the past. They are the vessels that hold the stories of the people that have come before us and tell how they lived, worked, and experienced life on a daily basis. They tell of the struggles, the accomplishments, and the innovative and pioneering nature of those who shaped Dallas from a small settlement on the Trinity River into the modern and diverse city that we know today. We need those historic places from all facets of Dallas's development so those incredible stories are not lost.

Architecture is something in which I have been interested since I was a child, and it took a college semester of studying in Italy for me to understand the importance of historic preservation and preserving our past. As I traveled through Europe, I marveled at how people there treasured the centuries-old buildings and how they were a major part of their daily lives. When I came back to Texas, I saw the opposite, as "old" buildings were discarded for new development. I was disheartened to see the loss of those unique structures and decided to focus my career on working to save as many historic buildings as I could from the wrecking ball.

With Dallas being a relatively new city, many people don't think we have historic architecture worth saving. But we do! Dallas actually has an amazingly rich diversity of historic buildings all over the city, in all shapes and sizes, from the late 1800s to the 1960s, and covering a wide range of architectural styles. Now and in the future, I would like people to be able to come to Dallas to experience the incredible historic architecture we have and the stories that go with those places. I want people to marvel at the level of craftsmanship and detail in those buildings that is hard to attain today and to learn about the people who built those places.

The mix of old and new buildings makes Dallas a vibrant and interesting city. However, as the city has grown over the years, many historic buildings have been lost in the quest for the newer-bigger-better of a rapidly changing city. That makes the historic places that remain all the more important for us to preserve, so we can save our past for our future.

David Preziosi

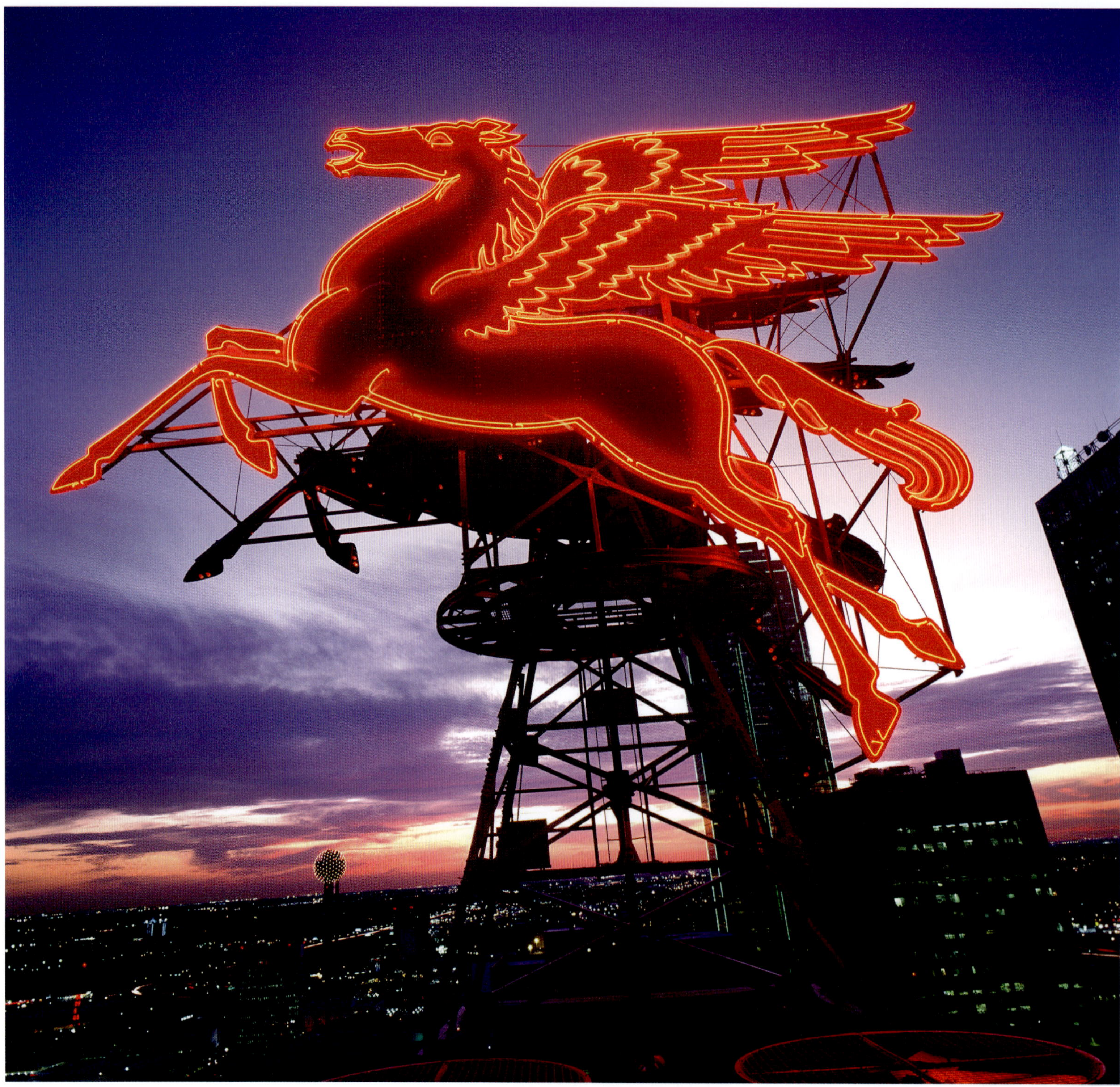

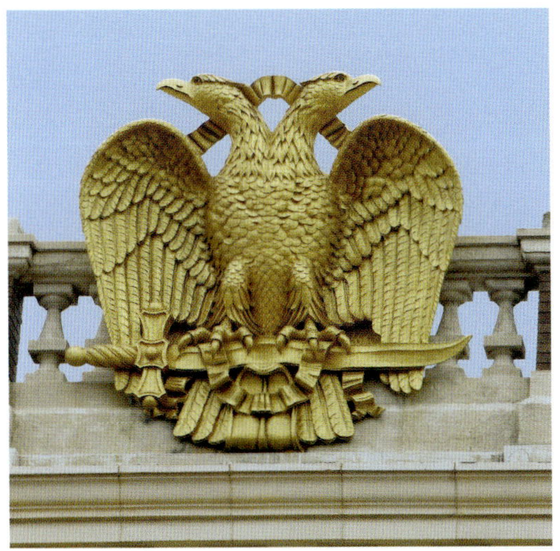

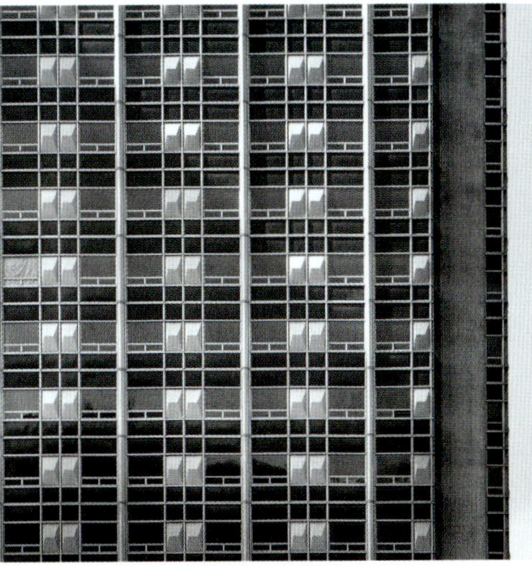

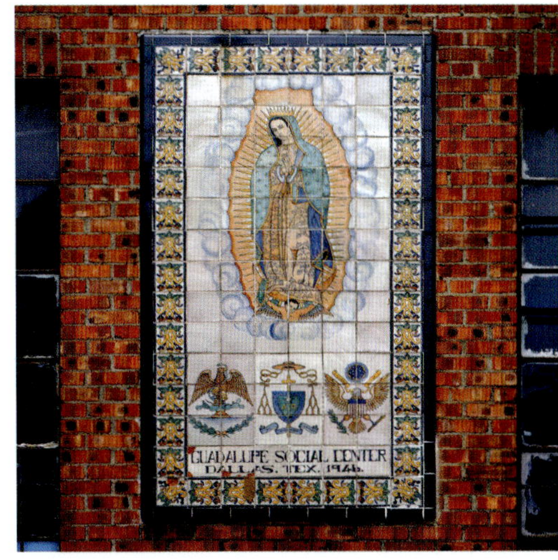

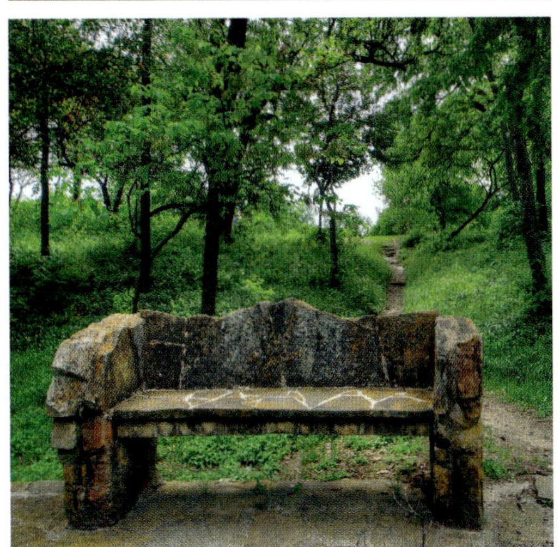

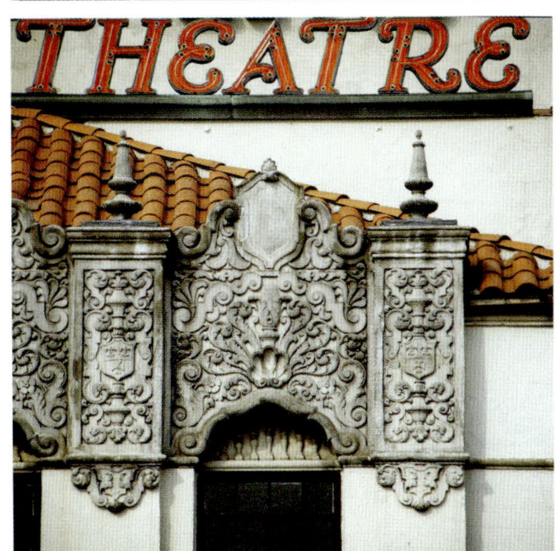

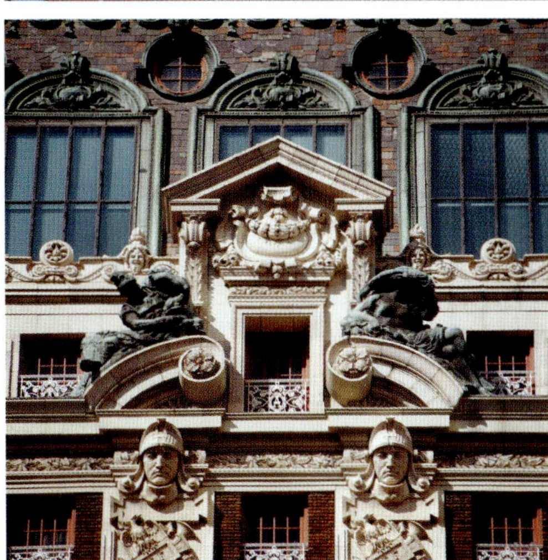

Above
Six close-up views of preserved historic sites in Dallas include a fraternal lodge, hotels, a former school, a theater, and a park.

Opposite
This massive red neon horse has kept watch over the city for over eighty years. Built in 1934 to rotate on top of the Magnolia Building, then Dallas's tallest building, the winged image of Pegasus has become the symbol of Dallas.

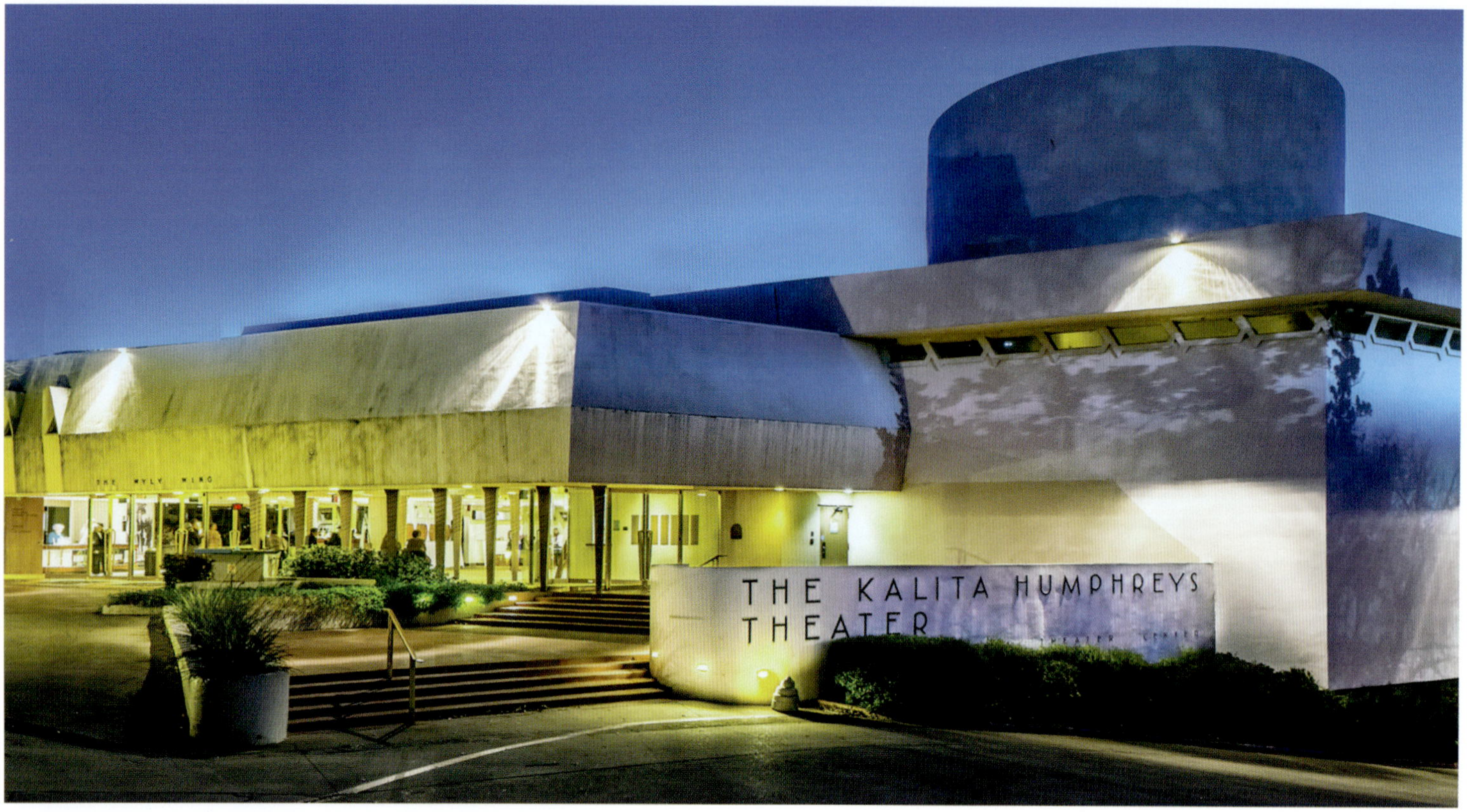

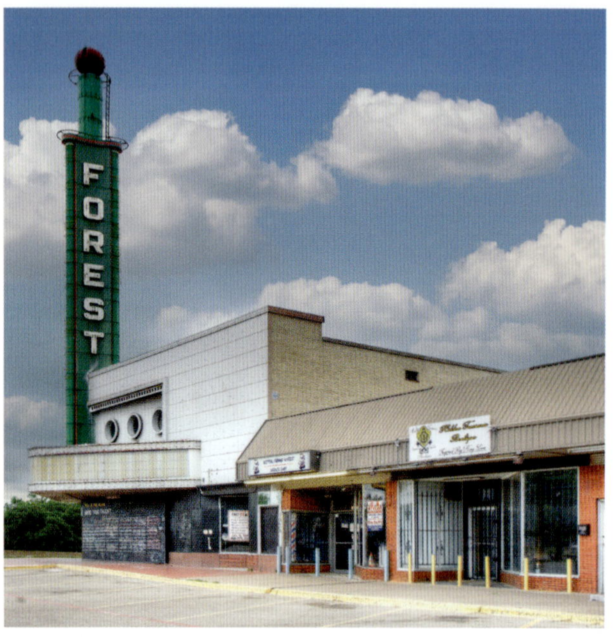

Above
The Kalita Humphreys Theater opened in 1959 and is the only freestanding theater designed by Frank Lloyd Wright.

Left
The Forest Theater on Martin Luther King Boulevard near Fair Park opened in July 1949 and was designed by H. F. Pettigrew of Pettigrew and Worley.

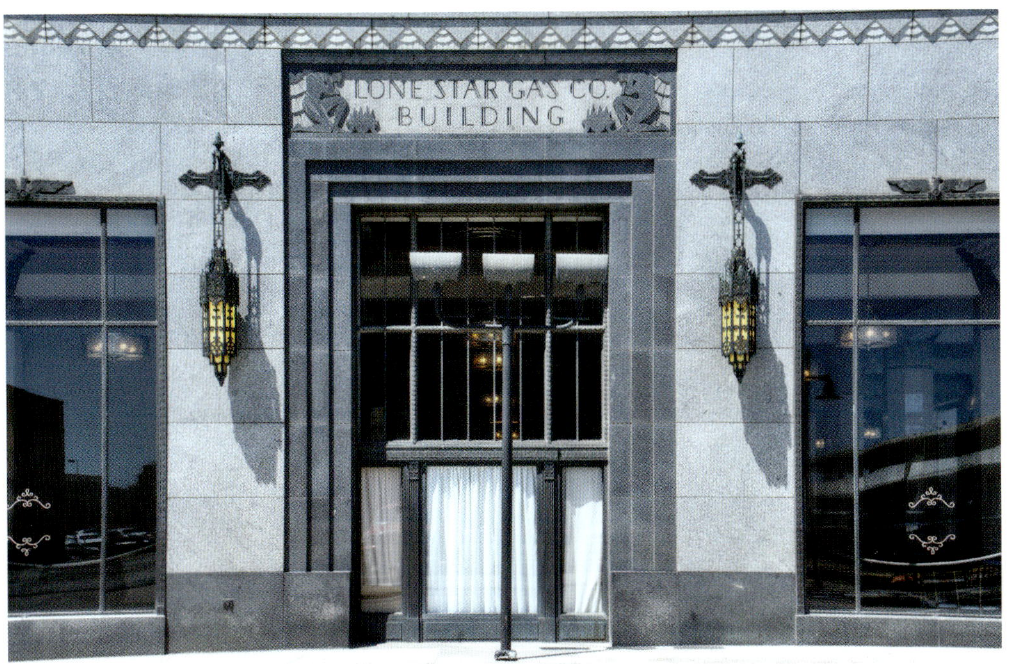

Left
The Lone Star Gas Co. Building was built in 1931 in the Art Deco style with richly detailed street entrances, ornate light fixtures, and a lobby of soaring columns and stone walls carved with bas-relief sculptures.

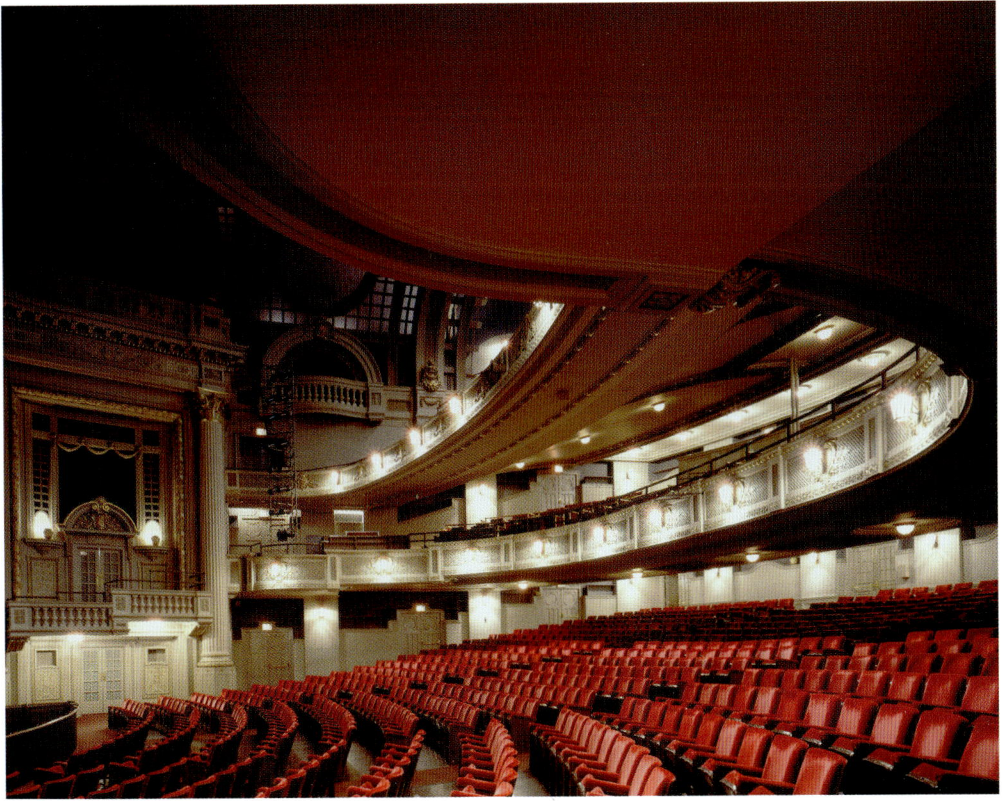

Left
The Majestic Theatre, designed by John Eberson in 1921, is a performing arts theater in downtown Dallas. It is the last remnant of Theater Row, the city's historic entertainment center on Elm Street, and is a contributing property in the Harwood Street Historic District. It was restored by the City of Dallas in 1983.

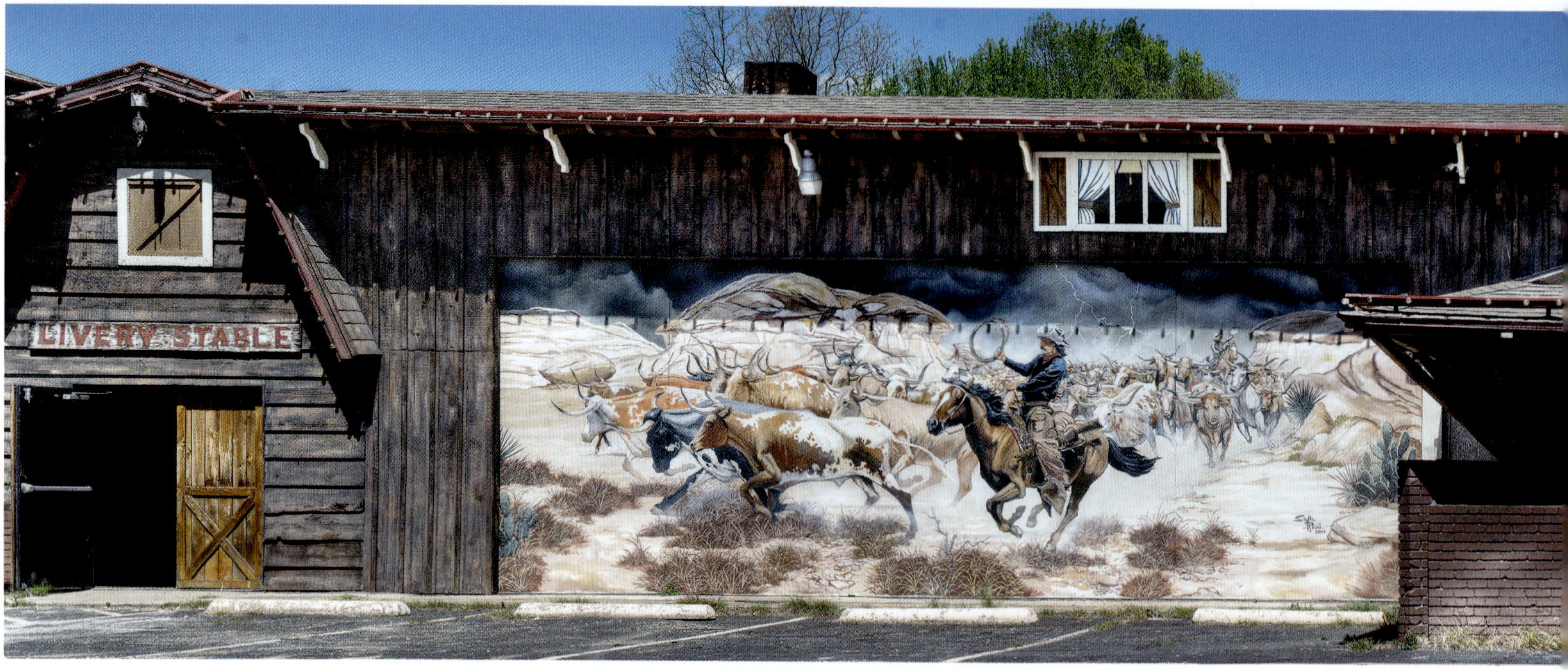

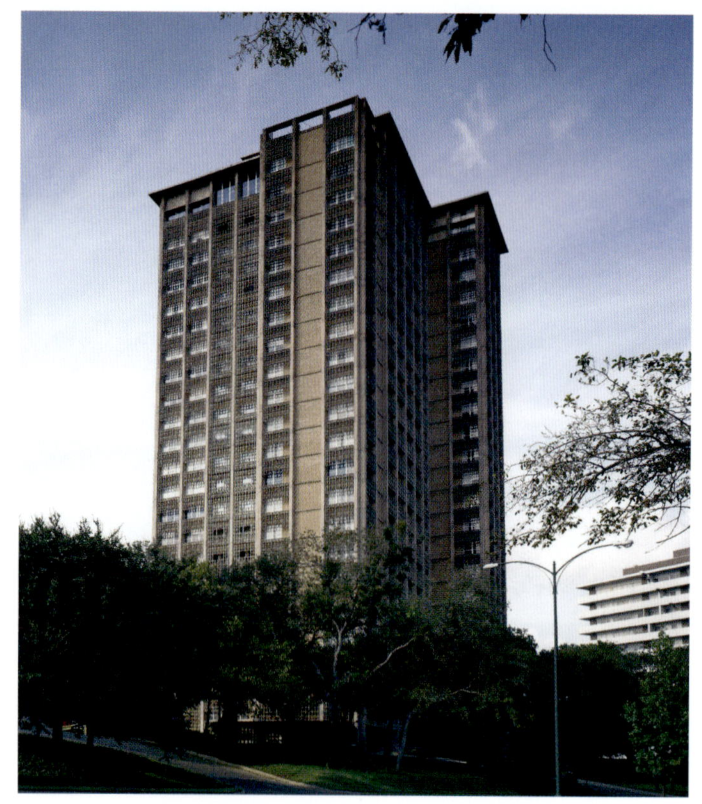

Above
The Longhorn Ballroom was originally built as the Bob Wills Ranch House in 1950 and was made famous by Dewey Groom, who renamed it the Longhorn Ballroom in 1958. He installed the quirky 250-foot-long western-themed façade in 1968. The popular music venue attracted famous musicians from country and western to punk rock and was dubbed the "Astrodome of Country and Western Music" for its size. Stylle Read completed the current murals on the building in 2019.

Right
Designed by Howard Meyer and known by the numerals of its street address, 3525, this was the first residential high-rise built on Turtle Creek in 1957.

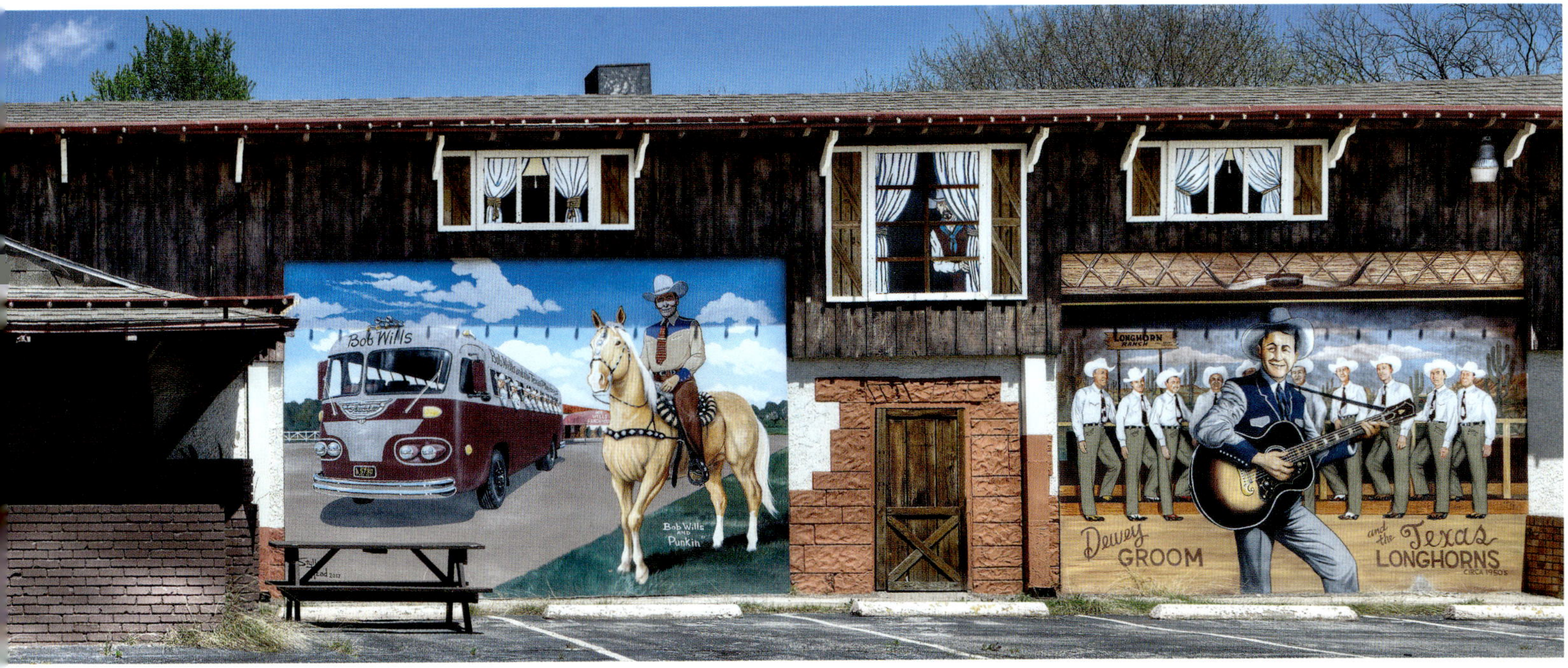

Right
St. Jude Chapel opened on Main Street in 1968 to provide a peaceful oasis in the midst of busy downtown Dallas. The colorful Genesis Mosaic is made up of hand-cut Smalti tile and was designed by MIT professor György Kepes. The chapel offers daily mass and confession, as well as a gift shop for religious articles.

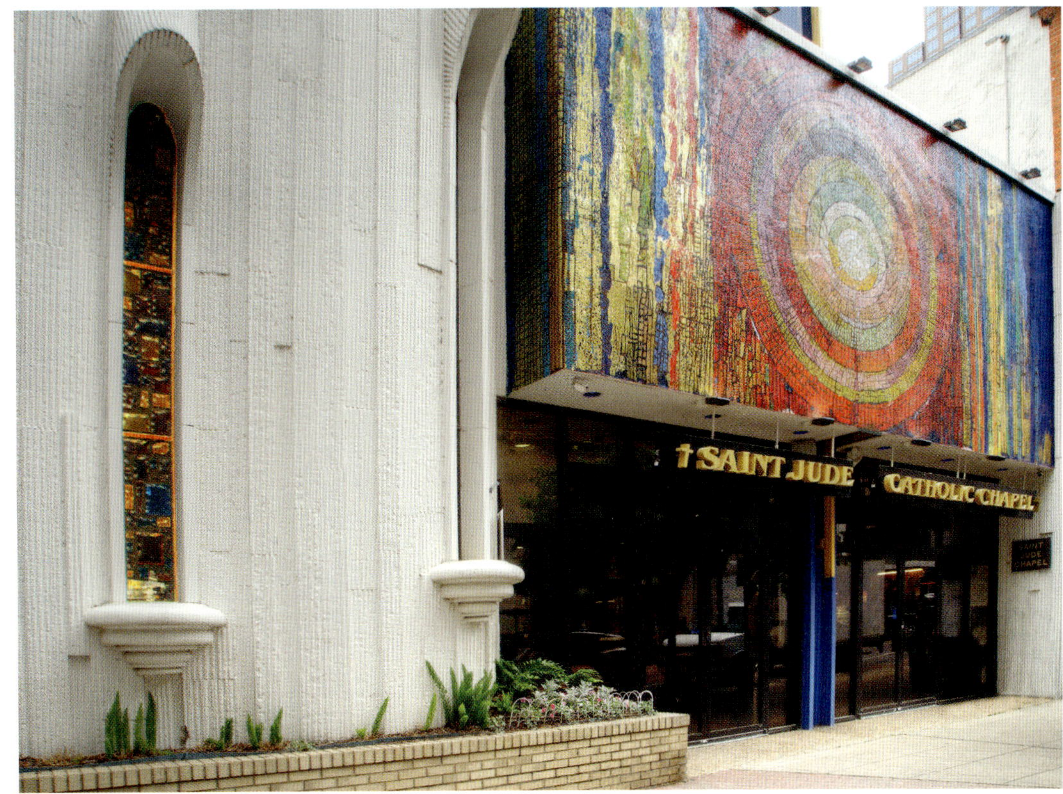

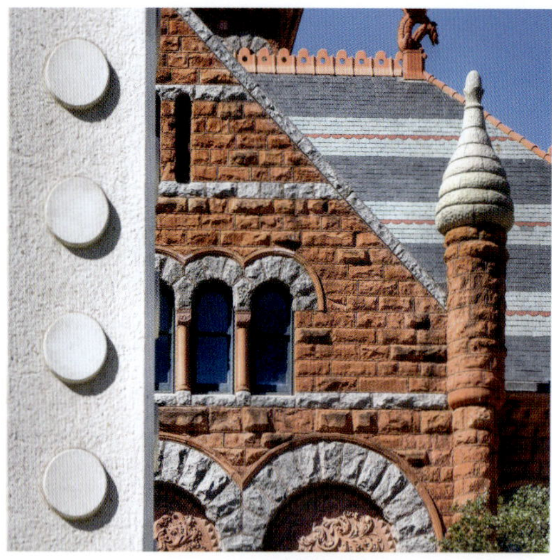

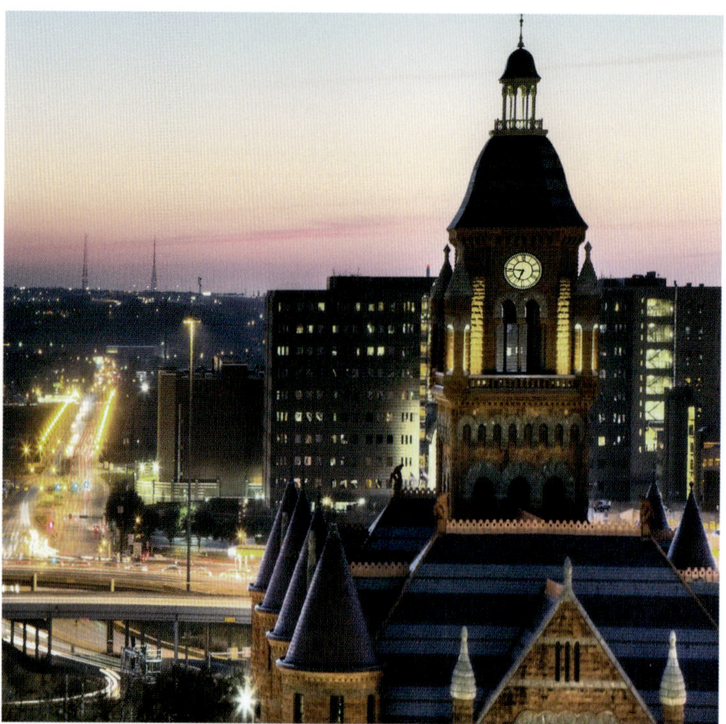

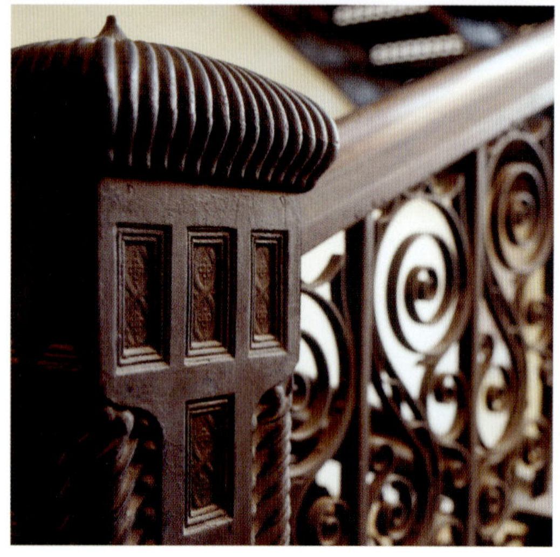

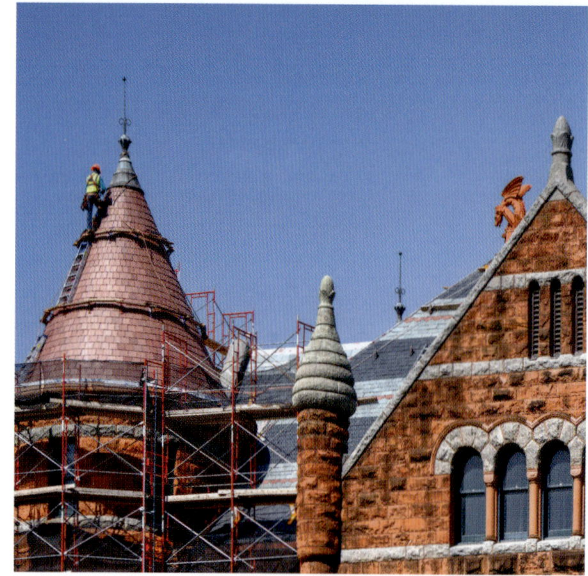

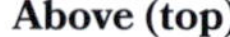

Above (top)
Old Red, Dallas County's sixth courthouse, is built of Pecos sandstone and Arkansas granite in a Romanesque Revival style. Construction began in 1890, and county officials moved in two years later.

Above (right)
Elevated view of Old Red at twilight.

Above
Closeup of a stairway with intricate metal work in Old Red.

Above
One of the Old Red wyverns on the slate roof watches as the conical roof of one of the towers is repaired.

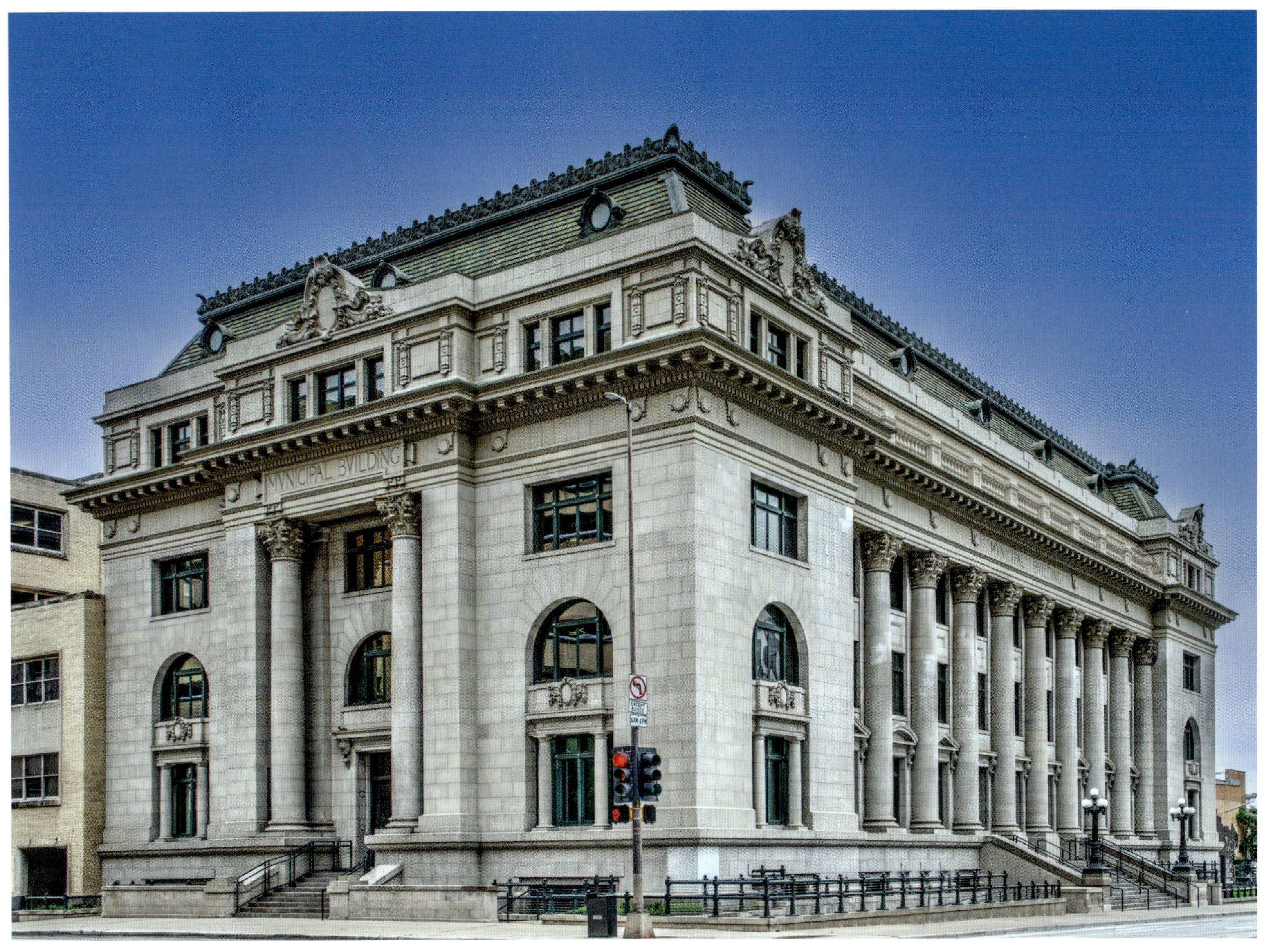

Above
The Dallas Municipal Building, located on Main Street in downtown, once served as the Dallas City Hall. The 1914 Beaux Arts-style structure is both a Dallas Landmark and a Recorded Texas Historic Landmark. It now serves as the home of the University of North Texas at Dallas College of Law.

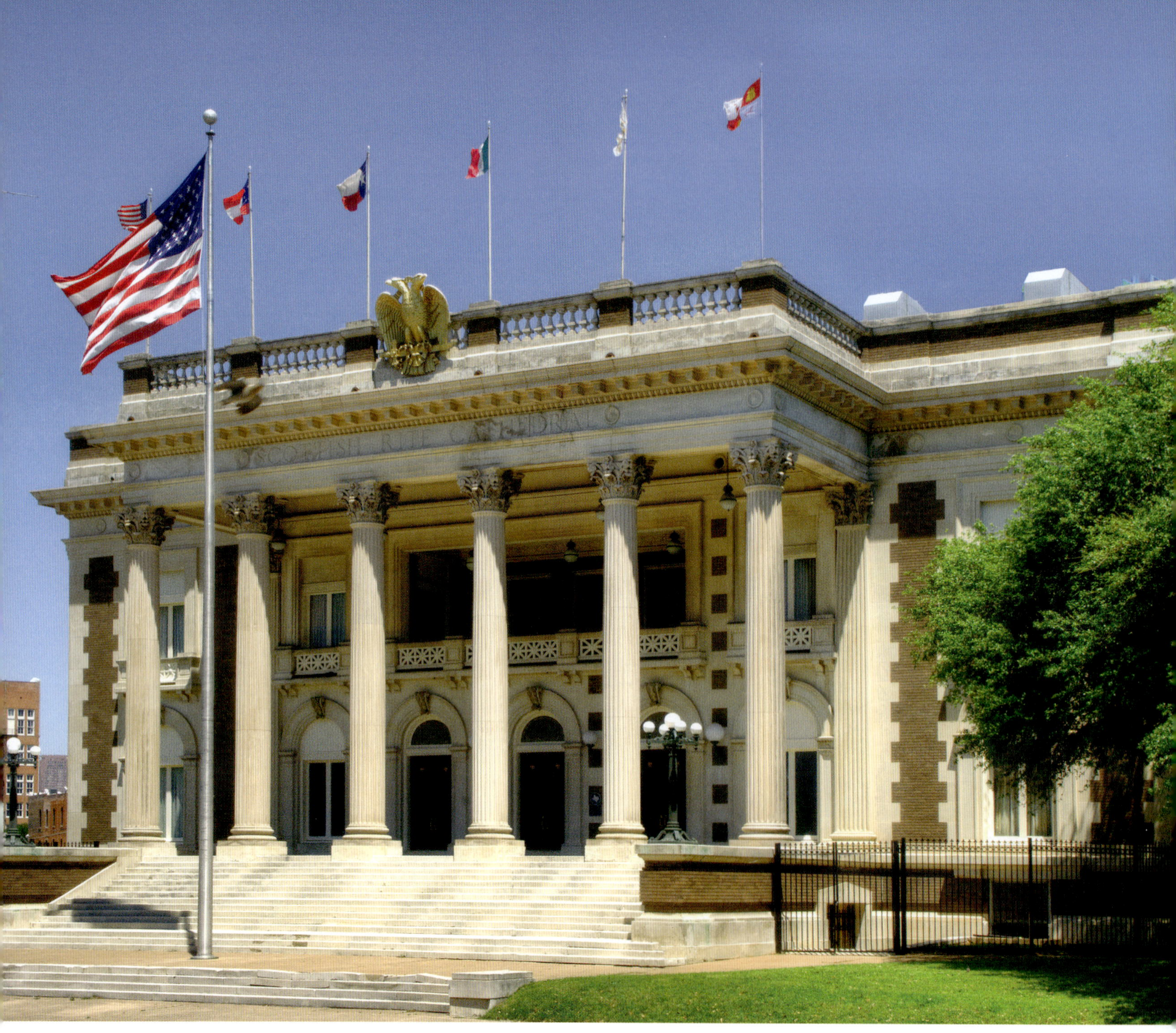

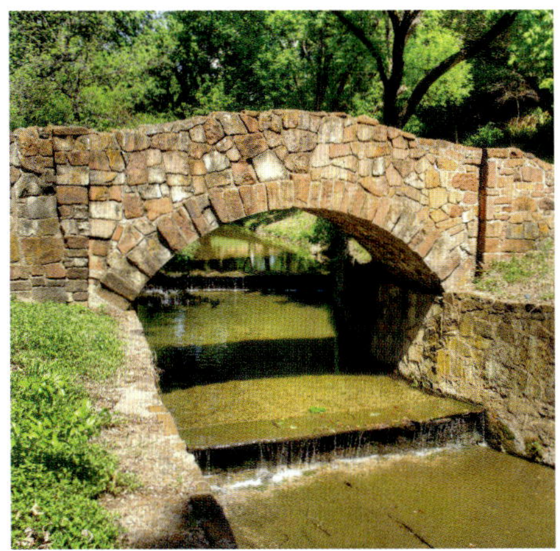

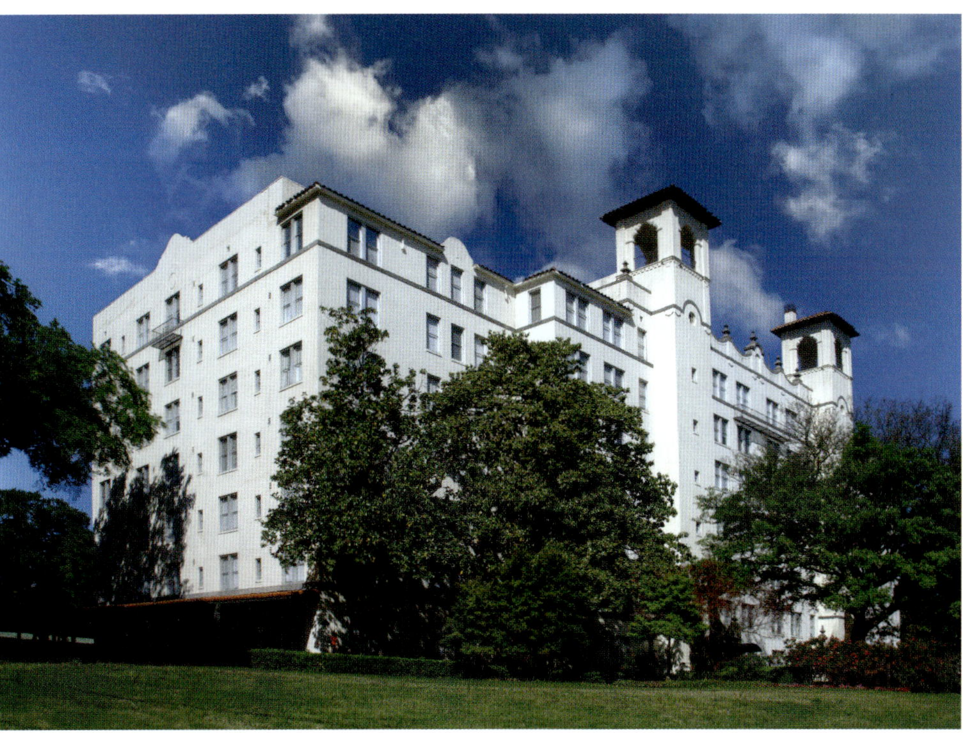

Above
Reverchon Park opened in 1915. The park was named for the French botanist Julien Reverchon, who came to Texas as a boy with the La Réunion colony in 1855. During the 1930s the WPA funded park improvements that included rock steps and pathways adjacent to Maple Avenue.

Opposite
The Dallas Scottish Rite Cathedral on Harwood Street began as a dream in 1903, and the Beaux Arts-style structure opened in 1913. It now stands as one of the finest Masonic buildings in the world devoted exclusively to the Scottish Rite.

Above (right)
Maple Terrace, designed by the English architect Sir Alfred Bossom in 1925, was Dallas's first luxury high-rise residence. The Mission Style building is considered the first "million-dollar apartment house" and has always attracted the city's cultural and creative elites.

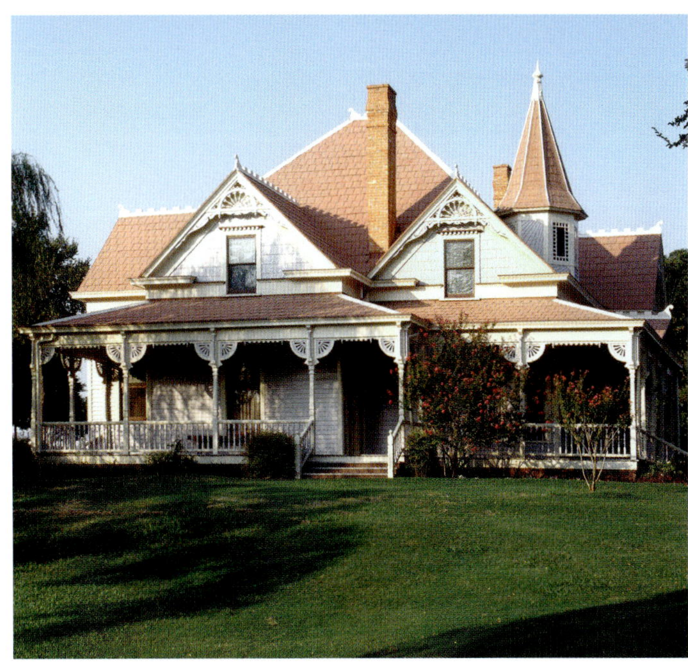

Right
Heritage Village is a twenty-acre park located south of downtown Dallas, that consists of pioneer and Victorian residences and structures moved from various locations in North Texas. Furnished with historic collections from the 1840s through the early 1900s, this city park presents programs and events for visitors and families.

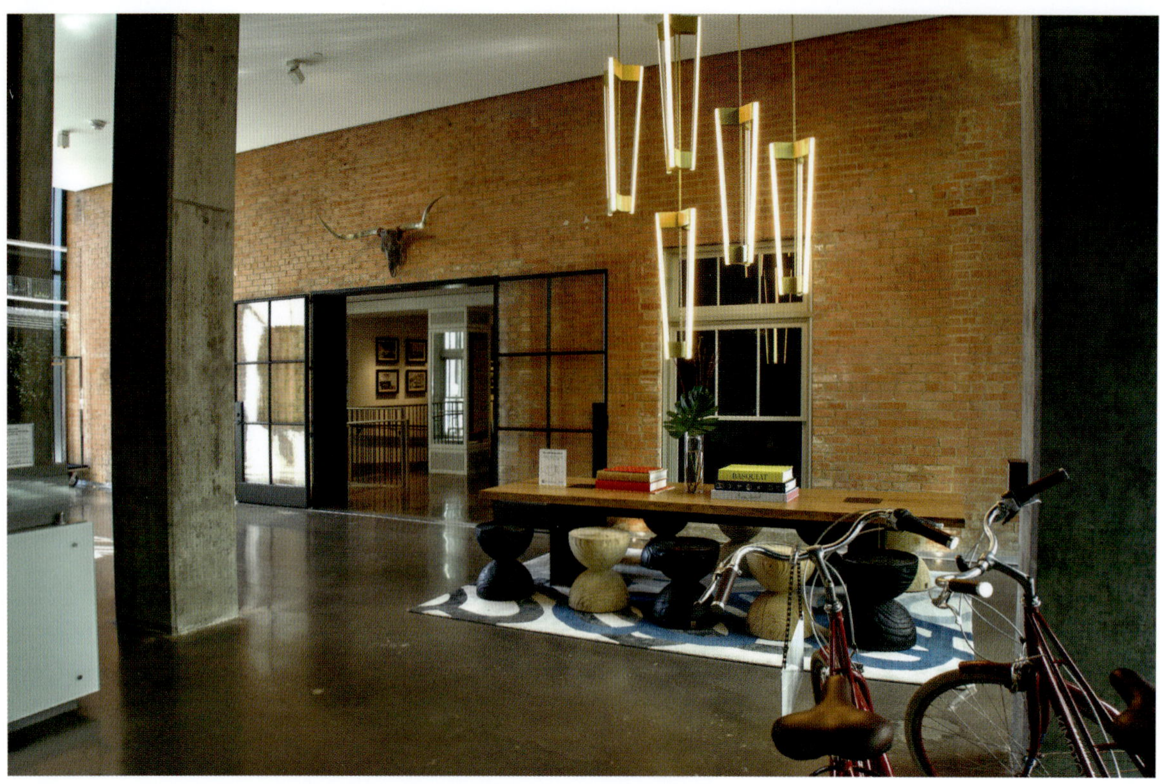

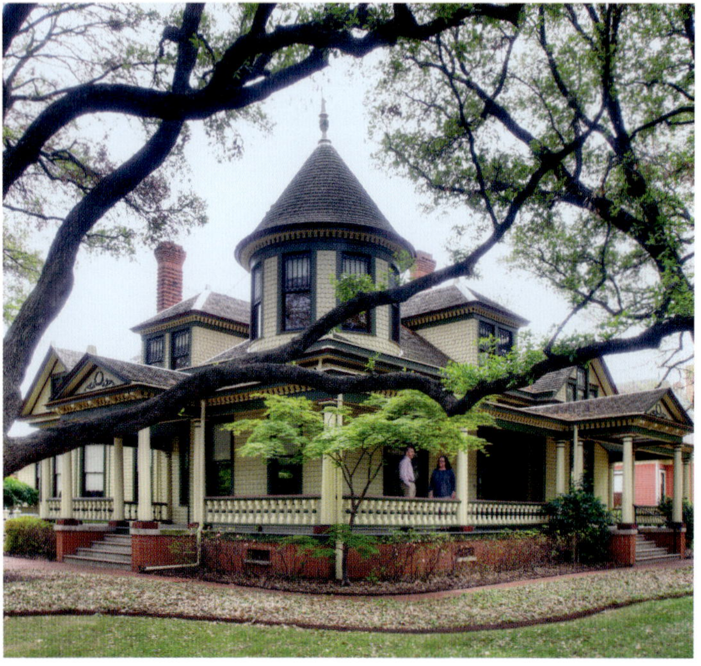

Above
The Pittman Hotel is located in Deep Ellum in a Beaux Arts building. The 1916 structure was formally the Knights of Pythias Temple, designed by Dallas's first African American architect, William Sidney Pittman.

Left
Built in 1899 as a family home, the Free Classic Queen Anne-style Wilson House on Swiss Avenue is now the centerpiece of the Wilson Block Historic District and headquarters of Preservation Dallas.

Opposite
Originally part of a chain owned by Howard Hughes, the Texas Theatre opened in 1931 on West Jefferson Boulevard in Oak Cliff. On November 22, 1963, Dallas police arrested Lee Harvey Oswald inside the theater minutes after he shot and killed Dallas police officer J. D. Tippit.

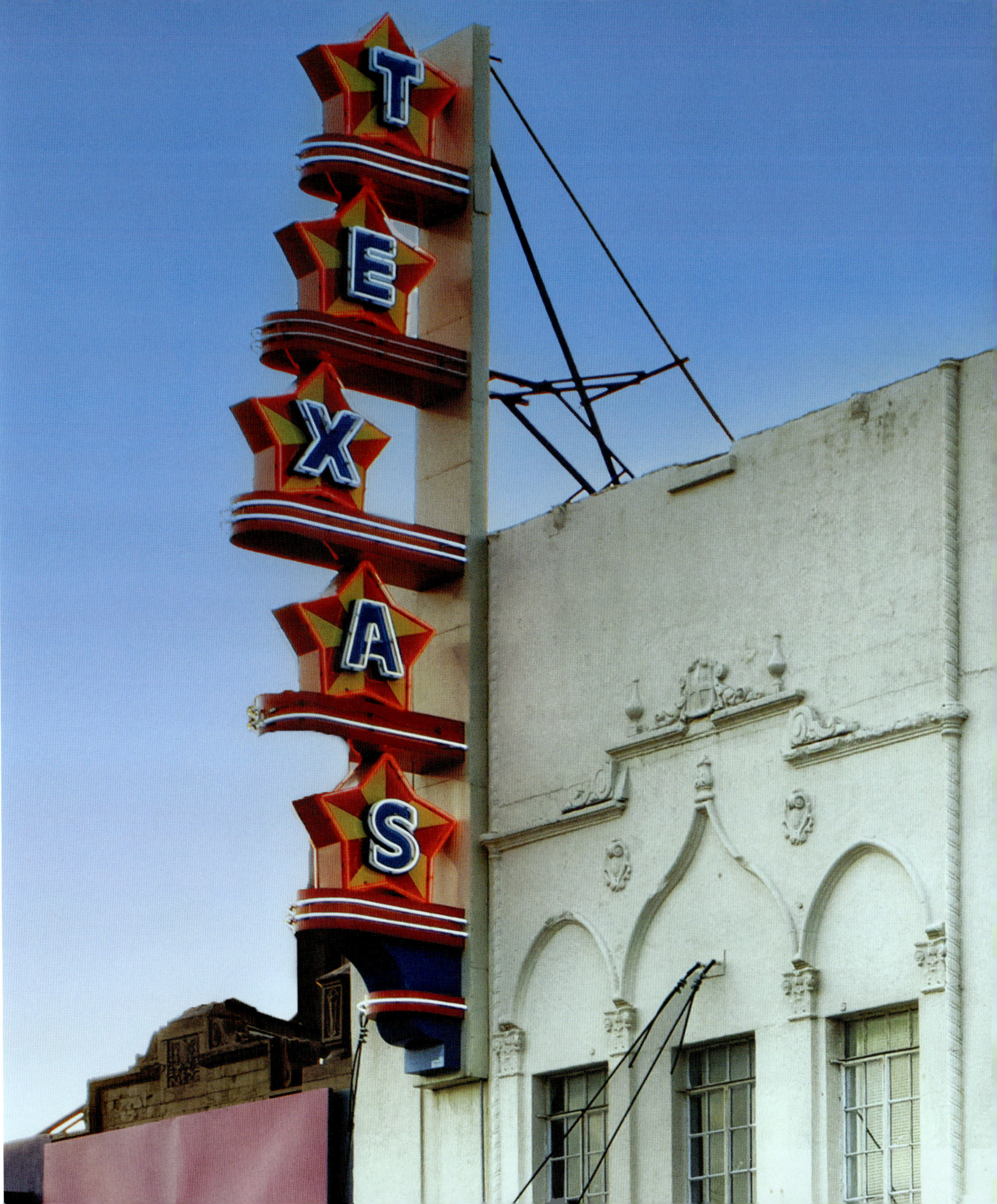
TEXAS

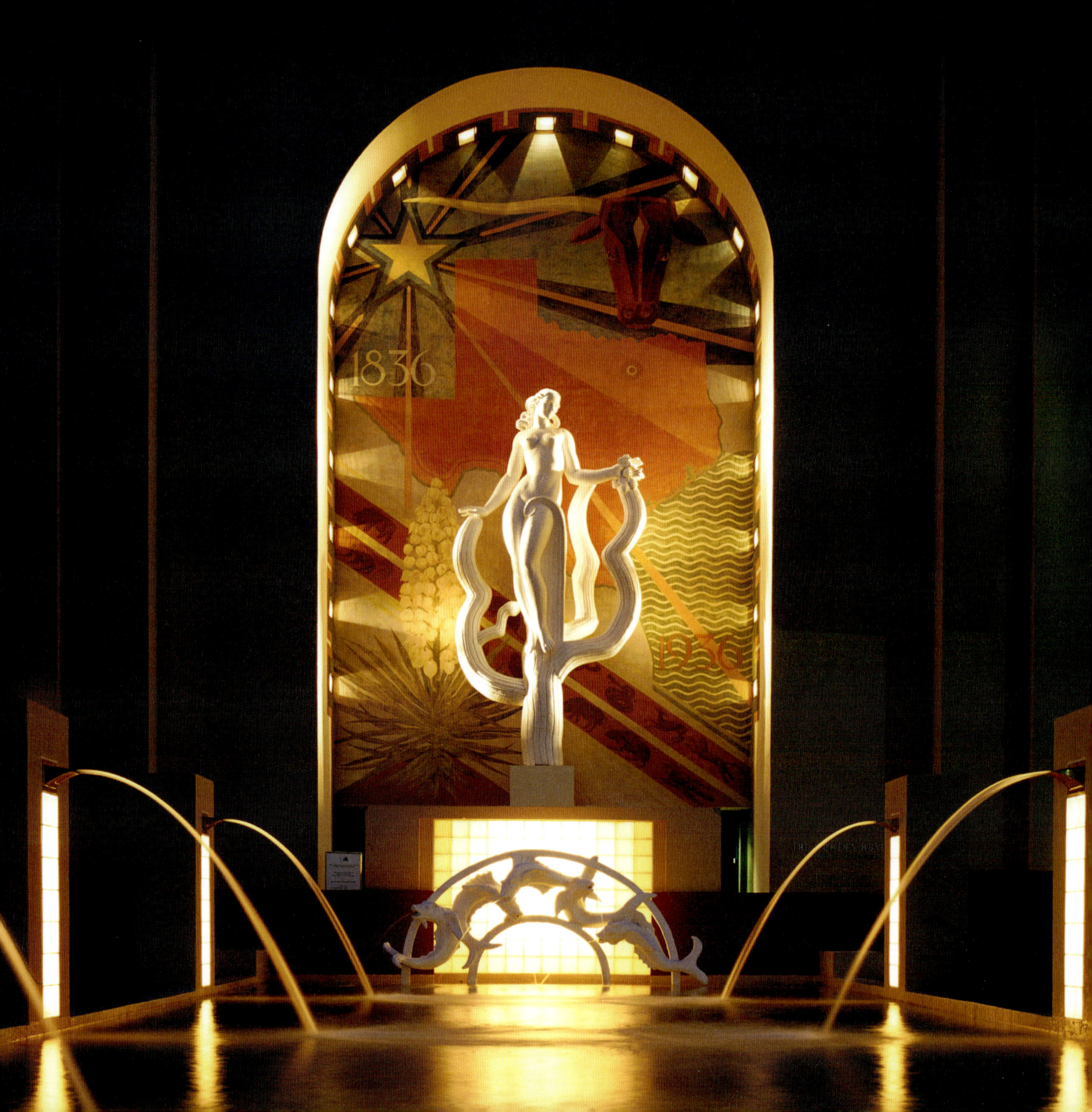
1836
1936

Protect

Willis Winters is an architect and the director emeritus of the Dallas Park and Recreation Department, having retired in 2019 following a twenty-seven-year career in public service. He is the author or co-author of seven books on the history of architecture and planning in Dallas and Texas.

Fair Park is a microcosm of Dallas. It encapsulates the city's relatively brief but colorful history within its glorious grounds and buildings. It reflects the myth and spirit of Dallas more than any other place or idea. Fair Park represents the ambition of a city on the prairie—with little reason for being—to be something more, something illustrious. When it was carved from the vast cotton fields that stretched eastward to the rising sun in 1886, few could comprehend what this place would mean for a neophyte community of twenty-five thousand still rough around the edges, with a rowdy, pioneer-town mentality. Its founding as the site for the State Fair of Texas was an audacious undertaking by the city's business elite that launched an entrepreneurial spirit still thriving almost a century and a half later. The annual fair brought visitors, commerce, and prestige to this undistinguished town, fostering its gradual emergence as the principal city of North Texas and nurturing it to assert its economic dominion over an entire region.

Then, fifty years later, Fair Park reaffirmed its vital importance in Dallas history when it was selected to host the Texas Centennial Exposition. The fairgrounds were transformed into a glittering national showplace that by itself lifted the city out of the throes of the Great Depression. The year 1936 was when America discovered Dallas. It was the first world's fair to provide air-conditioning within its gleaming, modernistic exhibition halls. Eighty-five years after the exposition, Fair Park is recognized as the last remaining intact site of exposition architecture from the 1930s and acclaimed as one of the greatest collections of Art Deco architecture and public art in the world. It is truly one of the great public spaces in America.

I feel very fortunate to have grown up in a city with a place like Fair Park, and to have had the opportunity each year over the past half-century to attend the State Fair of Texas. George Dahl's compelling Art Deco buildings—which he described in 1936 as "Texanic" in proportions, and as "exemplifying the color, romance and grandeur that had marked the development of Texas"—no doubt played a significant role in propelling me to first become an architect, and later in my career, to become a park professional (with the singular privilege of caring for Fair Park's buildings and legacy). It has played a big role in defining my life.

Willis Winters

Opposite
Raoul Josset created this graceful sculpture of a woman, entitled *Spirit of the Centennial*, in 1936 for the Texas Centennial Exposition. The sculpture and the Texas-themed mural behind it, by artist Carlo Ciampaglia, were restored in honor of Calvert Collins, the first woman to serve on the Dallas City Council.

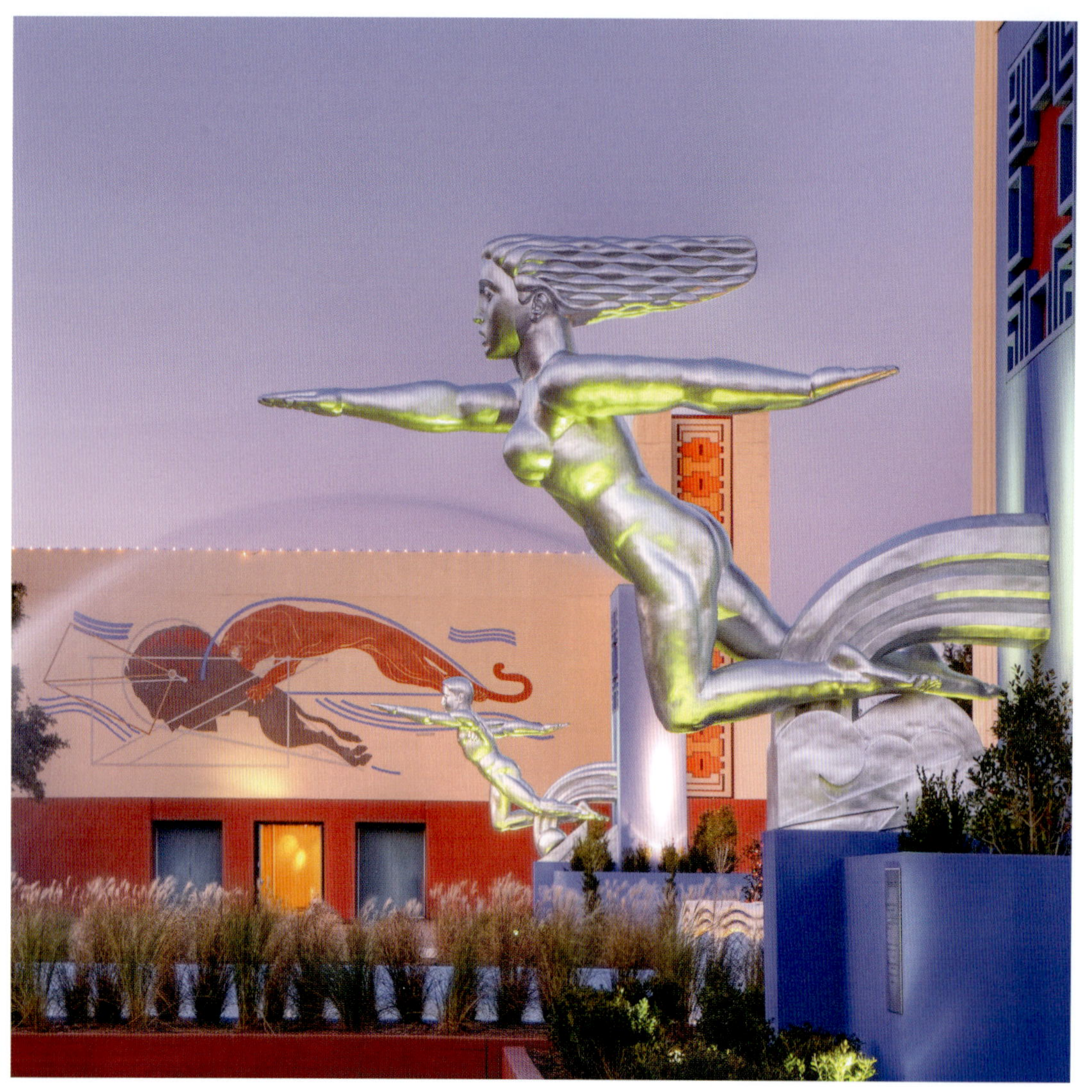

Above
Re-creations of Lawrence Tenney Stevens's 1936 sculptures appear to fly above the Esplanade's reflecting pool at Fair Park. Fabricated by artist David Newton, *Contralto* and *Tenor* were installed in 2009.

Opposite
This is one of four colorful plaster sculptures on the stucco walls of the current-day Centennial Building, executed in dimensional bas-relief by the French American artist Pierre Bourdelle. The piece is entitled *Man and Angel*, representing the artist's depiction of "speed" as the theme for the Hall of Transportation at the 1936 Texas Centennial Exposition.

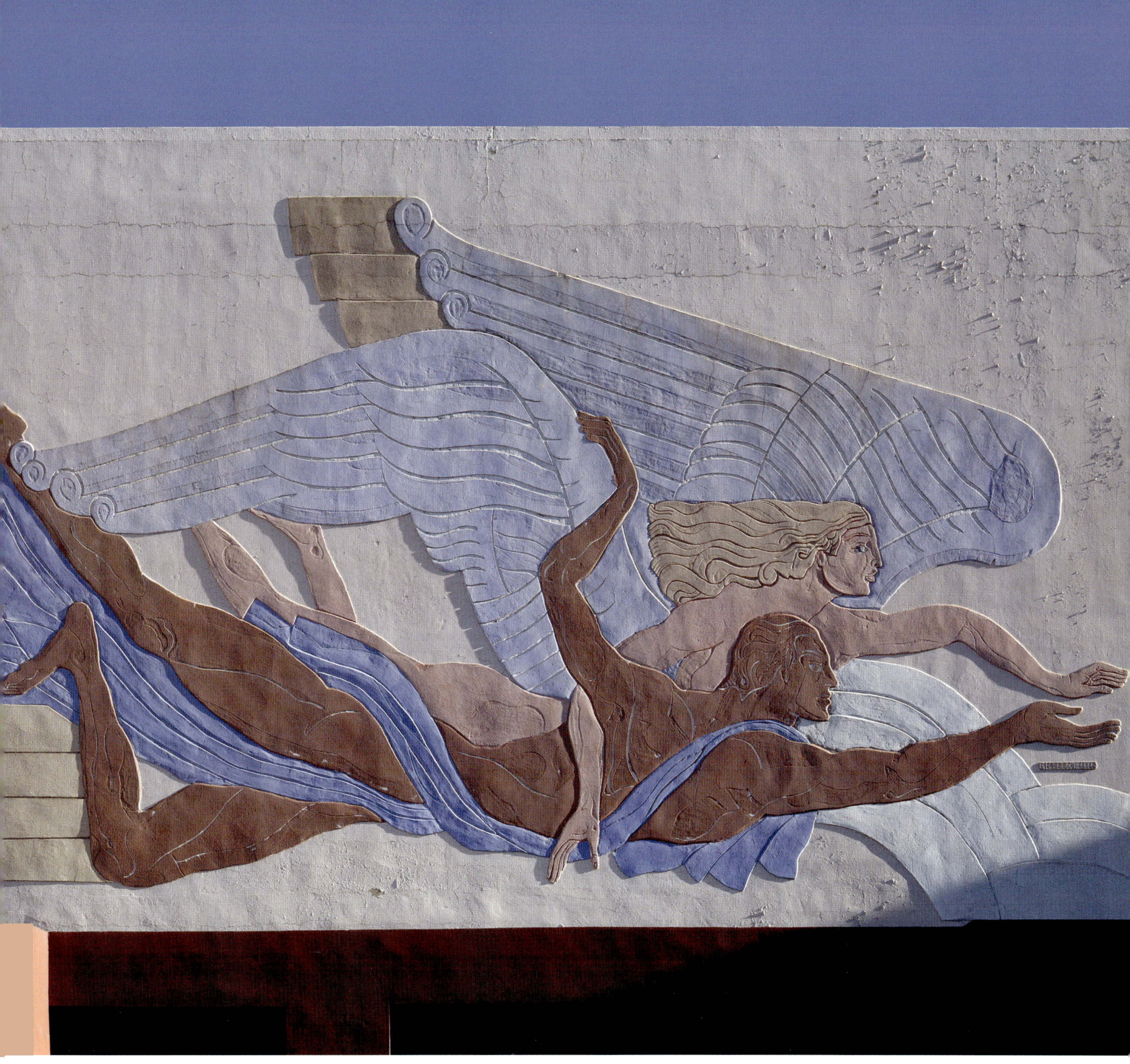

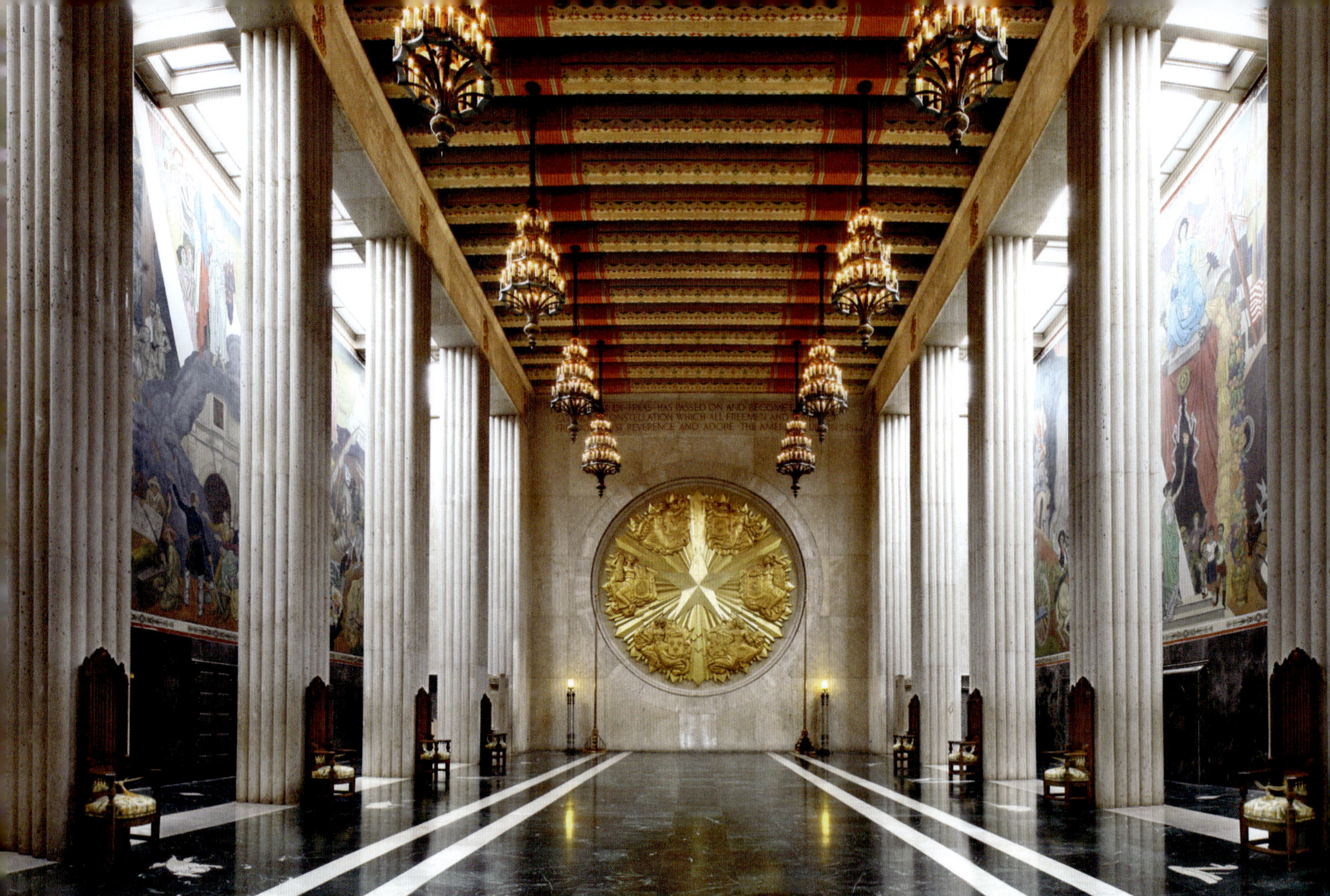

Above
The Great Hall is the largest room in the Texas Hall of State, considered by many to be the symbolic and architectural centerpiece of the entire Texas Centennial Exposition. Two of the largest oil murals ever painted adorn the two side walls, and the centerpiece is a gold medallion sculpture by artist Joseph Renier that depicts the six nations that ruled Texas throughout its history.

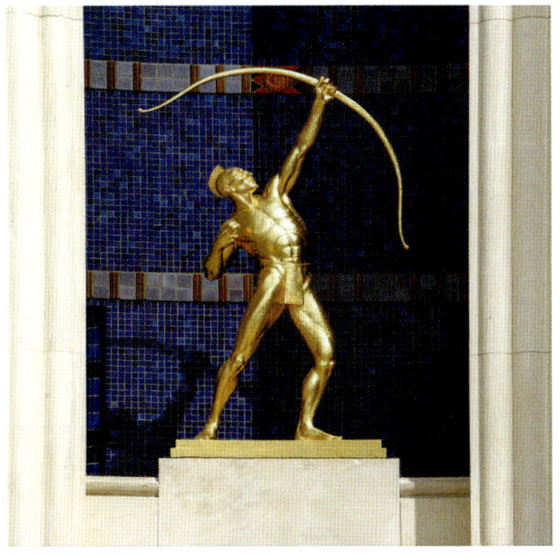

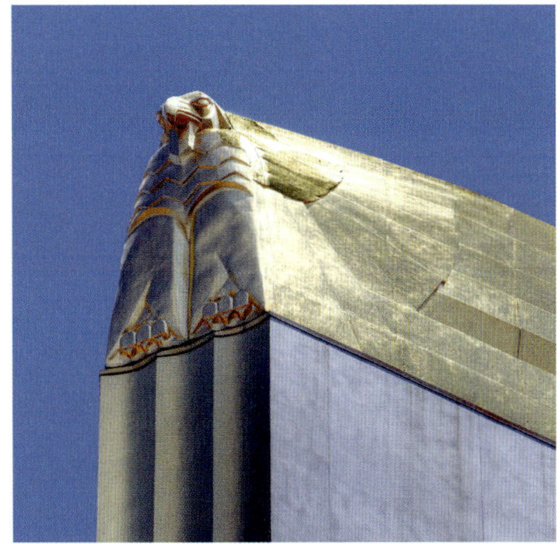

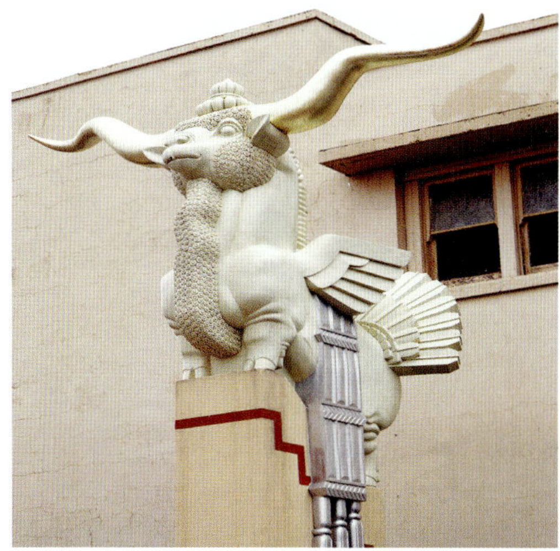

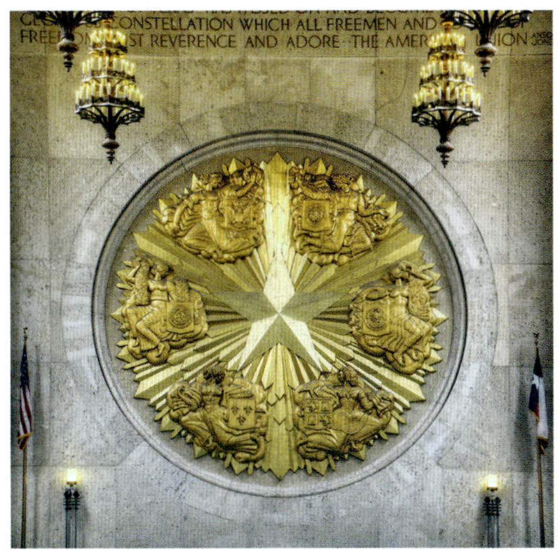

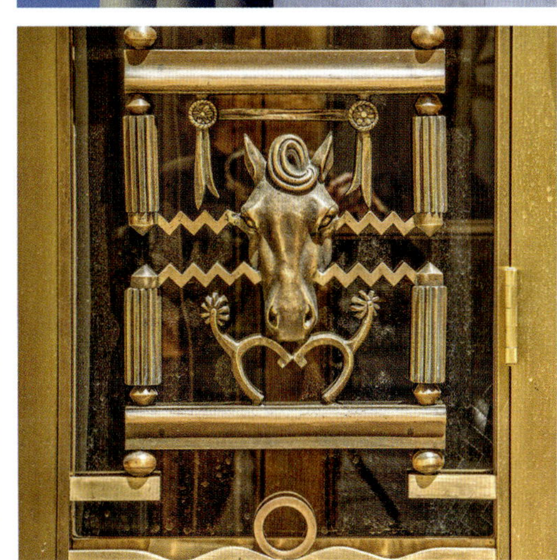

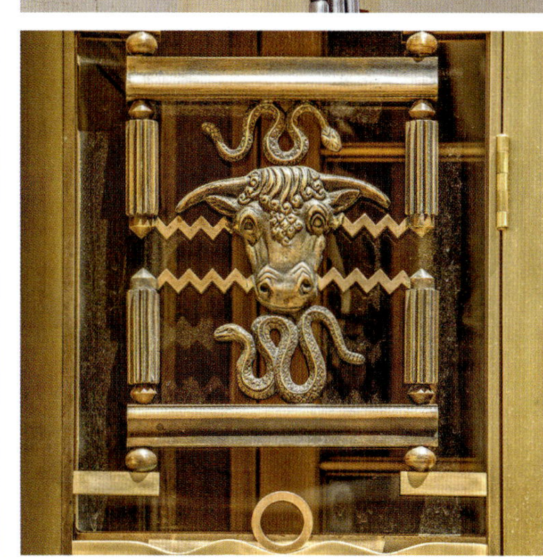

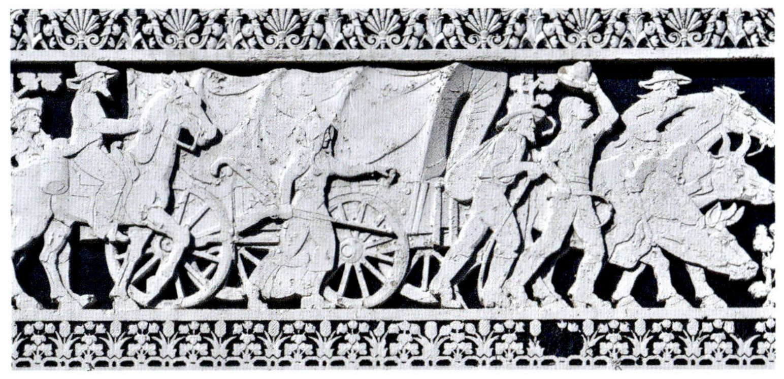

Above
Architecture details from Fair Park include these from the Hall of State, the Tower Building, and sculptor Lawrence Tenney Stevens's *Woofus* statue (top right).

Left
The Fair Park entrance pylon off Parry Avenue features a detailed carved bas-relief of early Texas pioneers by artist James Buchanan Winn Jr.

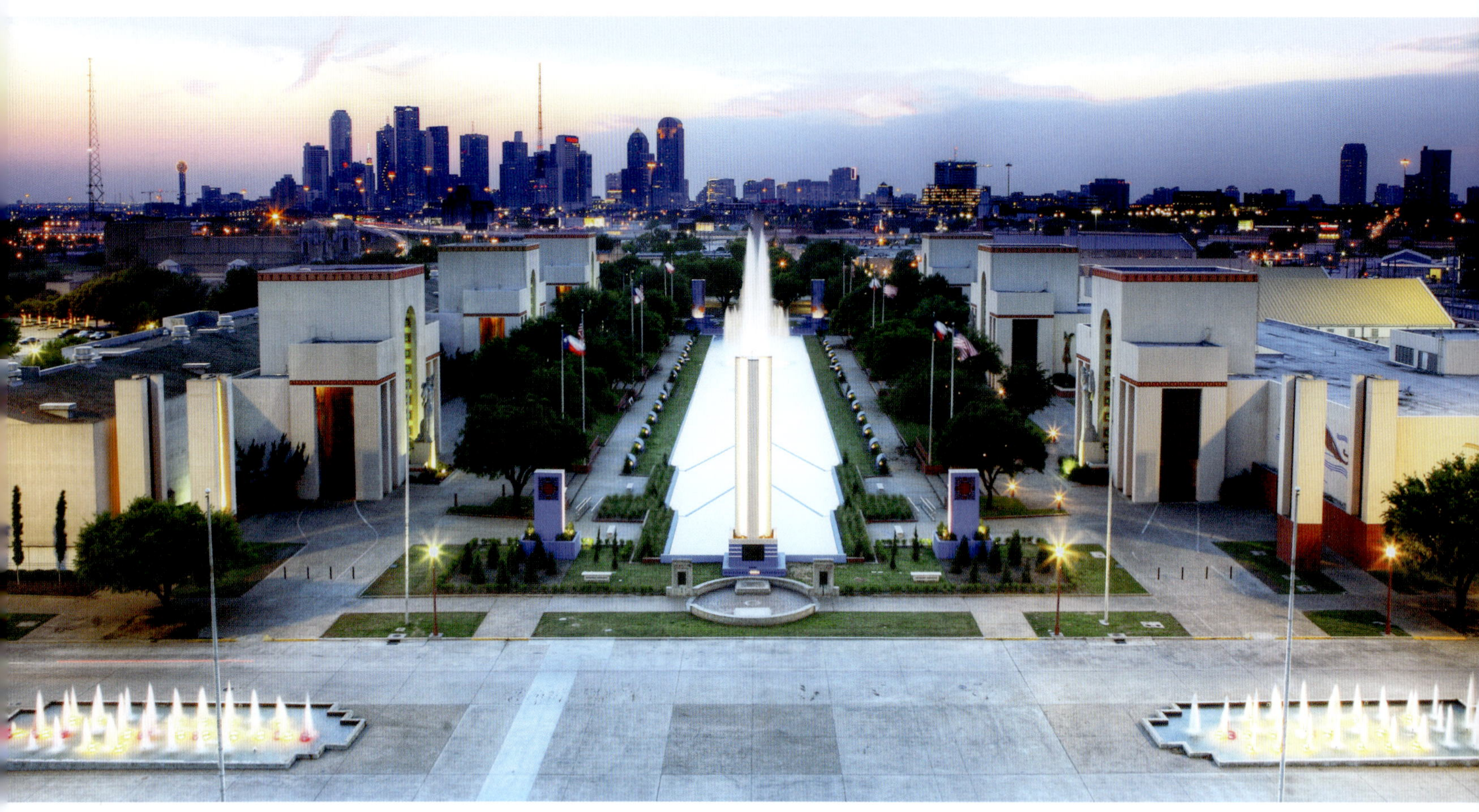

Above
The Esplanade at Fair Park. With a seven-hundred-foot-long reflecting pool and fountains flanked by exhibition buildings, the Esplanade was designed by George Dahl to be the centerpiece of the Texas Centennial Exposition in 1936. The current Dallas skyline glows in the distance.

Opposite
Allie Tennant's golden *Tejas Warrior* aims his bow to the sky over the entrance to the Hall of State. The Dallas Historical Society occupies the building, presenting special exhibits and programs relating to local and state history. Its extensive historical archives are available to researchers.

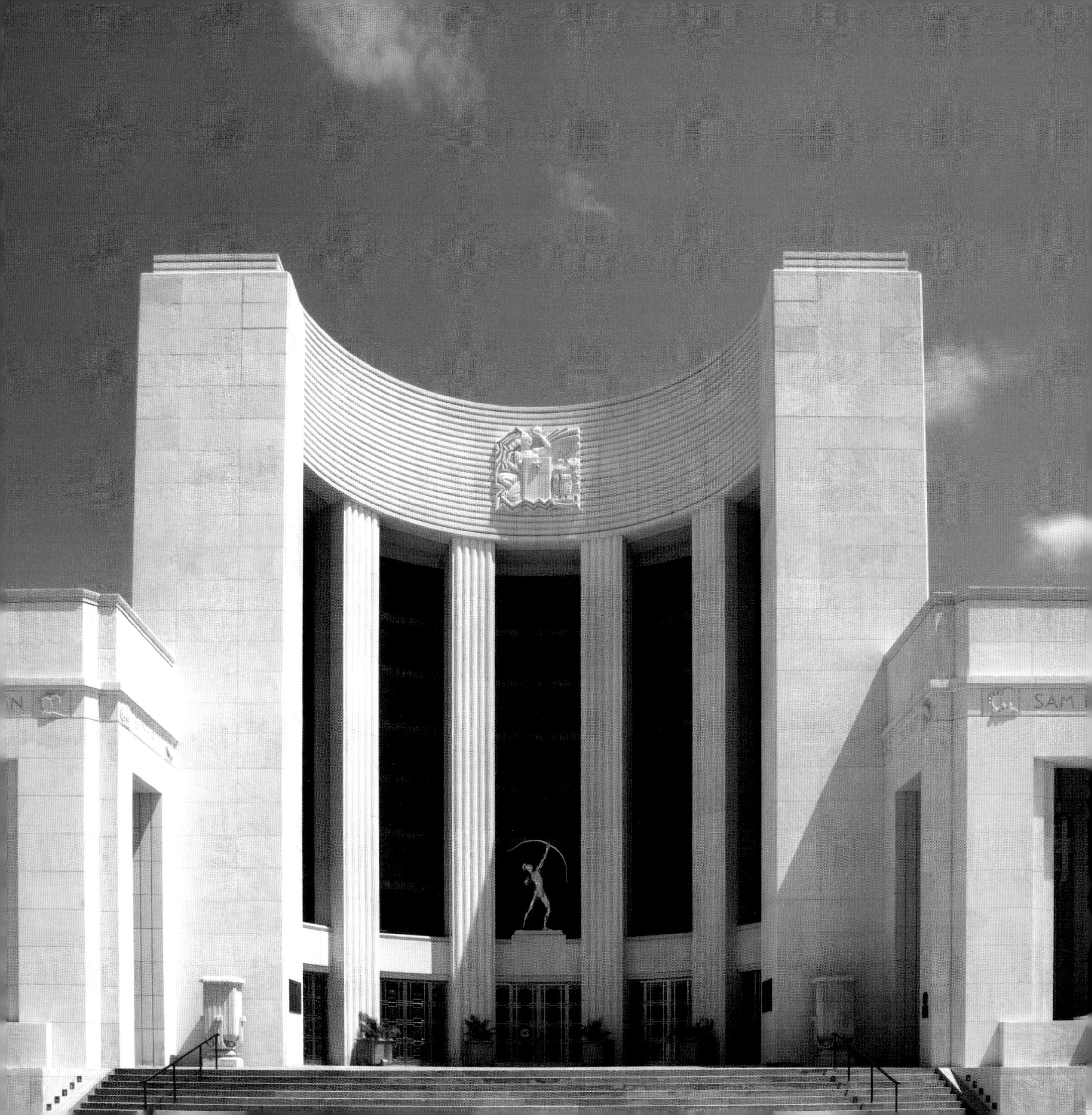
SAM

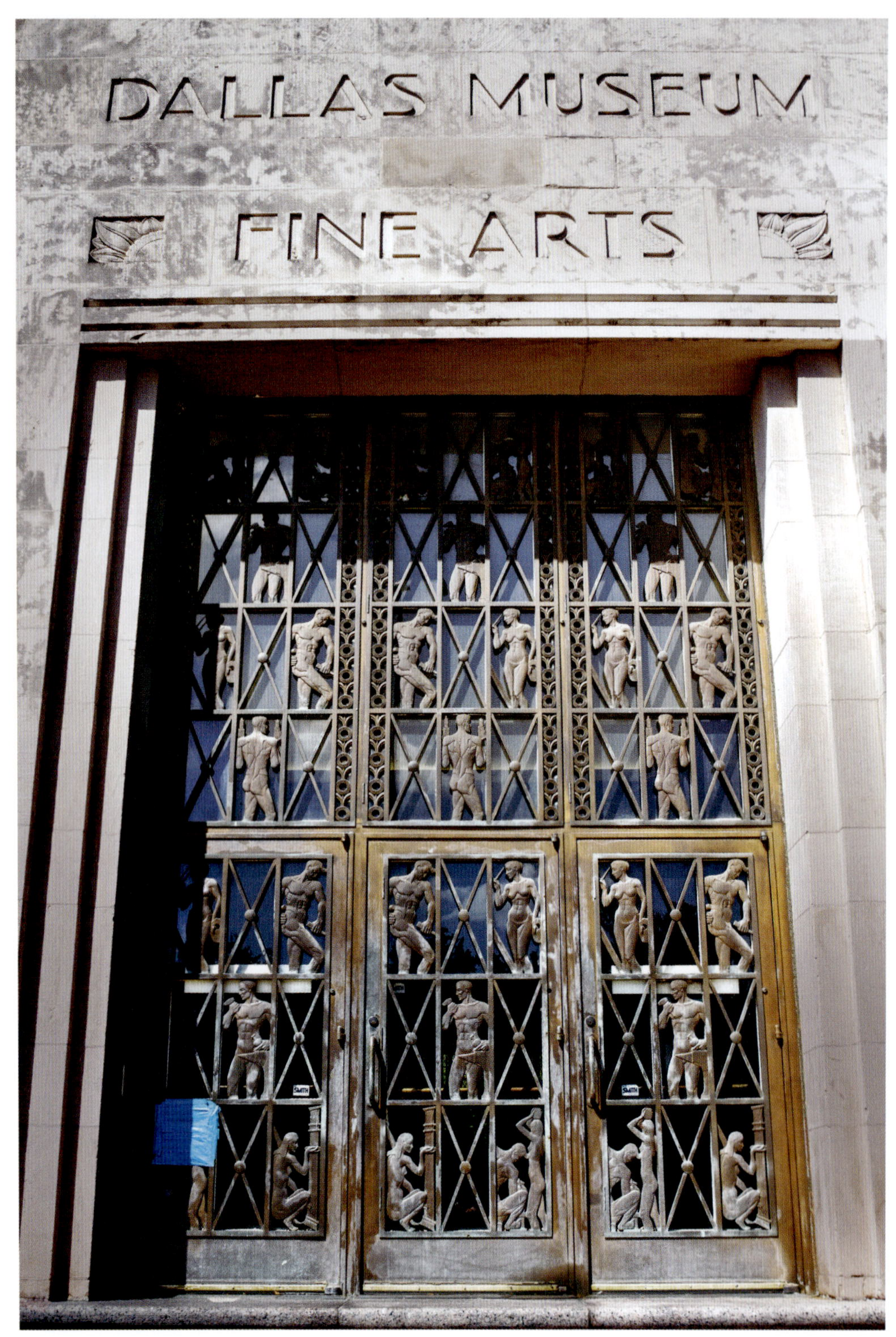

Left
Metal grills with male and female figures were created by Madelyn Miller in 1936 for the doorways of the original Dallas Museum of Fine Arts at Fair Park.

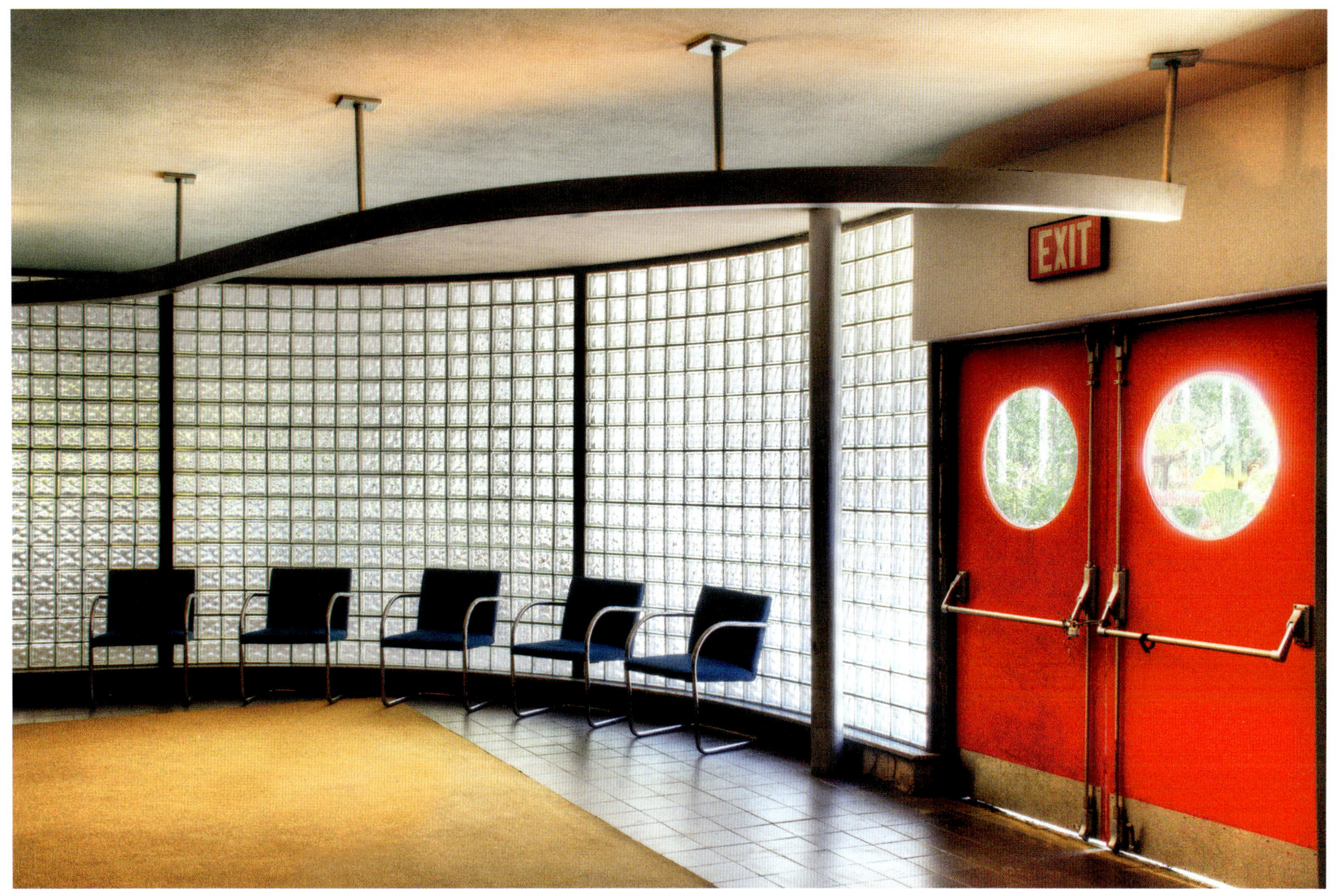

Above
The Magnolia Lounge, the first important modernistic building in Texas, was designed by the Swiss American architect William Lescaze for the 1936 Texas Centennial Exposition. Magnolia Oil provided an air-conditioned visitor's center in this space. In 1947 the Magnolia Lounge took on a new life as the location where theater director Margo Jones launched the American Regional Theatre movement.

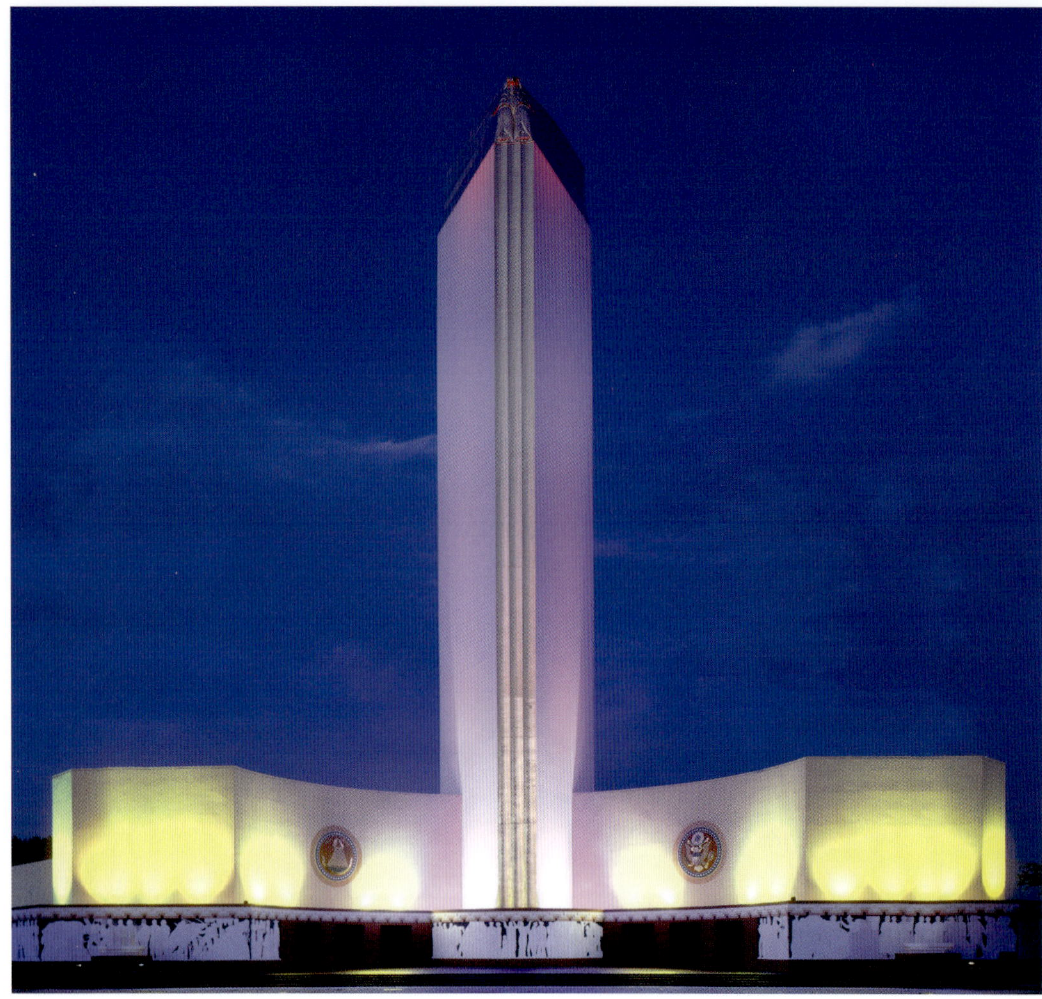

Above
The Tower Building, a Dallas landmark built in 1936 for the Centennial Exposition, originally housed United States government exhibits. The tower is topped by a sculpted eagle designed by artist Raoul Josset.

Opposite
The *Woofus*, a combination of six different Texas farm animals, was created for the 1936 Centennial Exposition by artist Lawrence Tenney Stevens but later disappeared. The sculpture was re-created utilizing historic photographs.

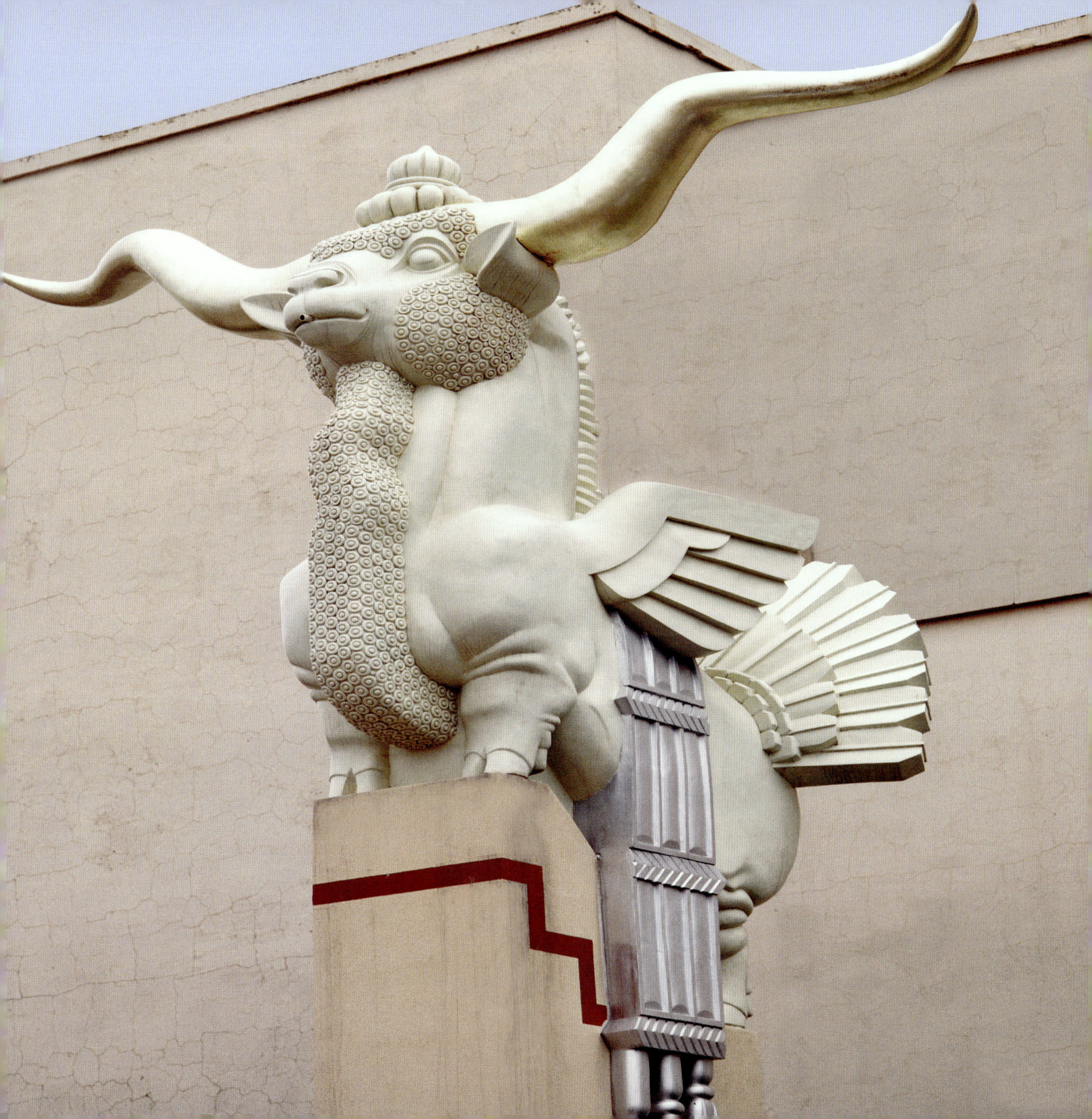

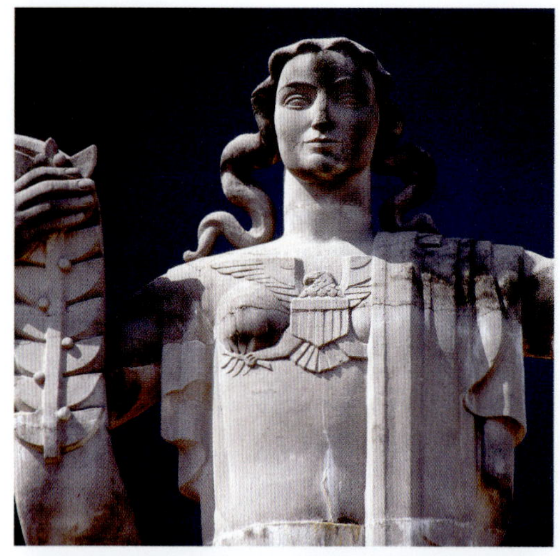

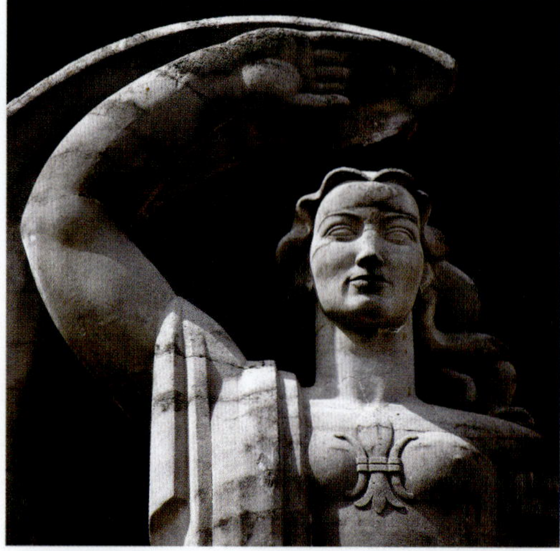

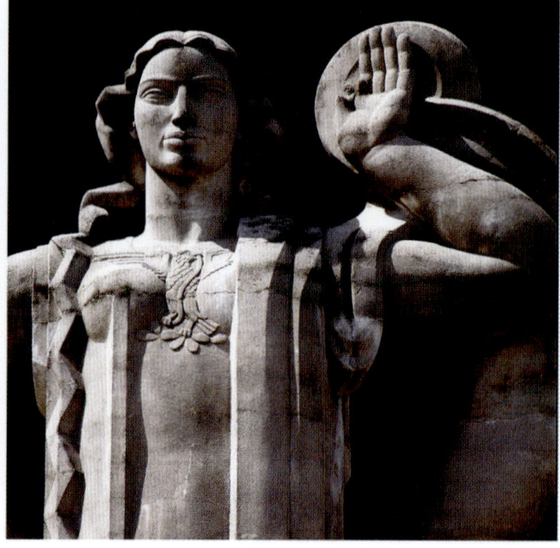

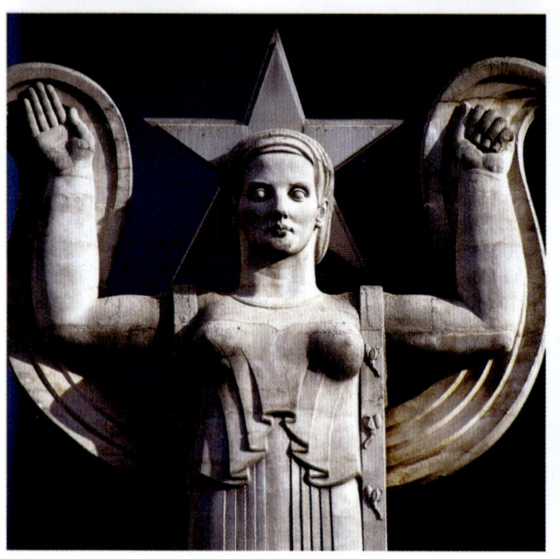

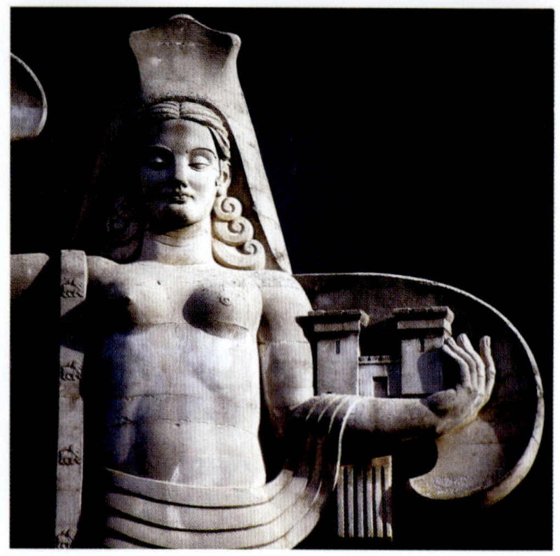

Left and Above
Each figure represents a nation whose flag has flown over Texas: the United States, France, Mexico, Texas, and Spain.

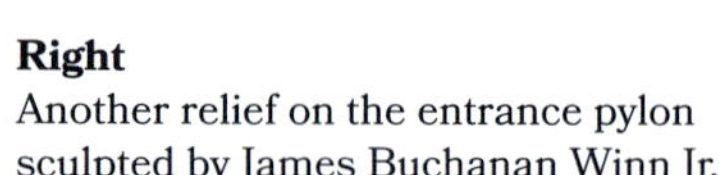

Right
Another relief on the entrance pylon sculpted by James Buchanan Winn Jr.

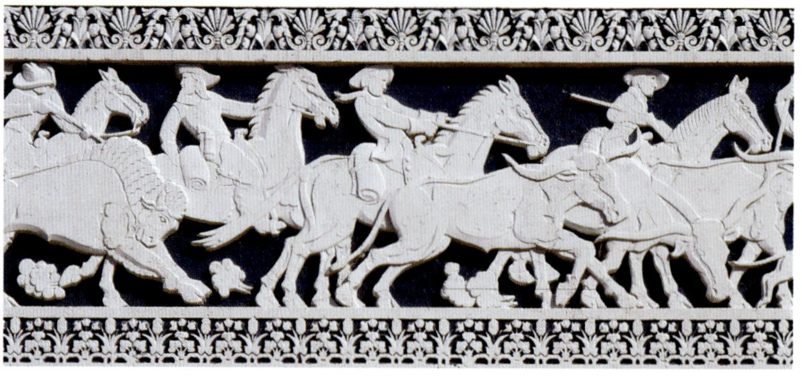

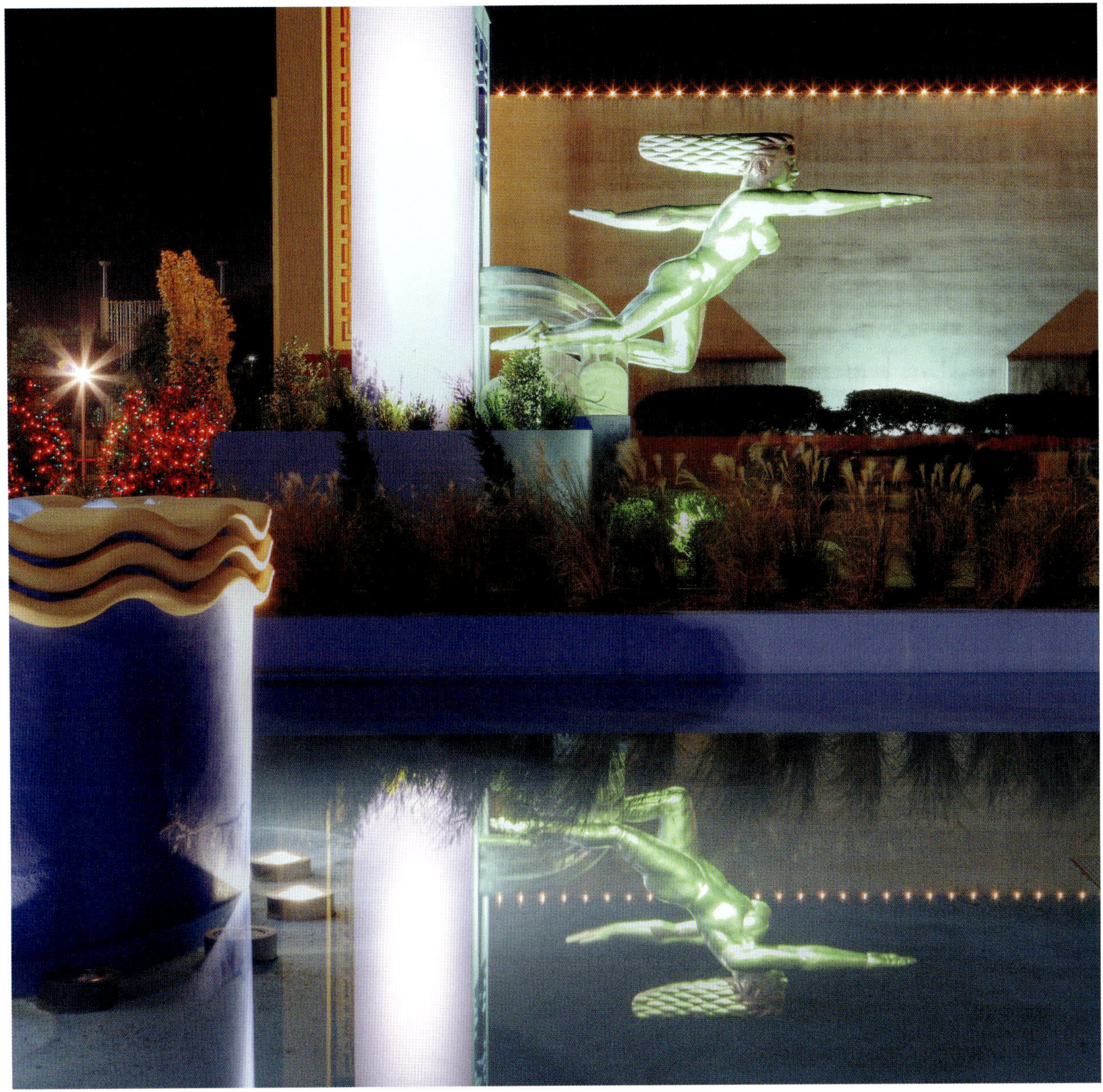

Above
The *Contralto* sculpture soars above the Esplanade's reflecting pool, while her reflection floats below.

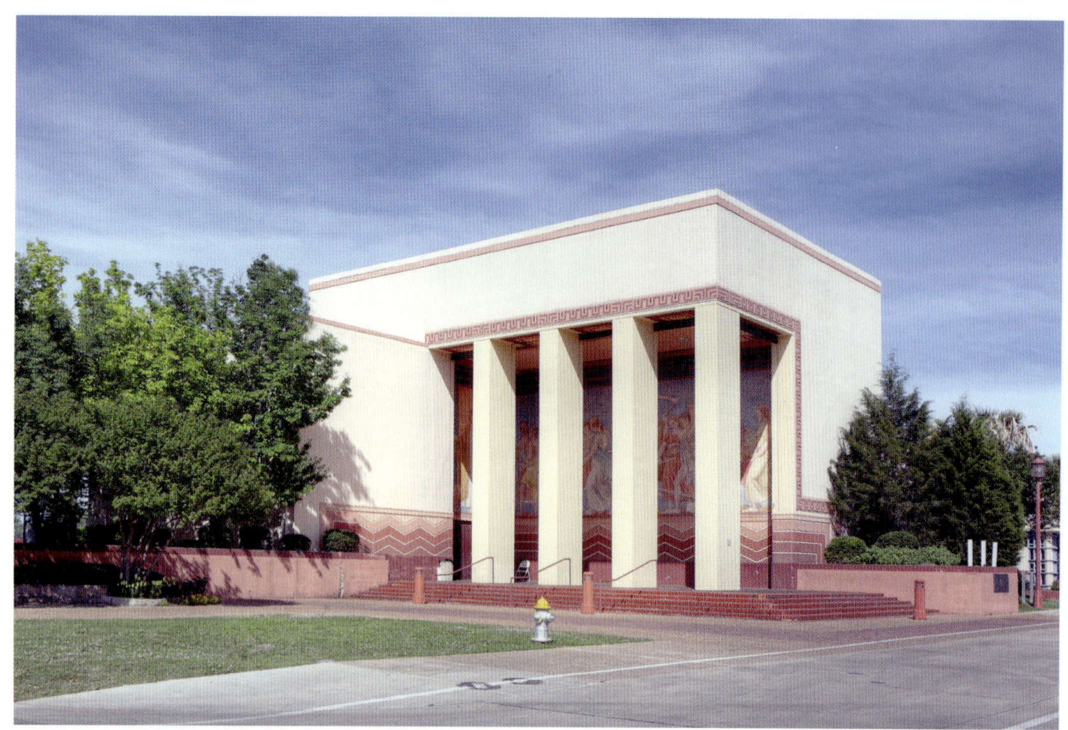

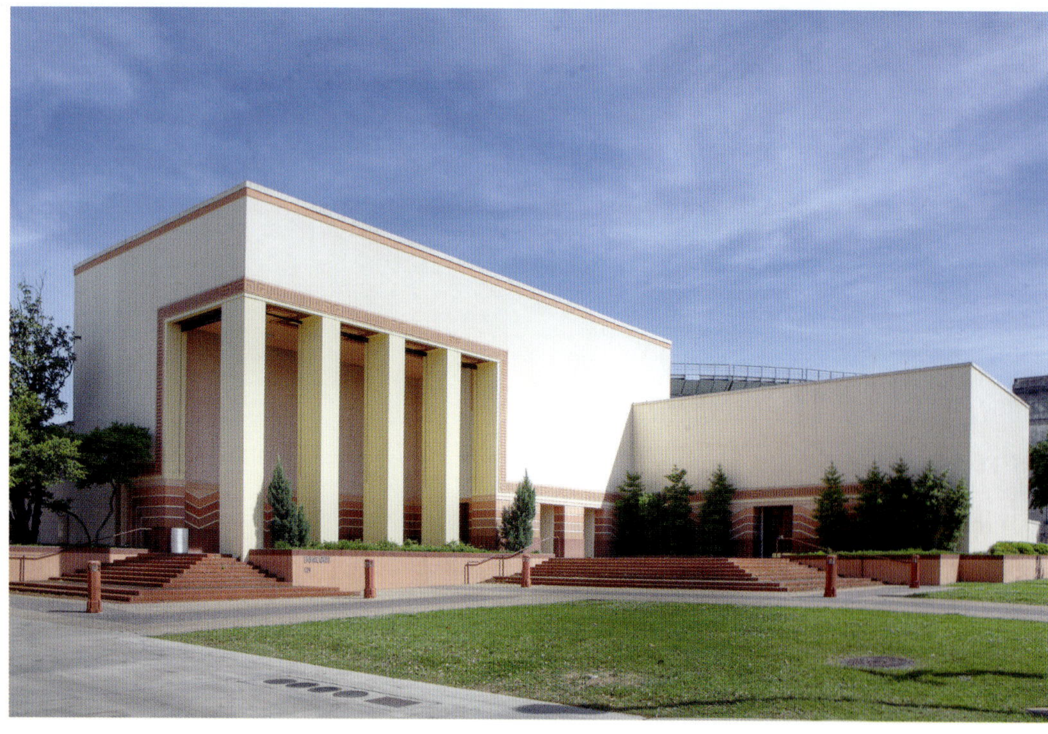

Left
Two buildings form an impressive gateway to the Agrarian District at the 1936 Texas Centennial Exhibition. The buildings are currently named the Food and Fiber Building and the Embarcadero Building.

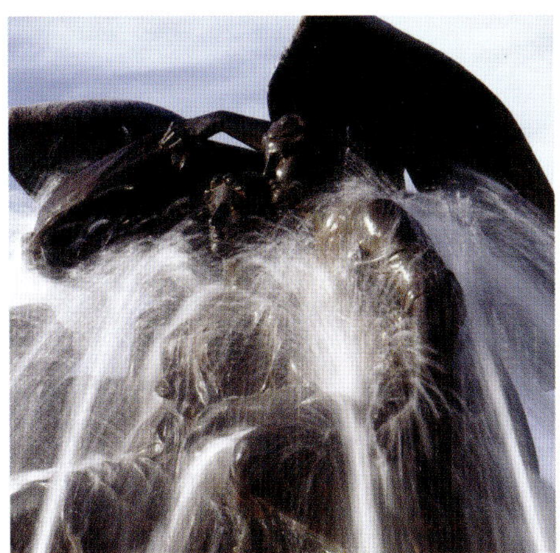

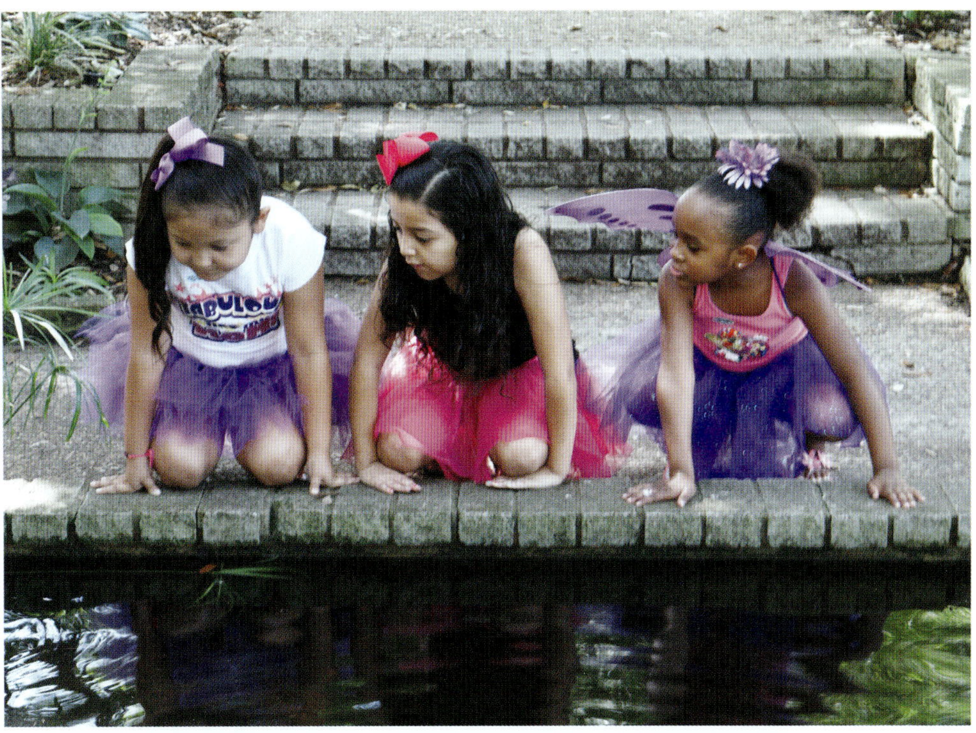

Above
Gulf Cloud, a bronze and granite fountain sculpture by Miss Clyde Chandler, was commissioned by the State Fair of Texas in 1912. The four female figures symbolize four Texas landscapes: the Gulf of Mexico, coastal plains, tablelands, and mountains.

Right (above)
Texas Discovery Gardens, an urban oasis of 7.5 acres within Fair Park, is filled with native flora. Within the Rosine Smith Sammons Butterfly House are found hundreds of free-flying butterflies. Three little girls dressed as butterflies carefully observe fish in the pond.

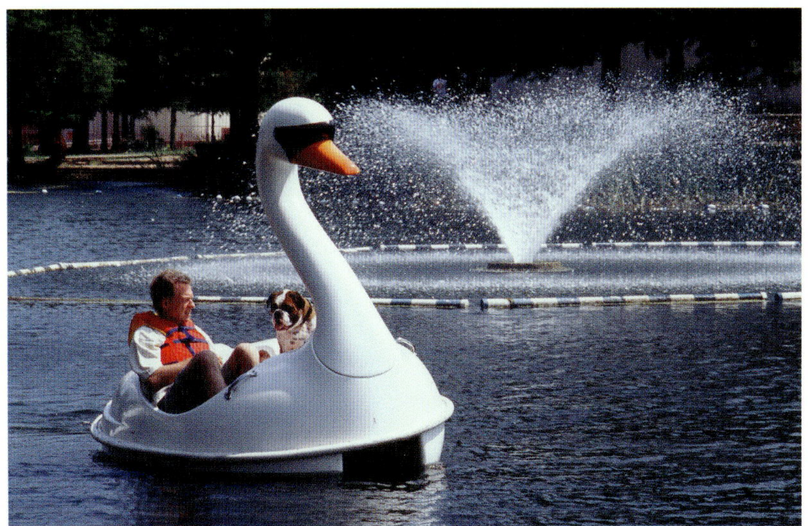

Above
A man and his dog enjoy a journey on a swan boat at the Fair Park Lagoon.

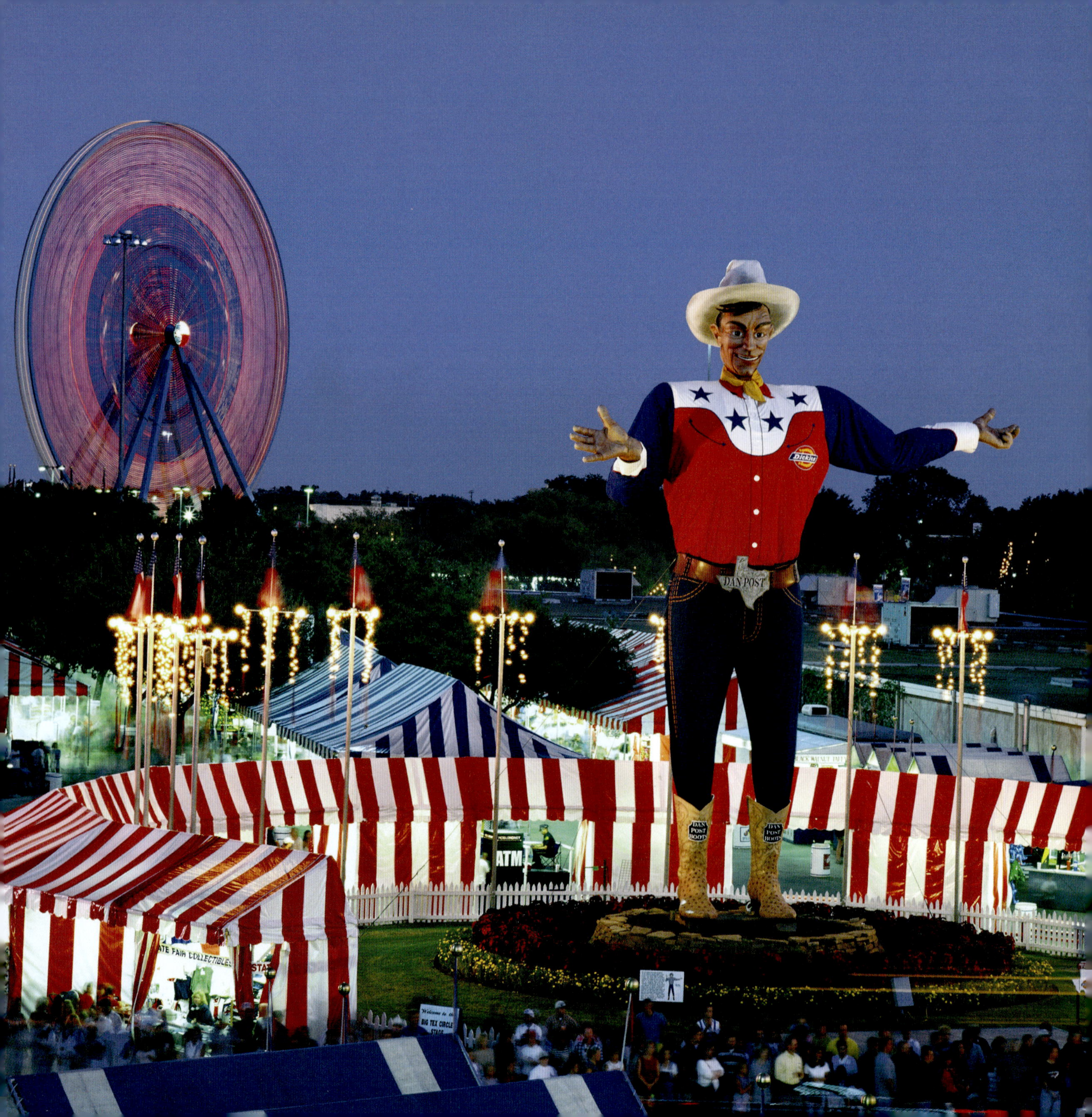
Dickies
DAN POST
DAN POST BOOTS
DAN POST BOOTS
ATM

Celebrate

Gina Armour Norris served as board chair from 2019 to 2022 at the State Fair of Texas, where she has volunteered since 2004, raising funds for the annual Big Tex Youth Livestock Auction & Scholarship Program. Born and raised in the rural Midwest, she spent her career in financial services, private equity, and real estate. She is a CFA charterholder and serves on public, private, and nonprofit boards.

Howdy, folks! Nothing in Dallas is so personal and yet so communally shared as the State Fair of Texas. Folks say it's legendary. Established in 1886, the State Fair's history is the history of Dallas, catapulting onto the national scene during the Texas Centennial Exposition held at Fair Park in 1936. In this new millennium, the State Fair embraces its role as an impactful nonprofit, striving to be a good neighbor and supporting agriculture, education, and community involvement. I like to say that the State Fair is the heart and soul of Texas—a diverse kaleidoscope of Texas culture and fun where folks share the community spirit of Big Tex in Big D.

Being elected the first chairwoman of the State Fair is a dream come true. I really got swept up by the Big Tex spirit almost twenty years ago. Before that, I happily took in the fair each year with my young daughters, along with more than two million other fans. But in 2004, I was introduced to the nonprofit mission of the fair and after attending my first Big Tex Youth Livestock Auction & Scholarship Committee meeting, I came home and told my family, "I finally found my people!" In addition to raising funds for rural youth from across Texas, I am enthusiastic about the fair's educational and community initiatives right here in Dallas.

The State Fair of Texas means so much to so many in Dallas. I will forever be grateful for Big Tex's big heart and open arms to everyone, including this dairy farmer's daughter.

See you at the fair!

Gina Armour Norris

Opposite
Big Tex has been greeting visitors to the State Fair of Texas since 1952. Following a fire in 2012, he was completely reconstructed and updated. His clothes, by the Fort Worth firm of Williamson-Dickie, are designed to last three seasons. In the background, the Texas Star Ferris Wheel spins.

Right
The State Fair provides a colorful panorama in the nighttime sky and is visible for miles.

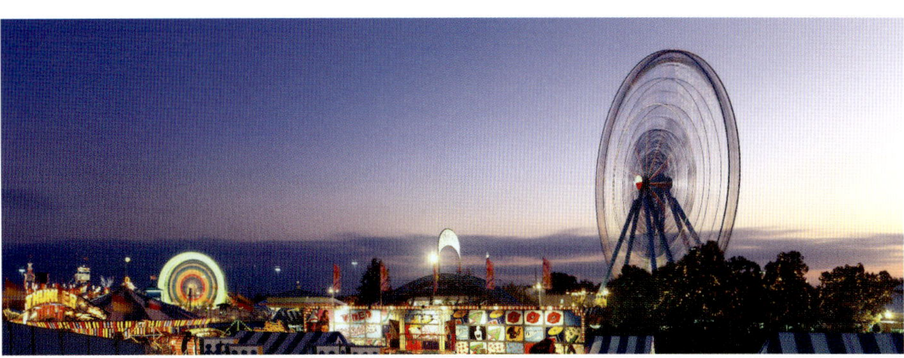

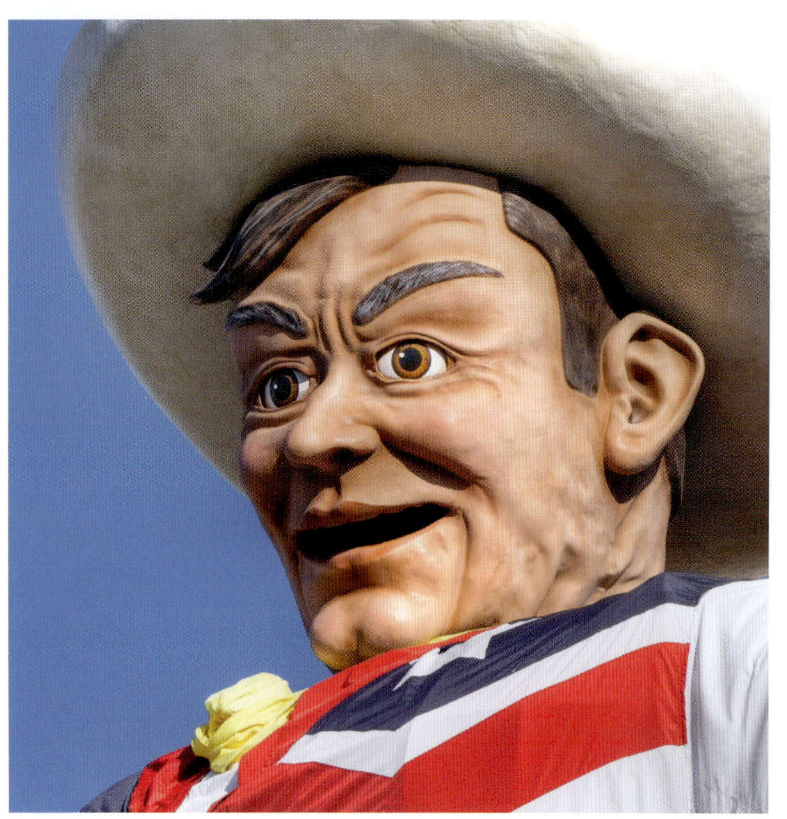

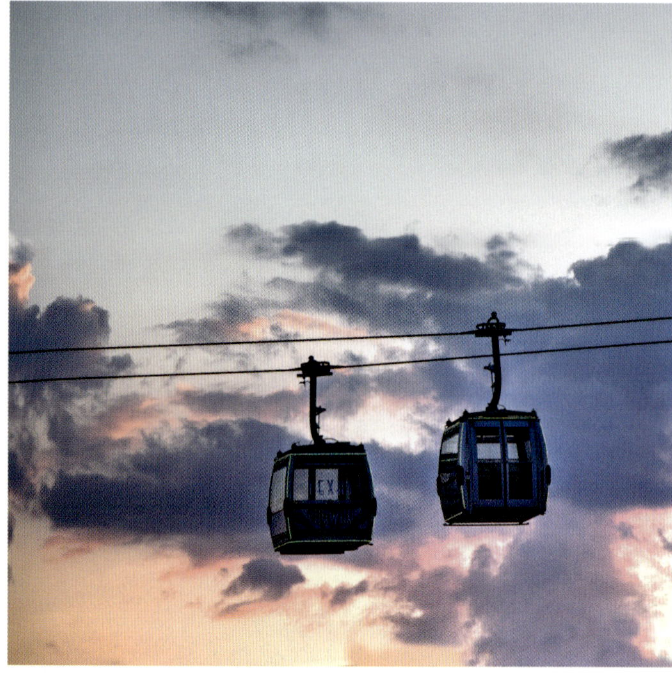

Above
The State Fair's iconic Big Tex wears a ninety-five-gallon hat. He has been altered considerably since he was created as Santa Claus in 1949.

Above
Two Texas Skyway carts move in seclusion above vibrant State Fair activity.

Opposite
Big Tex's boots are size ninety-six and are a replica of a 1949 Lucchese boot. Their design incorporates images of the Texas state flower and bird, the flags of Texas and the United States, and even the State Capitol in Austin.

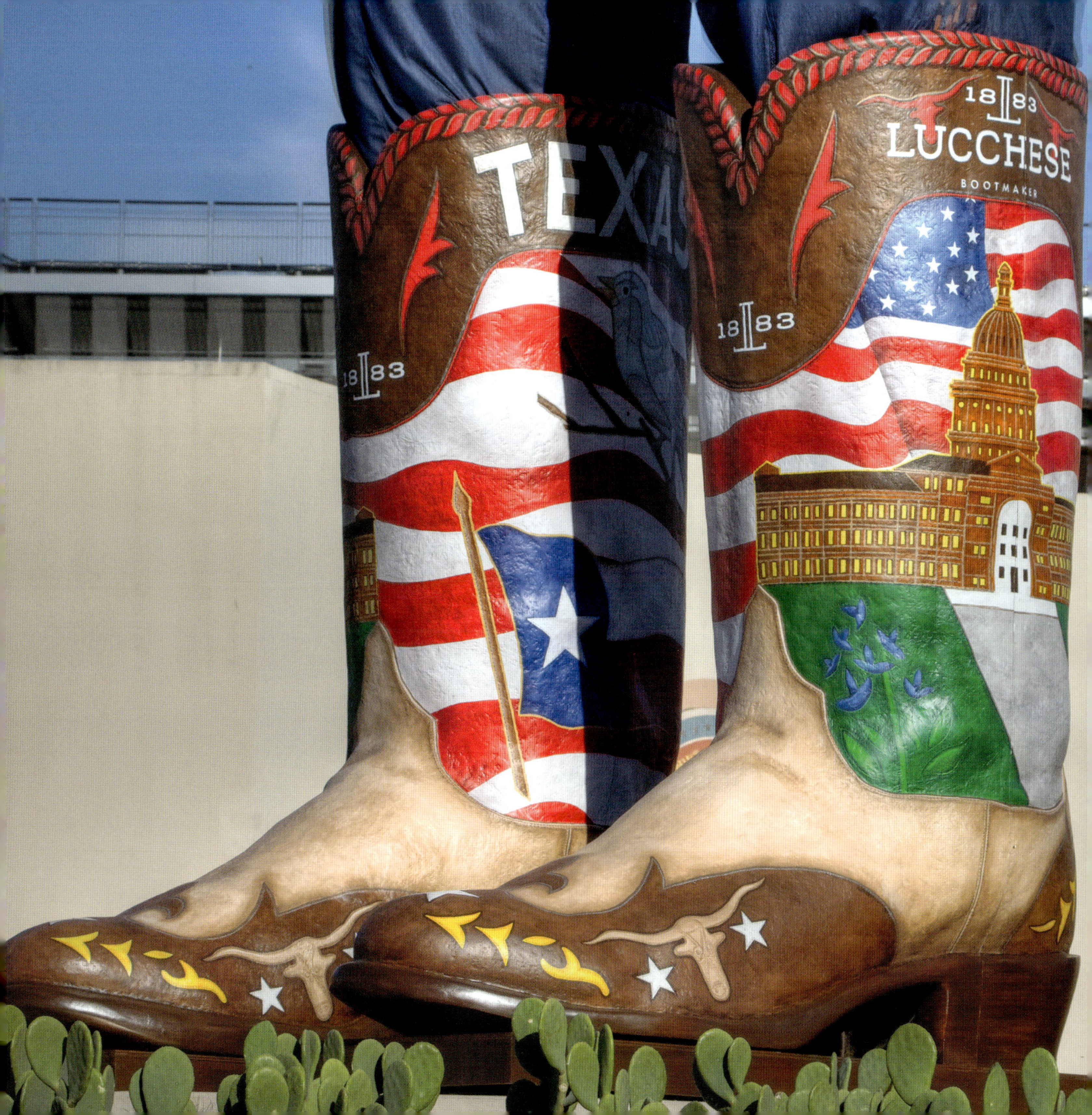
TEXAS
18 L 83
18 L 83
LUCCHESE
BOOTMAKER
18 L 83

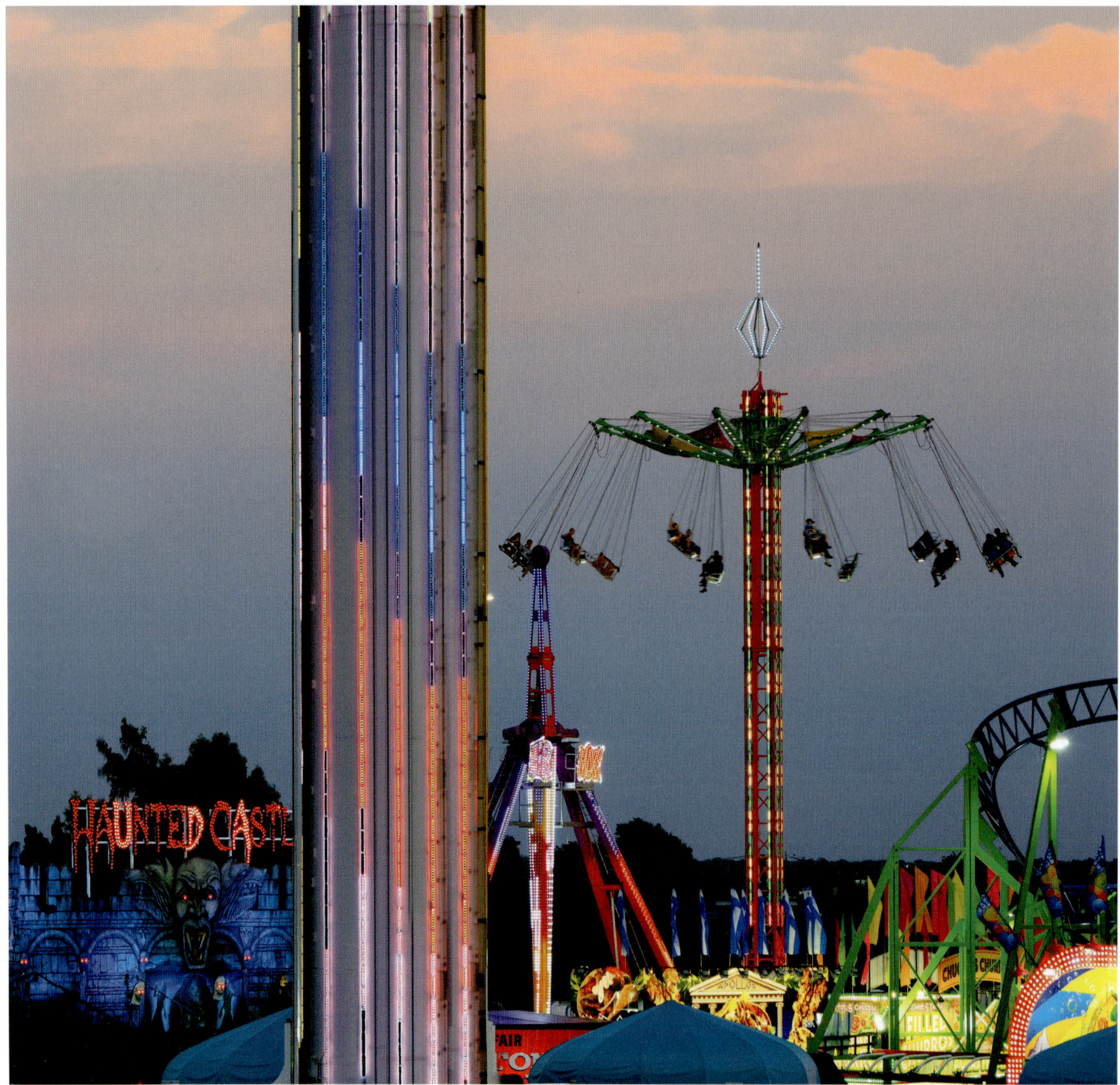
HAUNTED CASTL

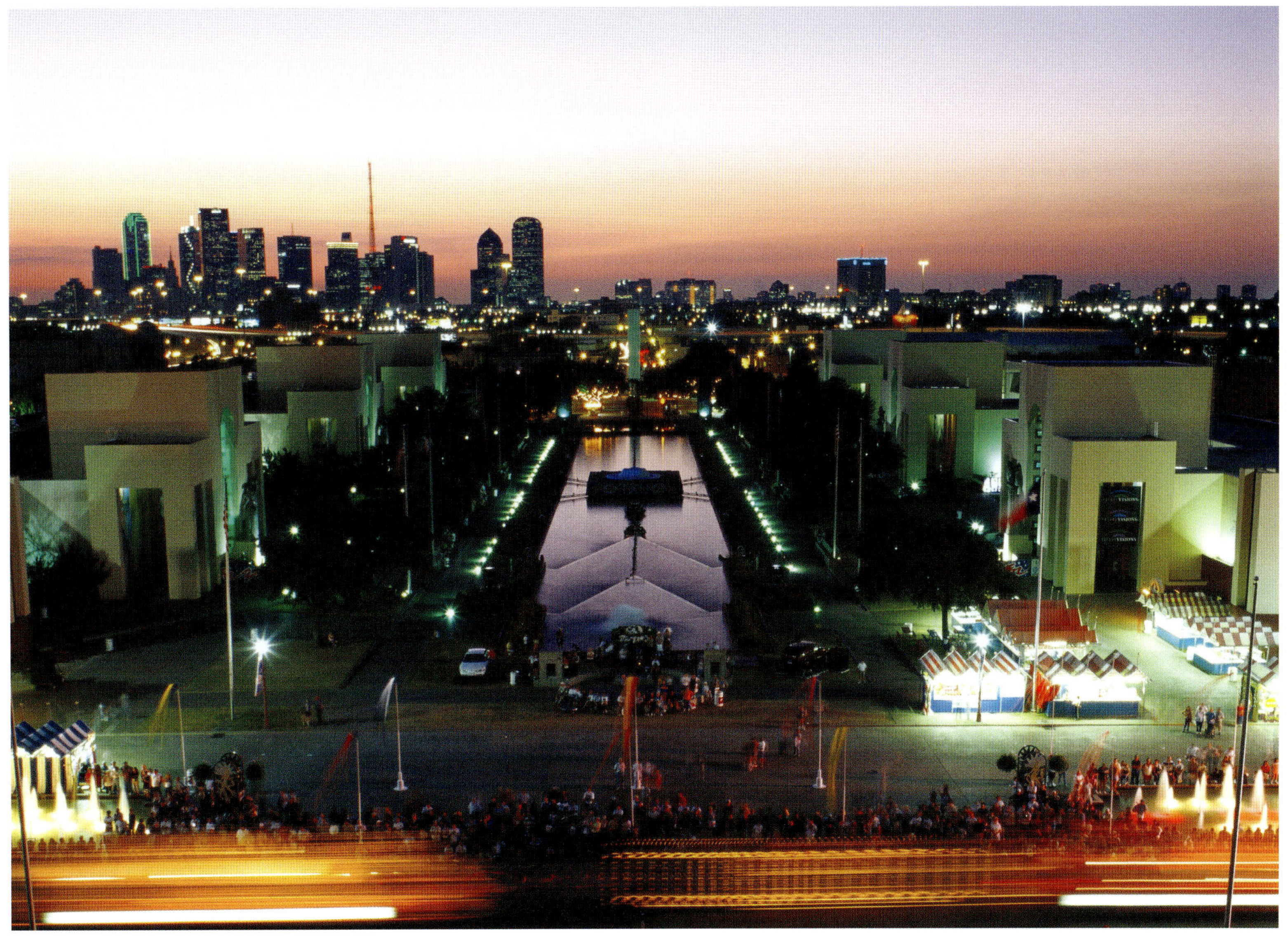

Above
Sunset view of the Esplanade at Fair Park with downtown Dallas glowing in the background.

Opposite
The sun sets on fairgoers as they participate in games on the midway. This area is among the most colorful spots during the State Fair, with neon signs beckoning visitors to rides, games, and food.

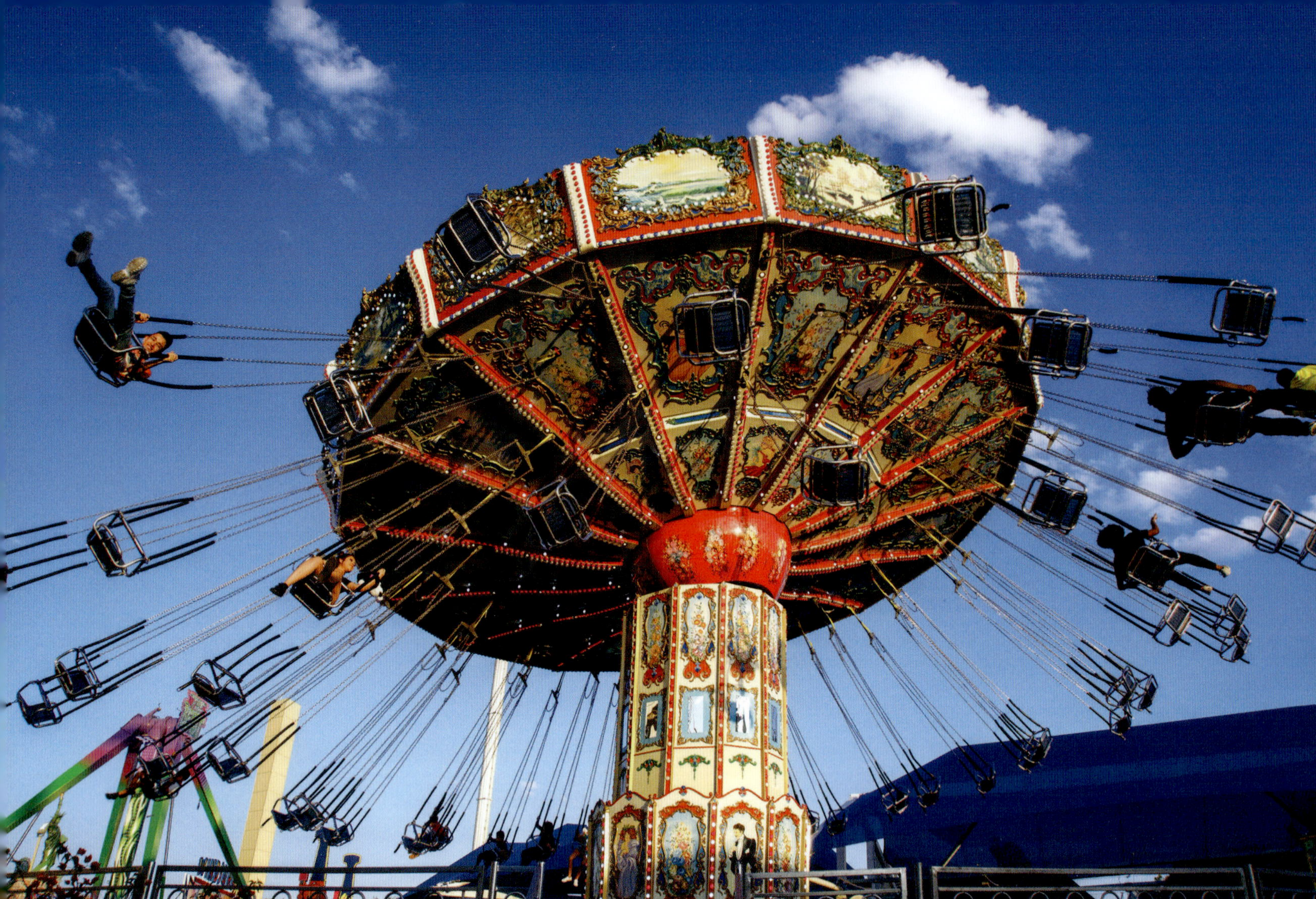

Above
The Swing Ride at the State Fair of Texas has a rotating top that also tilts for additional variations of motion.

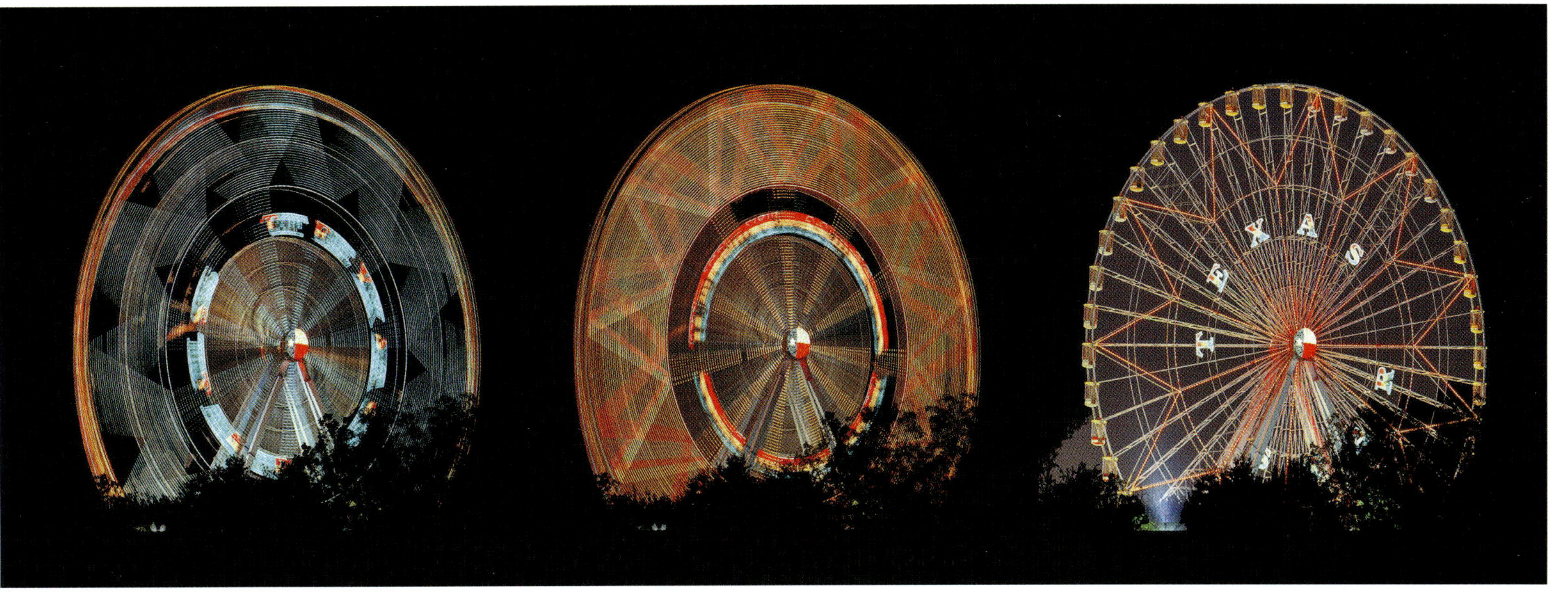

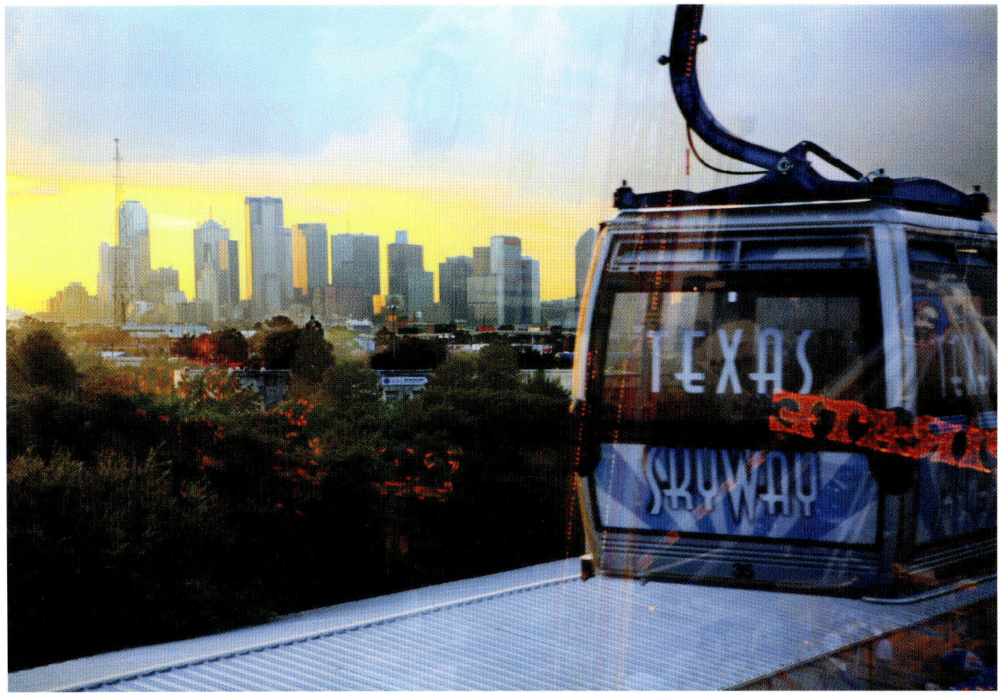

Above
No two photos of the Texas Star®
are the same due to the constantly
changing lights.

Right
A trip on the Texas Skyway provides a breathtaking view of Fair Park. The aerial track stretches 1,800 feet between two stations, where the ride soars high above the sights and sounds of the colorful midway below.

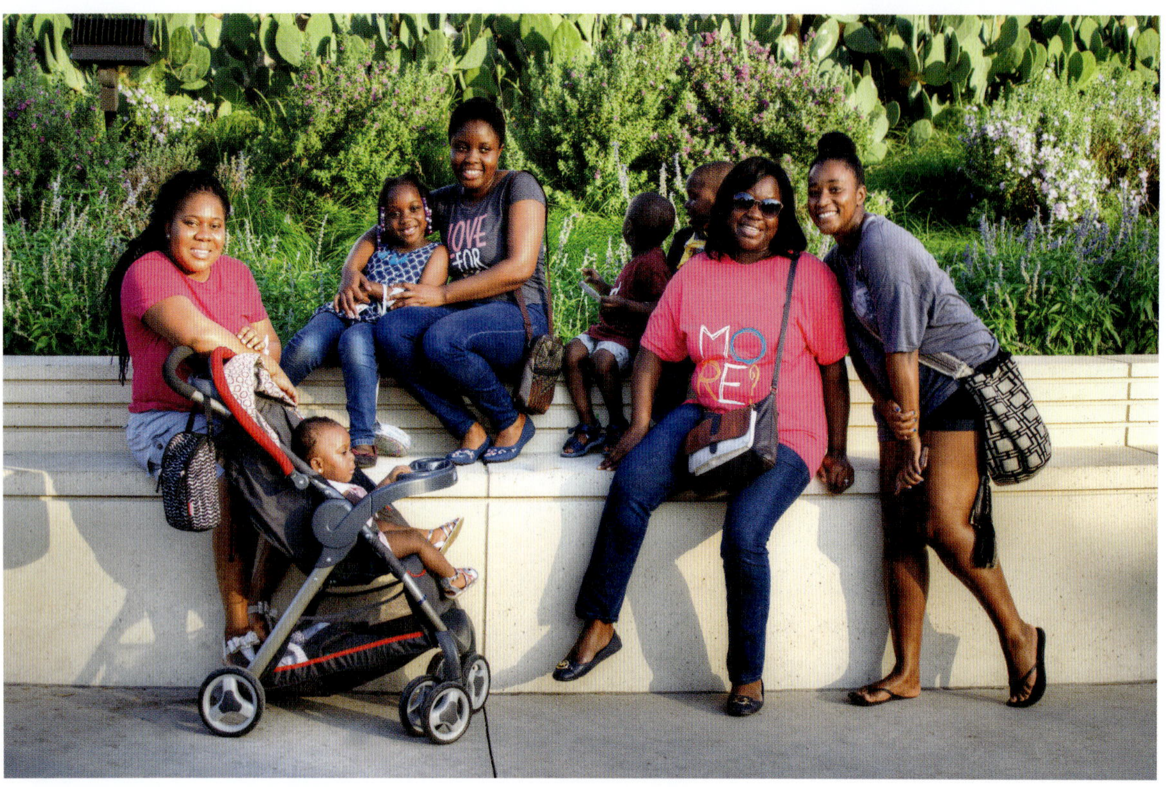

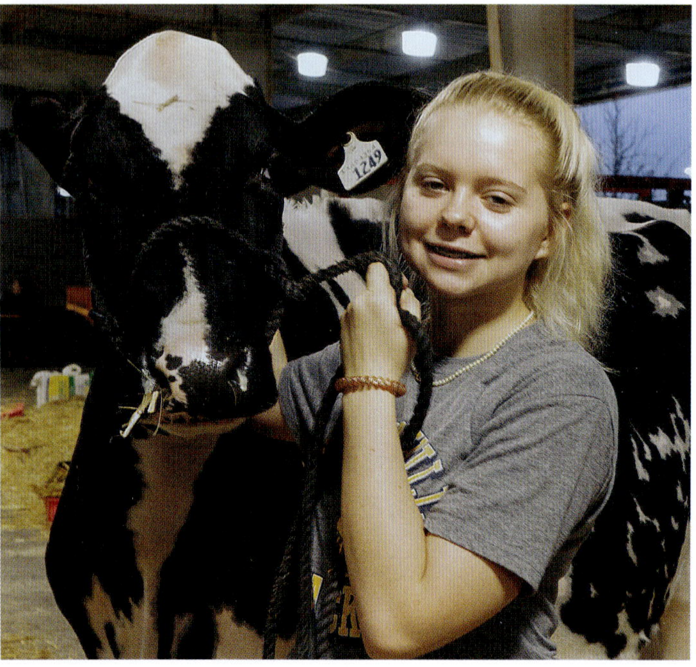

Above
Moms and kids take a break from the State Fair activities.

Left
Young people from across the Lone Star State exhibit their animals each year at the Big Tex Youth Livestock Auction.

Opposite
The State Fair Midway features more than seventy rides including the Thrillway and the Kidway, in addition to the iconic Texas Star Ferris Wheel.

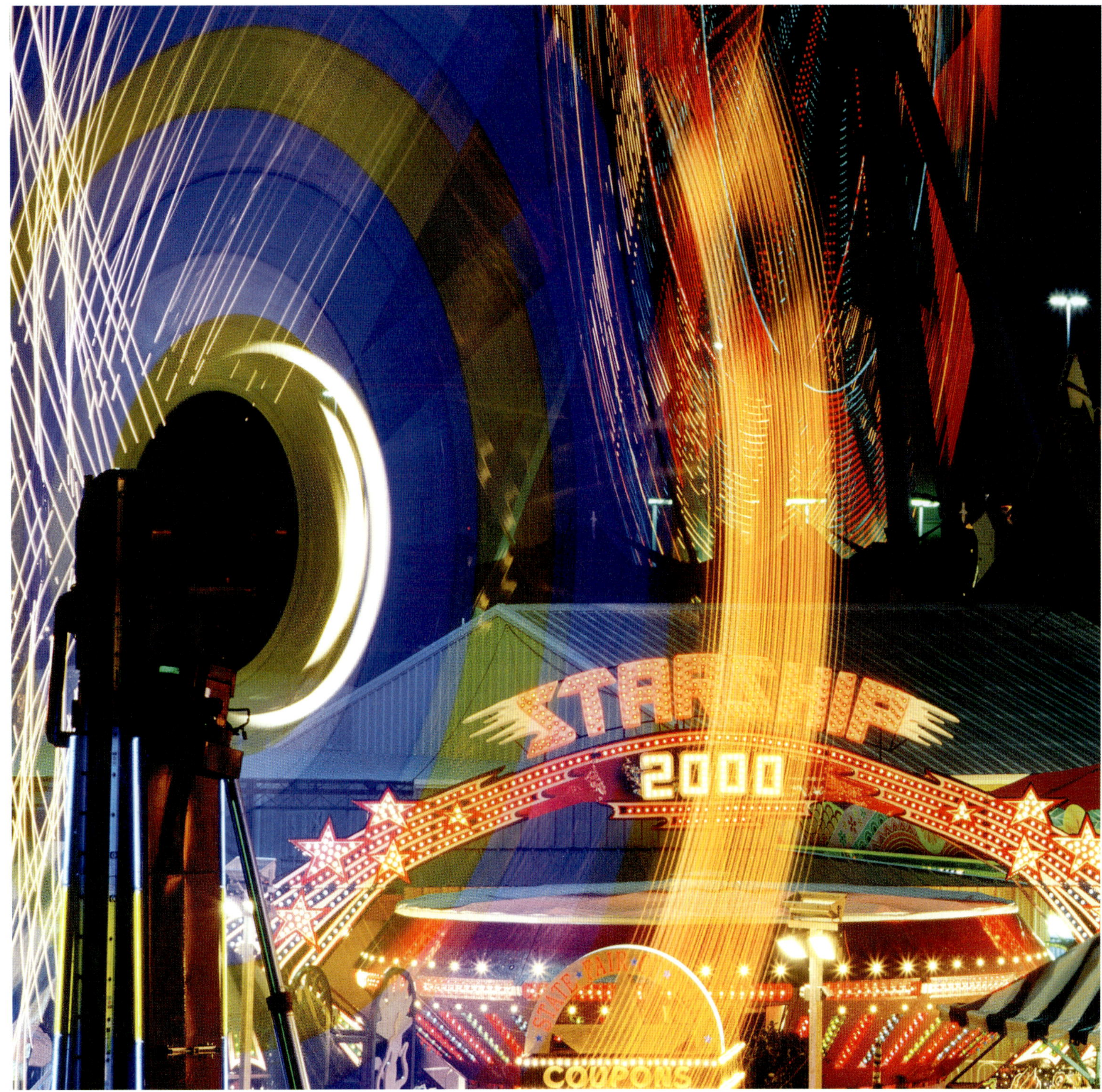
STARSHIP
2000
STATE FAIR
COUPONS

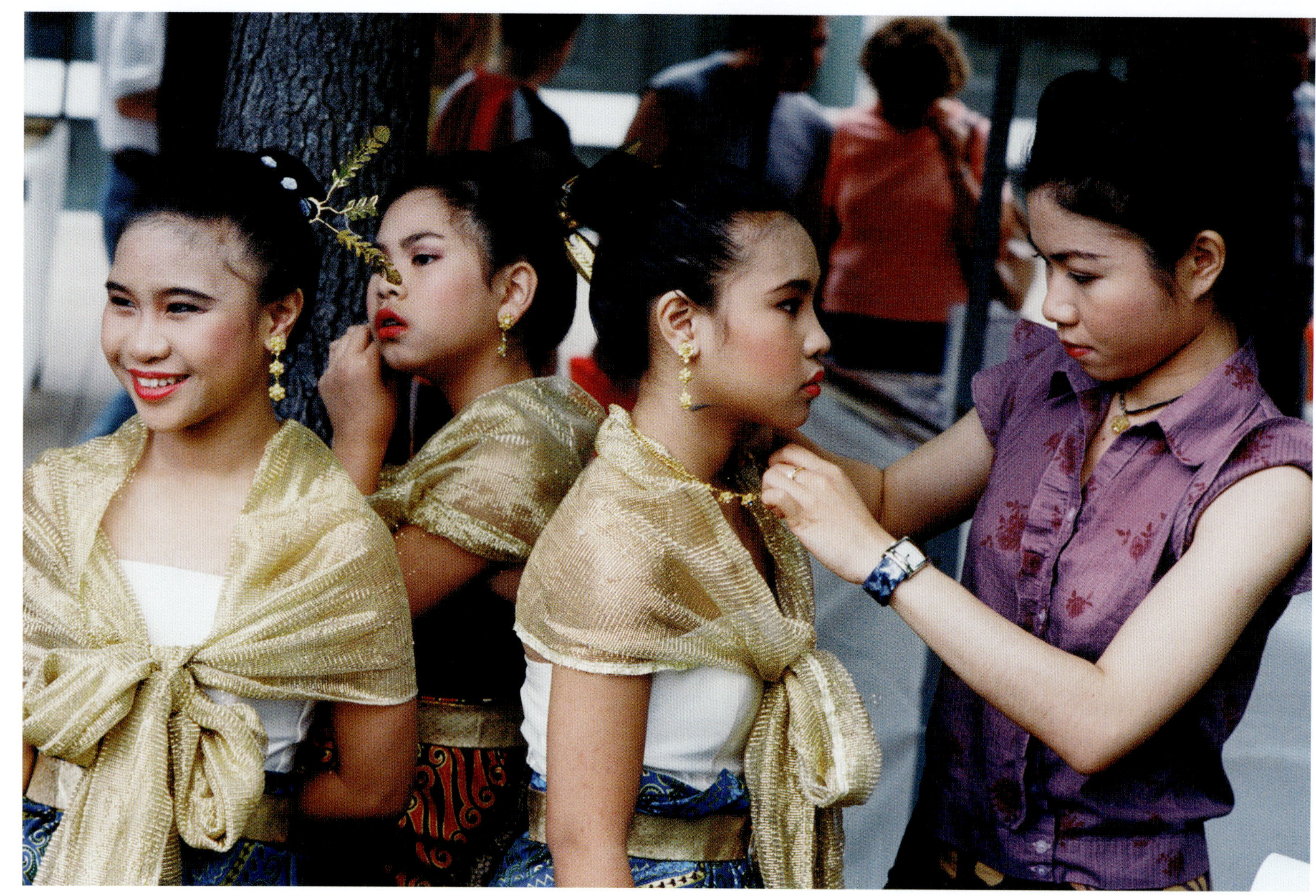

Above
Dancers prepare to perform at a popular Dallas Festival.

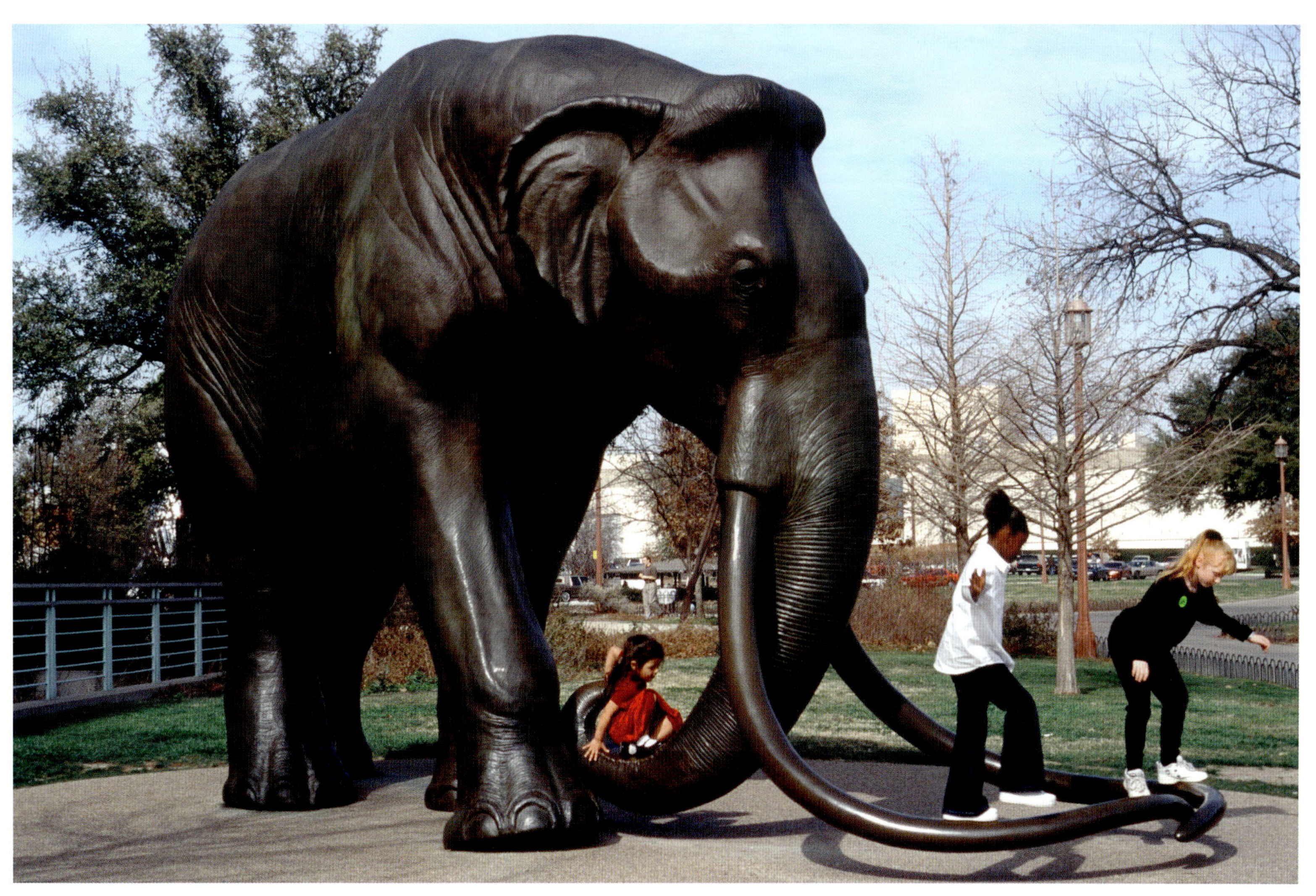

Above
Children enjoy the Mammoth sculpture at Fair Park.

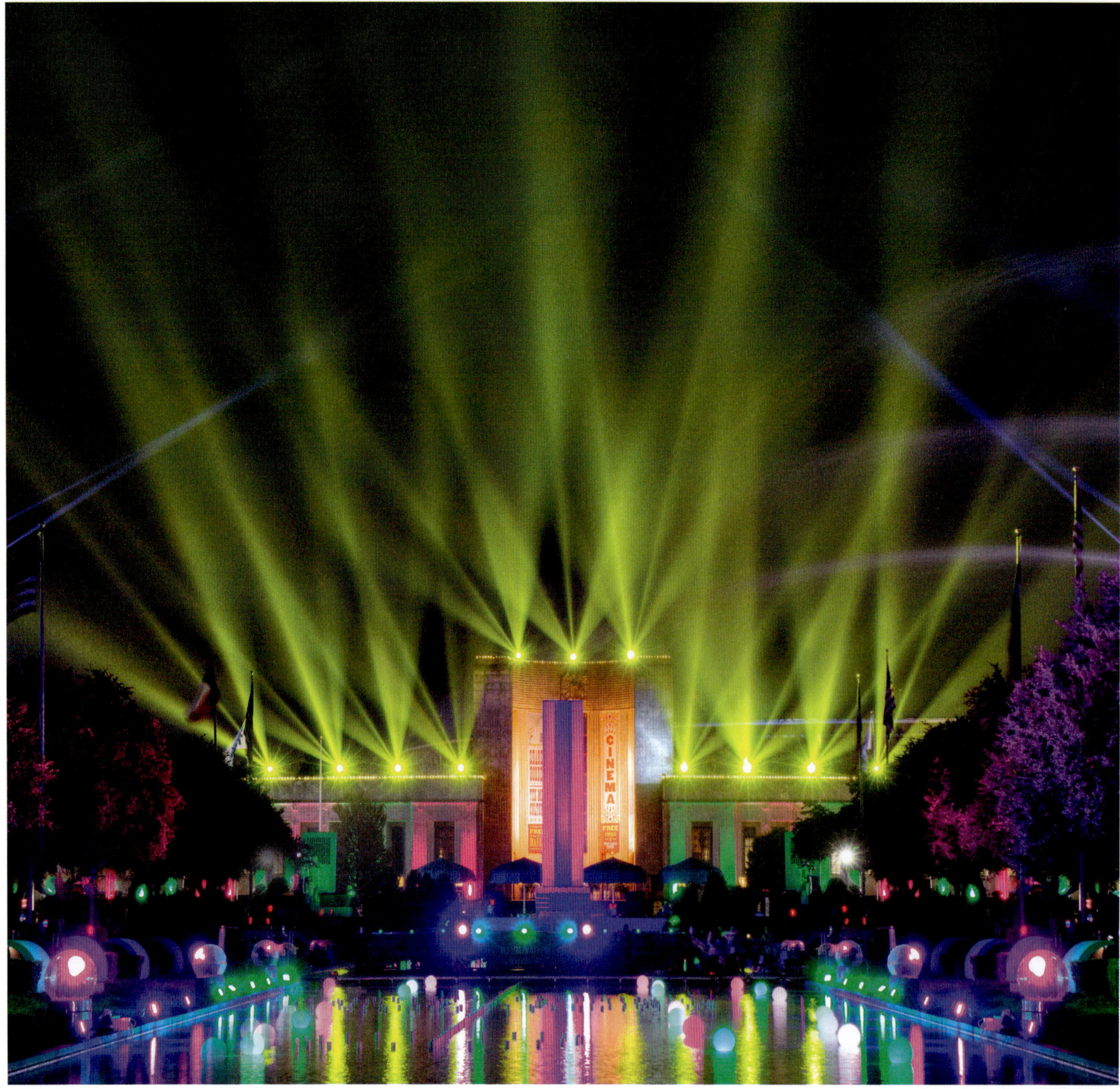
CINEMA
FREE

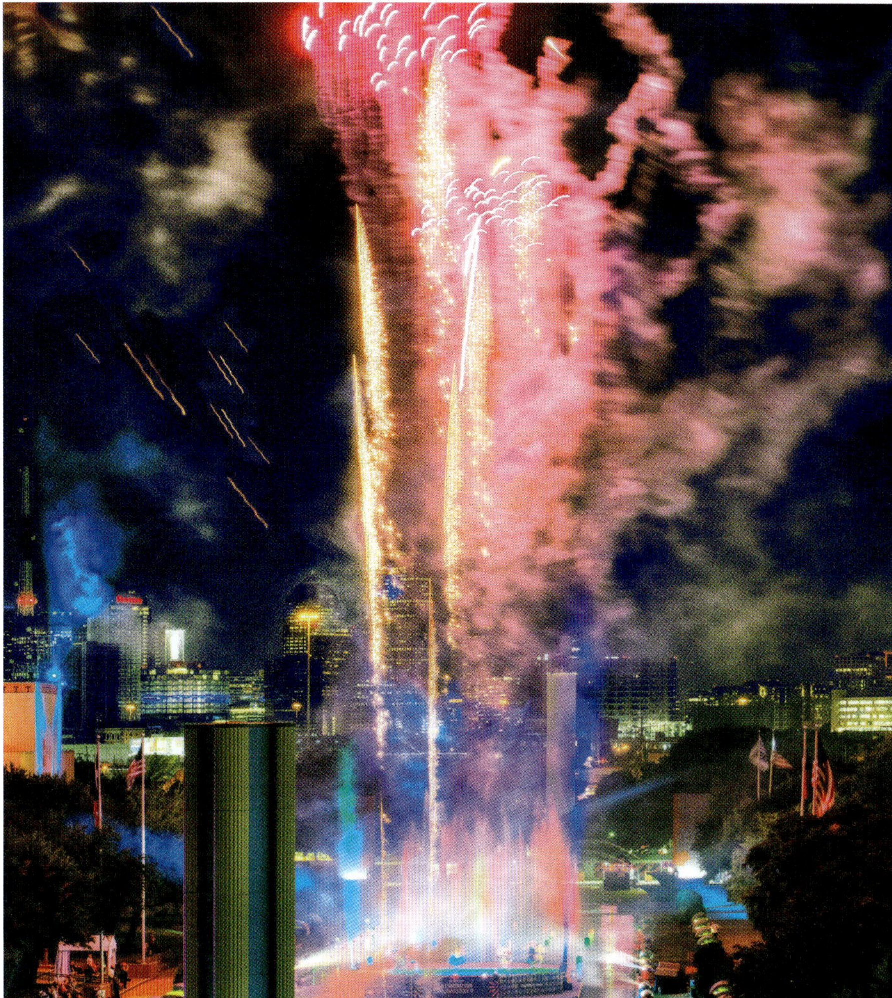

Right
On opening night, fireworks, dancers, and music fill the air at the State Fair of Texas.

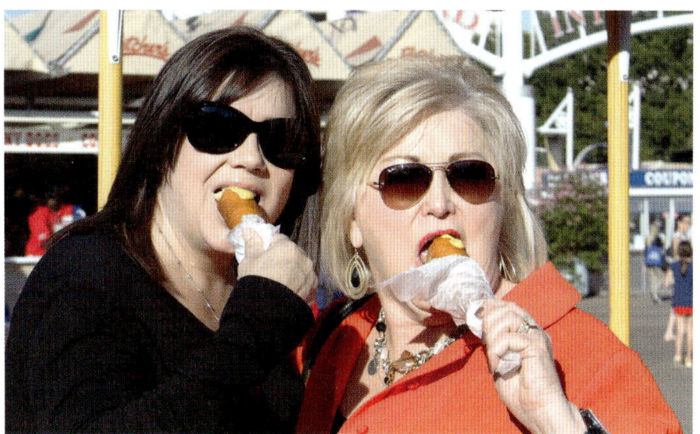

Right
Two women enjoy corny dogs at the State Fair of Texas.

Opposite
Lights beaming from the Hall of State onto the Esplanade provide a view reminiscent of the Texas Centennial Exposition in 1936.

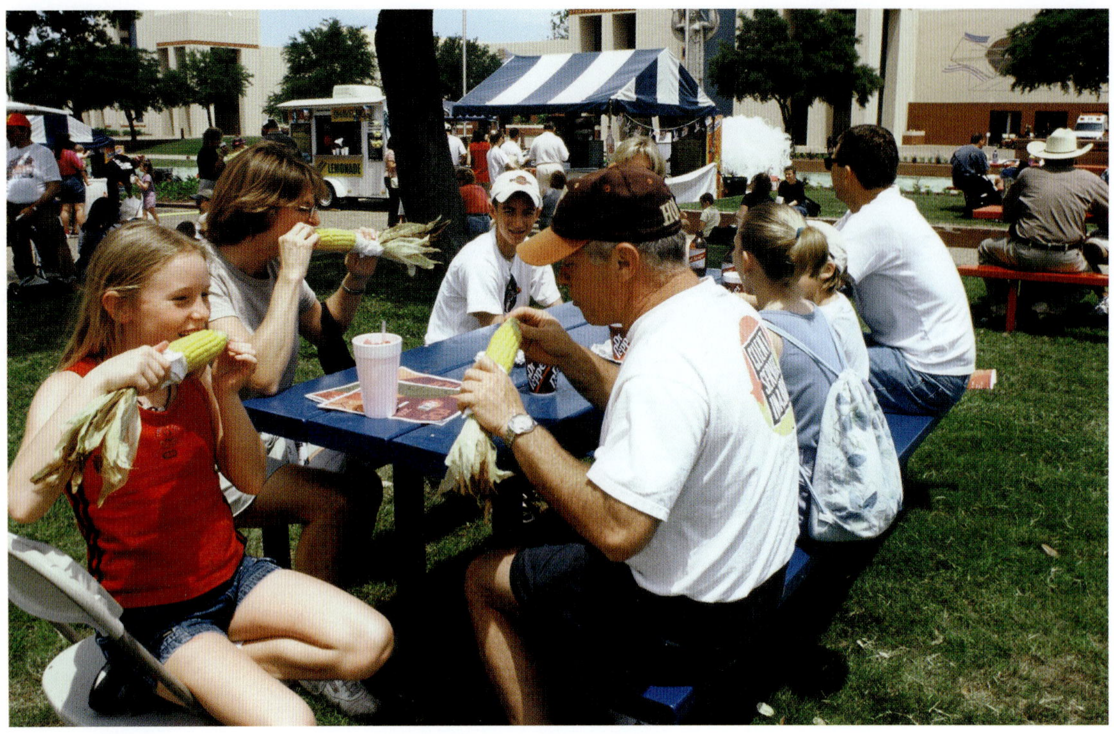

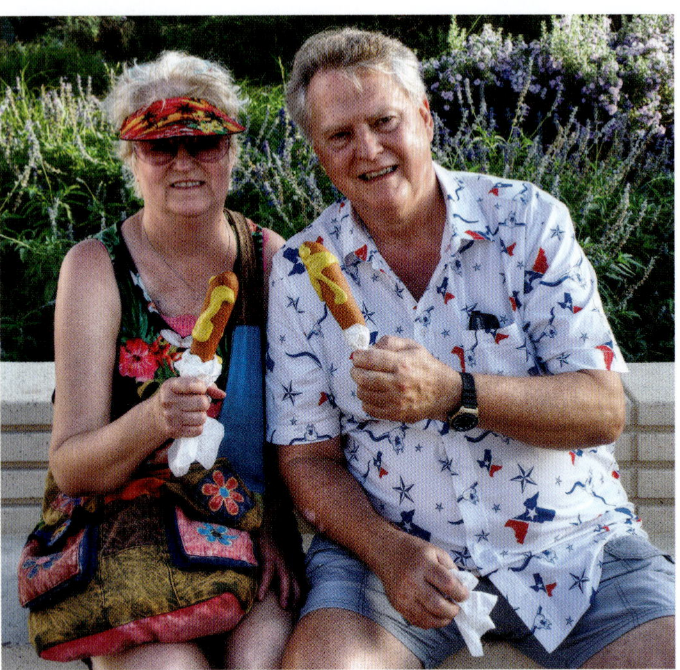

Above
Eating roasted corn at the State Fair of Texas is a family affair.

Left
Carl and Neil Fletcher introduced a hot dog dipped in cornmeal batter and deep fried at the State Fair of Texas in 1942. The “corny dog” has become a classic, enjoyed by half a million hungry consumers every year.

Opposite
The Texas Star® is the most popular ride at the fair. With forty-four gondolas, it can transport 264 passengers to a dazzling view and is one of the largest Ferris wheels in the United States (second only to the High Roller in Las Vegas).

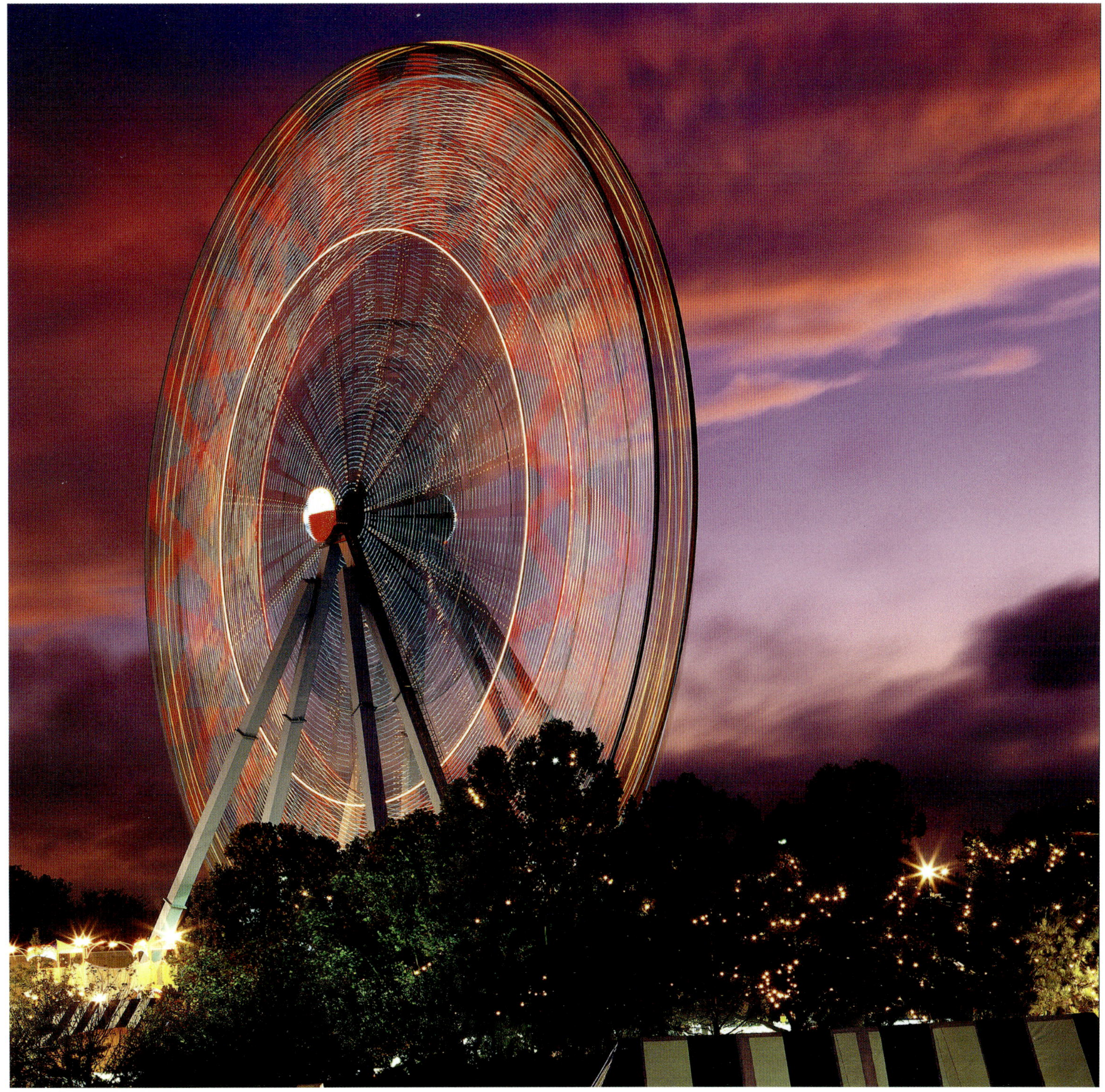

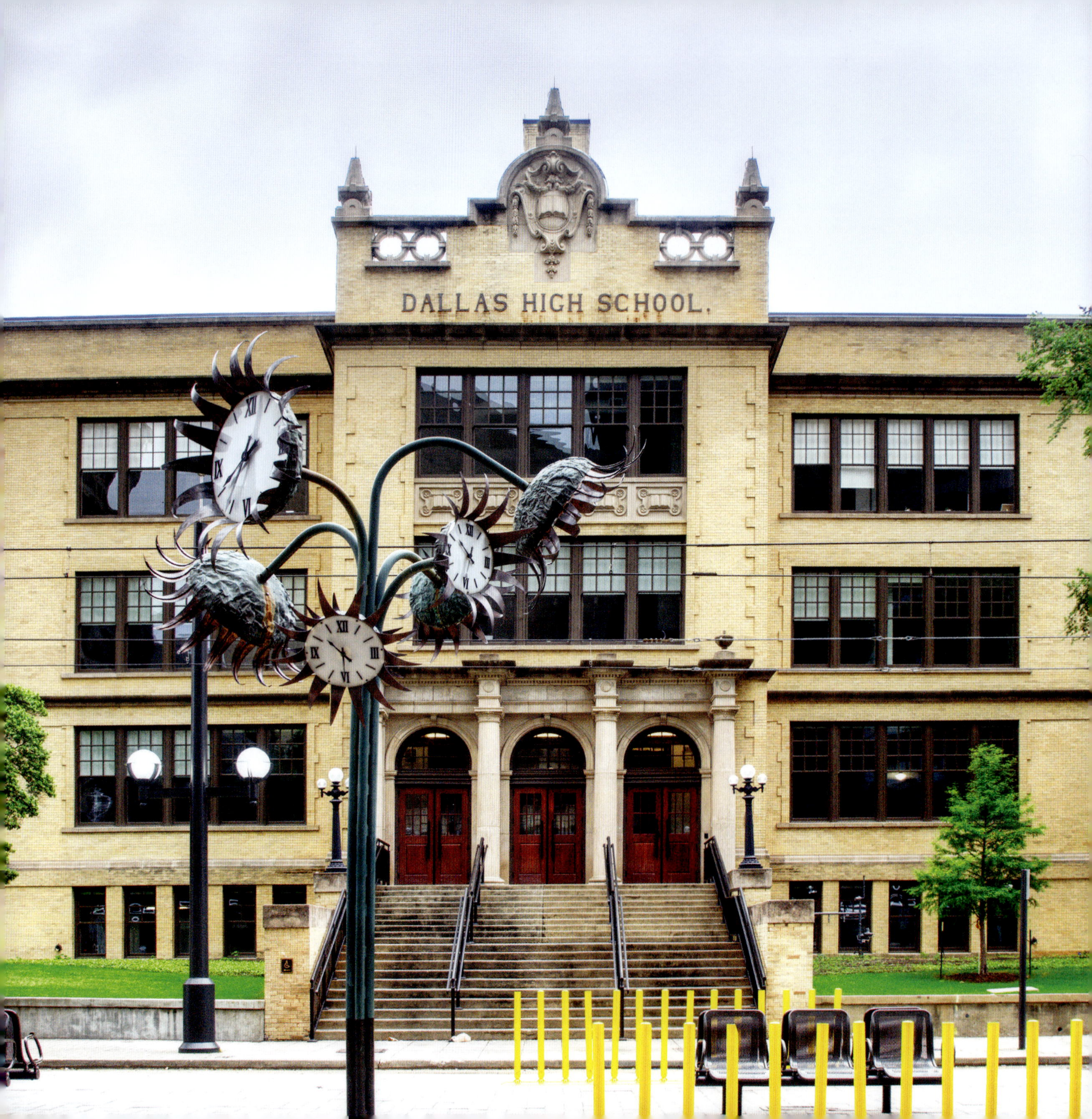
DALLAS HIGH SCHOOL.

Learn

Michael Hinojosa, EdD, in his twelfth year and second term as Dallas Independent School District superintendent, is a sought-after thought leader on issues ranging from public school funding to the concerns of urban school districts at the state and national levels.

Each of us is born with limitless potential. What we make of our lives—and how we serve the world—is often determined by circumstance, but we are not without the power to forge our own destiny. The difference is in what we learn. In my experience, education, not environment, is the key to success.

As an immigrant, I can speak to the power of education. My parents moved our family to this country when I was a young boy. When we eventually made it to Dallas, our first stop was the West Dallas housing projects, before moving to Oak Cliff and eventually buying a house there.

My parents had a dream for each of us to be able to build better lives and experience the art of the possible. Education was the catalyst for me, as it is for every student well served by any educational system. Through education, we are creating conditions for success, one student at a time.

Students look to adults for a path forward. Great teachers and leaders can show them how to experience the art of the possible. It is critical that we provide that guidance. Equitable opportunities, coupled with high expectations and the commitment to guide students, should be the goal of every educator, parent, and community member. Together, we can build guiding coalitions to bring real transformation to students' lives.

A great city like Dallas requires an educated public. Ensuring that its residents can access a thorough, well-rounded education shapes the destiny of a city every bit as much as its geographic location, wealth, or natural resources. The Dallas Independent School District is striving to be that public education system that provides the first-class education required for all our students to learn.

Michael Hinojosa

Opposite
Dallas High School is the oldest high school building in Dallas. Several notable Americans are graduates, including former US Attorney General and Supreme Court Justice Tom C. Clark. It was built in 1907 and renovated as office space in 2018. The 3 1/2-story Classical Revival structure is located downtown next to the Pearl/Arts District DART light-rail station.

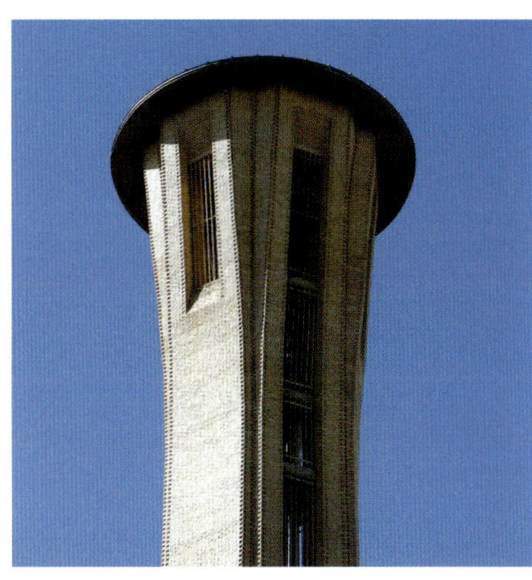

Above
The Campanile of the University of Dallas was designed by the renowned Texas architect O'Neil Ford. The university is a private, Catholic, liberal arts institution in Irving, an inner suburb of Dallas.

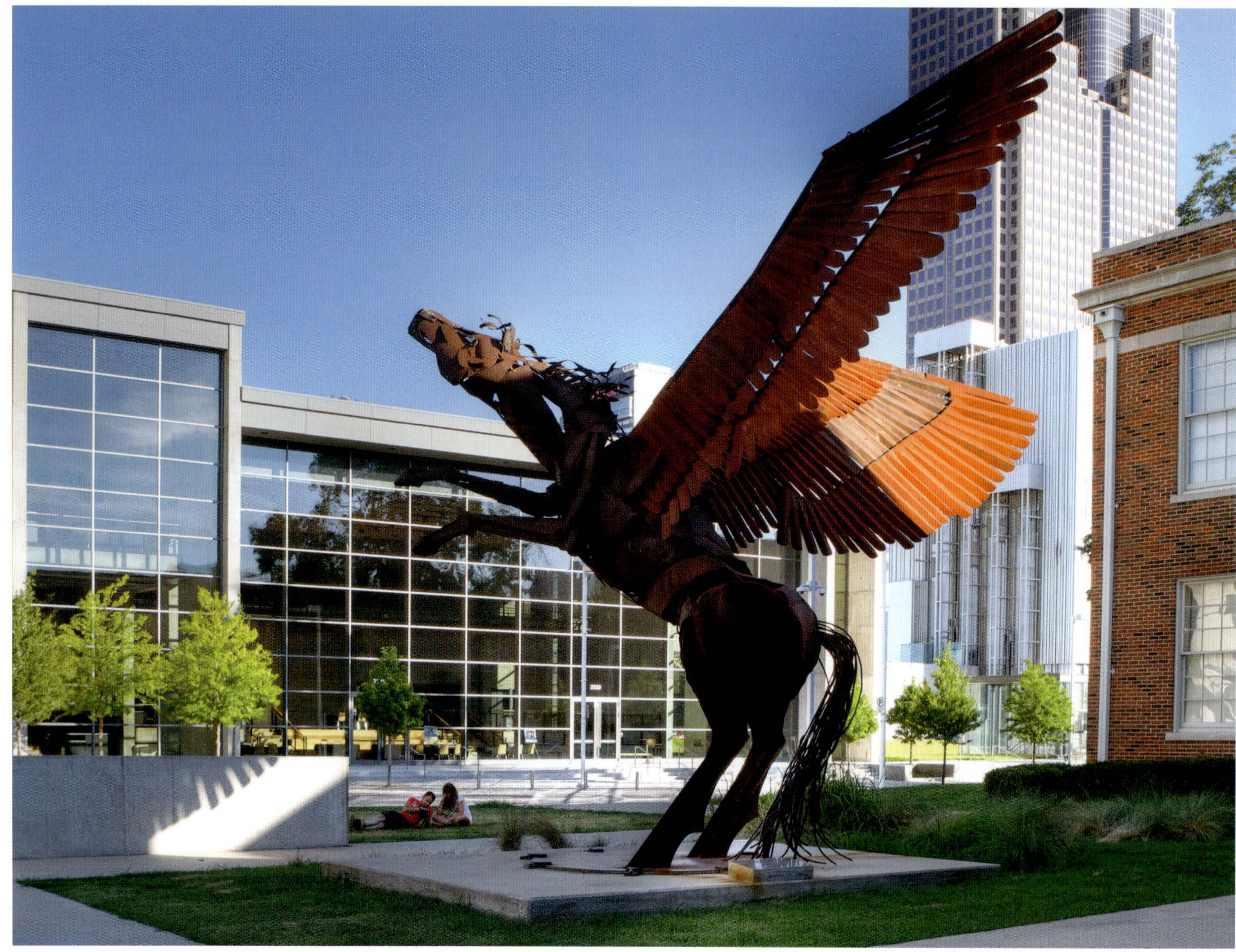

Above
Booker T. Washington High School for the Performing and Visual Arts is located in the Arts District of downtown Dallas. It is a magnet school for grades 9–12. Competitive and demanding, it educates promising young artists from around the city.

Opposite
The Dallas Institute of Humanities and Culture seeks to enliven the practical life of the city with wisdom and imagination. The institute's campus, located on Routh Street in Uptown, draws students of all ages to classes, events, and conferences.

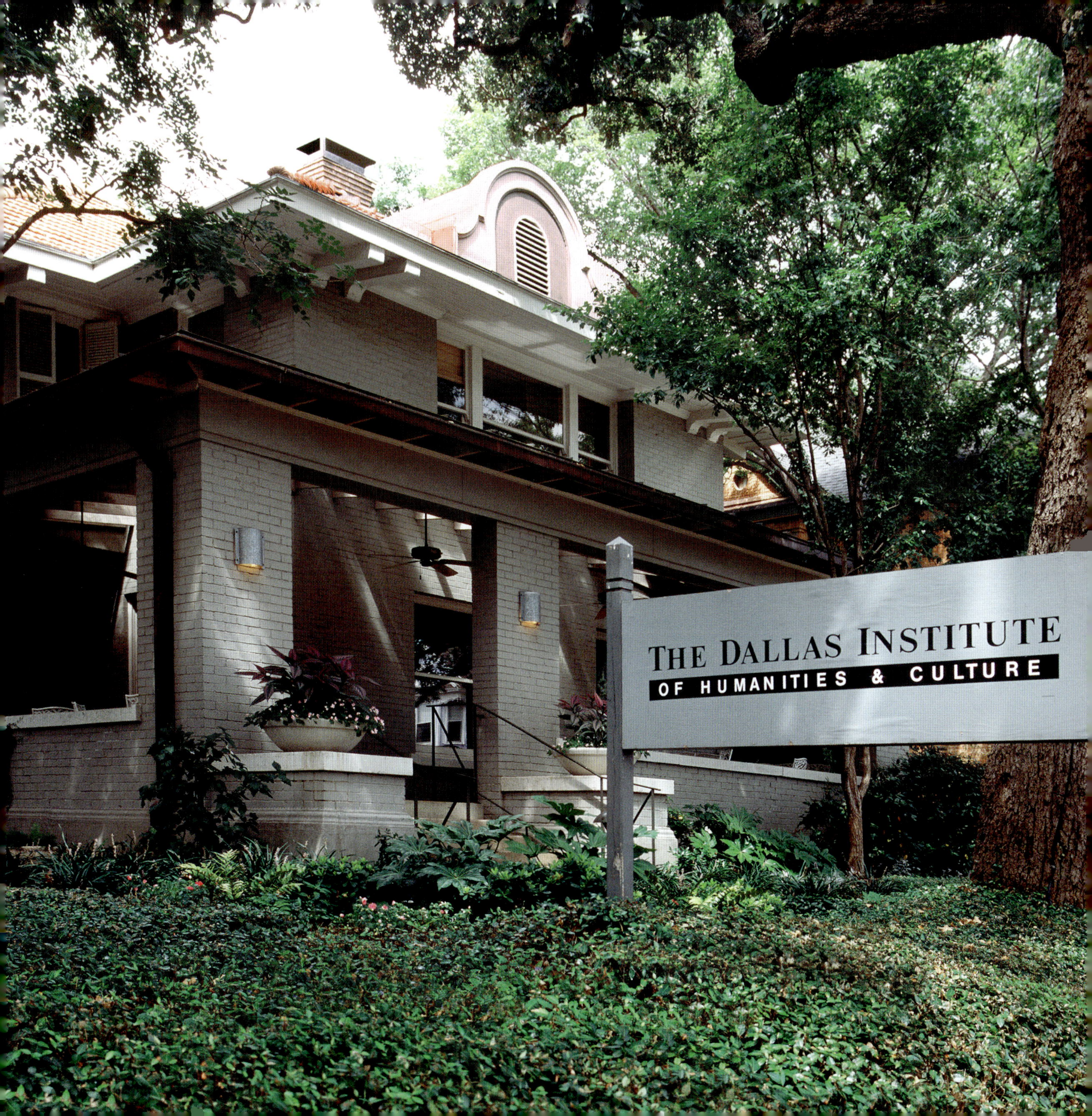
THE DALLAS INSTITUTE
OF HUMANITIES & CULTURE

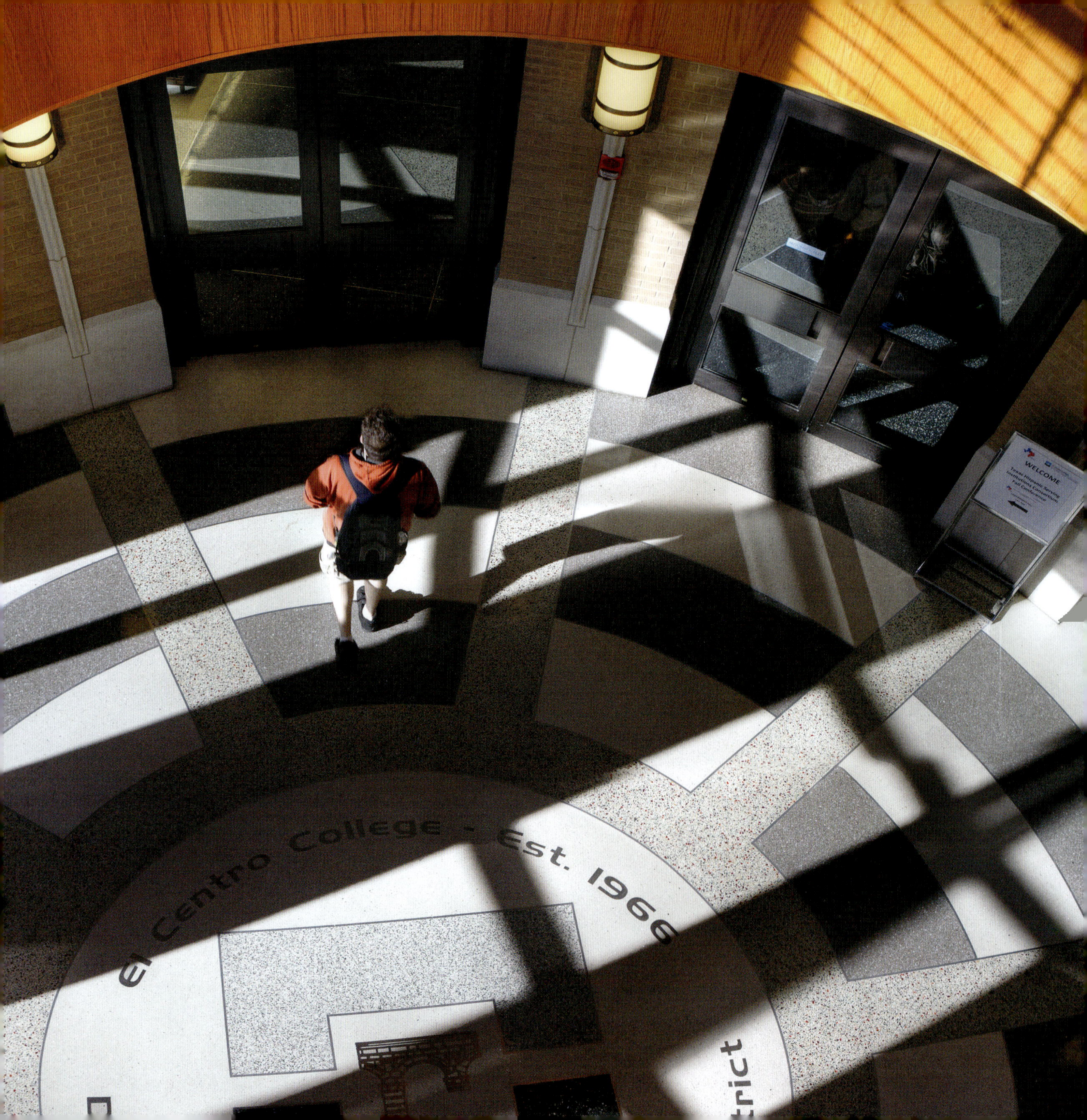
WELCOME
El Centro College - Est. 1966

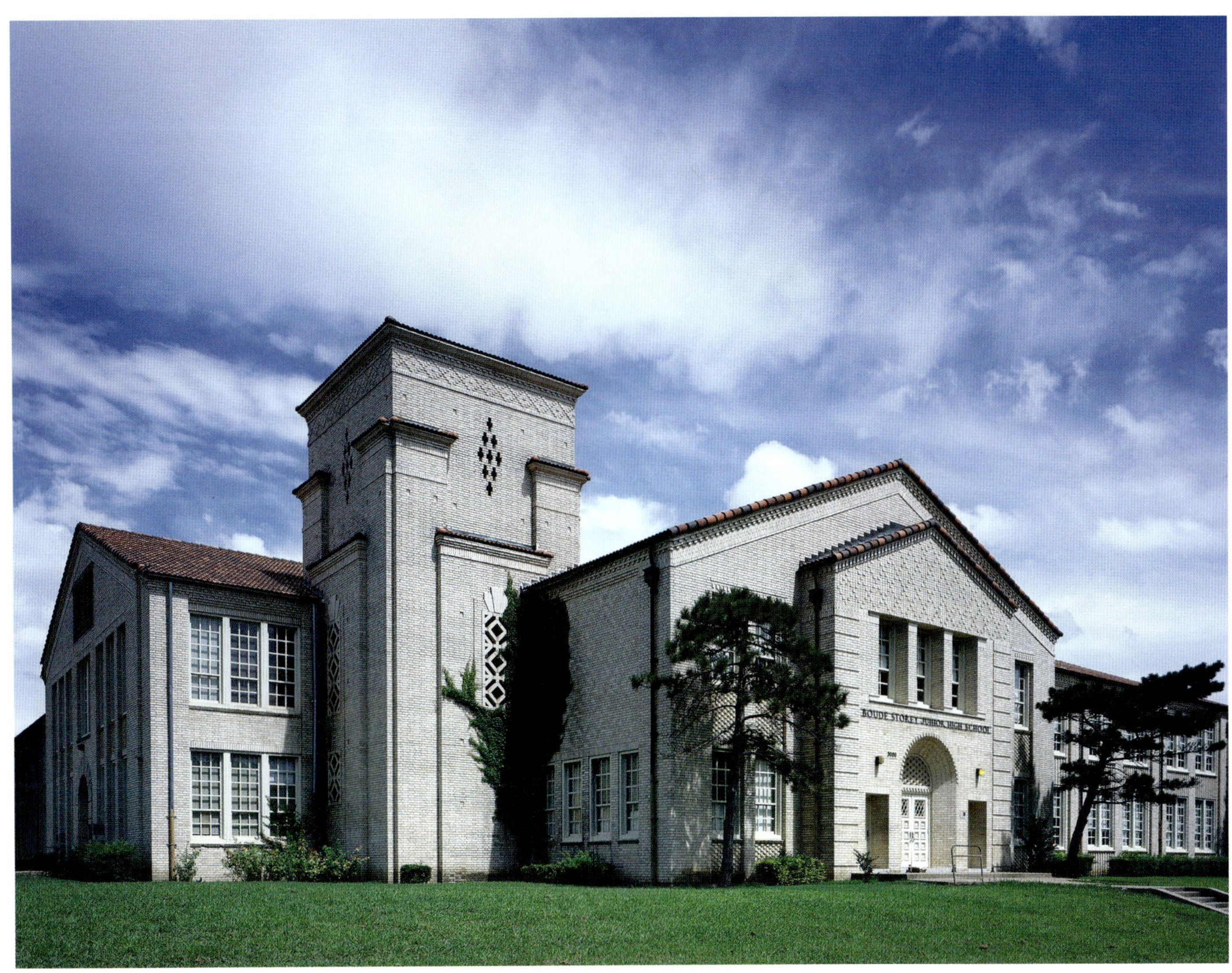

Above
Boude Storey Middle School, designed by Dallas architect Mark Lemmon, was built in 1933 in Oak Cliff

Opposite
The first Dallas County Community College, "El Centro," opened in 1965 in a renovated department store downtown.

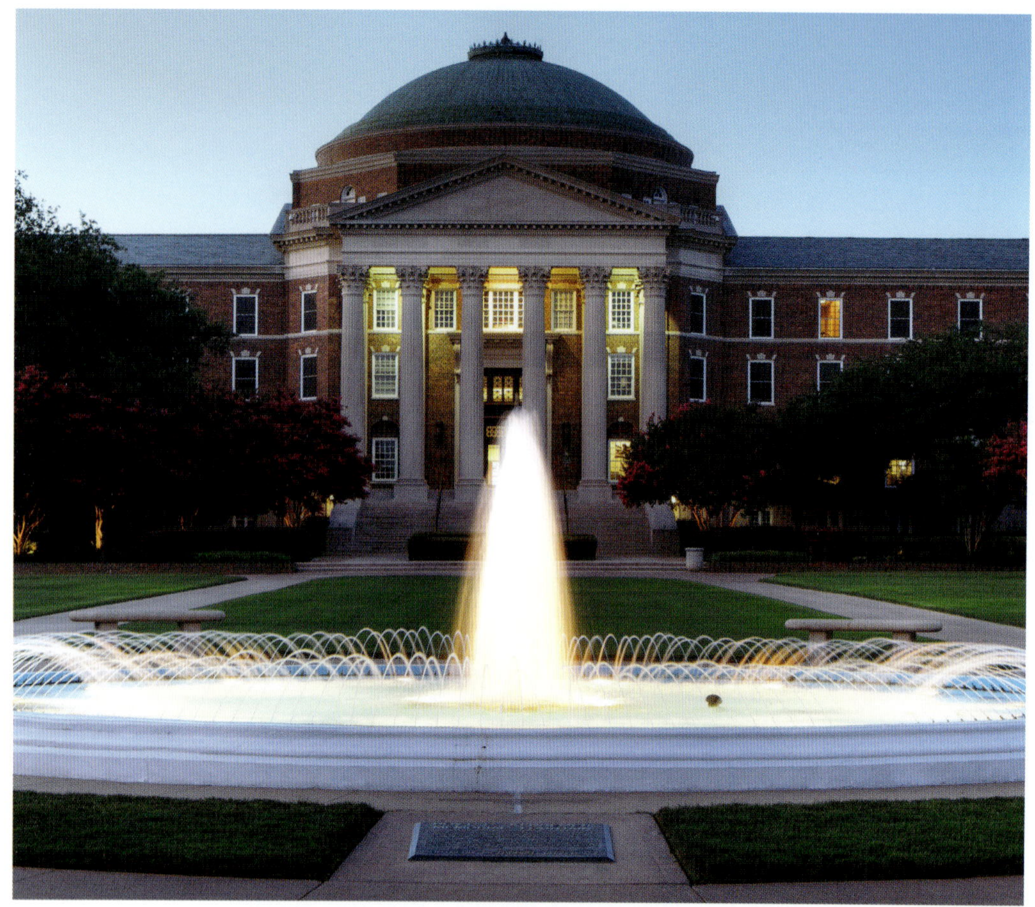

Left
Southern Methodist University was founded in 1911, with Dallas Hall as its centerpiece. The domed structure was inspired by Thomas Jefferson's rotunda at the University of Virginia.

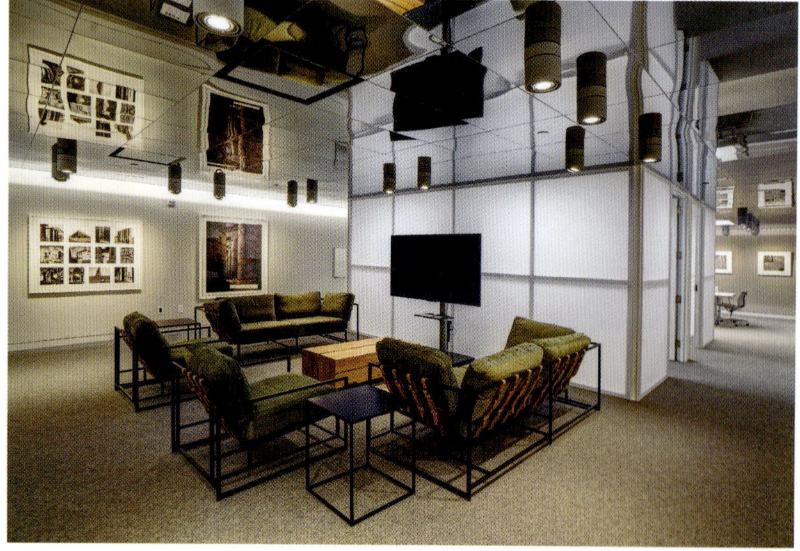

Left
The Edith O'Donnell Institute of Art History was founded by Dr. Richard Brettell at the University of Texas at Dallas in 2014, with a generous endowment from arts patron Edith O'Donnell. Her charge was to invent a new kind of art history that she called "Art History, UT Dallas style." A branch of the UTD program is located at the Dallas Museum of Art (pictured).

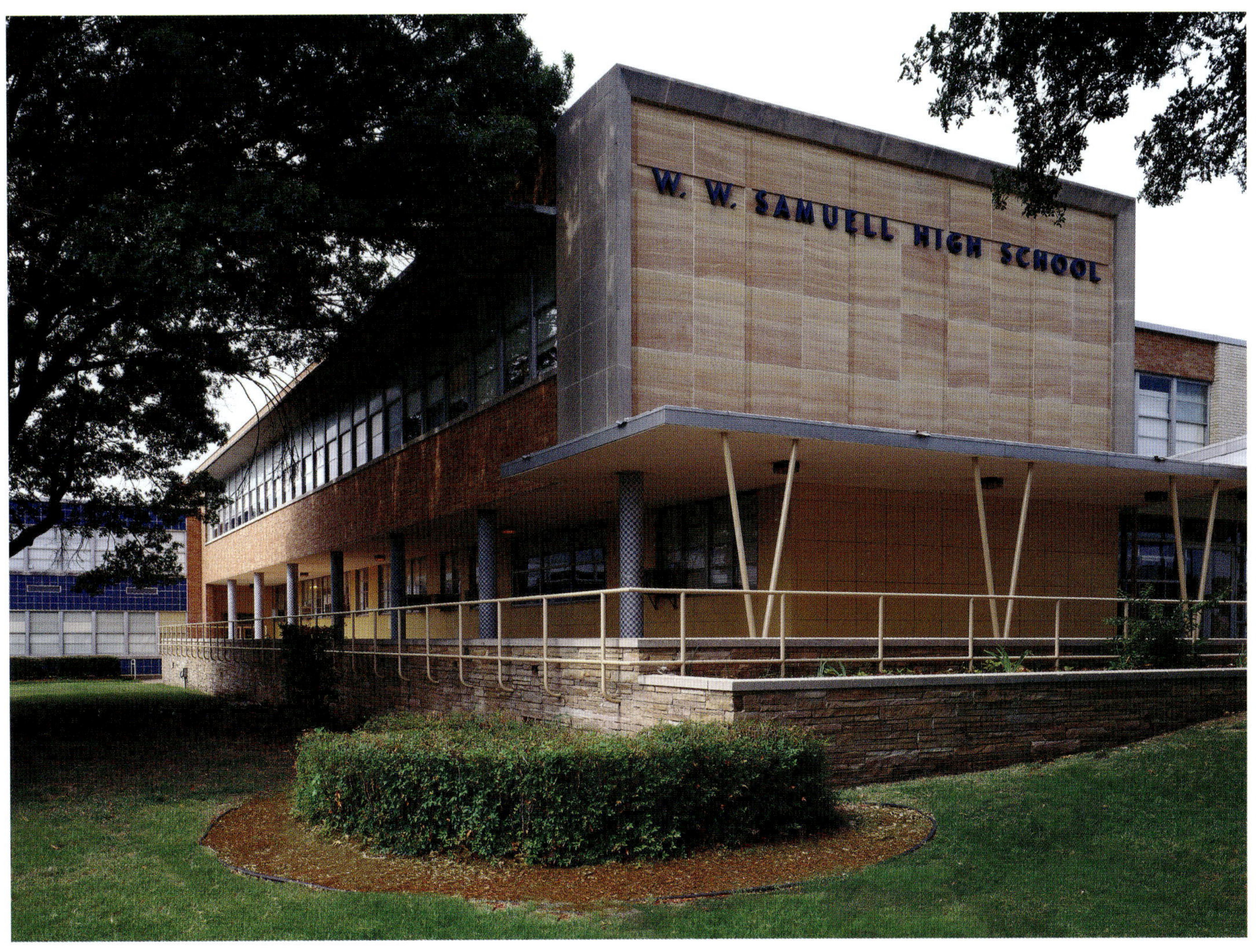

Above
W. W. Samuell High School, designed by Dallas architect Mark Lemmon, is located in the Pleasant Grove area of southeast Dallas and enrolls students in grades 9–12. The school serves portions of southeast Dallas and the nearby city of Balch Springs.

Following Pages
With a long history in Denton, the University of North Texas opened a South Dallas campus in 2010. It is the only public university located within Dallas city limits.

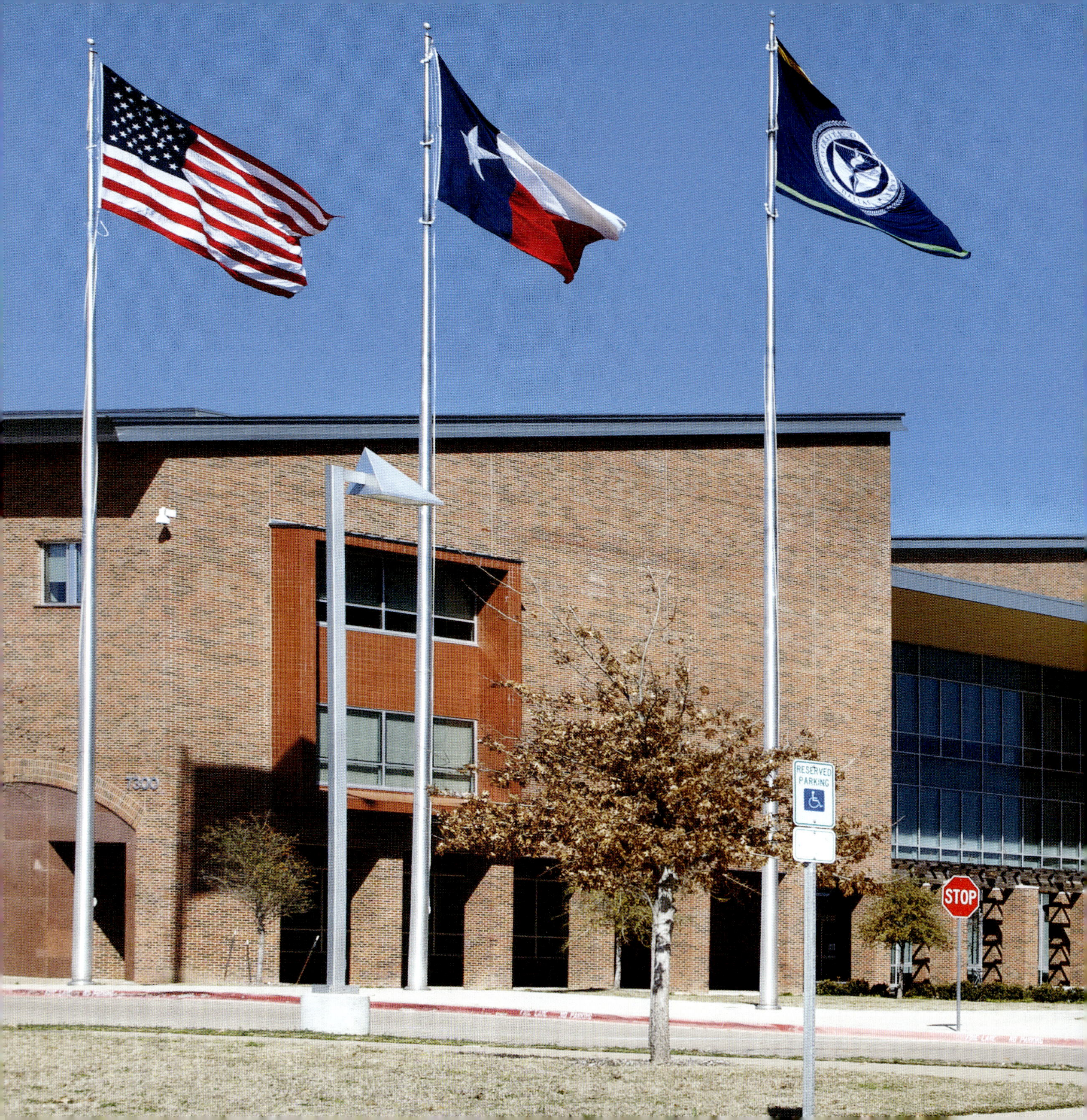
7300
RESERVED
PARKING
STOP

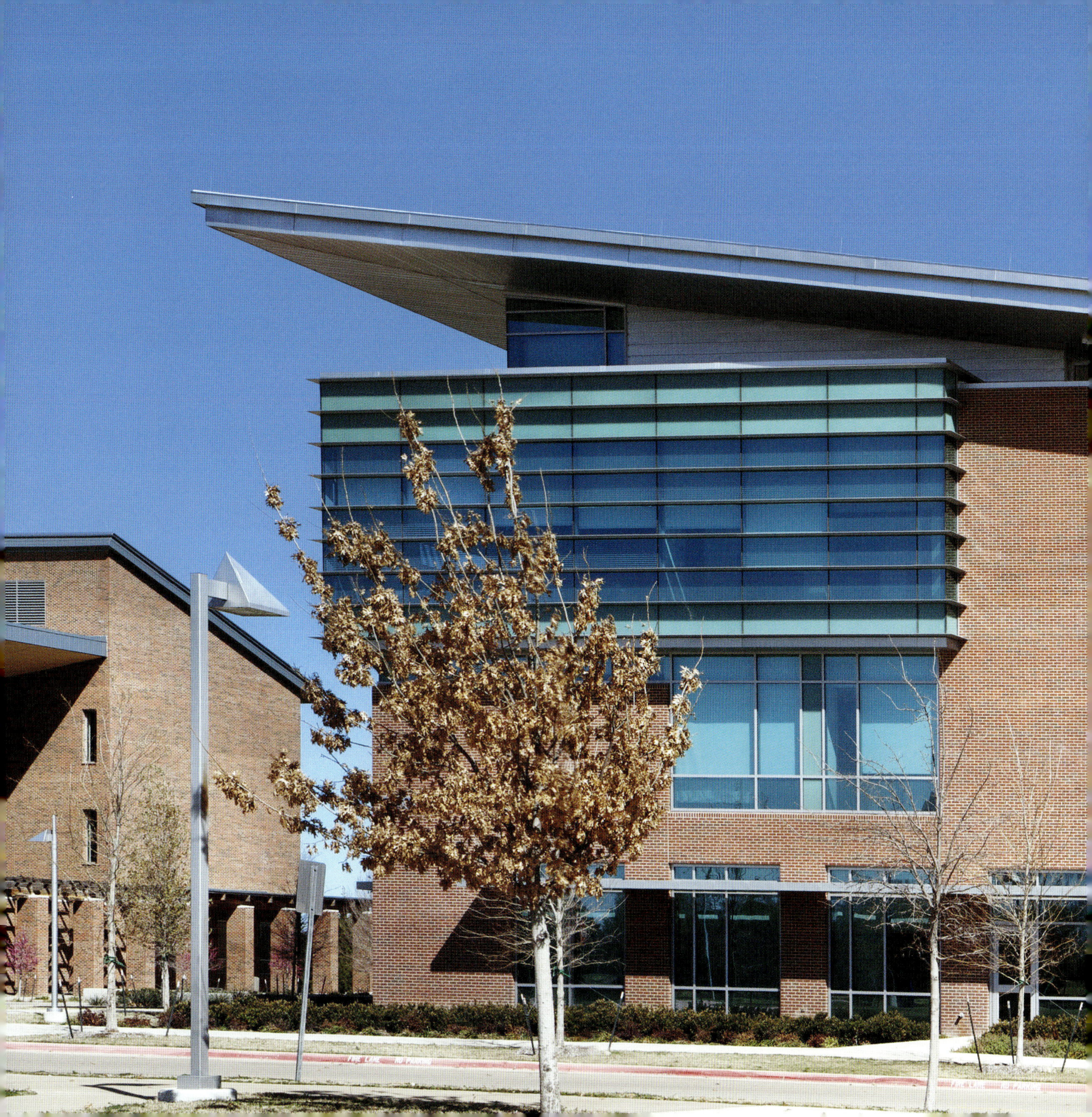

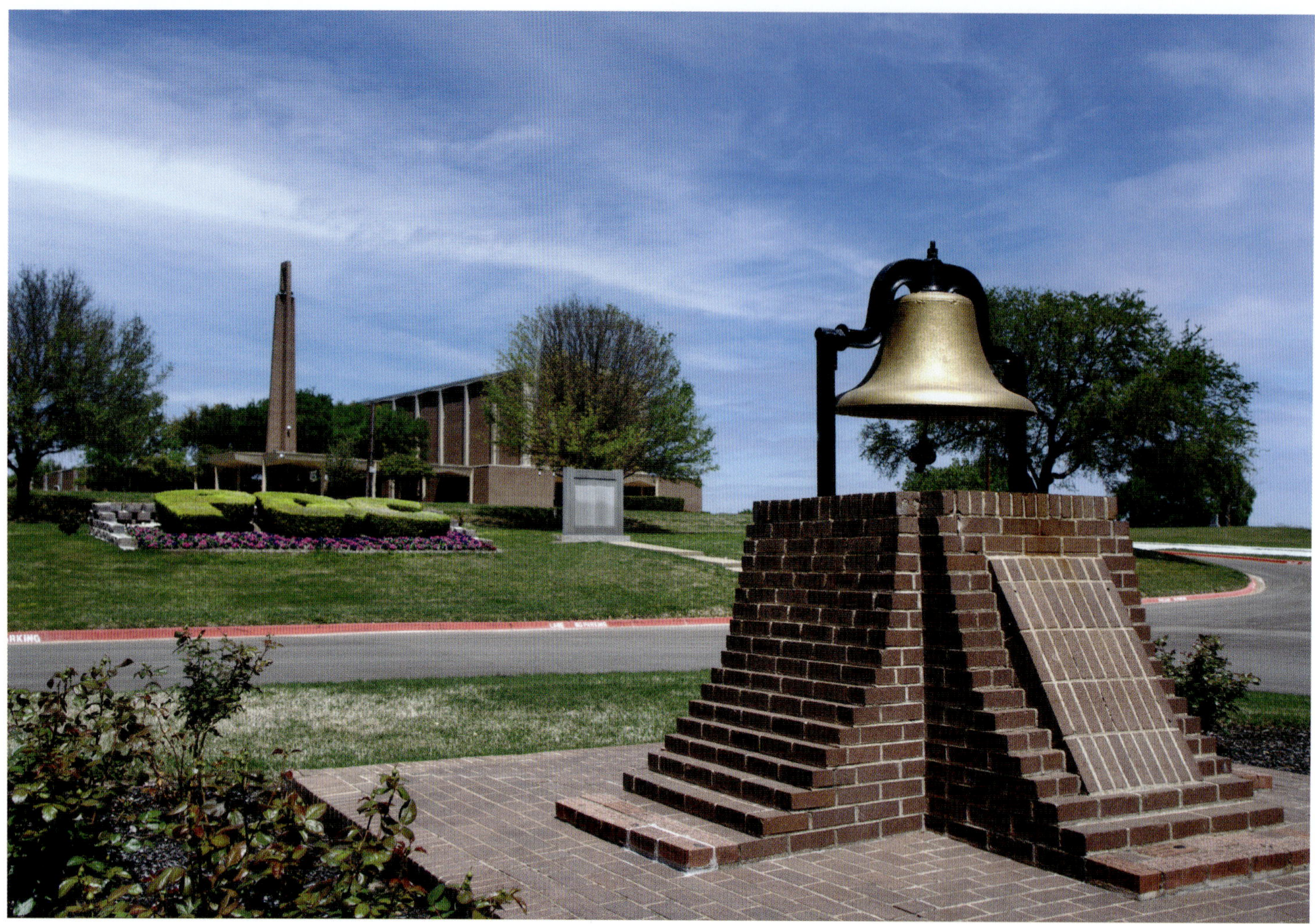

Above
On April 4, 1872, the Connectional High School and Institute was founded by a small group of African Methodist Episcopal preachers in Austin, Texas, to educate freed slaves and their progeny. When the college's name was changed to Paul Quinn College in 1881, it was located in Waco, Texas, on land that was the old Garrison Plantation. There, on the plantation, was a bell that had once been used to alert the enslaved when it was time to head to the fields to work and when they could end work for the day. It was also used to alert the enslaved when it was time to eat or when danger was approaching. That bell now sits on the campus and it's called the "Heritage Bell." It was relocated when Paul Quinn College moved to Dallas in 1990, and now rests at the foot of the PQC Avenue of Roses. The bell, once a symbol of the tyranny of enslavement and bondage, was transformed into a symbol of light and hope. Students touch the bell twice while in the "Quinnite Nation": once, when they join the nation, and again, during graduation week, as they finish their journey.

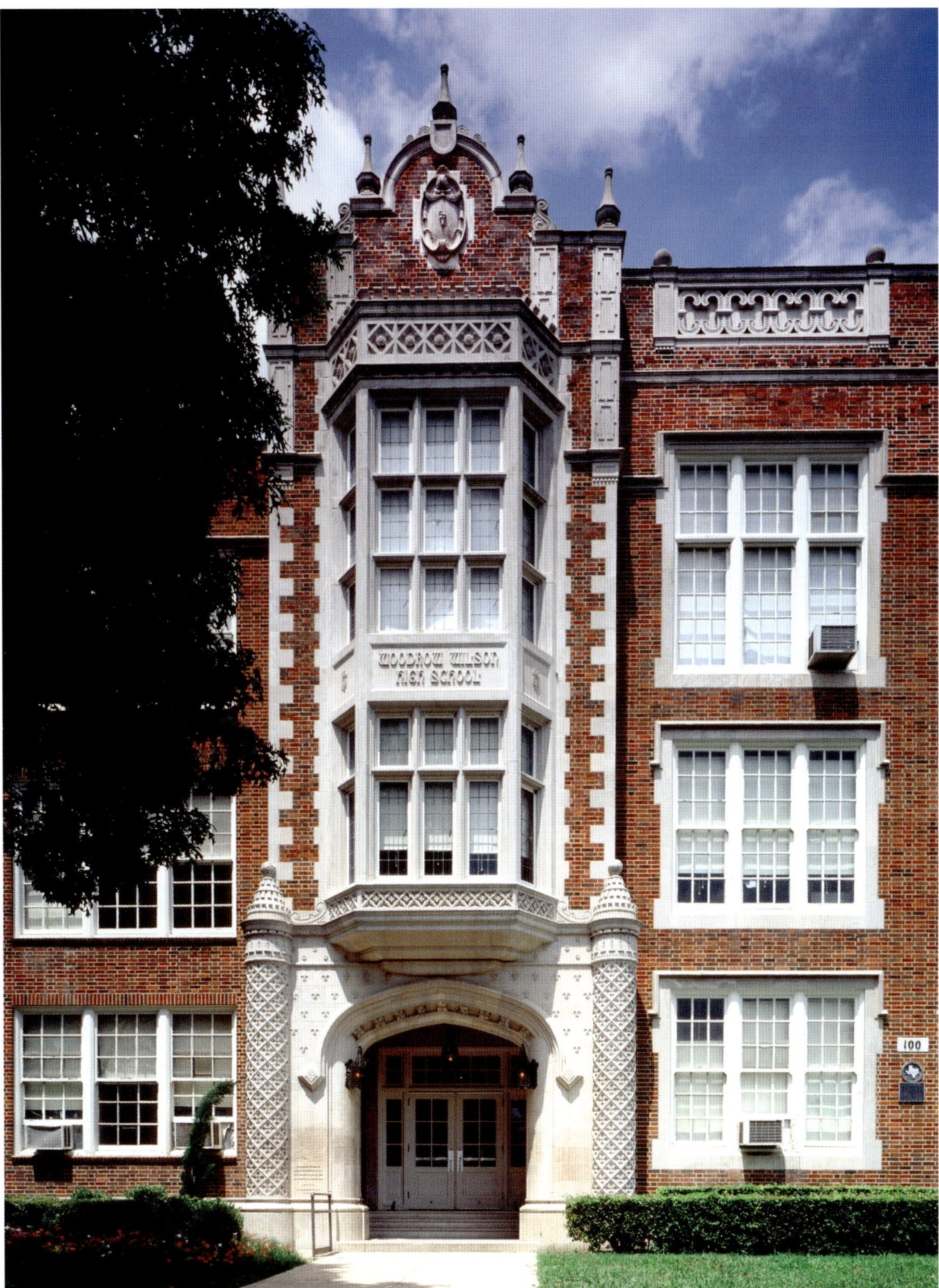

Right
Woodrow Wilson High School, designed in 1928 in a Jacobean style by Mark Lemmon and Roscoe Dewitt, remains the educational centerpiece of its East Dallas neighborhood.

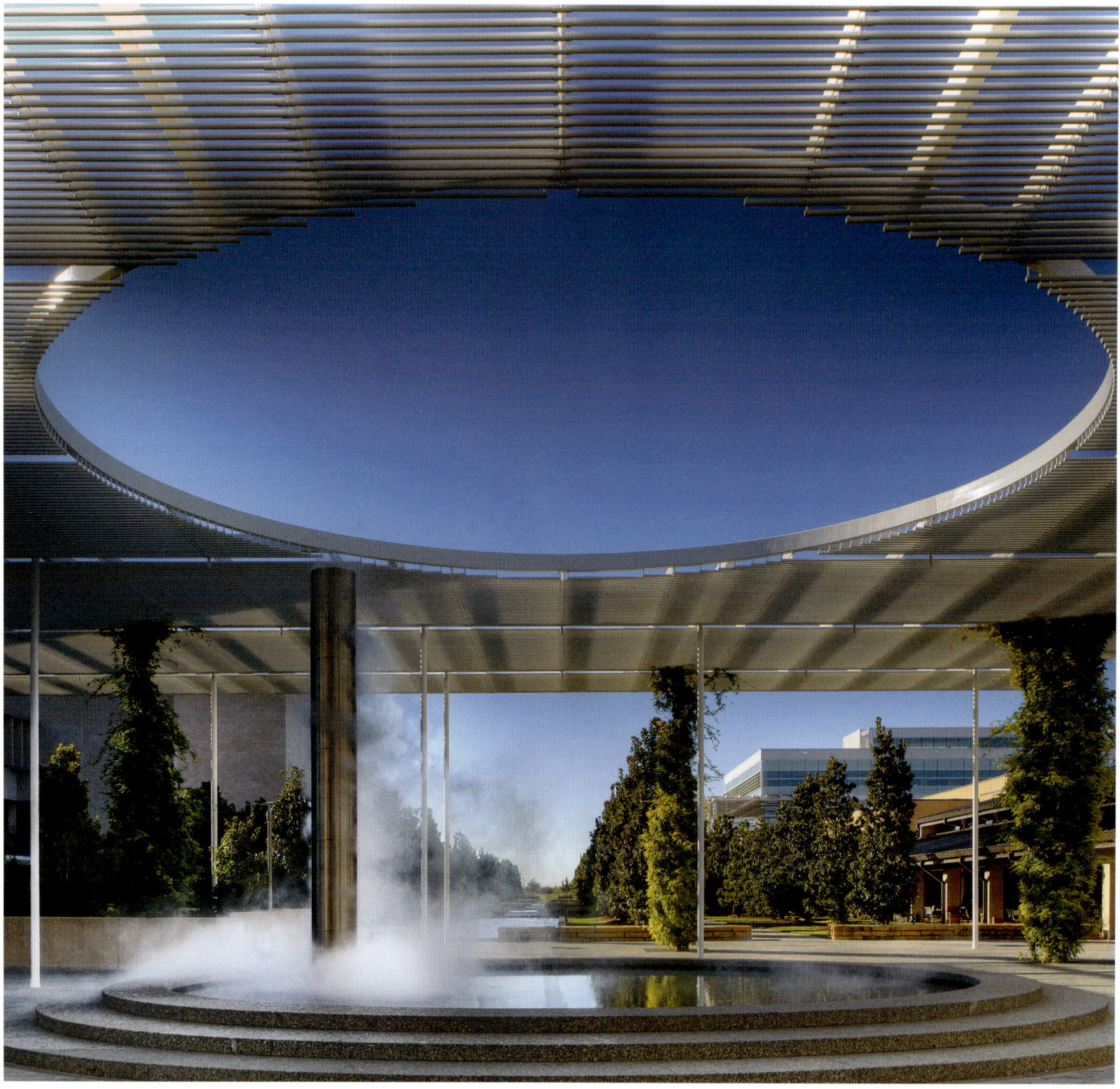

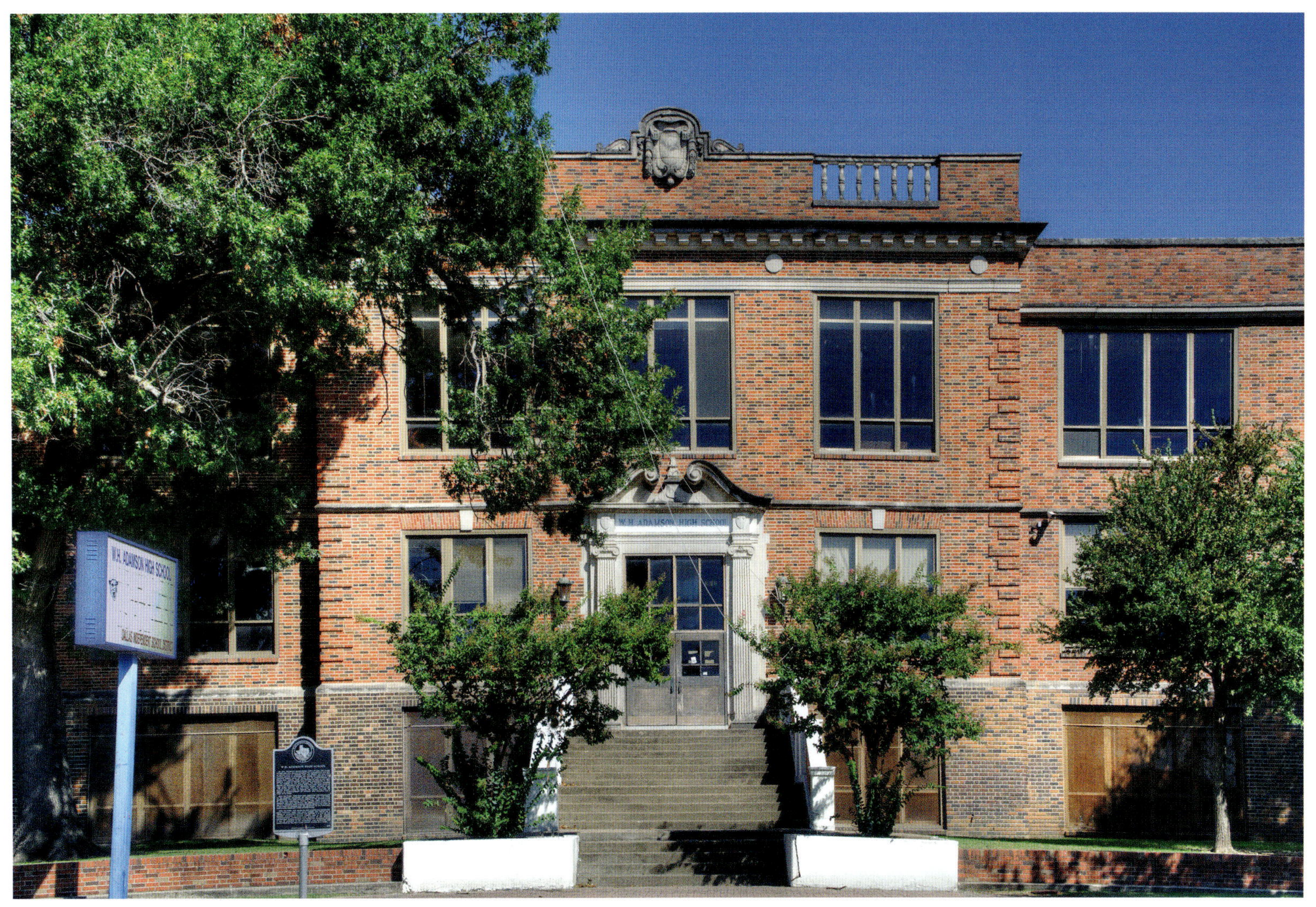

Above
Adamson High School is a public DISD school located in the Oak Cliff area of Dallas.

Opposite
Eugene McDermott, one of the legendary founders of Texas Instruments, also founded the University of Texas at Dallas. This trellis area of the campus mall is named in his honor.

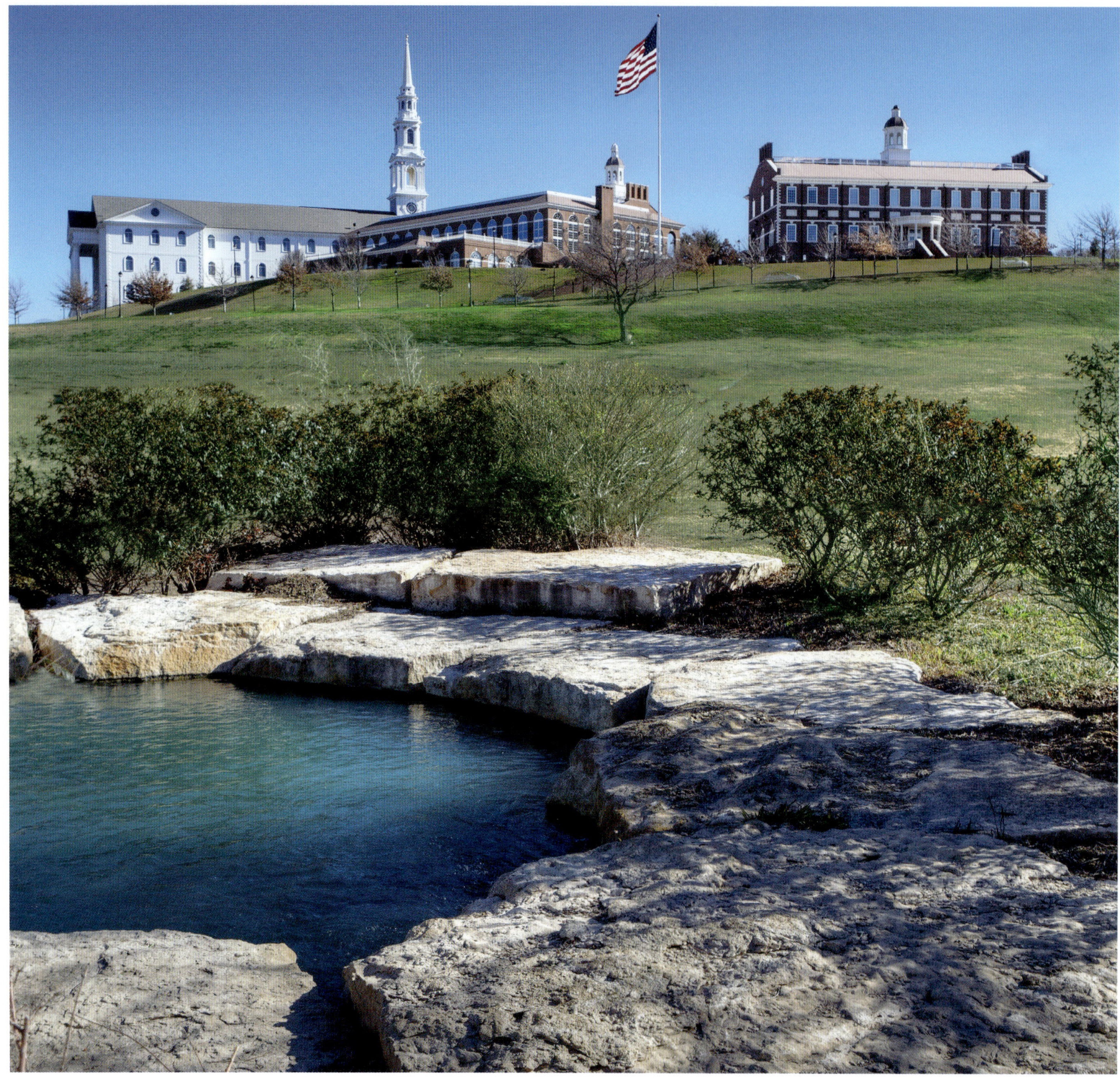

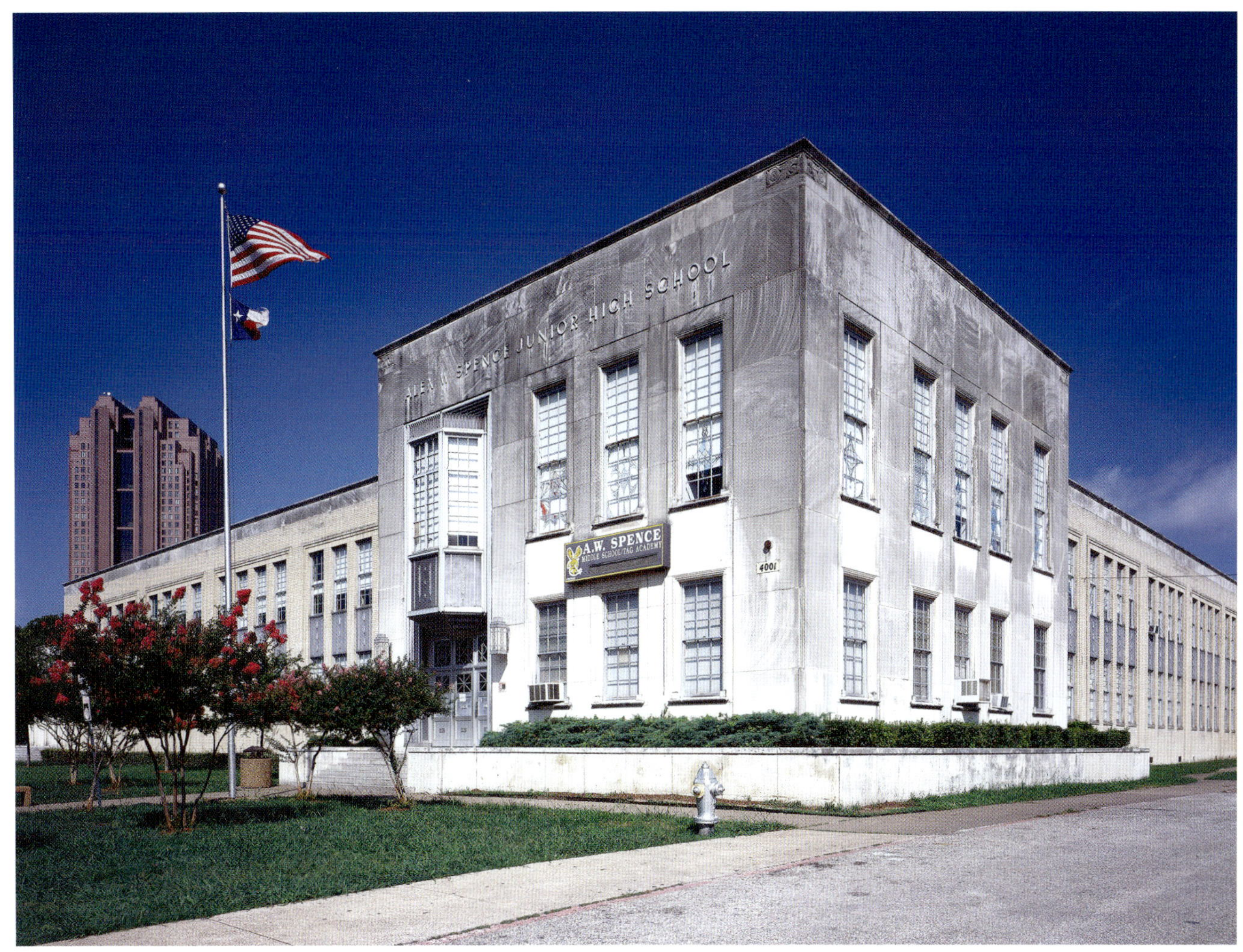

Above
Alex W. Spence Academy, a middle school for talented and gifted students, was named for a Dallas lawyer and soldier who served in WWI. Designed in 1939 in the Art Deco style by Mark Lemmon, the building was designated a Dallas Landmark in 1996.

Opposite
Dallas Baptist University occupies 293 acres of rolling hills that overlook Mountain Creek Lake in southwestern Dallas.

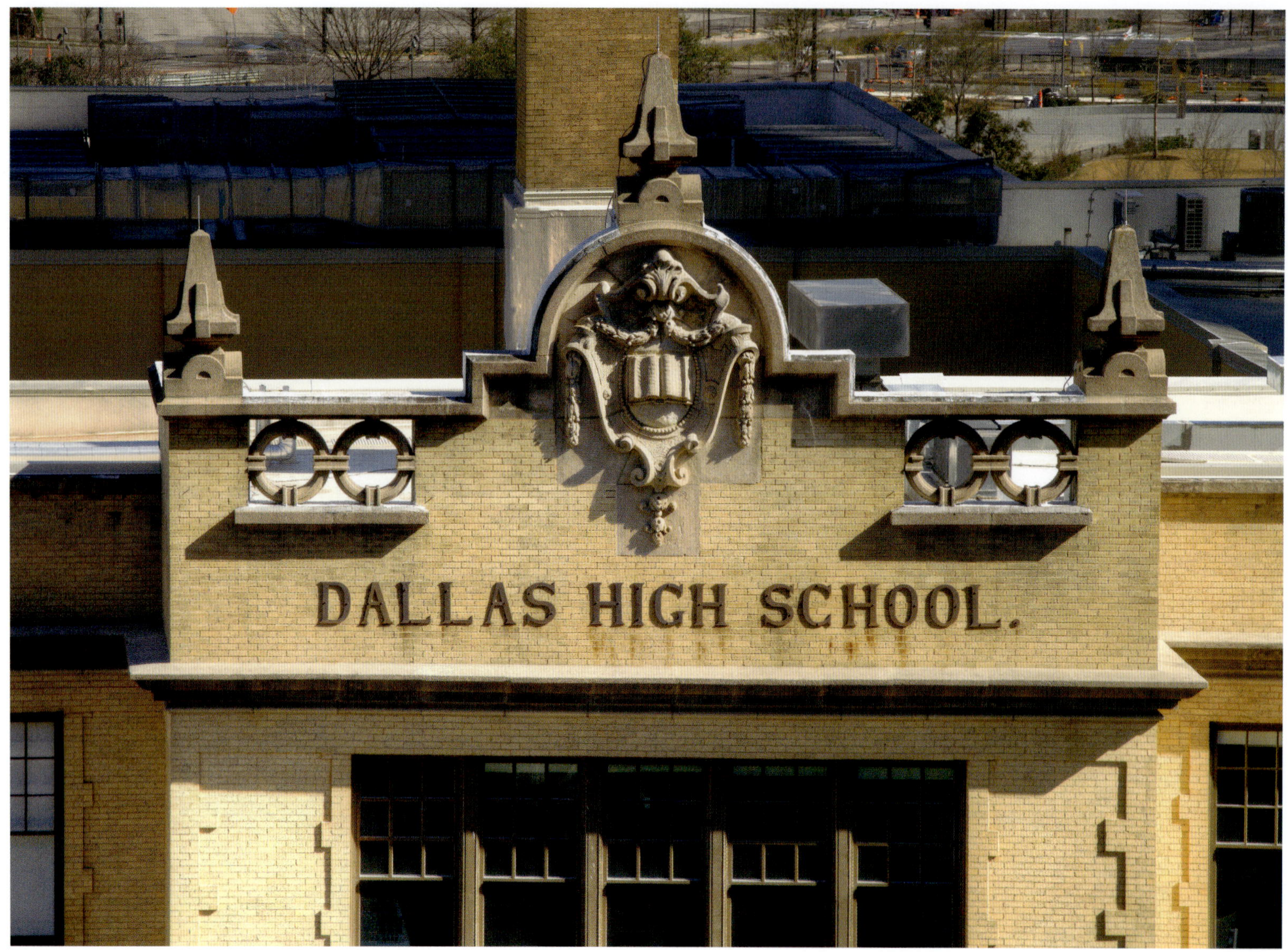

Above
Detail relief on façade of Dallas High School, the oldest high school building in Dallas

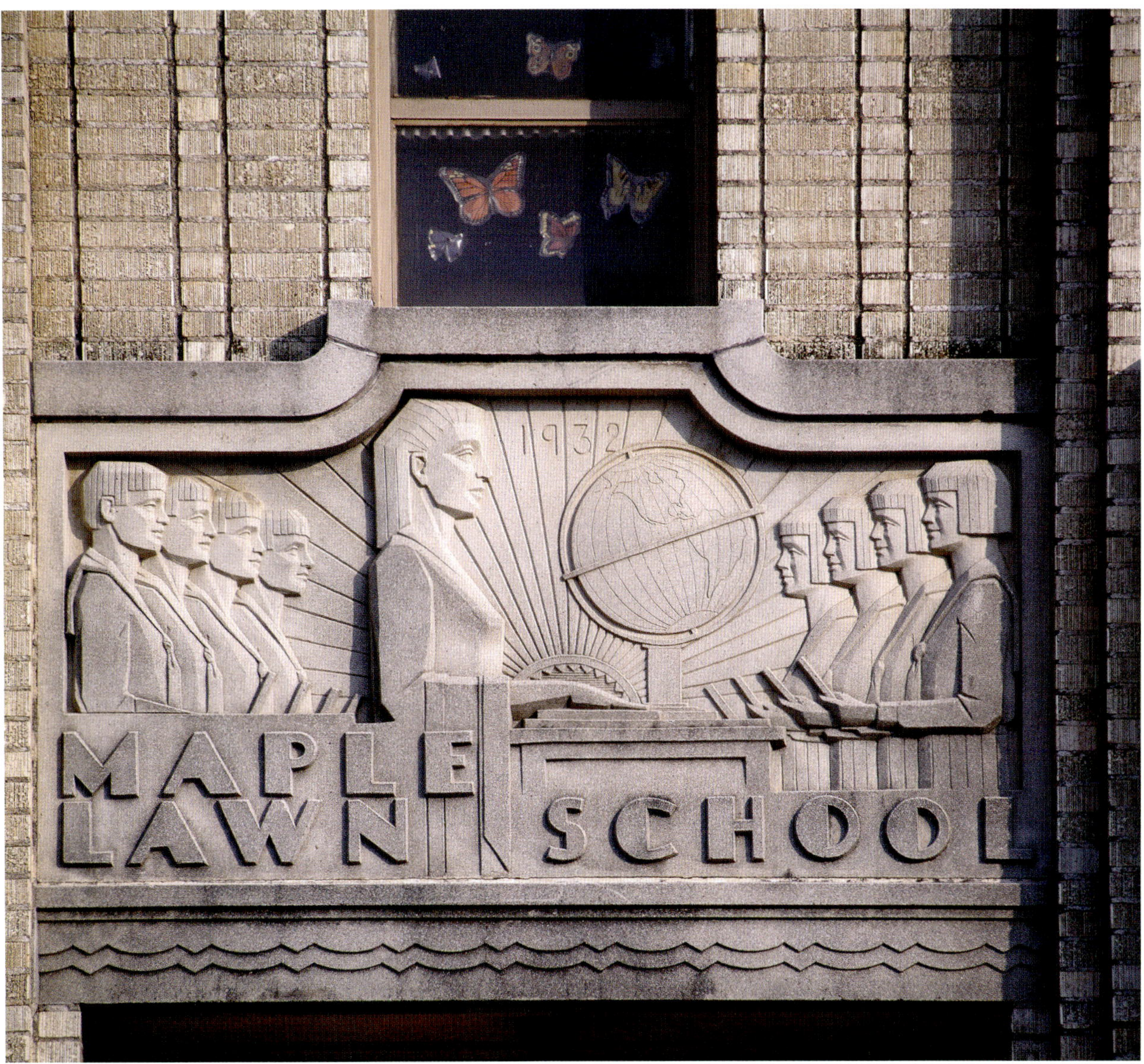

Above
Maple Lawn Elementary School is one of the oldest school structures in Dallas. It has welcomed students since 1932.

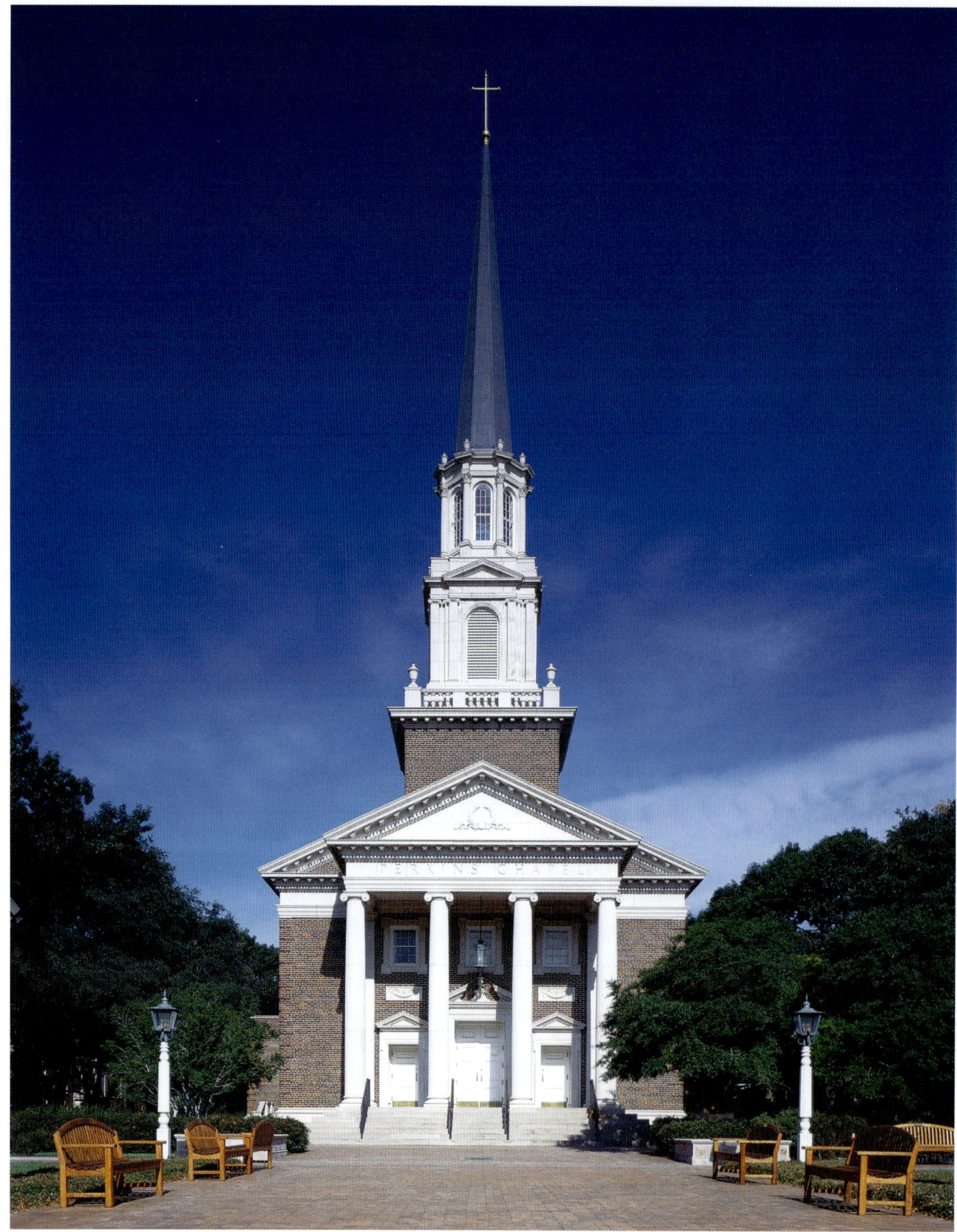
PERKINS CHAPEL

Believe

William B. Lawrence is professor emeritus of American Church History at Southern Methodist University's Perkins School of Theology, where he served as dean for fourteen years. He is an ordained minister in the United Methodist Church, a clergy member of the North Texas Annual Conference, the former president of the denomination's global Judicial Council, and currently a research fellow at the Center for Studies in the Wesleyan Tradition at the Divinity School of Duke University.

Opposite
Perkins Chapel is the primary worship space for the Perkins School of Theology at Southern Methodist University. Dedicated in 1951, the chapel is one of seven buildings donated by Joe and Lois Perkins of Wichita Falls, Texas. It was designed by Mark Lemmon.

Expressing Dimensions of Spirituality

Dallas developed as diverse people came to the city with ambitions and aspirations. They also brought their religious convictions. And they expressed all of it in architecture and art.

Many religious traditions are observed by believers at their homes. Jews share Passover meals, Muslims break the Ramadan fast, and Hindus have shrines in homes where they live.

Jews, Hindus, Muslims, Buddhists, Christians, and others also practice their spirituality in places of prayer they create for their constituents and for the communities that they serve. They build structures that respect the texts they treasure and honor the history through which they have traveled. Some of their buildings dominate city blocks. Others are intimate and elegantly simple.

The cathedrals of Catholic and Episcopal Christians, sanctuaries of Baptist and Lutheran congregations, and stone structures of Methodist and Presbyterian communities can be grand and magnificent. So can mosques, temples, synagogues, and shrines. But serene spaces for prayer and study are cherished, too. Theological schools ponder the immensity of faith and value soulful meditation, with space for both. St. Teresa of Ávila suggested that an infinite God is infinitely bigger than the cosmos and yet infinitely small enough to hide in the human heart.

Some sacred structures soar skyward, pointing to the heavens. Some are enclaves giving sanctuary from the troubles of the world. Some have windows telling sacred stories. Others have clear views of the community they are called to serve. Some were funded by those who guided or governed the city. Some were founded by those who could not worship as they wished until they were liberated from enslavement.

In a city of boundless hope, sacred structures testify to all the diversities of spirituality.

William B. Lawrence

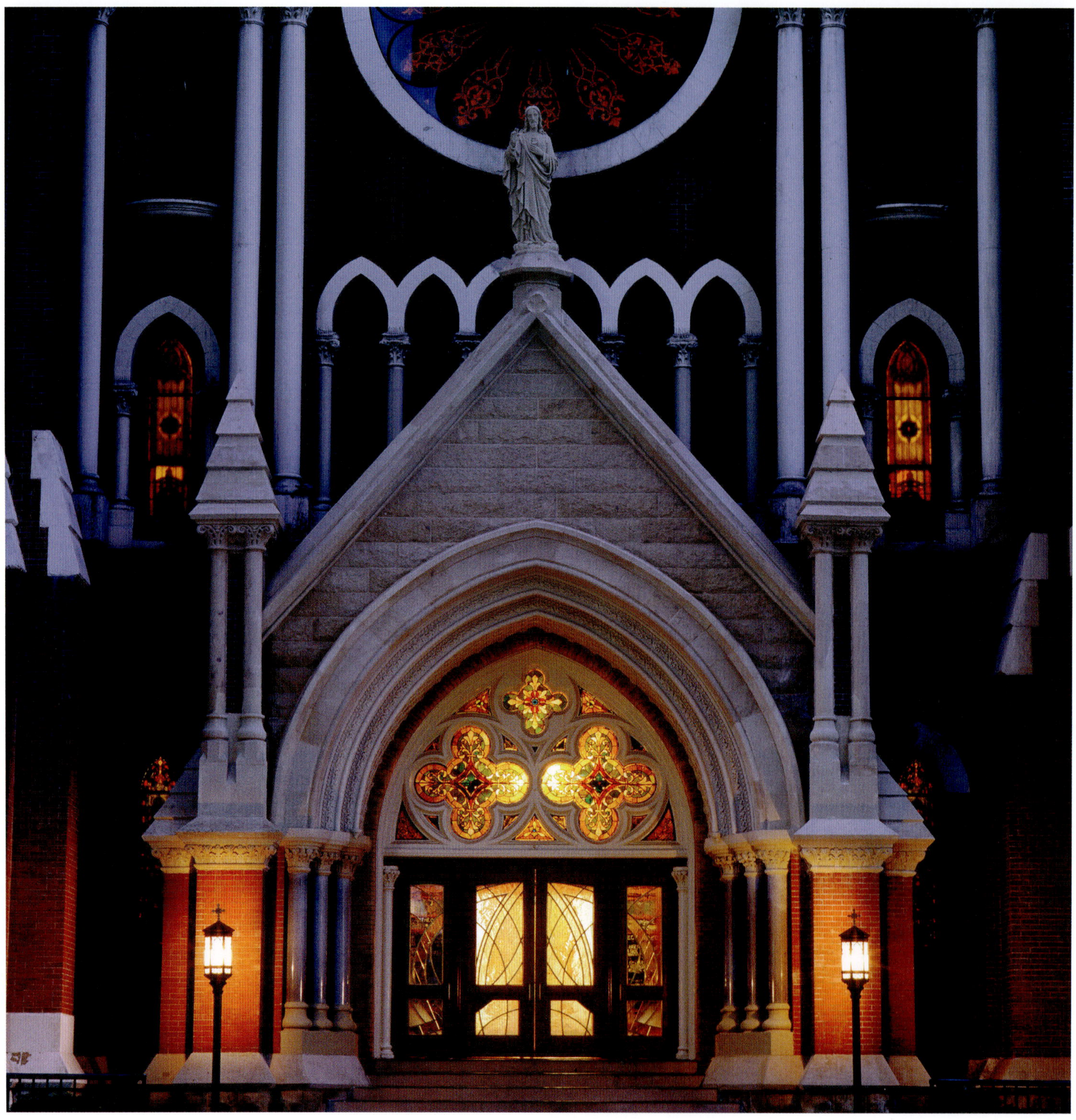

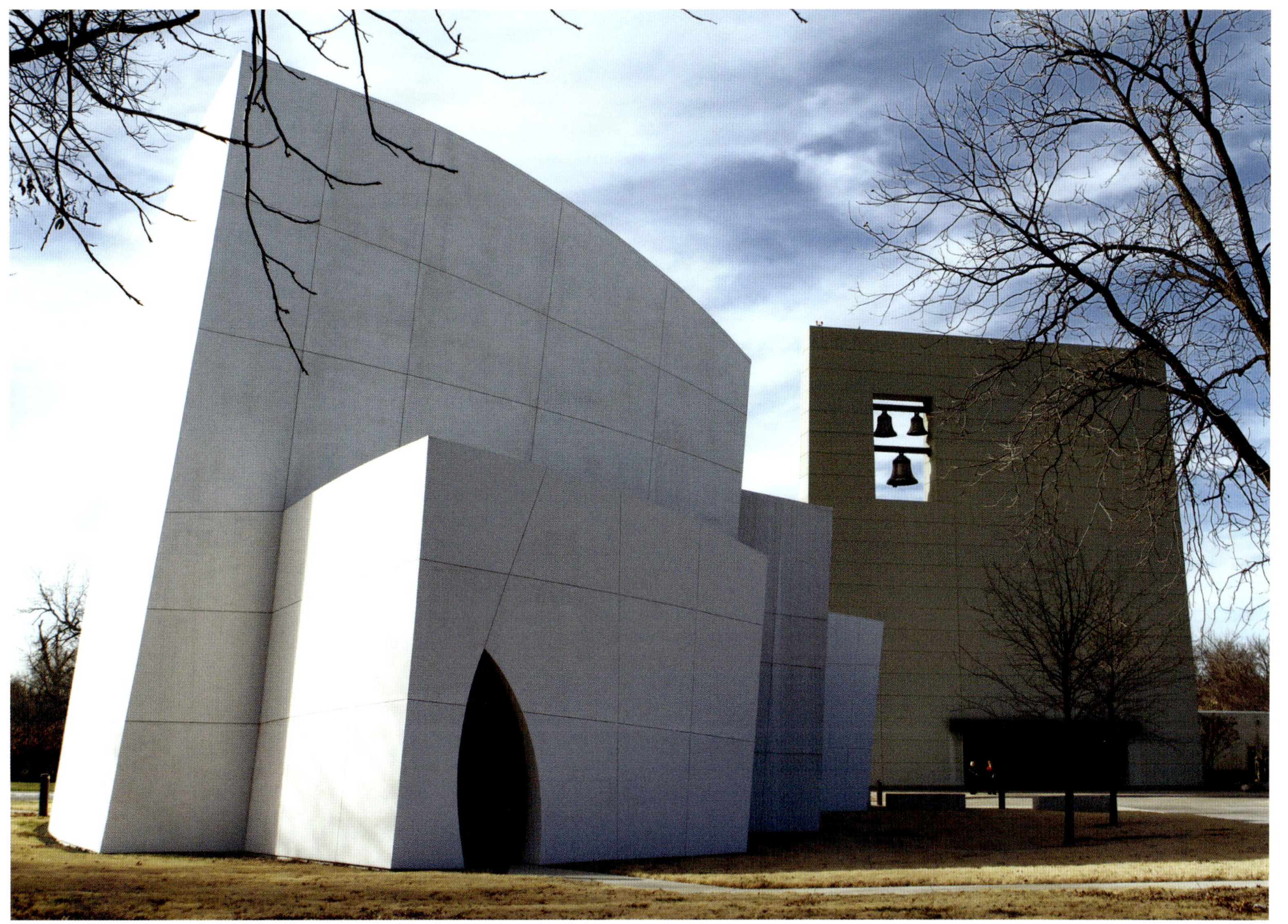

Above
The Cathedral of Hope, known as the "world's largest gay church," was designed by architect Philip Johnson in 1995 and accepted into the United Church of Christ in 2006.

Opposite
The Cathedral Santuario de Guadalupe, designed by Texas architect Nicholas Clayton in the Gothic Revival style, opened in 1902.

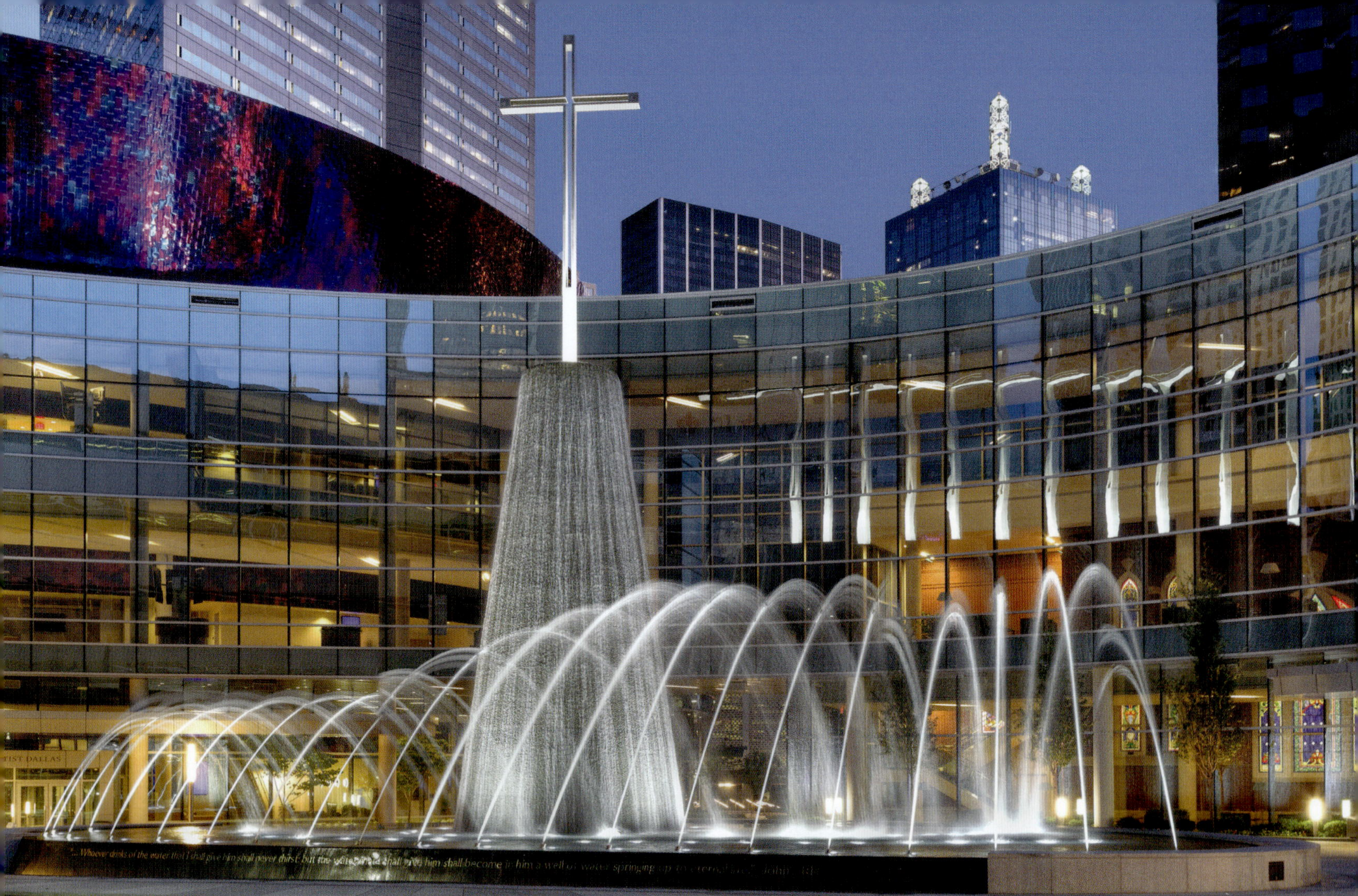

Above
A fountain on the six-square-block downtown campus of the First Baptist Church of Dallas. Music accompanies the water as it flows from the base of a sixty-eight-foot-high cross to the edge of the pool and over a biblical verse, "Whoever drinks of the water that I give shall never thirst," which is etched in steel.

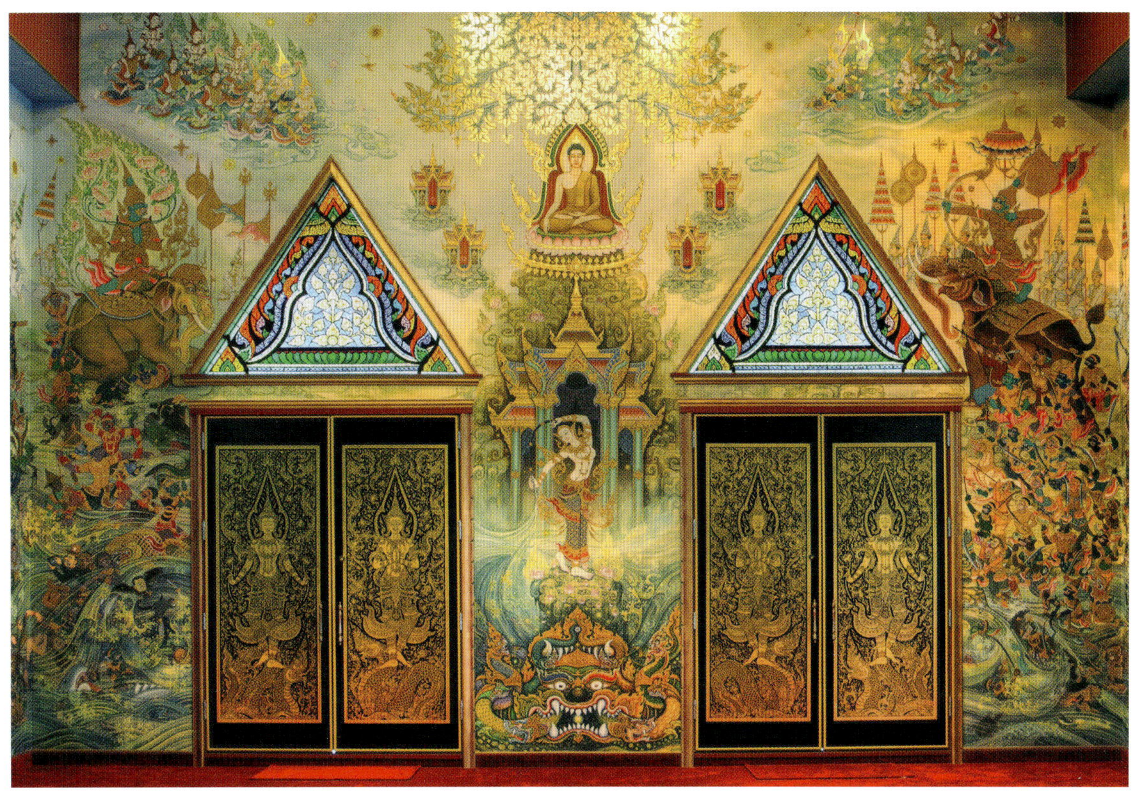

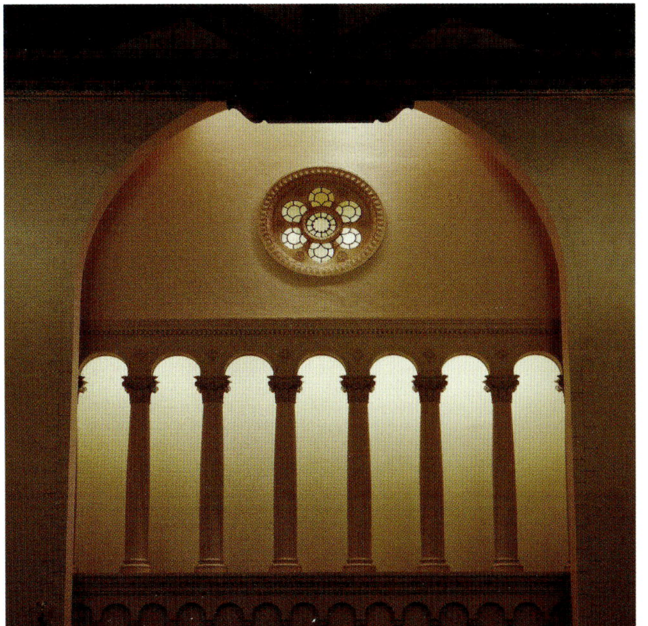

Above
The Buddhist Center of Dallas, organized in 1982, follows the Thai tradition and offers a space for chanting, meditation, and discussion.

Left
Detail of the Third Church of Christ, Scientist, designed by Mark Lemmon in the Romanesque style and constructed in 1931 on Oak Lawn Avenue, south of Highland Park.

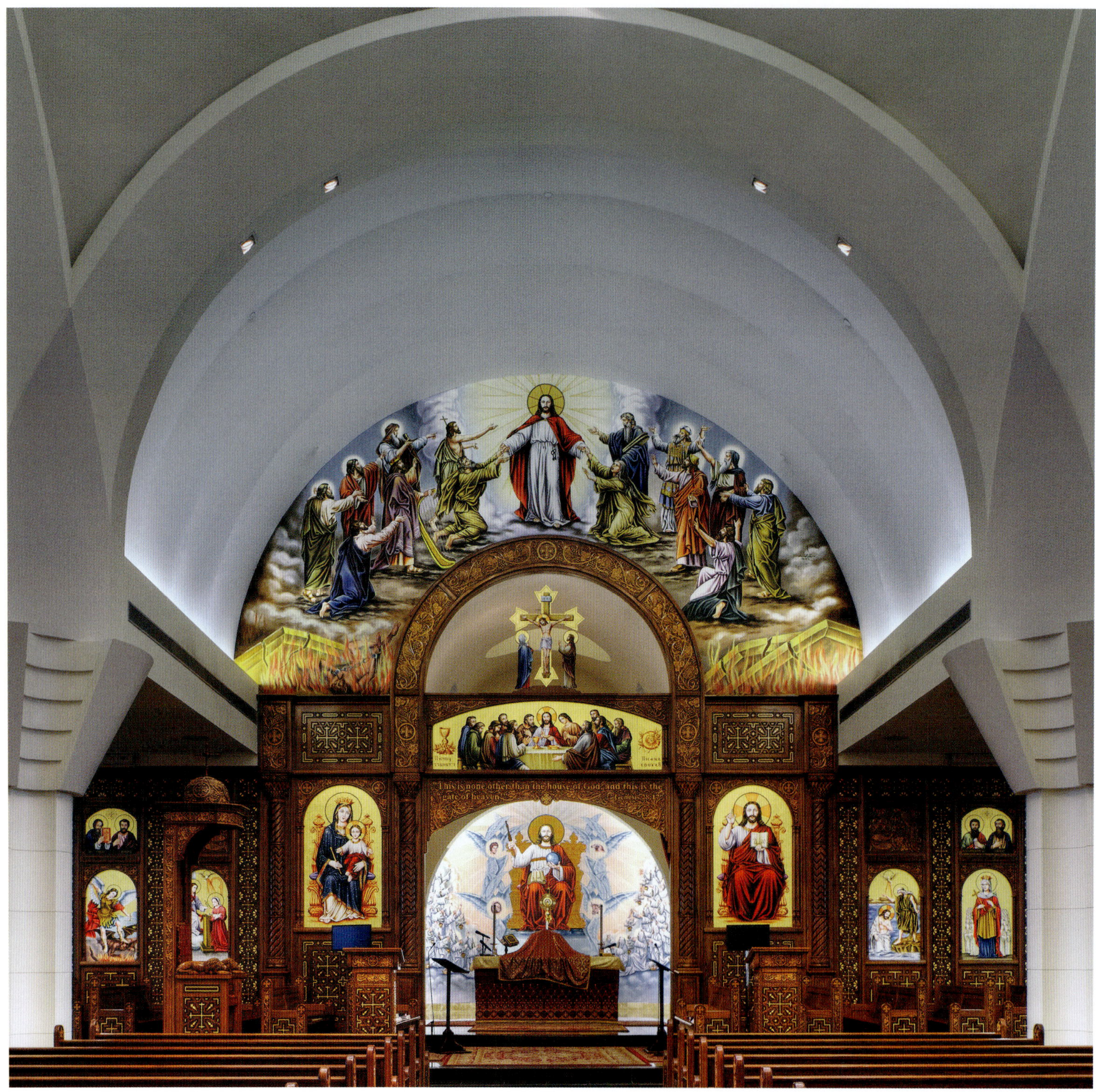
"This is none other than the house of God, and this is the
gate of heaven" Genesis 28:17

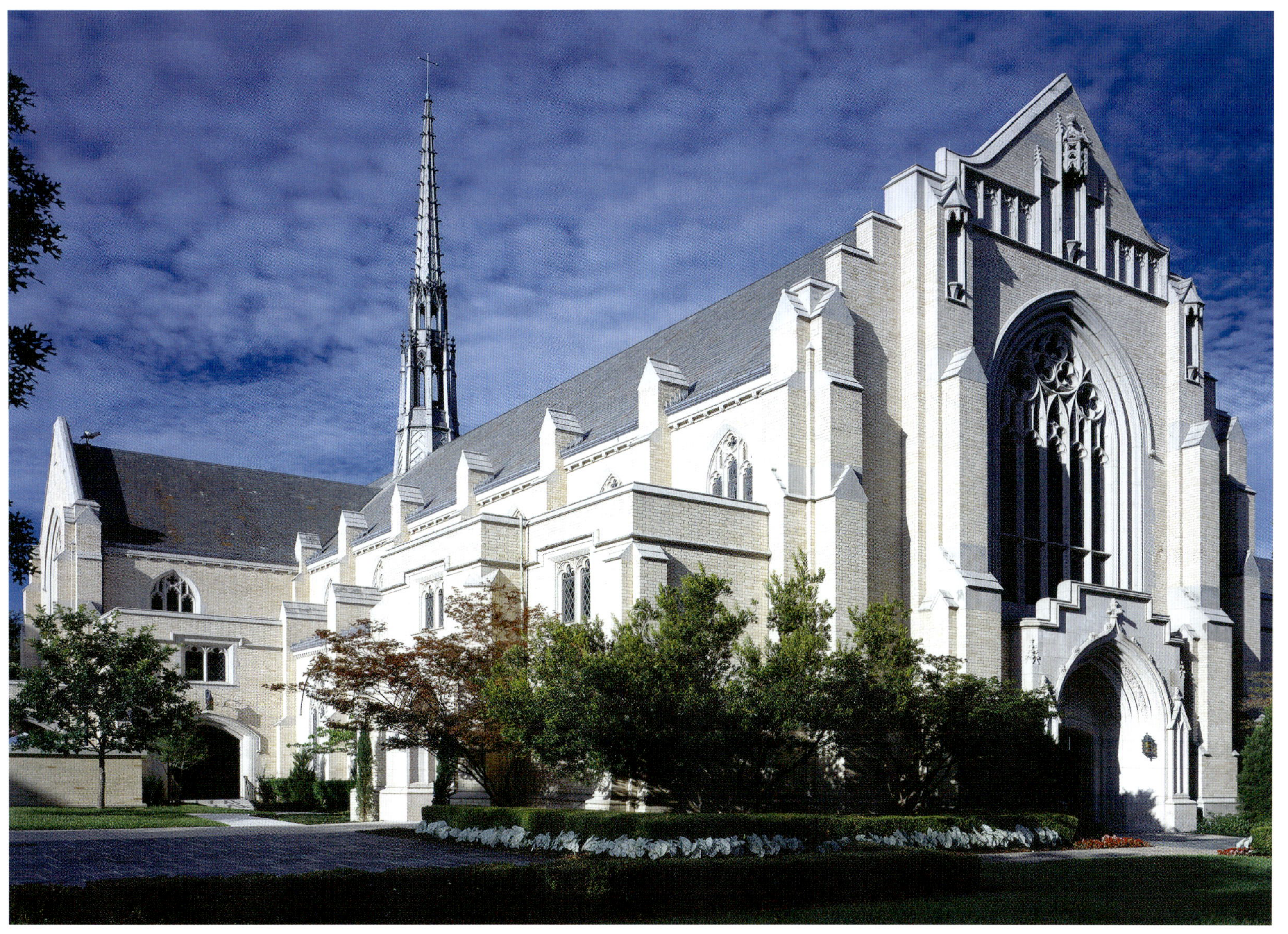

Above
The Highland Park Presbyterian Church was designed in the Gothic Revival style by Mark Lemmon in 1929. The church once had the largest Presbyterian congregation in the United States.

Opposite
St. Philopateer Coptic Orthodox Church was consecrated in 2010 in Richardson, an inner suburb of Dallas.

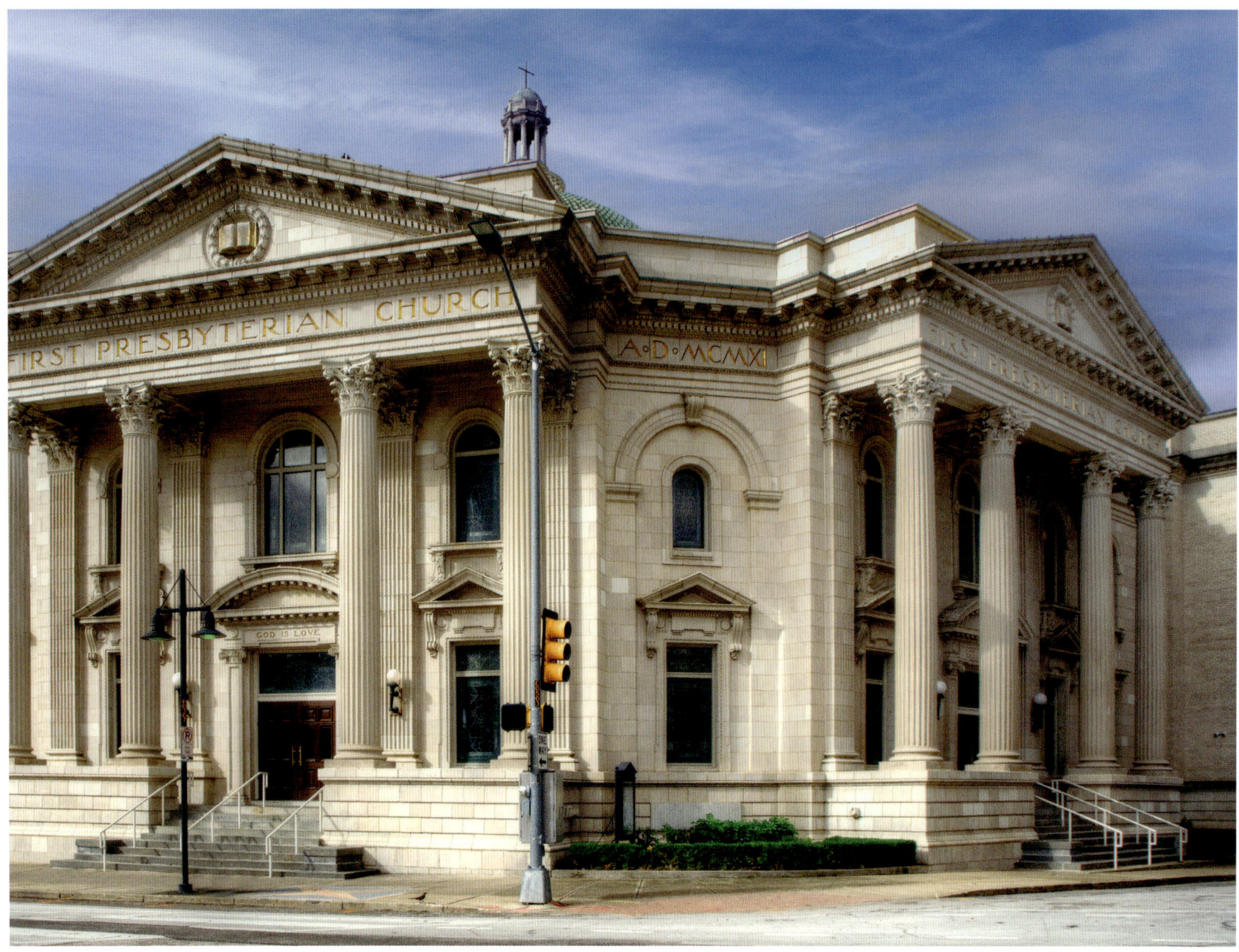

Above
First Presbyterian Church is a Dallas Landmark building in the Farmers Market District of downtown. It is a neoclassical masterpiece designed in 1912 by the Dallas architect C. D. Hill.

Opposite
Interior of the dome of the Holy Trinity Greek Orthodox Church. Founded in 1915 in South Dallas, the parish relocated in 1992 to a new Byzantine Church and Community Center at Hillcrest Road and Alpha Road in North Dallas.

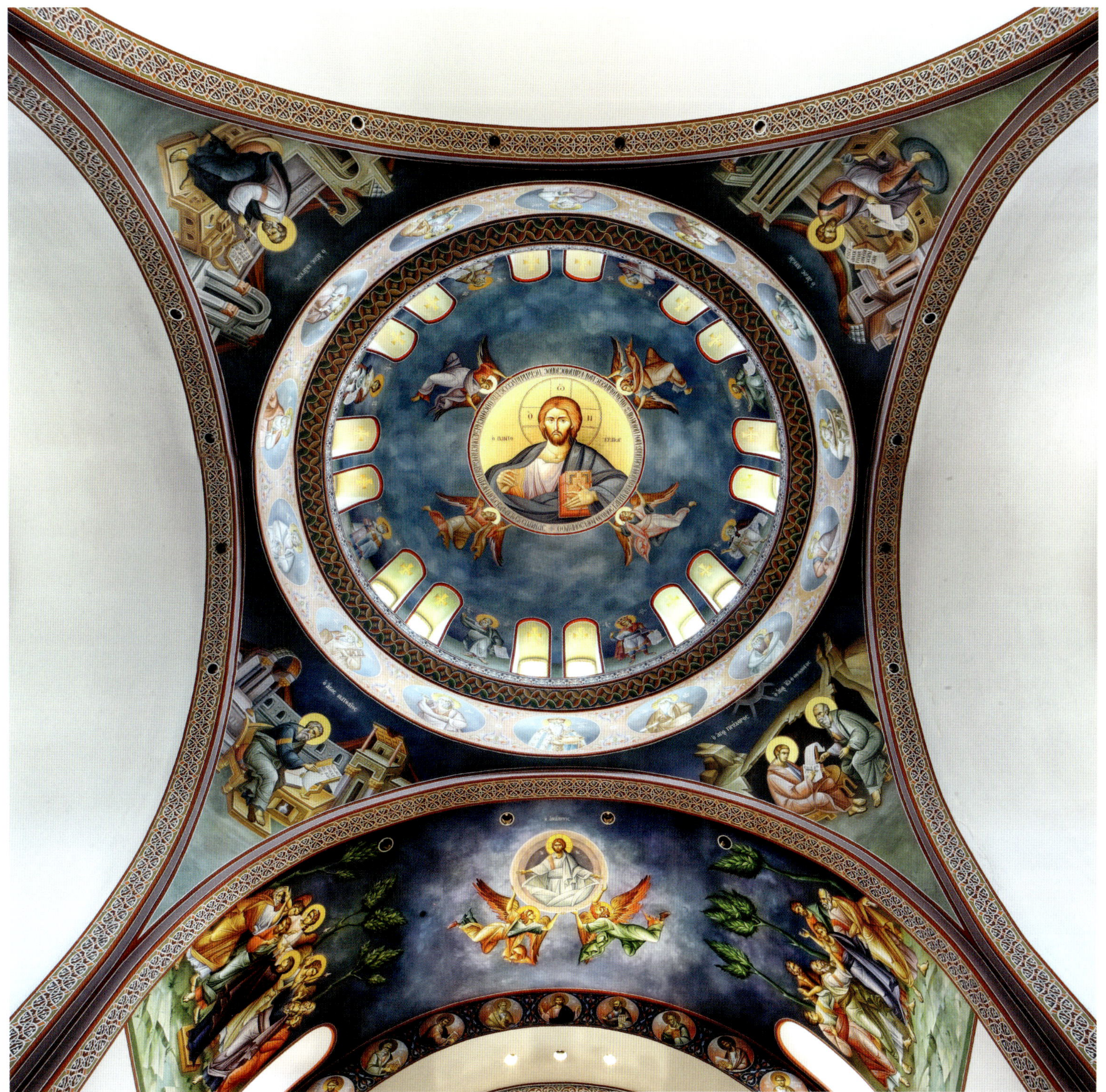

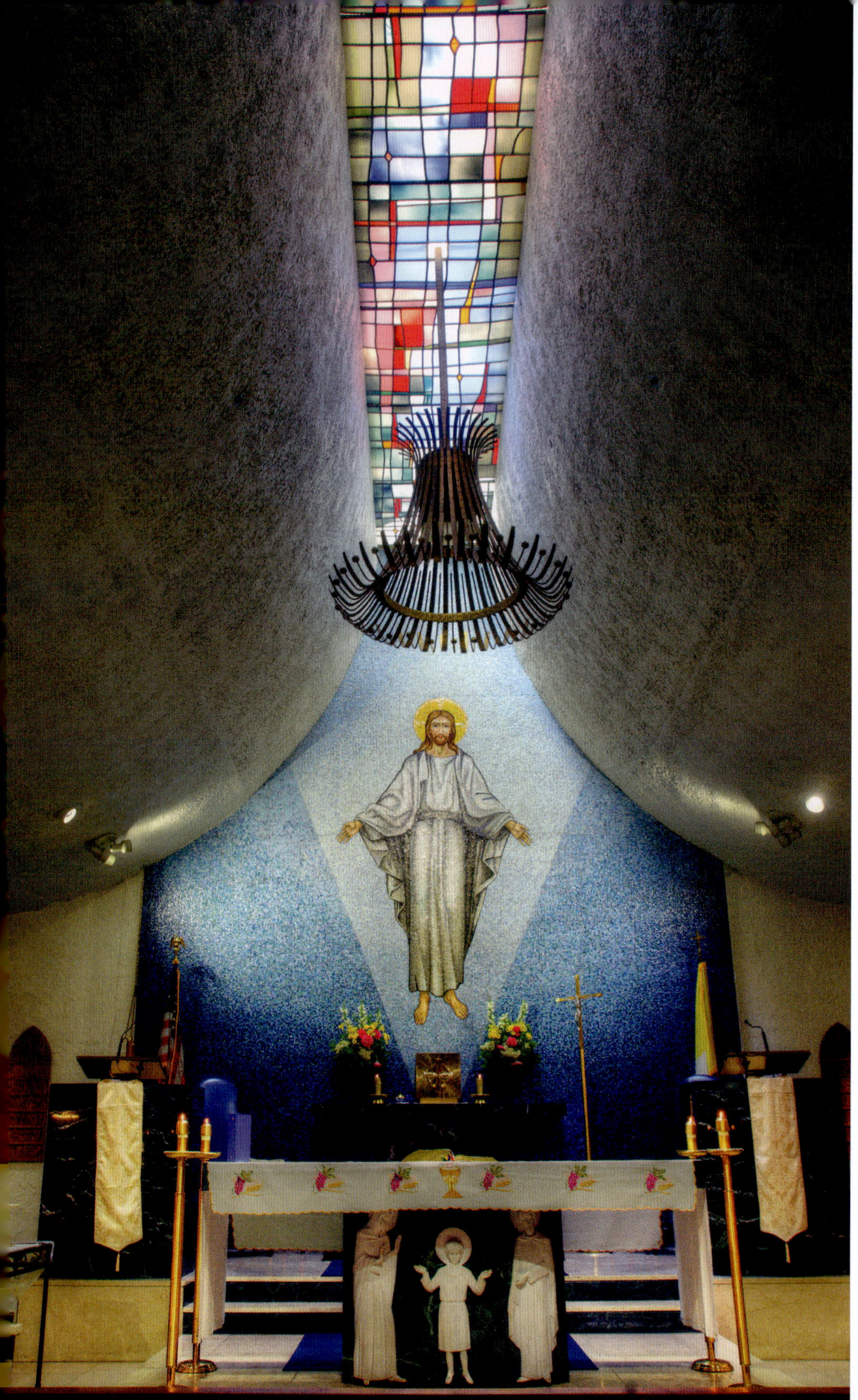

Left
St. Jude Chapel is a downtown Catholic parish that offers daily mass and confession. Established in 1968, the chapel can seat 350 people.

Opposite
The Dallas Central Mosque in Richardson provides the region's rapidly growing Islamic population a place for prayer and education.

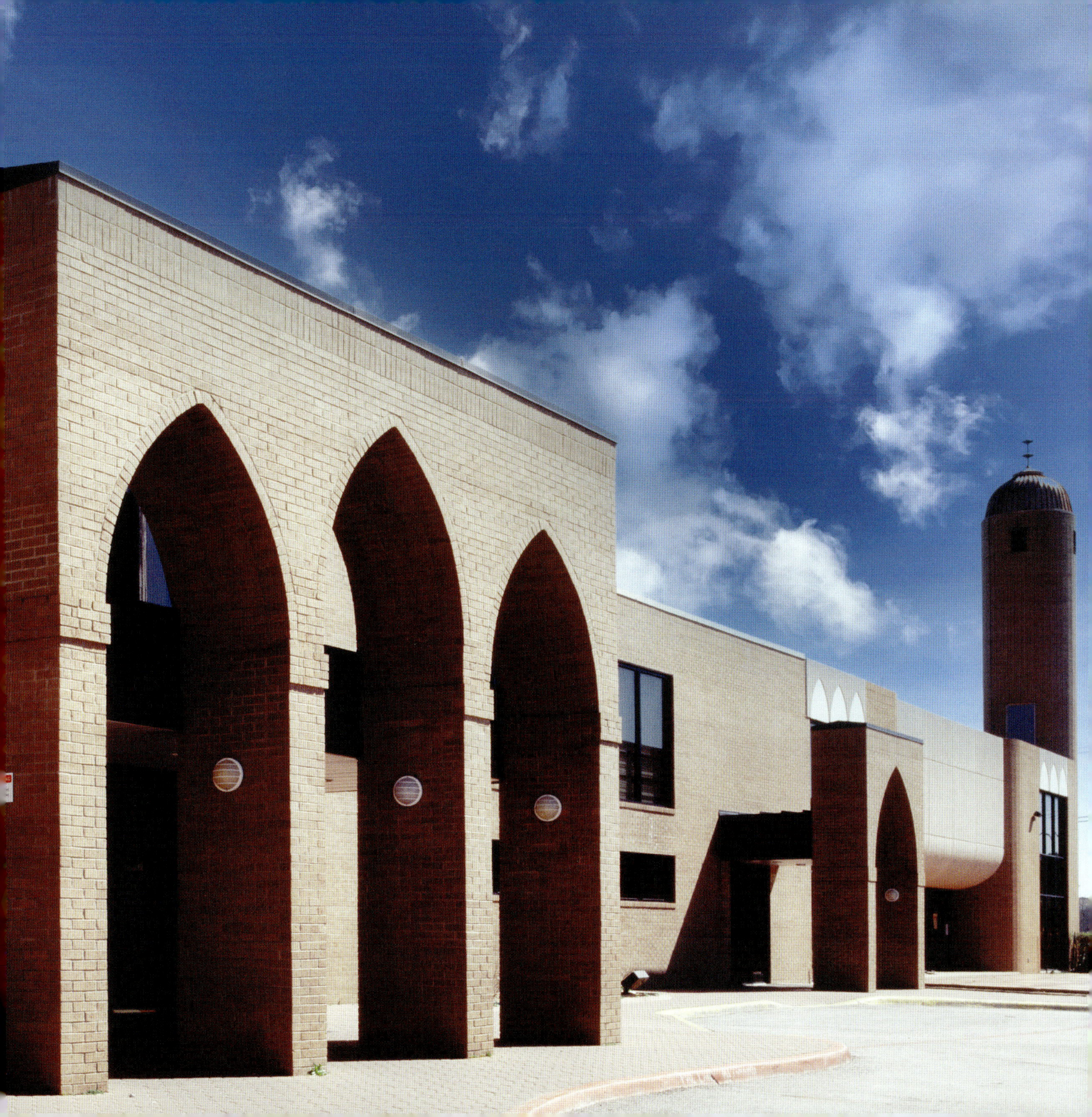

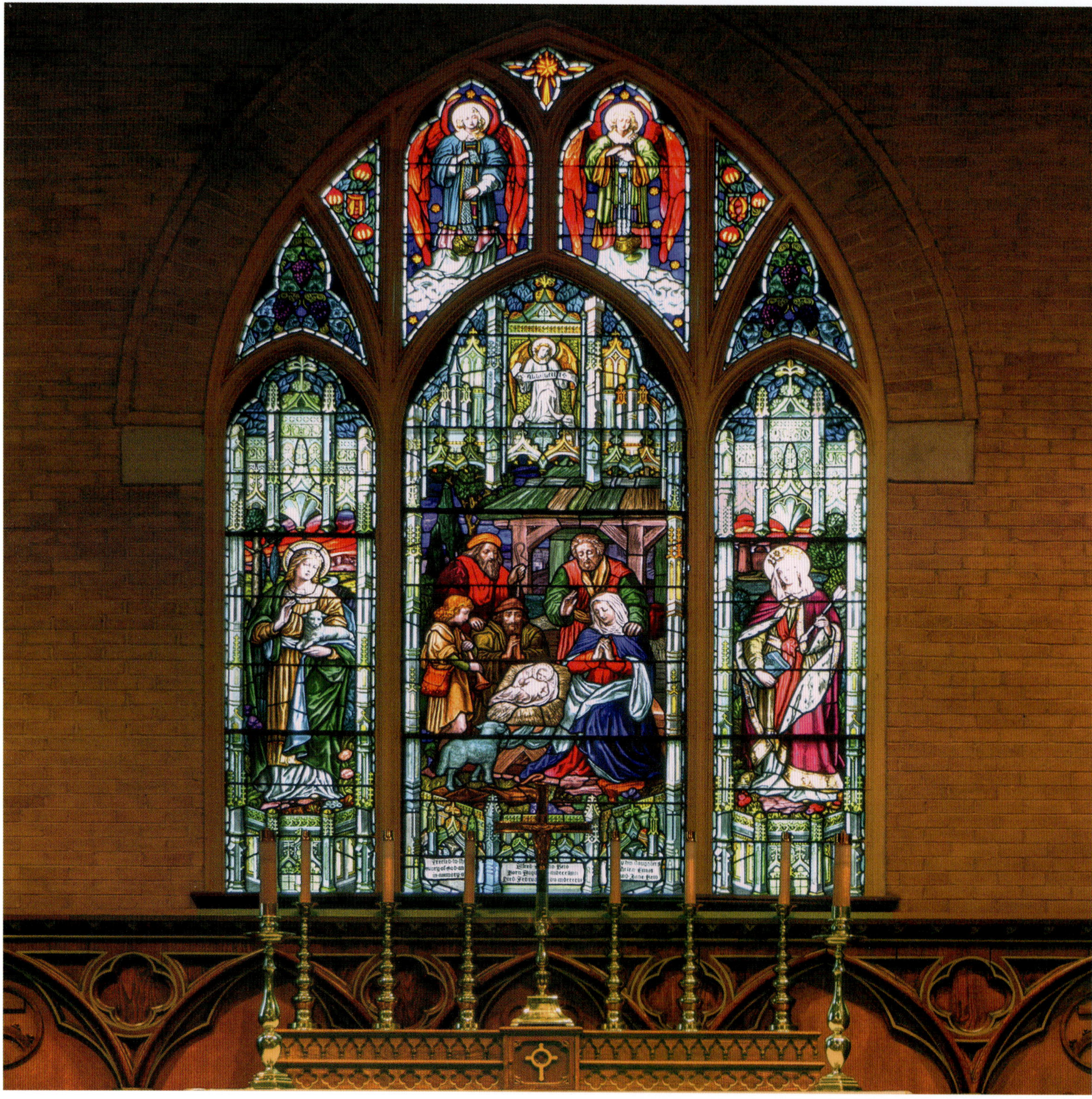

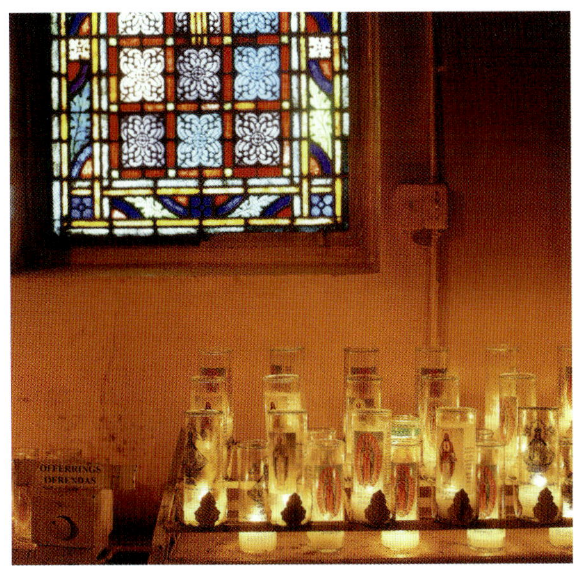

Above
In a side chapel of the Cathedral Santuario de Guadalupe, prayer candles glow beneath 100-year-old stained glass.

Opposite
The stained-glass windows in St. Matthew's Episcopal Cathedral on Ross Avenue date from the late 1800s and were a gift from St. Mary's Episcopal College for Women.

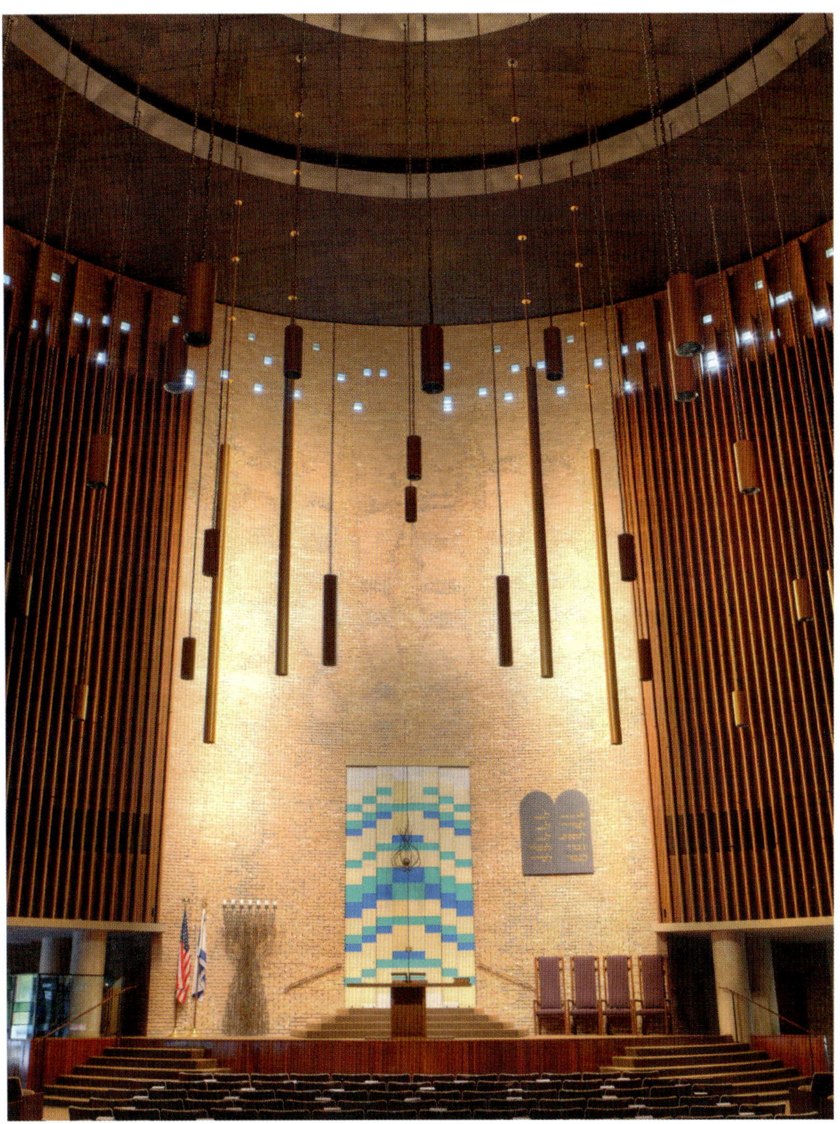

Above
Temple Emanu-El was founded in 1873 and moved to its present location at Hillcrest Road and Northwest Highway in 1957. The temple's sanctuary, designed by Dallas architect Howard Meyer, is ornamented with György Kepes's mosaic bricks and Anni Albers's altar tapestry.

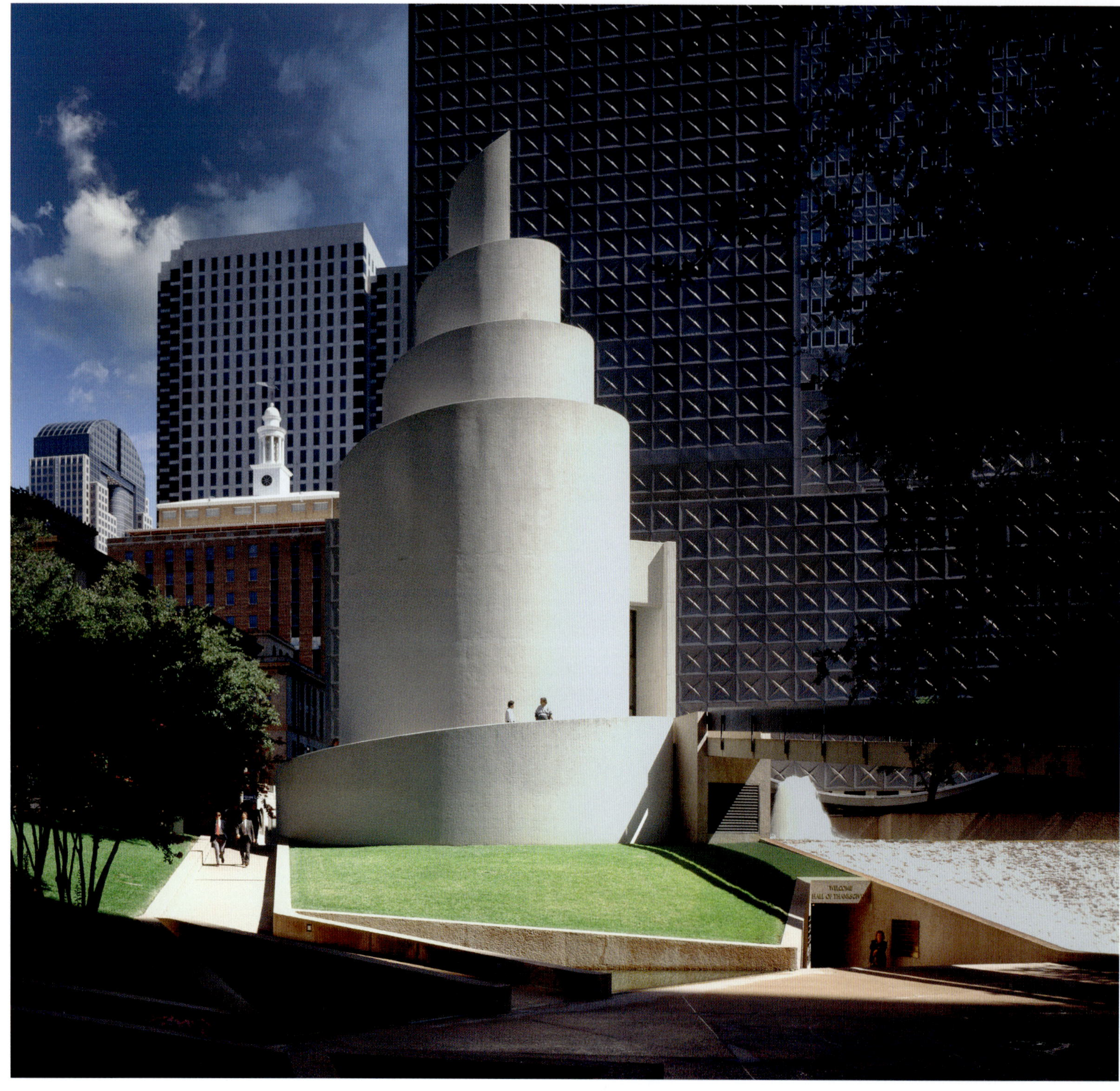
WELCOME

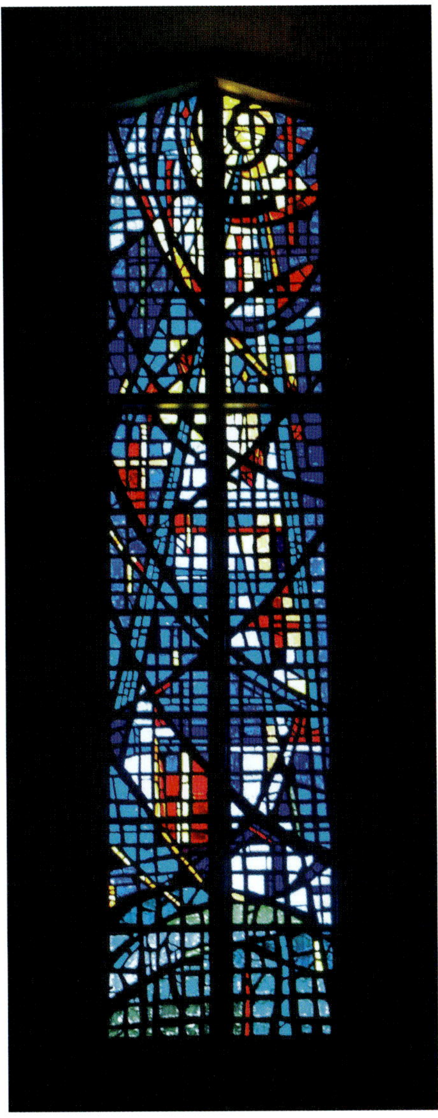

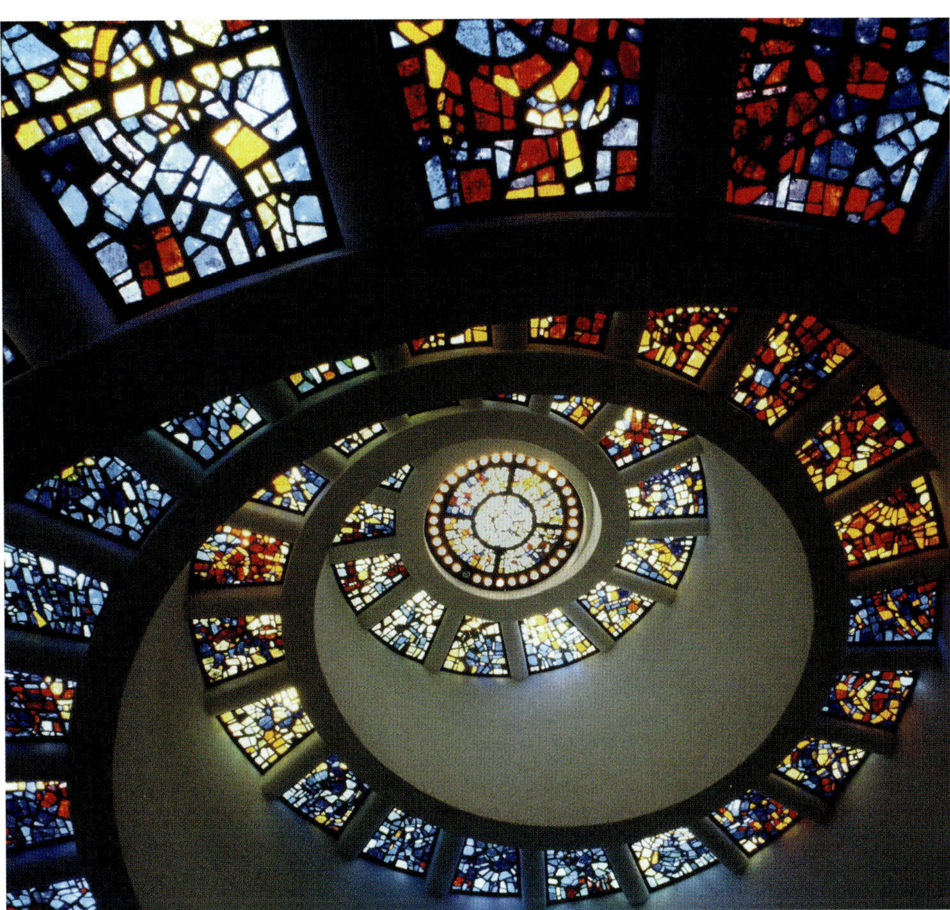

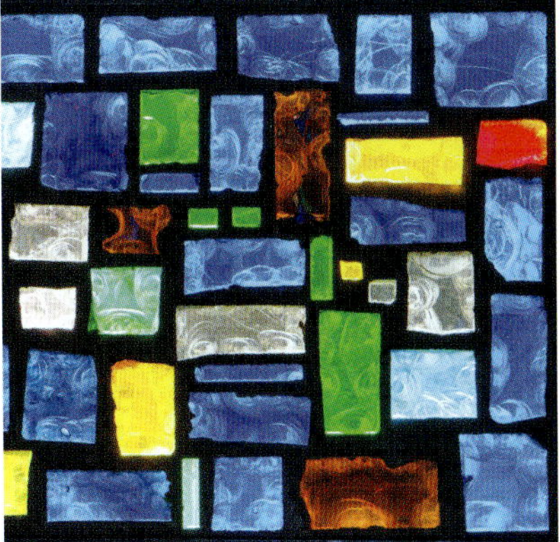

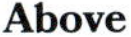

Above
Stained glass window at the Richard Allen Chapel at Paul Quinn College.

Right
The light filters through a colorful stained glass window at Saint Monica Catholic Church and School on Midway Road.

Above
The Glory Window in the sixty-foot-high ceiling of the chapel at Thanks-Giving Square was designed by French artist Gabriel Loire. It is one of the largest horizontally mounted stained glass windows in the world.

Opposite
Thanks-Giving Square in downtown Dallas was dedicated in 1976 and consists of a garden, a nondenominational chapel, and the Burlington Truck Terminal. It was the first public-private facility of its kind in Dallas.

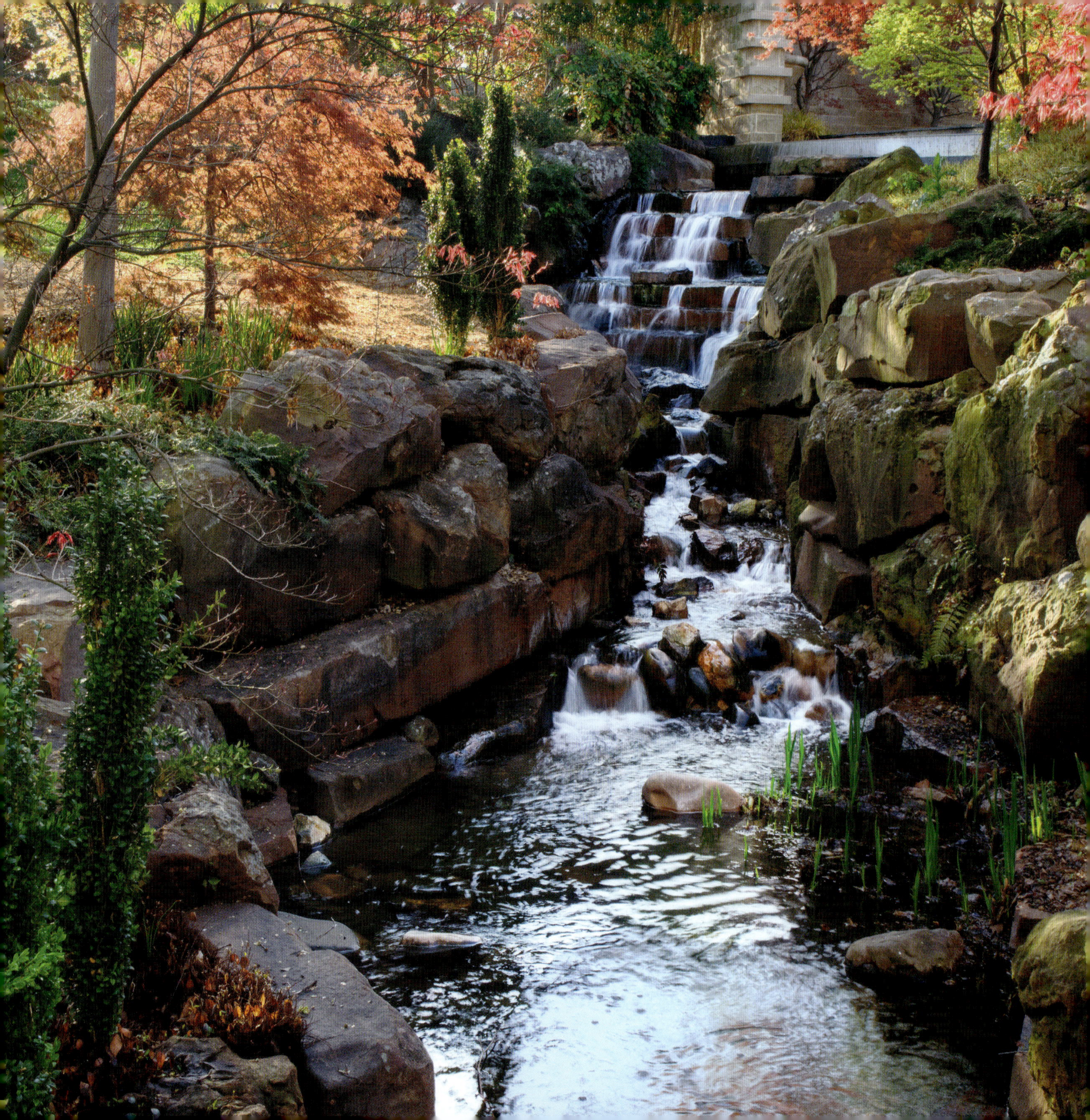

Enjoy

Calvert Collins-Bratton is a seventh-generation Texan, former television reporter, and healthcare foundation executive. The mother of three daughters, she serves as the president and District 13 representative for the Dallas Park and Recreation Board.

Opposite
The Dallas Arboretum and Botanical Garden is a sixty-six-acre botanical garden located on the southeastern shore of White Rock Lake in East Dallas.

Parks and Recreation

Wide-open green space—the proximity to nature, the smell of flowers or freshly cut grass, the hum of bees and chirps of birds. Parks are a feast for the senses and a respite from the chaos of everyday life. Whether it's a walk on the Katy Trail, cycling around White Rock Lake, hiking Cedar Ridge Preserve, or enjoying the sights and sounds of Klyde Warren Park, Dallas parks have something to offer everyone.

I personally love the diversity of the parks, trails, and other amenities in the park system. In a single weekend, I can take my family to the Dallas Arboretum, Dallas Zoo, Fair Park, Hillcrest Village Green, and the Trinity Skyline Trail, and not have the same experience twice.

With 400 parks, 200 playgrounds, 160 miles of trails, 43 recreation centers, and 32 pools and spraygrounds in the Dallas Park and Recreation system, we never run out of activities—most of which are free or very low cost. Investing in parks is investing in green infrastructure. Parks and amenities not only improve quality of life, but also the neighborhoods around them. They are gathering places where all are welcome—the most public of places.

I enjoy a park asset every day—the Northaven Trail. The first east-west trail in North Dallas has become a new mode of transportation. My family just moved to be closer to the trail so that our kids can bike and walk to school on it. We walk our dog every day on the trail, watching the wildflowers in the pollinator gardens grow, and teaching our kids about nature. It helps us slow down and appreciate the world around us. And it teaches us gratitude—for living in a city that values and invests in parks for all people.

Calvert Collins-Bratton

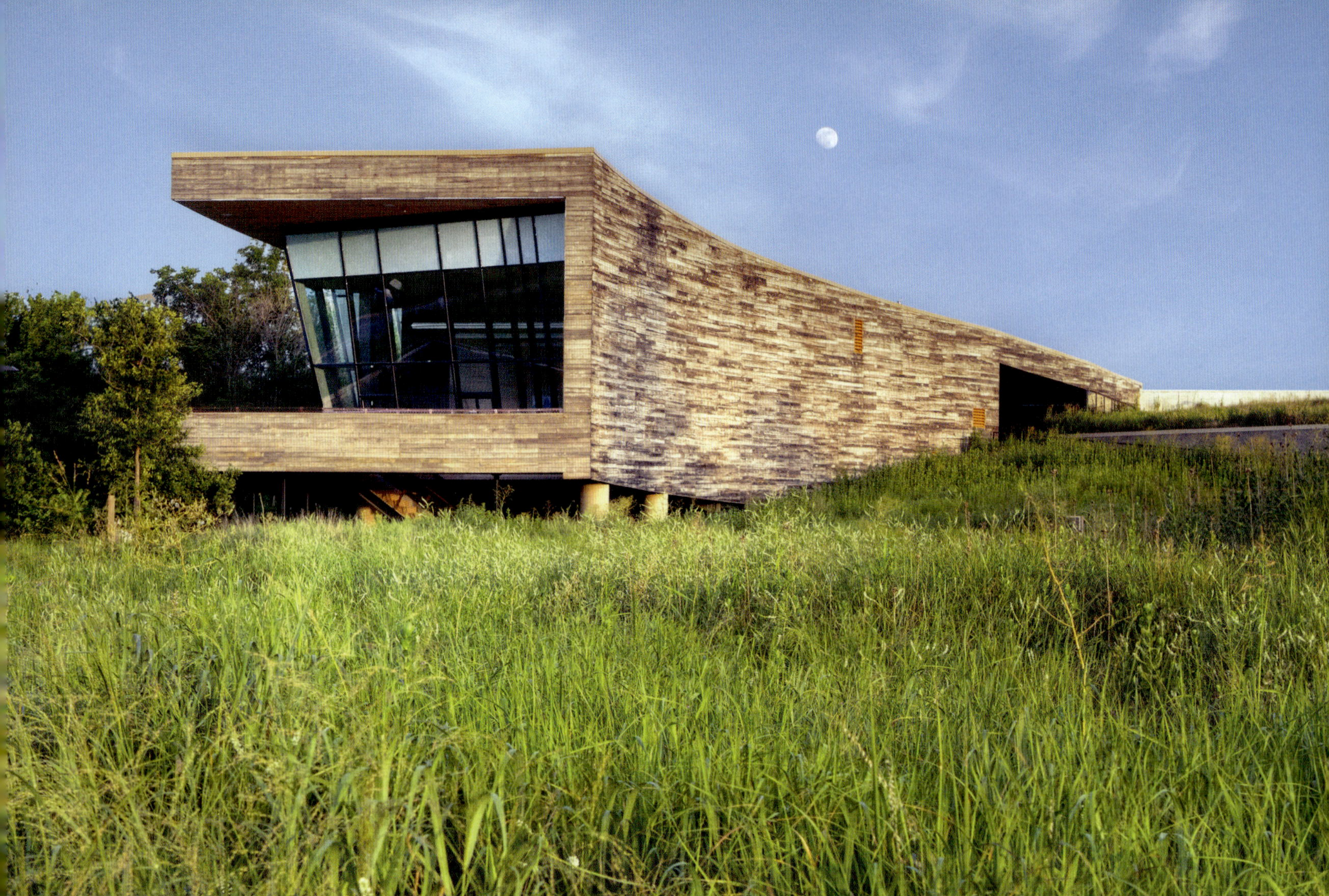

Above
Trinity River Audubon Center, located ten miles south of downtown Dallas, serves as gateway to the six-thousand-acre Great Trinity Forest, the largest urban hardwood forest in the United States.

Opposite
This sixty-seven-foot-tall giraffe, touted as the "Tallest Statue in Texas," stands at the entrance of the Dallas Zoo.

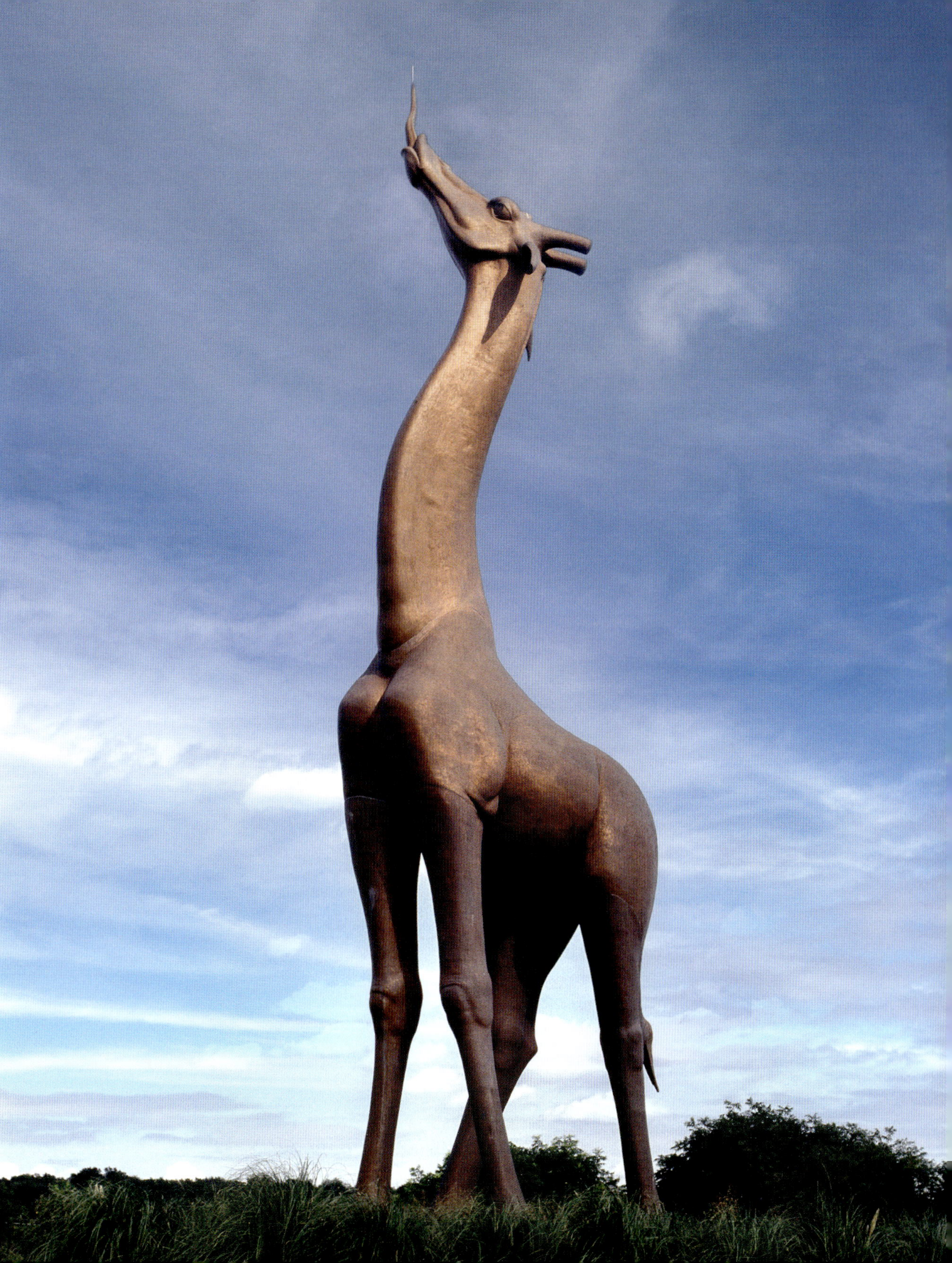

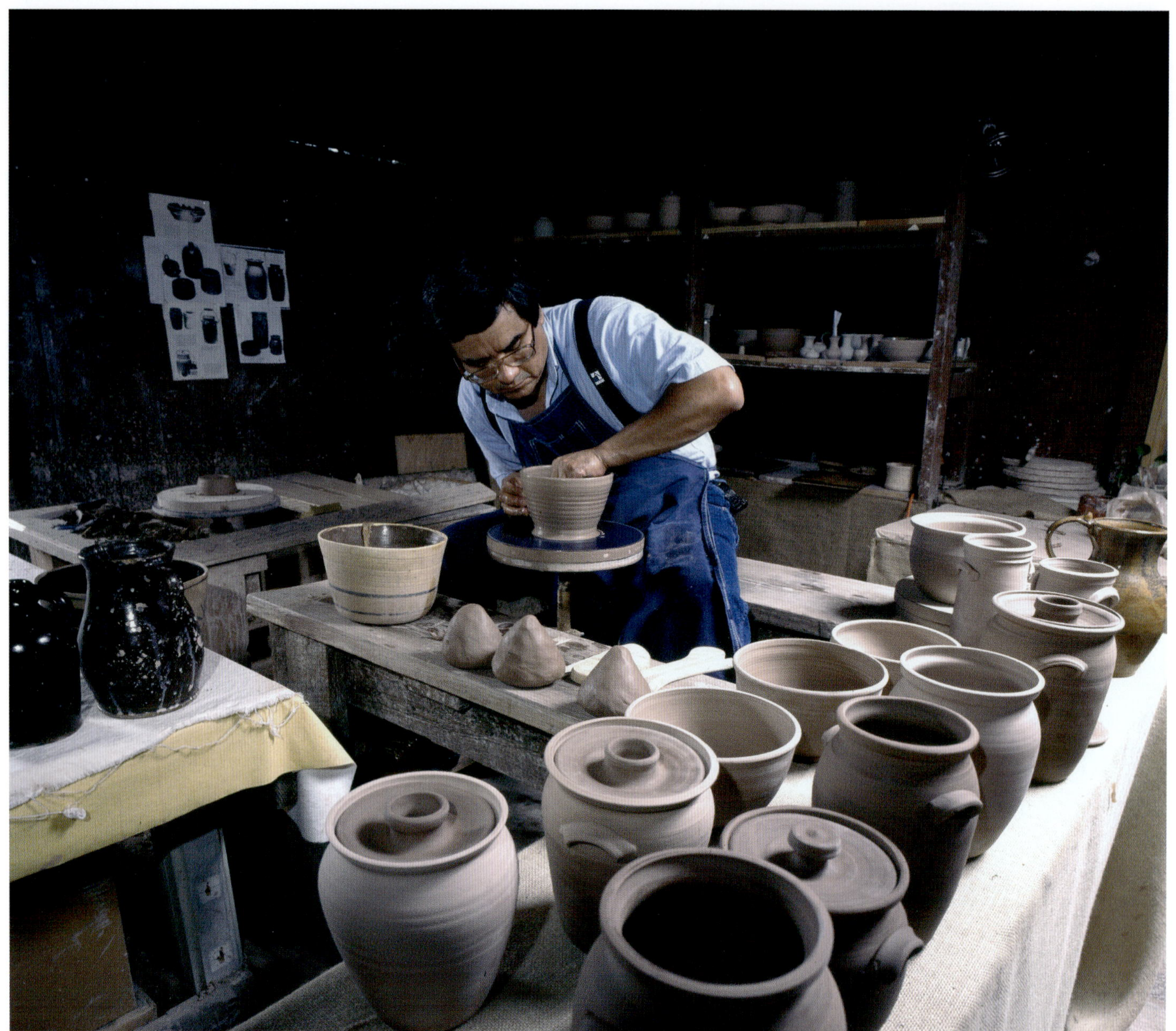

Above
A potter produces beautiful vessels at Dallas Heritage Park.

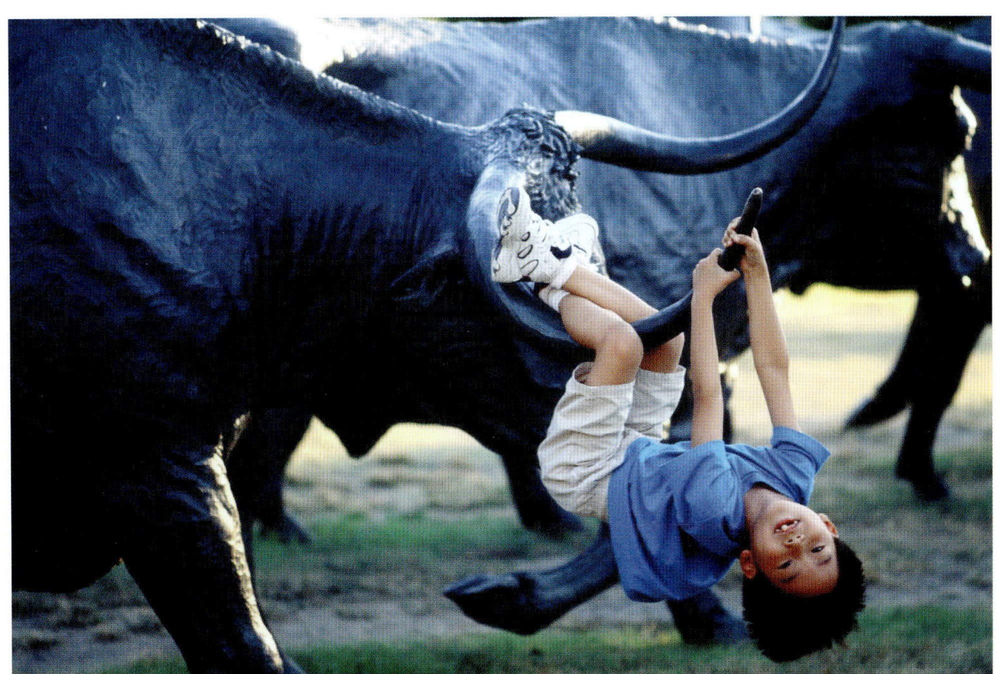

Right
A young acrobat practices hanging on to a steer at Pioneer Park.

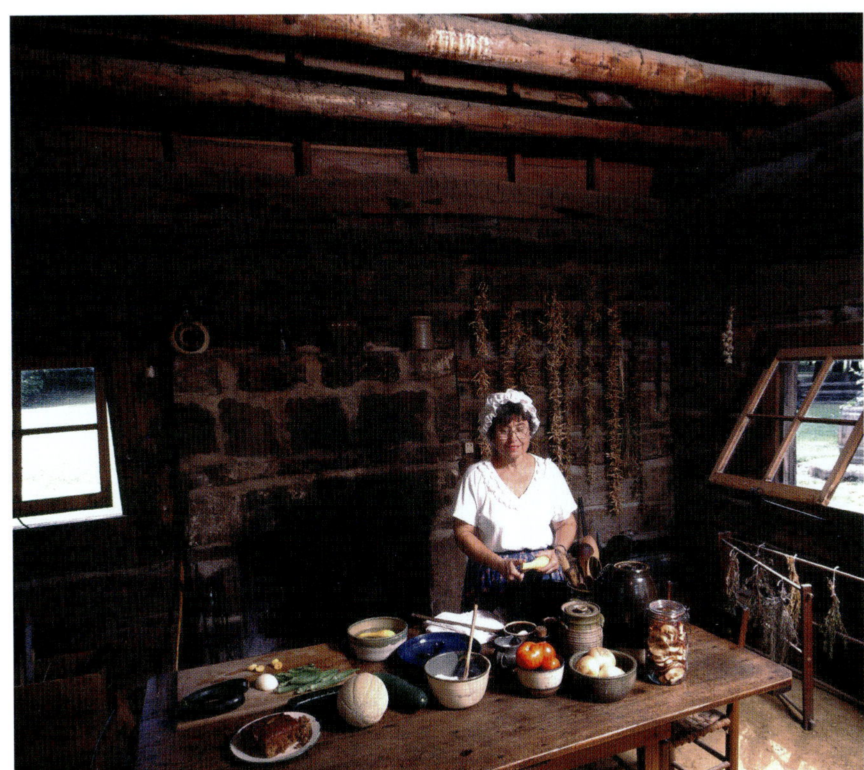

Right
A cook demonstrates pioneer cooking at Dallas Heritage Village.

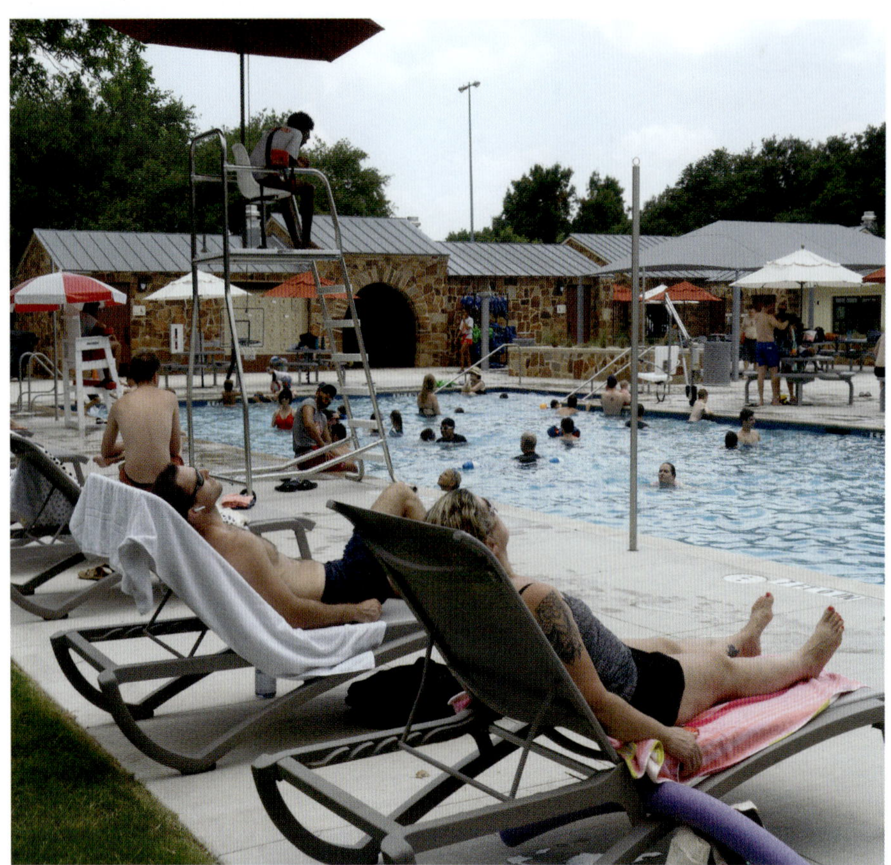

Left
Tietze Park has been one of the most popular parks in Dallas since 1924. Encompassing nine acres in the Lakewood area, it offers athletic fields, tennis and basketball courts, playgrounds, an aquatic center, an historic stone pavilion, and a walking path.

Opposite
Children enjoy crawling on this elephant sculpture at the Dallas Zoo.

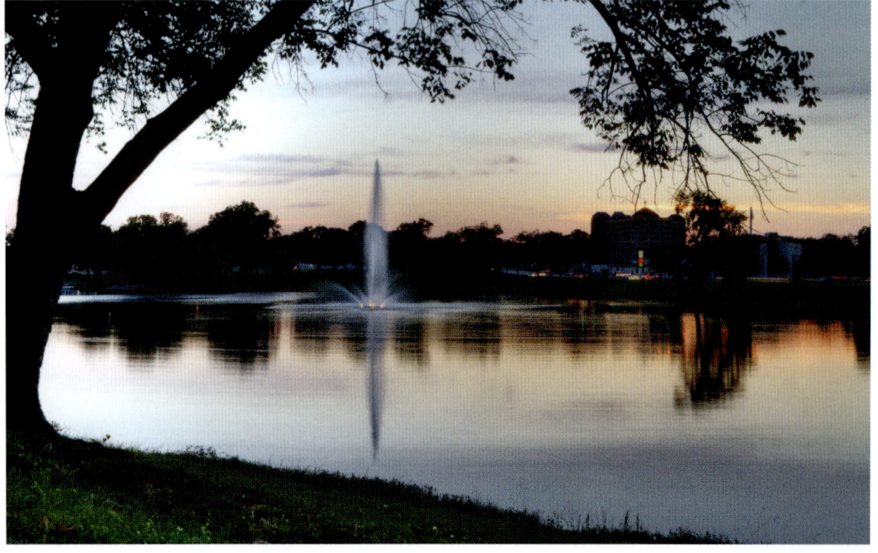

Left
Created as a private amusement park in 1906, Lake Cliff Park was acquired by the city and transformed into a municipal park that now anchors an historic residential district.

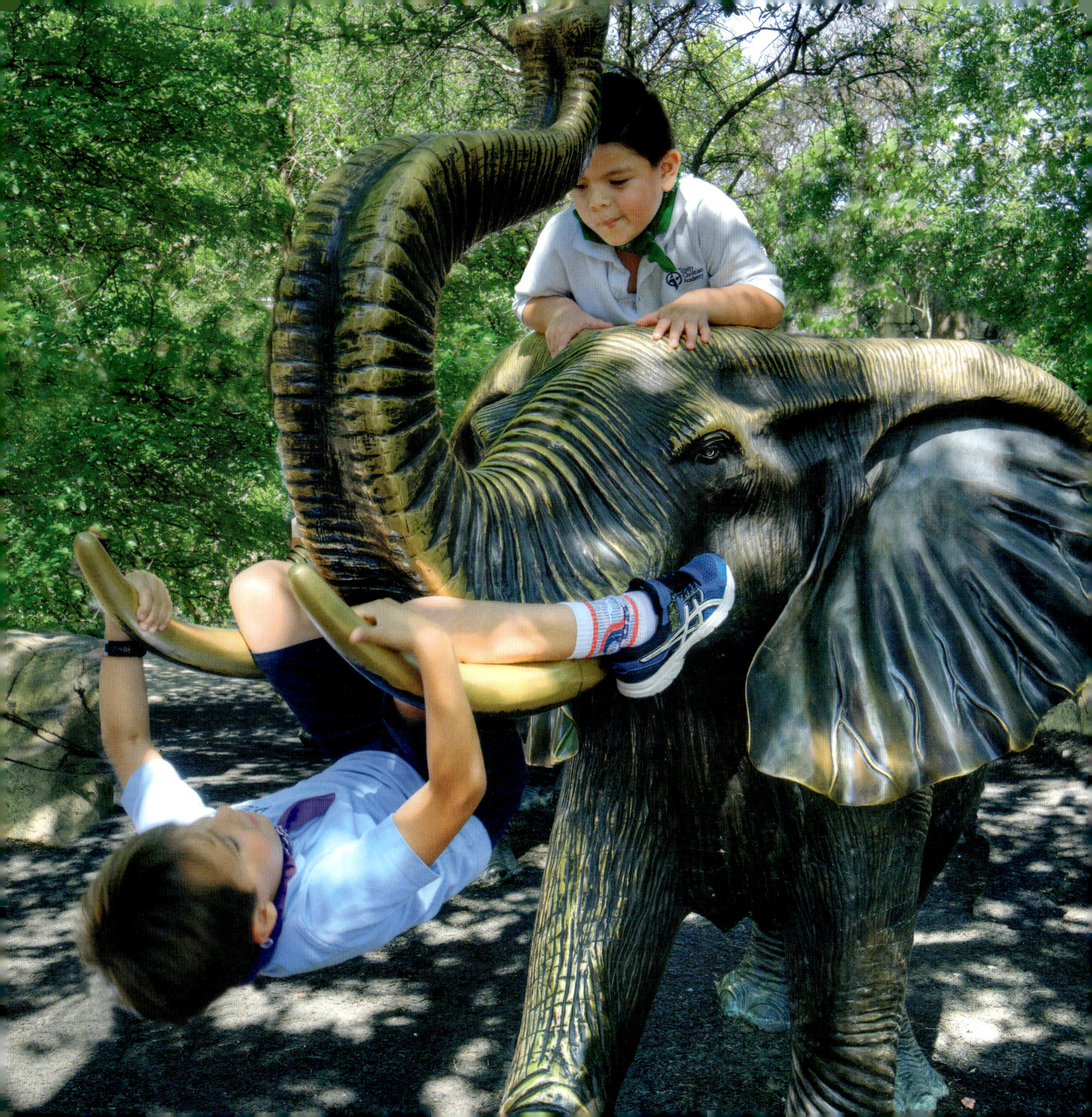

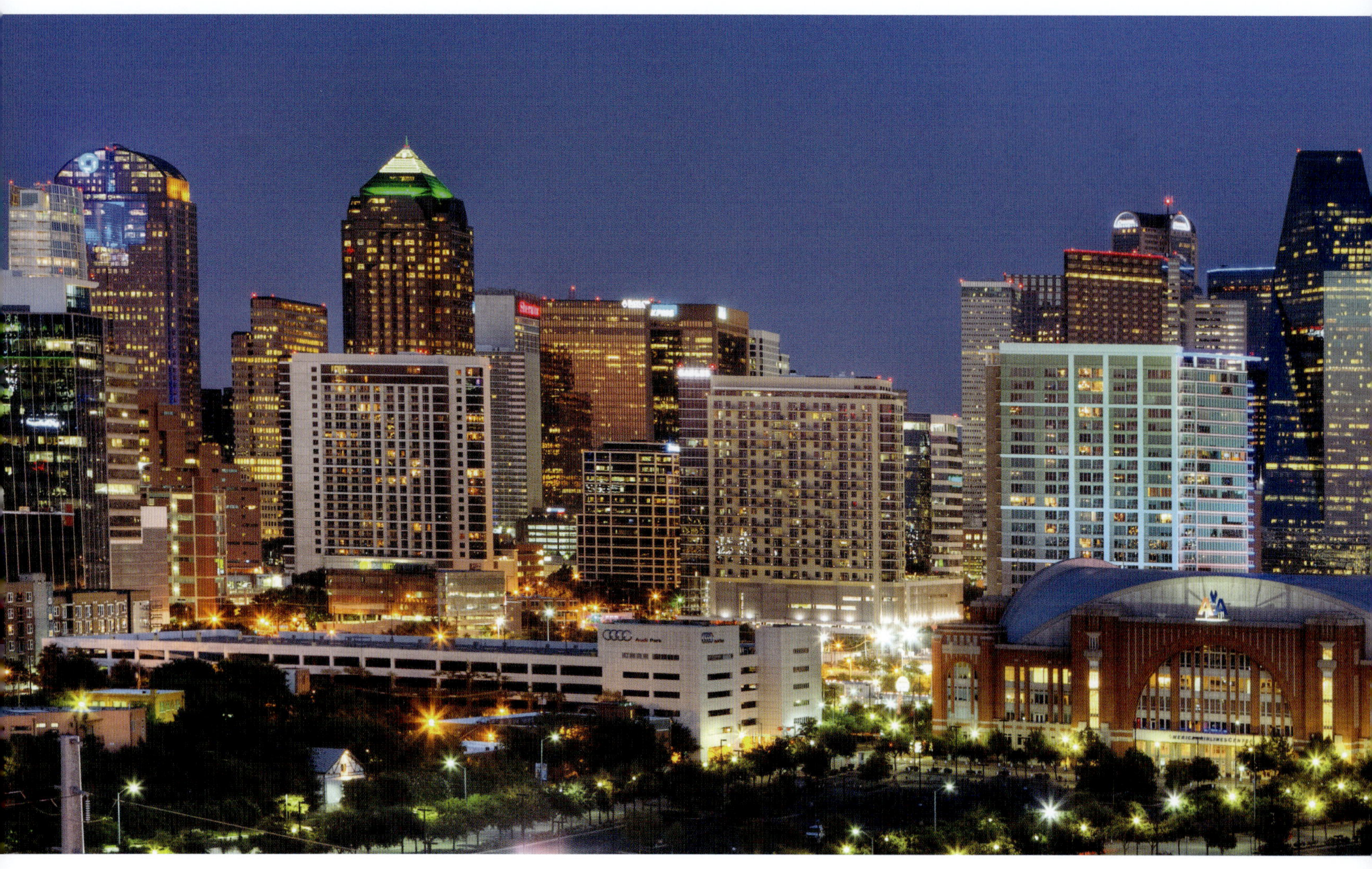

Above
A panorama of downtown Dallas shows Victory Park in the foreground. The park is anchored by American Airlines Center, a multipurpose arena which opened in 2001 as home to the Dallas Mavericks (basketball) and Dallas Stars (ice hockey), as well as a venue for live entertainment.

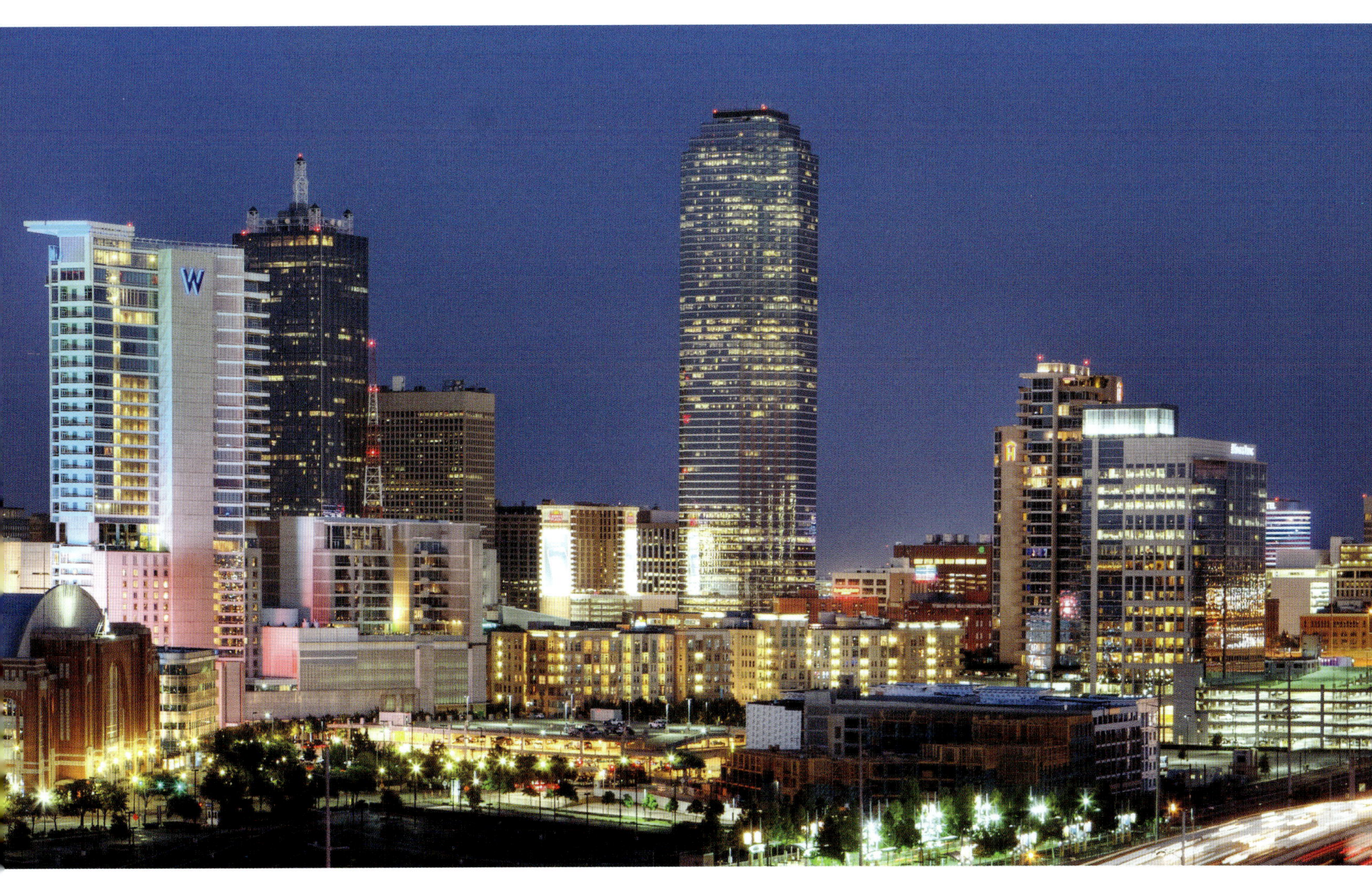

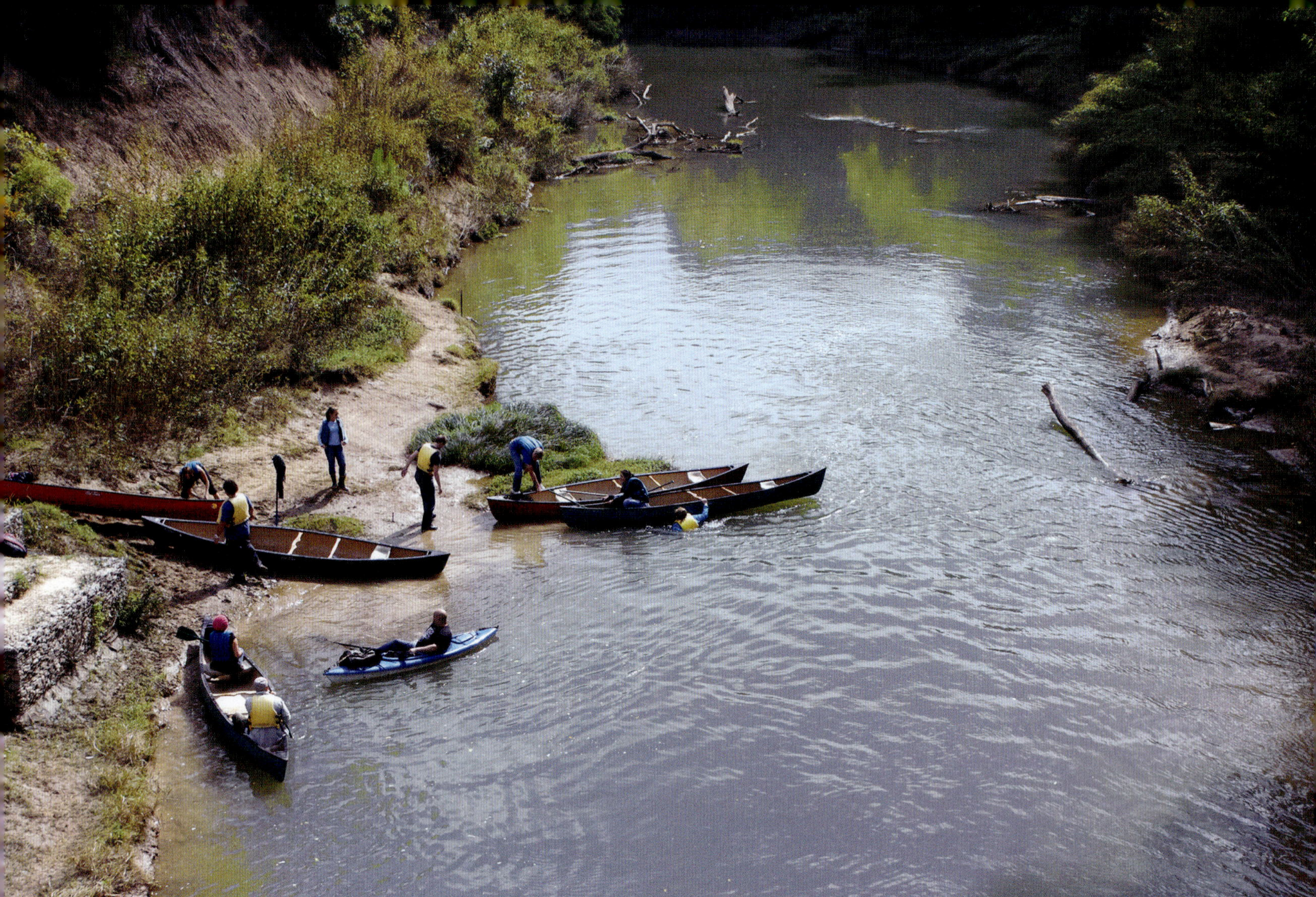

Above
In the middle of the city, guided canoe trips along the Trinity River allow glimpses of the natural world.

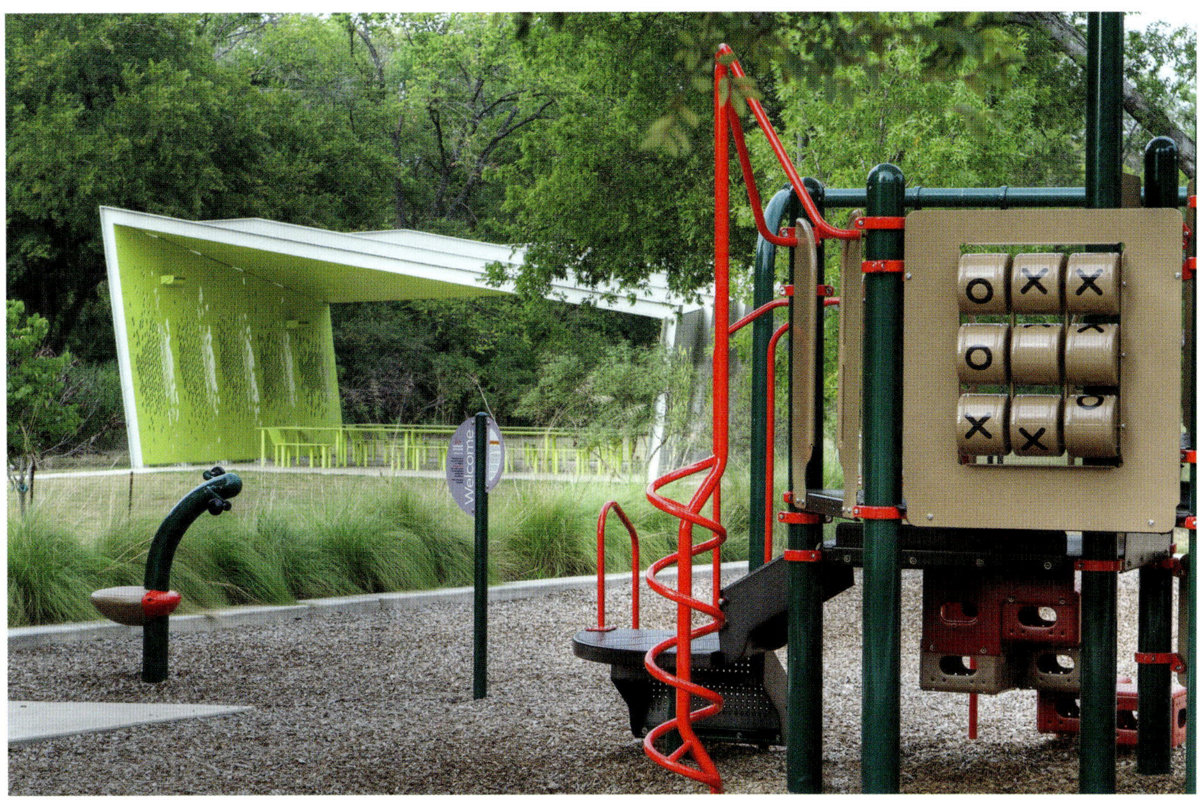

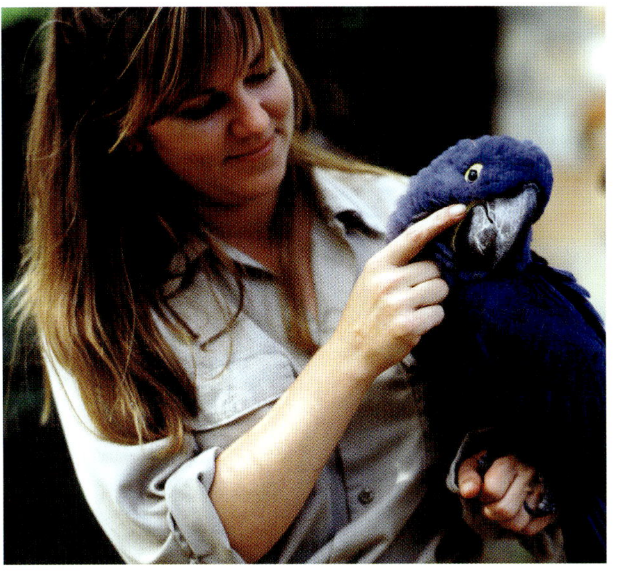

Above
College Park sits next to Five Mile Creek in South Dallas. The park pavilion, designed by Snøhetta, won an AIA design award. It is positioned to frame a quiet meadow view.

Left
A zoo attendant plays with a blue parrot.

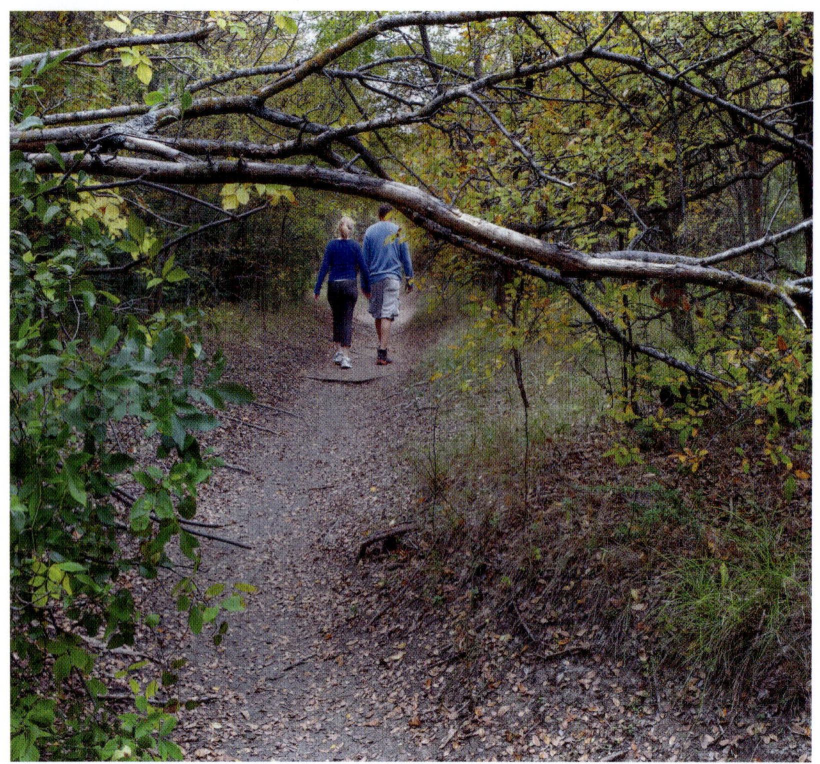

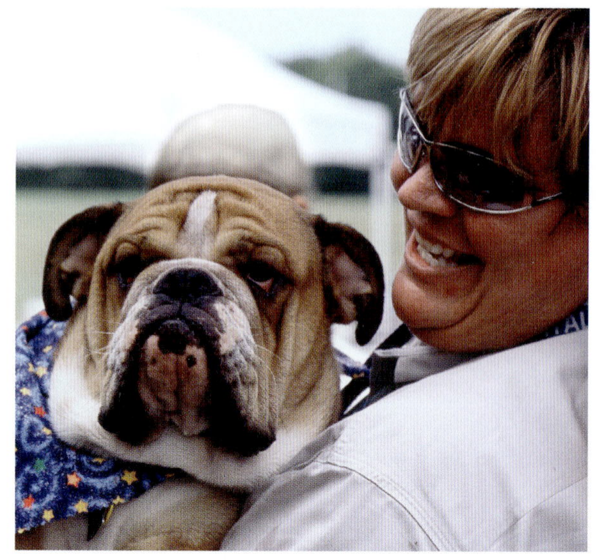

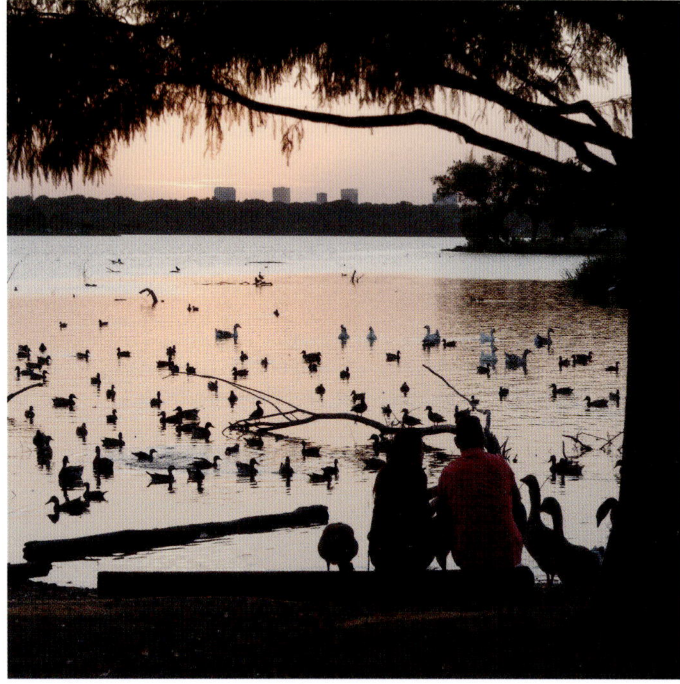

Above (left)
The Great Trinity Forest, one of the largest urban forests in the nation, offers miles of tranquil paths near the Trinity River.

Above
A woman proudly holds her precious English Bulldog at a Fair Park event.

Left
White Rock Lake, created a century ago as a water supply for the city, quickly became a playground for Dallas residents and home to a wide variety of waterfowl. It offers picnic pavilions, fishing piers, sailboat marinas, and hike-and-bike paths.

Opposite
A fountain in Turtle Creek delights visitors. The creek meanders through Highland Park and flows through Dallas into the Trinity River.

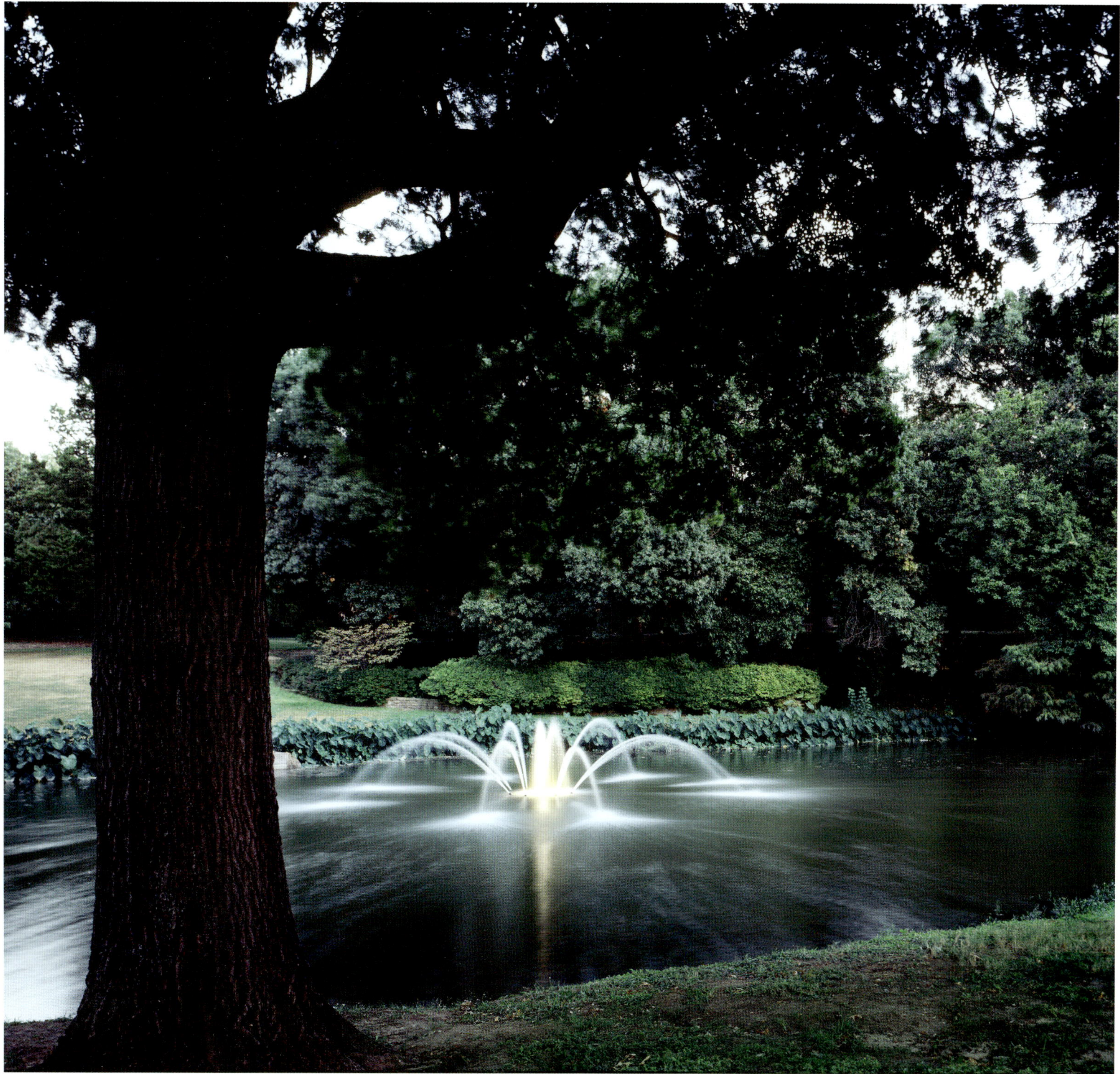

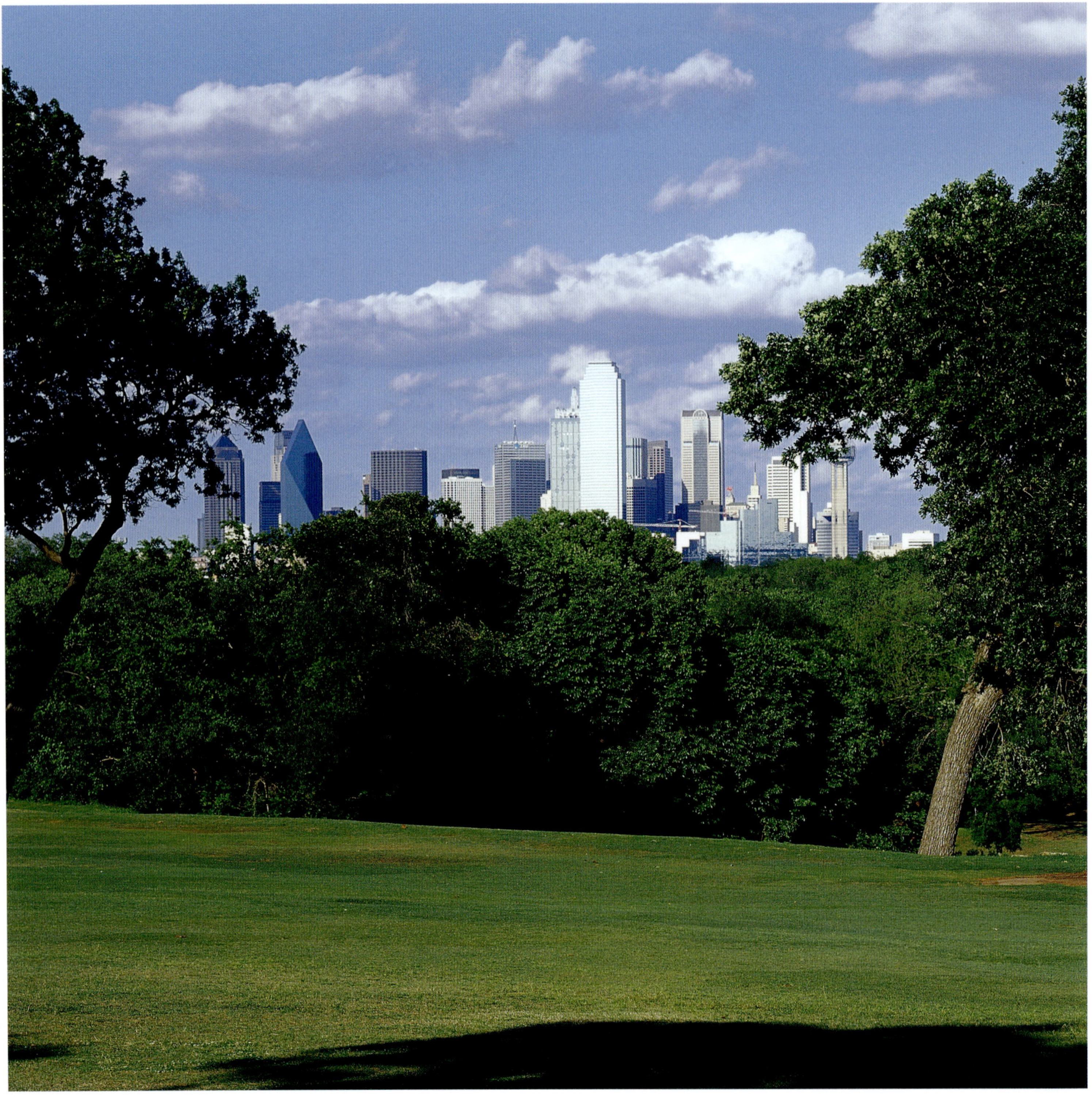

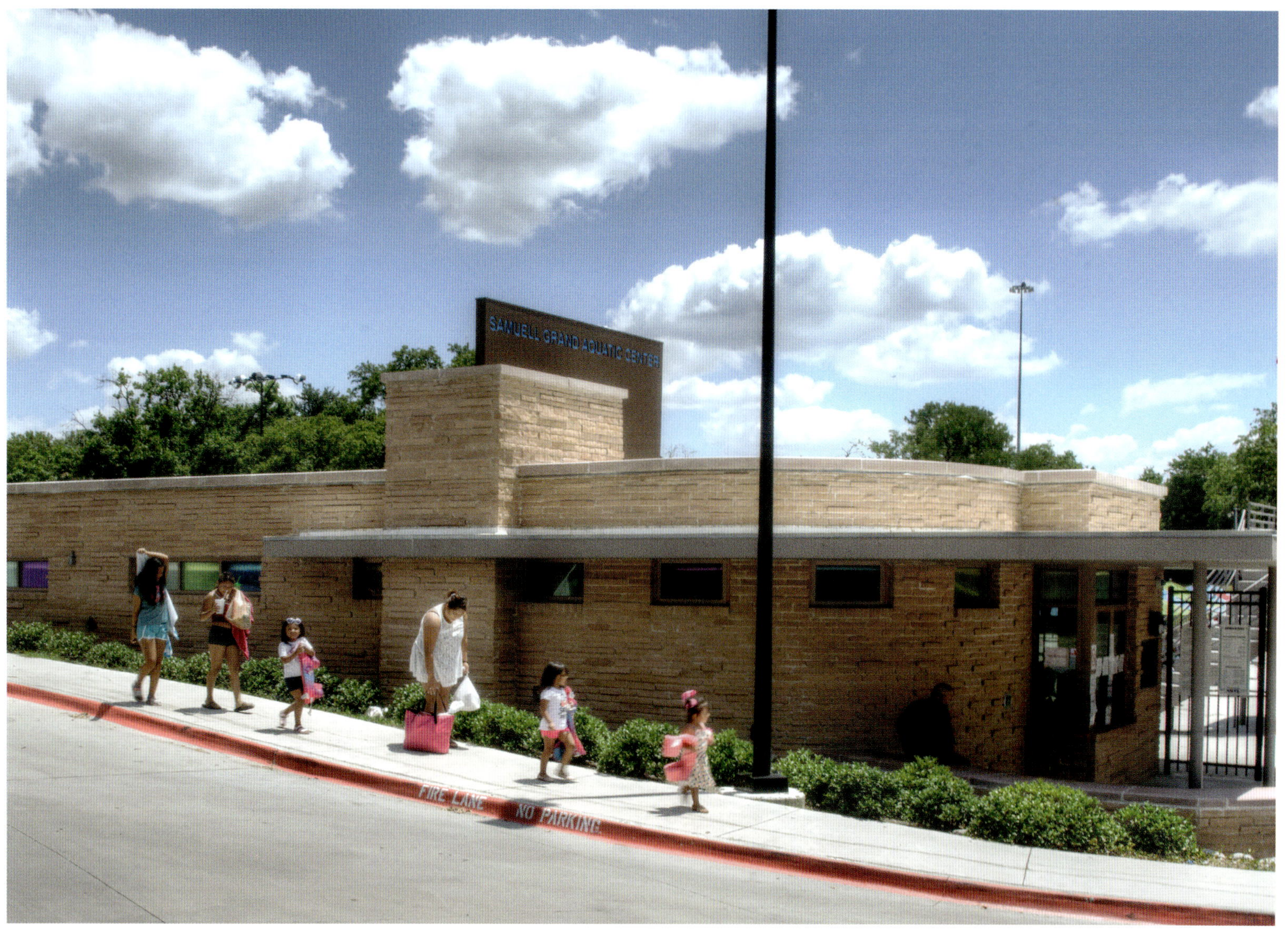

Opposite
Stevens Park Golf Course is one of the premier public golf destinations in the Dallas-Fort Worth Metroplex and ranks among the Top 20 Texas public golf courses.

Above
The Samuell Grand Aquatic Center, originally an historic 1960s bathhouse, has been preserved and enlarged to serve the surrounding community.

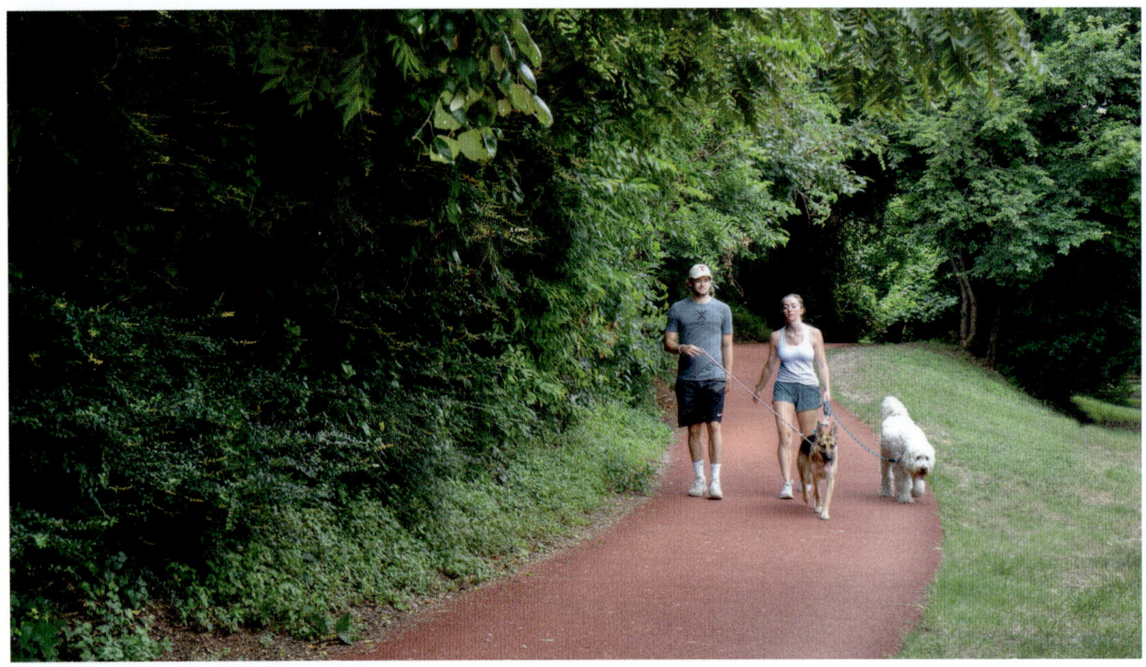

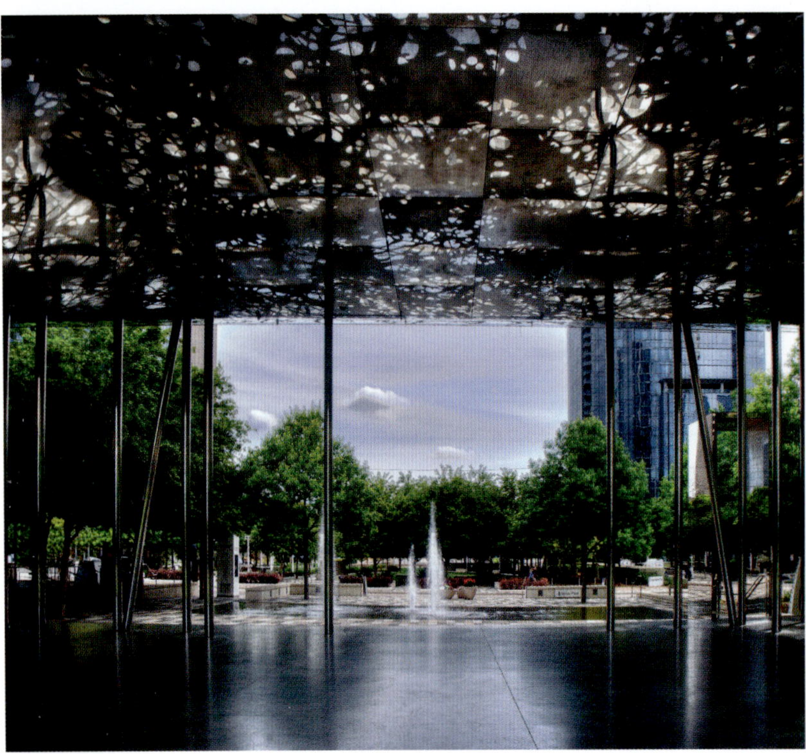

Above
Once an abandoned railroad line, the Katy Trail is now an iconic Dallas destination. With 3.5 miles of well-maintained path, it serves more than 1.5 million visitors a year.

Left
Klyde Warren Park is a 5.2-acre park built over a recessed freeway bordering the Dallas Arts District. It has become one of the most dynamic urban parks in America since its dedication in 2012.

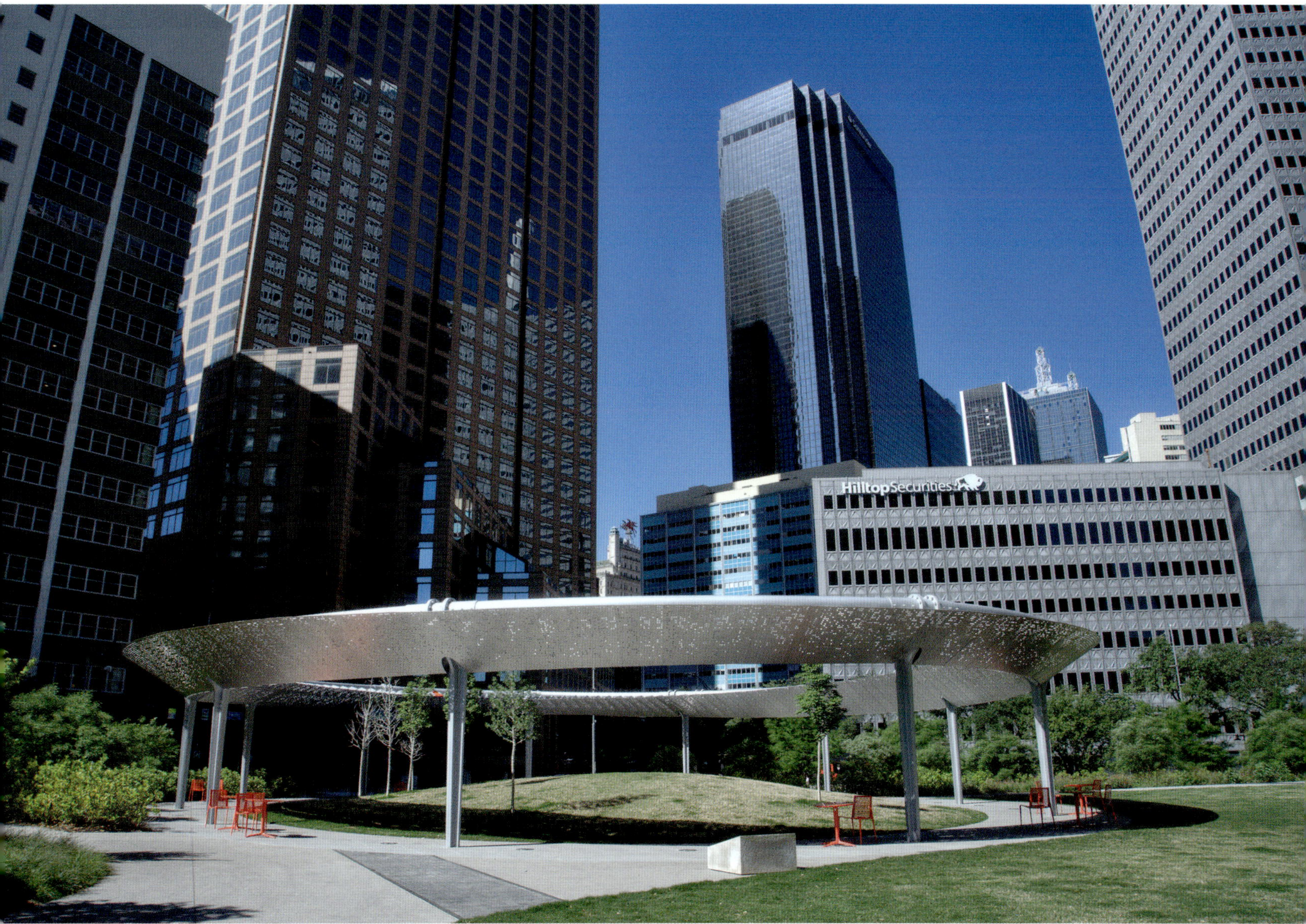

Above
Pacific Plaza is a public park located downtown between St. Paul and Harwood Streets. Its 3.7 acres opened to the public in 2019.

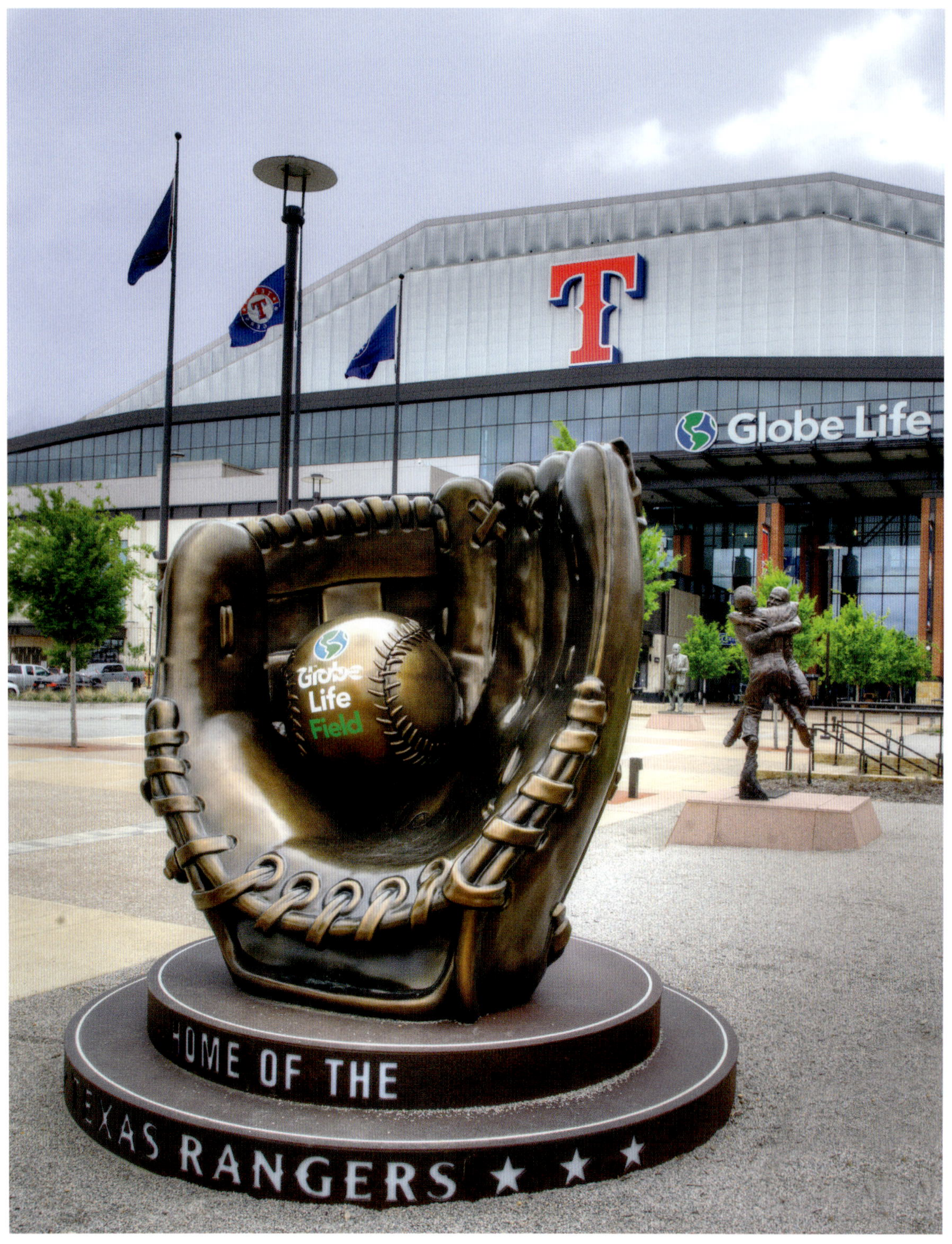

Left
Located between Dallas and Fort Worth in Arlington, Texas, Globe Life Field is the new home of the Texas Rangers baseball team, replacing Globe Life Park across the street.

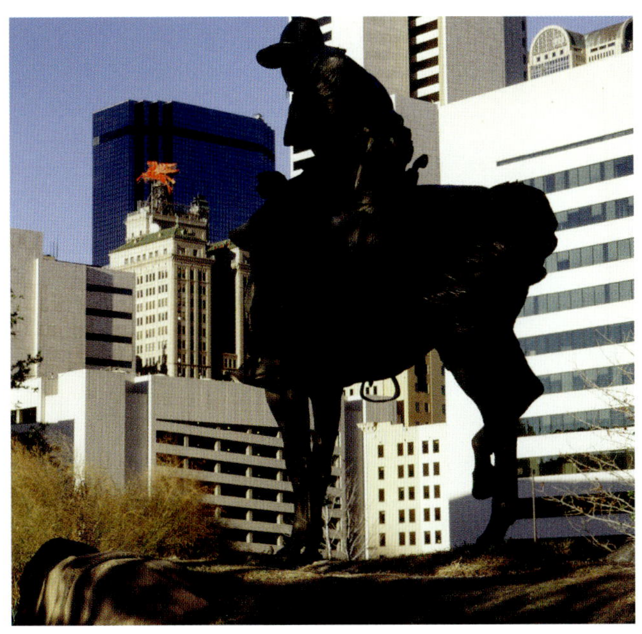

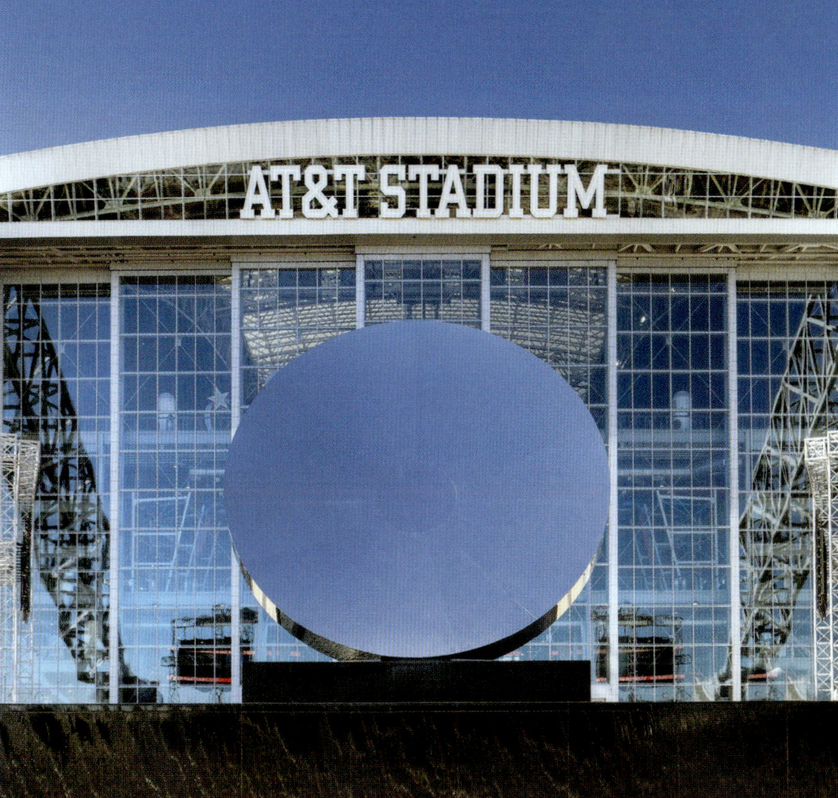

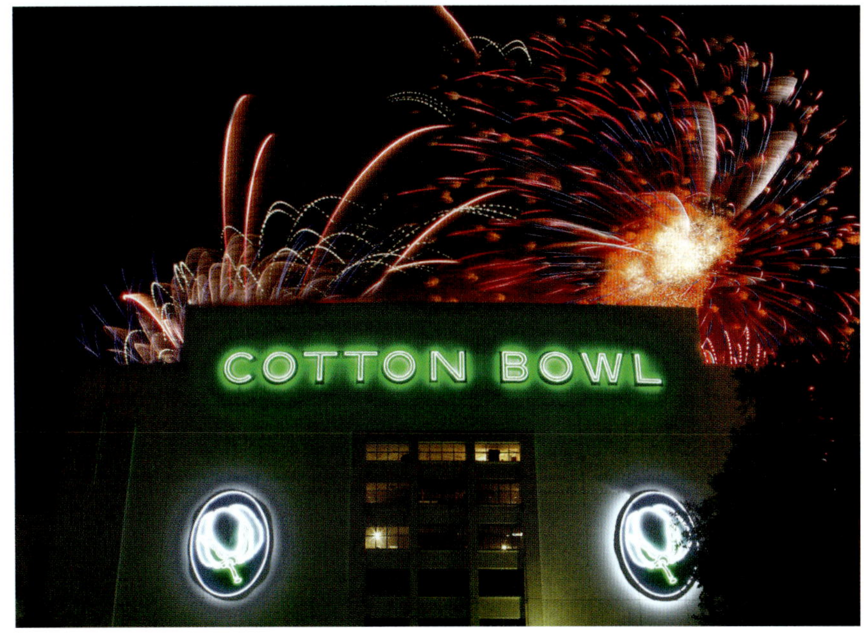

Above
Pioneer Plaza is located across from the Dallas Convention Center. A heavily visited tourist site, it is the largest public open space in the central business district and features a bronze sculpture of a cattle drive created by the artist Robert Summers.

Above (right)
AT&T Stadium, home of the Dallas Cowboys, opened in Arlington in 2009. Designed by the Dallas architects HKS, Inc., the stadium can seat eighty thousand fans and boasts a retractable roof and the world's largest column-free interior.

Right
The Cotton Bowl Stadium at Fair Park opened in 1930 and is known for hosting fabled football rivalries and outdoor concerts.

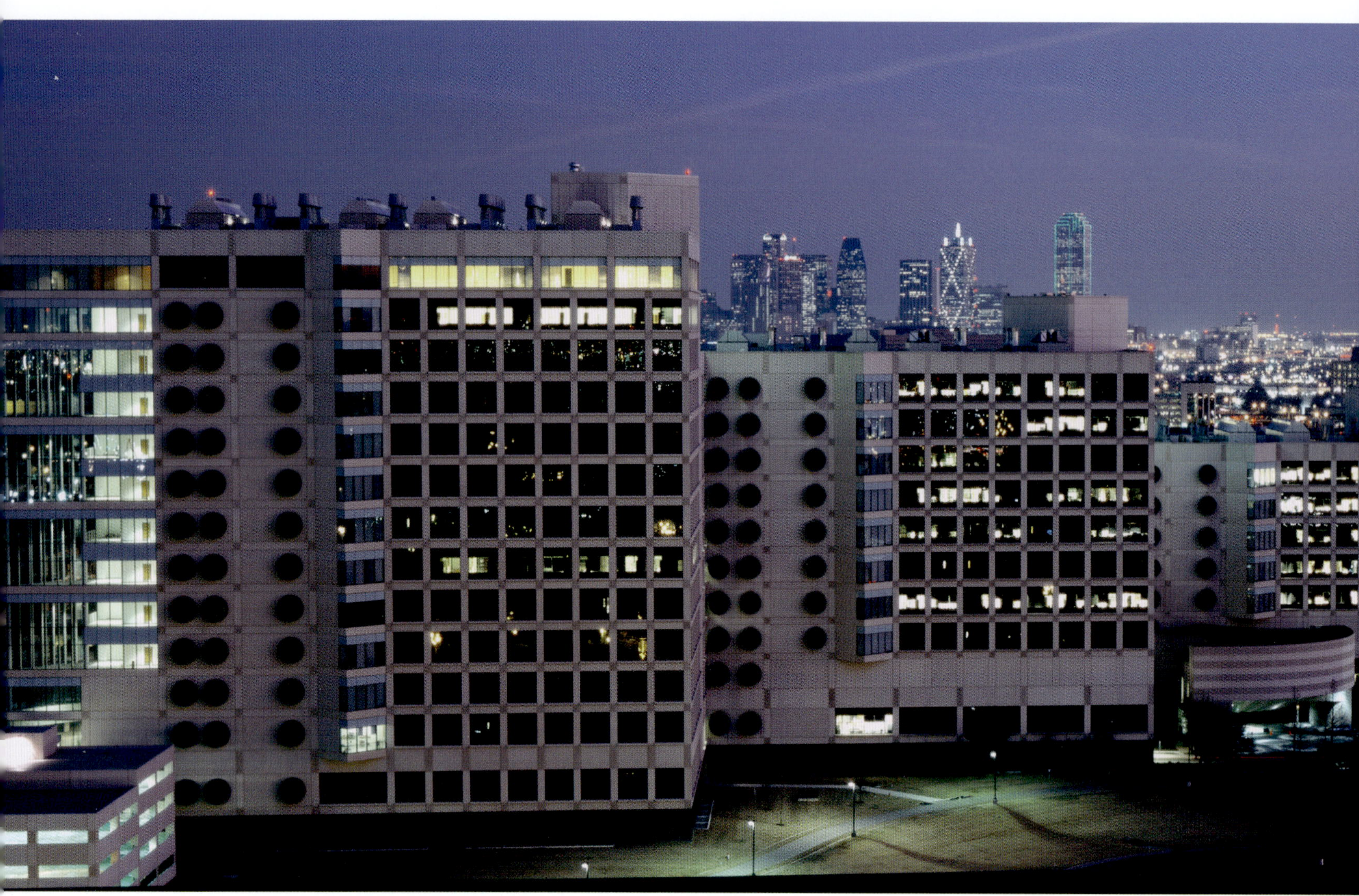

Heal

Kern Wildenthal, MD, PhD, a graduate of UT Southwestern Medical Center and Cambridge University, joined the UT Southwestern faculty in 1970. After serving from 1976 to 1986 as dean, he was president of the Medical Center for twenty-two years, until his retirement in 2008. Post-retirement, he served as president of Southwestern Medical Foundation from 2008 to 2012 and of Children's Medical Center Foundation from 2013 to 2016. He was the interim general director and CEO of the Dallas Opera in 2017–18. He continues his work at Children's as past president and consultant for the Foundation, and at UT Southwestern as president emeritus.

Opposite
The University of Texas Southwestern Medical Center in Dallas is a burgeoning complex that covers six hundred acres and includes Parkland, Children's, Zale Lipshy, and William P. Clements hospitals. It is home to six Nobel laureates.

1961

A young West Texas boy looks at the campus of UT Southwestern Medical Center at Dallas, where he has just completed his first year of medical school. He sees two small education and research buildings on sixty-five acres of land, next to the new Parkland Memorial Hospital—an eight-year-old county facility that is already inadequate.

His class numbers ninety students. The faculty of just over one hundred physicians and scientists includes excellent teachers whose clinical expertise and research discoveries are slowly beginning to become noticed nationally.

2021

That West Texas boy, no longer young, looks back at sixty years of transformational change in Dallas medicine. With the strategic acquisition between 1988 and 2005 of three hundred acres of nearby land, UT Southwestern has been able to expand to fifty modern academic buildings, hospitals, and clinics, with others underway. In 2015, Parkland completed the nation's largest new clinical construction project. Children's Medical Center has moved to the campus (now known as the Southwestern Medical District) and has become the country's eighth-largest pediatric hospital. Texas Scottish Rite Hospital, Texas Woman's University, and UT Dallas have dramatically expanded their facilities in the district. And the district institutions have added satellite sites throughout Dallas and in Tarrant, Collin, and Denton Counties.

Three thousand faculty members provide care for a million patients; teach two thousand trainees; and conduct four thousand research projects. Since 1985, six have become Nobel Prize winners—more than at any other medical school in the world.

Elsewhere in Dallas, excellent hospitals such as Baylor, Presbyterian, and Methodist have expanded broadly and developed into major regional health systems that provide service to millions of patients in North Texas and beyond.

Dallas's rapid transformation from a good local medical center into a place of the highest international esteem has been remarkable. The foundation laid by our predecessors was solid; our growth in size and stature has been beyond what anyone could have dreamed; the brightness of our future is unsurpassed. The fuel for this explosion has been philanthropy: no community is more generous in supporting medical excellence. Dallas's continuing status as a leader in worldwide medical care, education, and research is guaranteed.

Kern Wildenthal

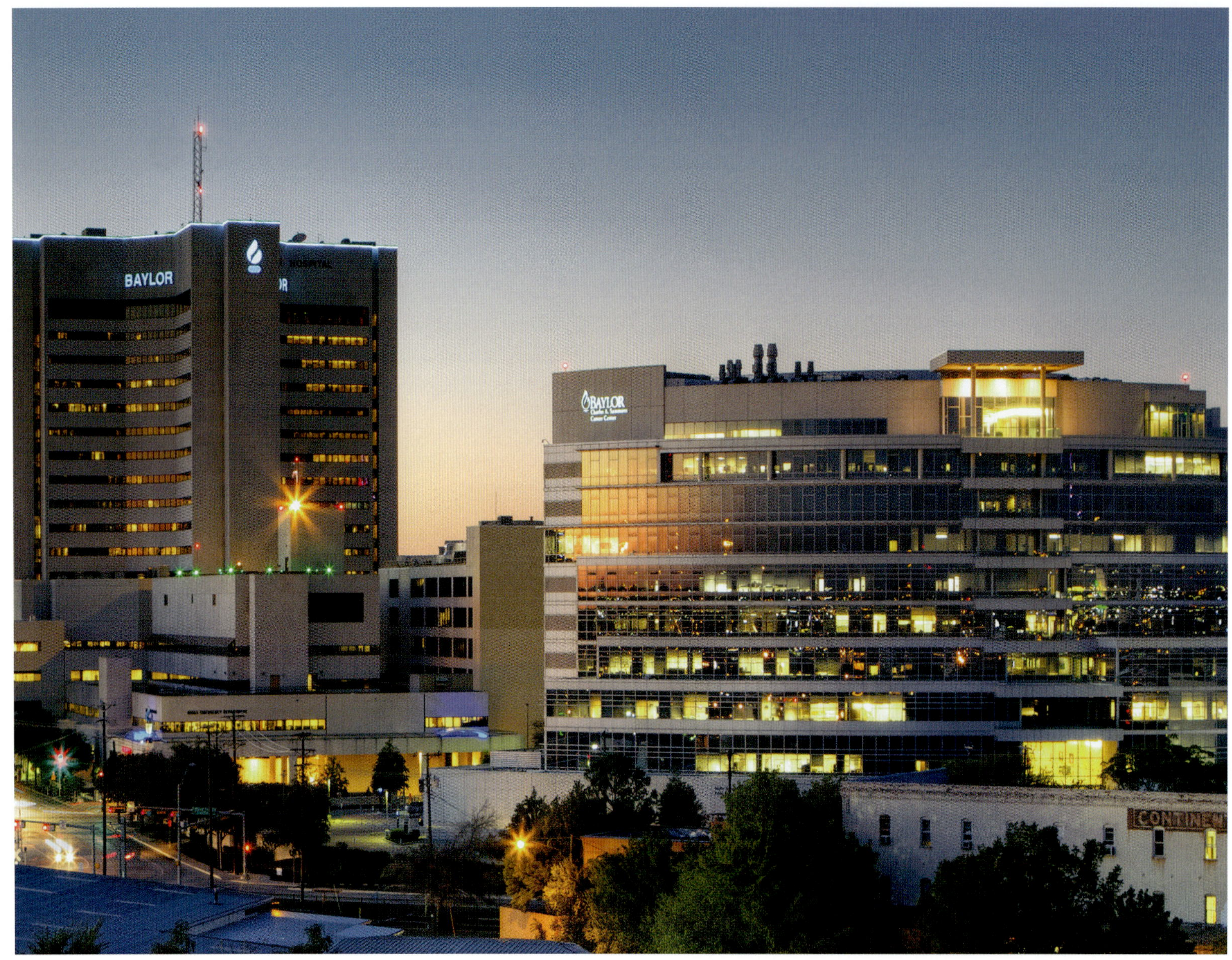

Above
Baylor University Medical Center, aglow at twilight.

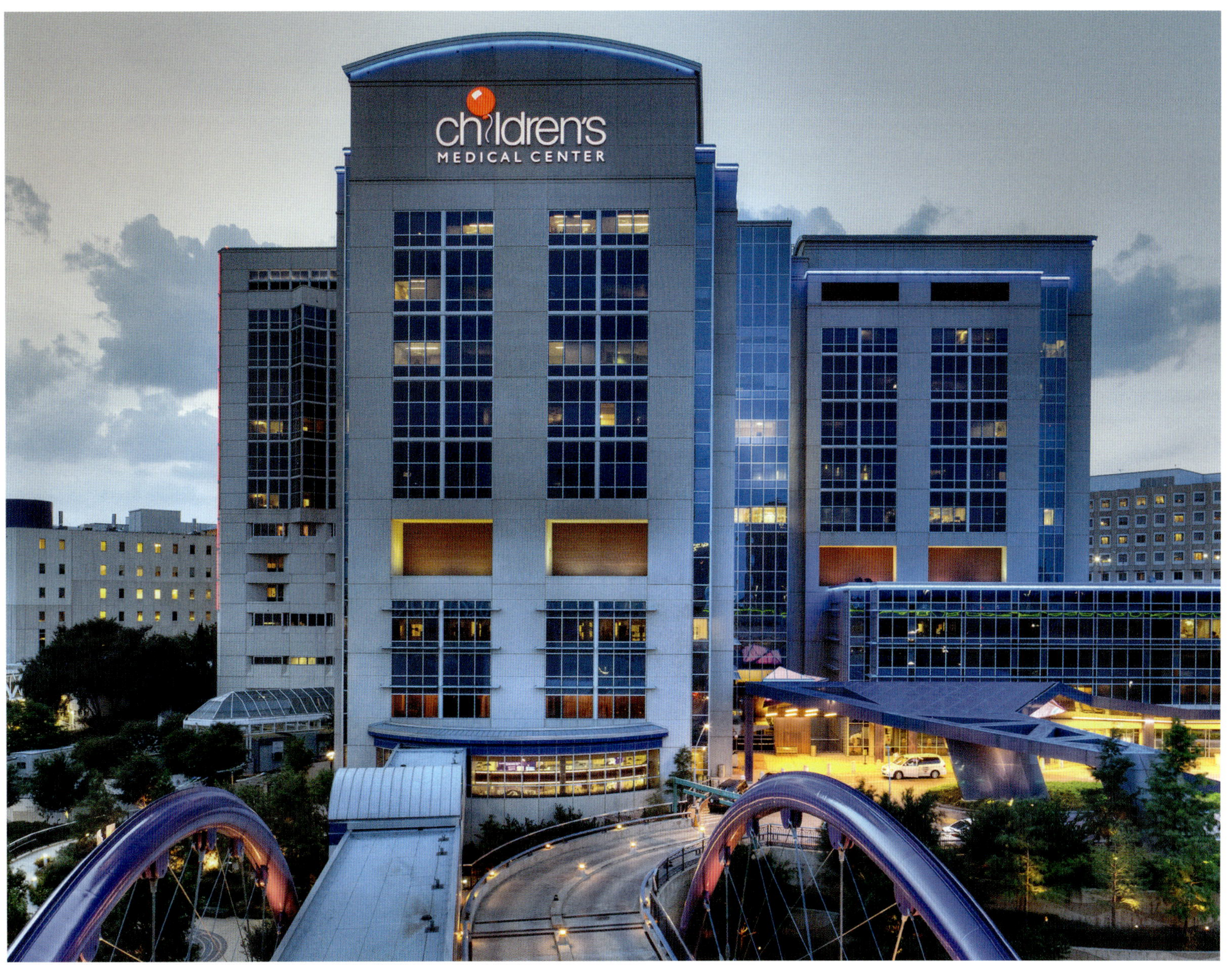

Above
Children's Hospital, founded in 1913 and now part of the not-for-profit UT Southwestern Medical Center, is the seventh-largest pediatric health care provider in the United States.

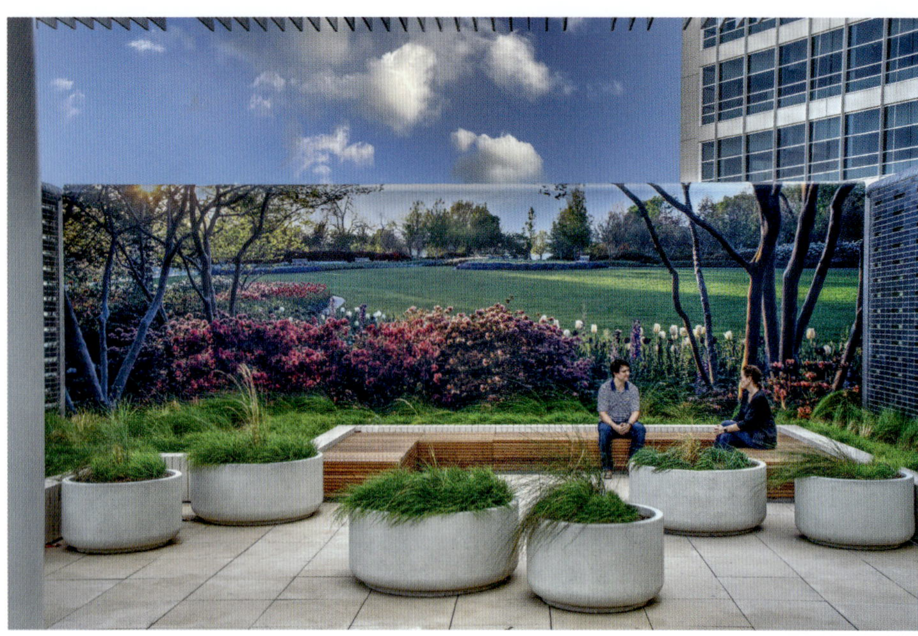

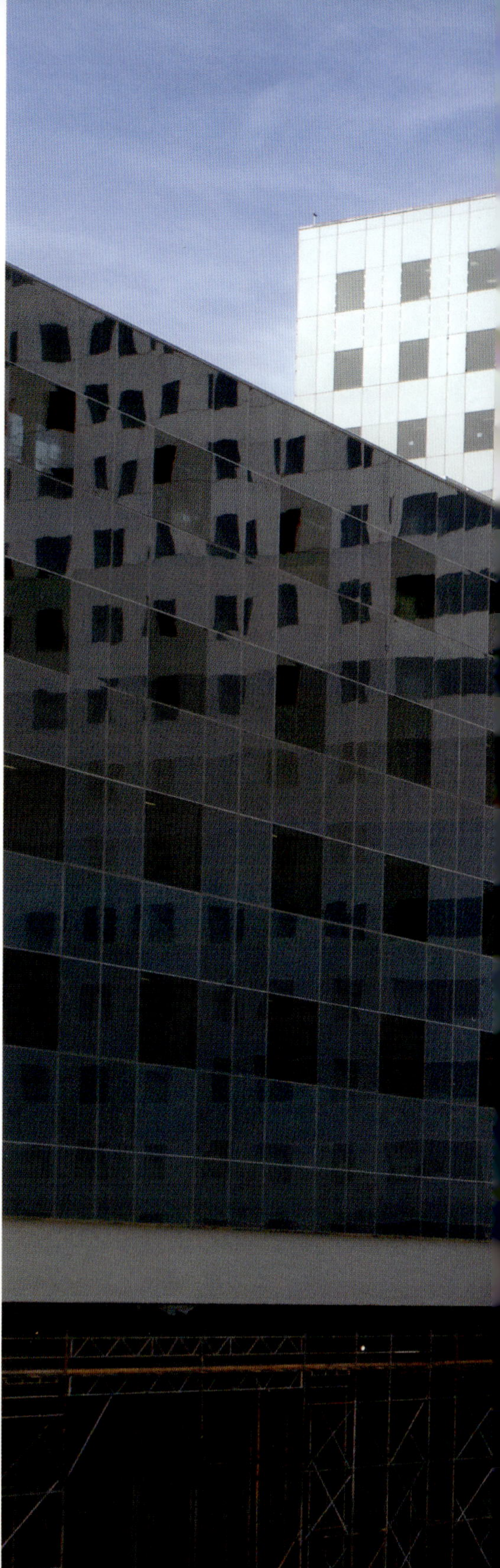

Above
A newly installed mural at the William P. Clements Hospital at UTSW was installed so patients can enjoy the outdoors without leaving the hospital.

Right
With a goal to provide medical care for all in need, Parkland Hospital has been Dallas County's public hospital for more than 125 years. The twenty-first century opened with construction of new state-of-the-art facilities.

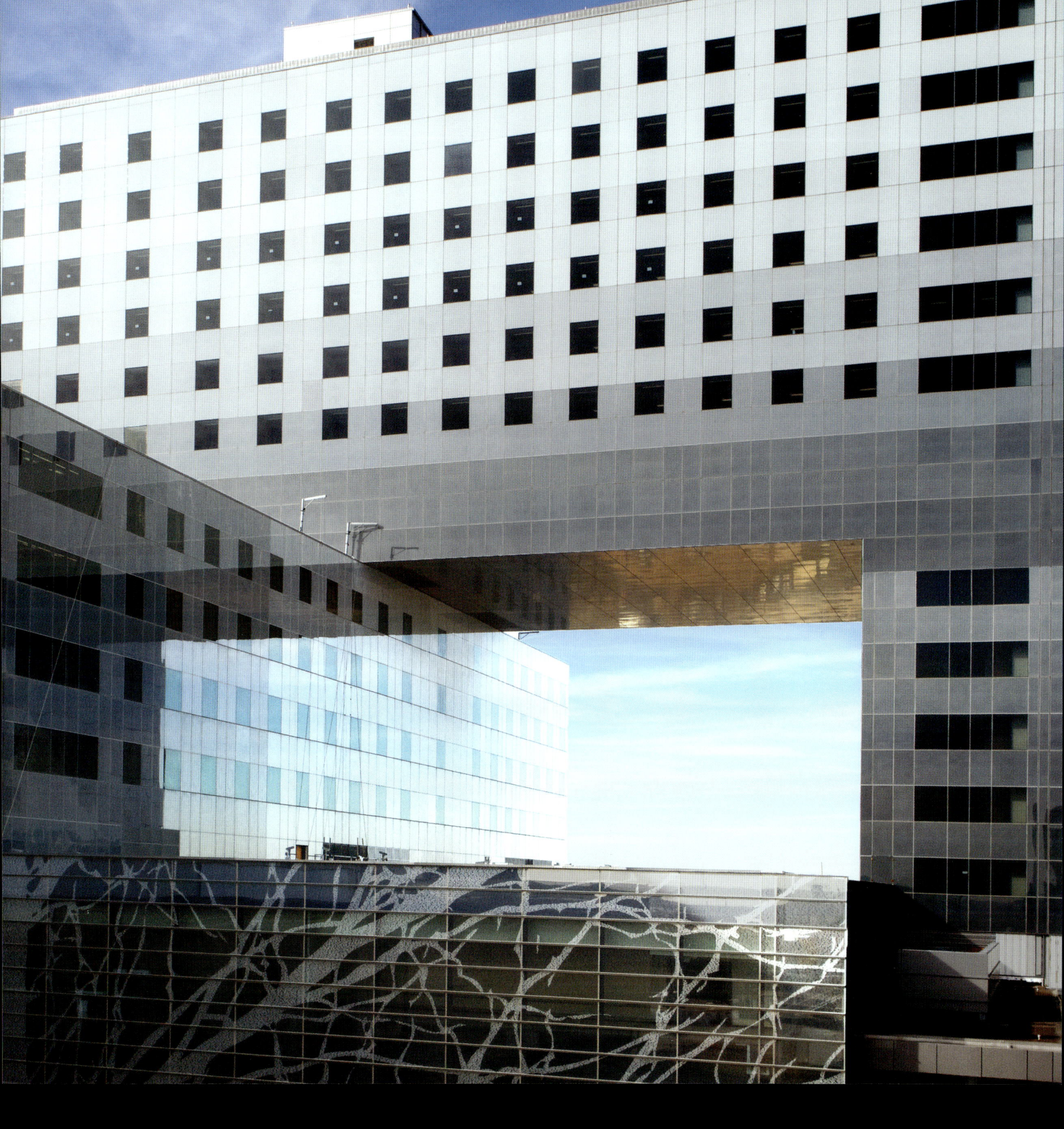

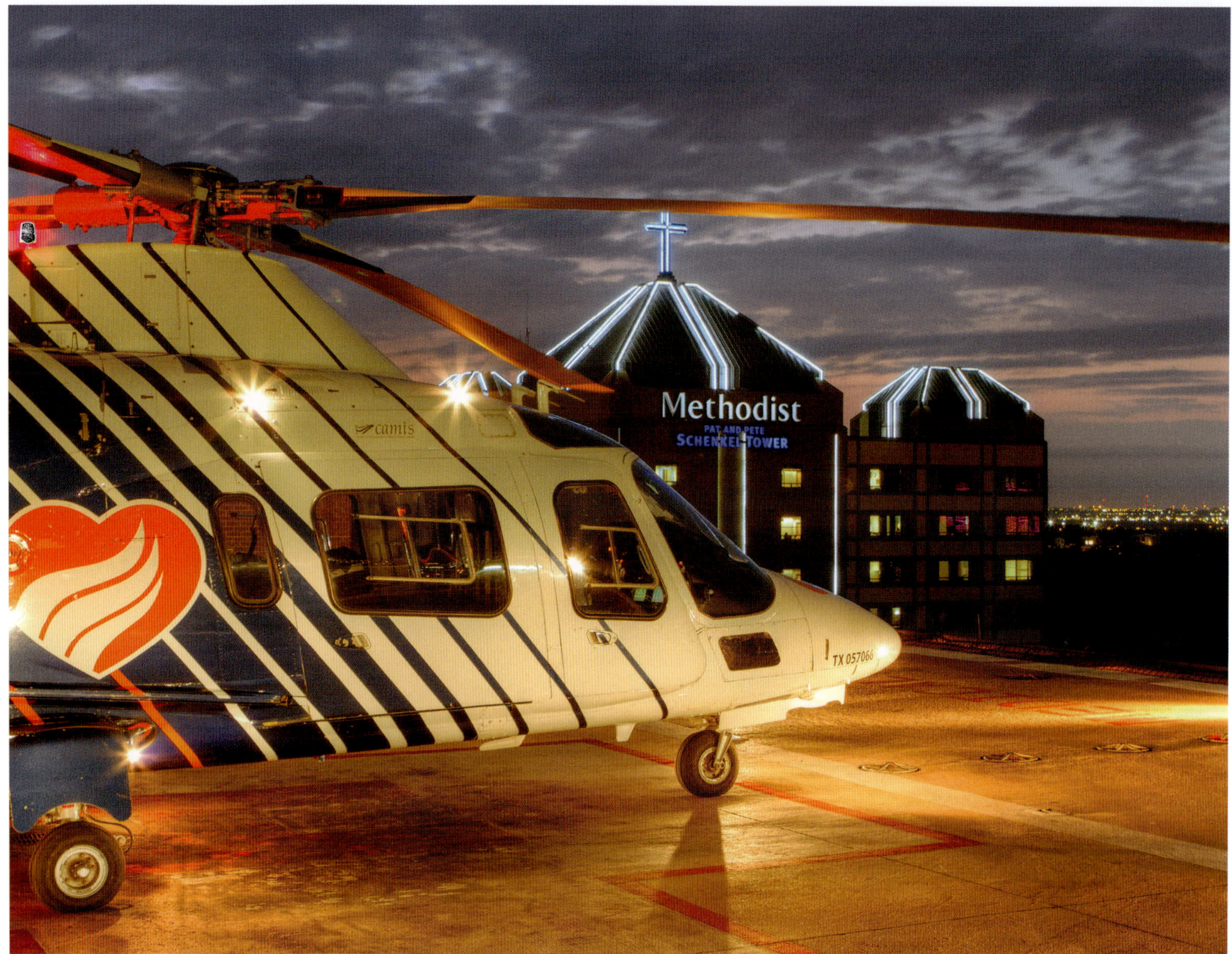

Above
Methodist Hospital, founded in 1927, provides quality care to residents of Oak Cliff and other communities west of the Trinity River.

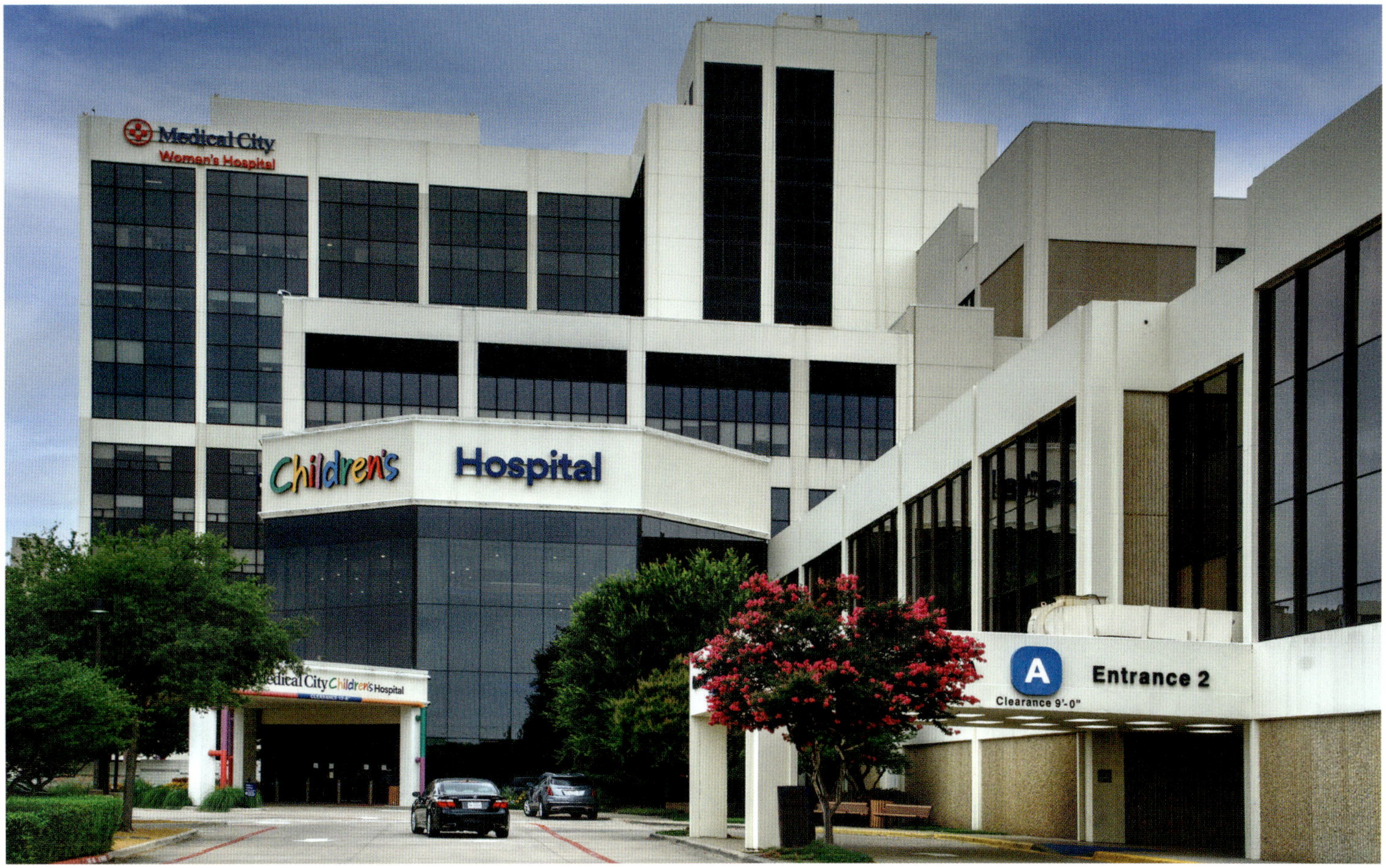

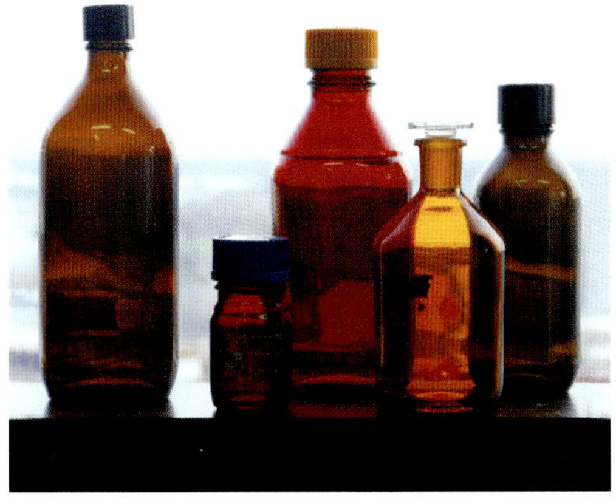

Above
Medical City Dallas is an award-winning hospital located on Forest Lane. More than 1,700 physicians office and work here. Many are world-renowned experts in their fields.

Left
Five amber medicine bottles on a windowsill at UT Southwestern Medical School.

Following Pages
Presbyterian Hospital opened in 1966 and has grown into one of Dallas's major health facilities. The Fogelson Pavilion was donated by the estate of Academy Award-winning actress Greer Garson.

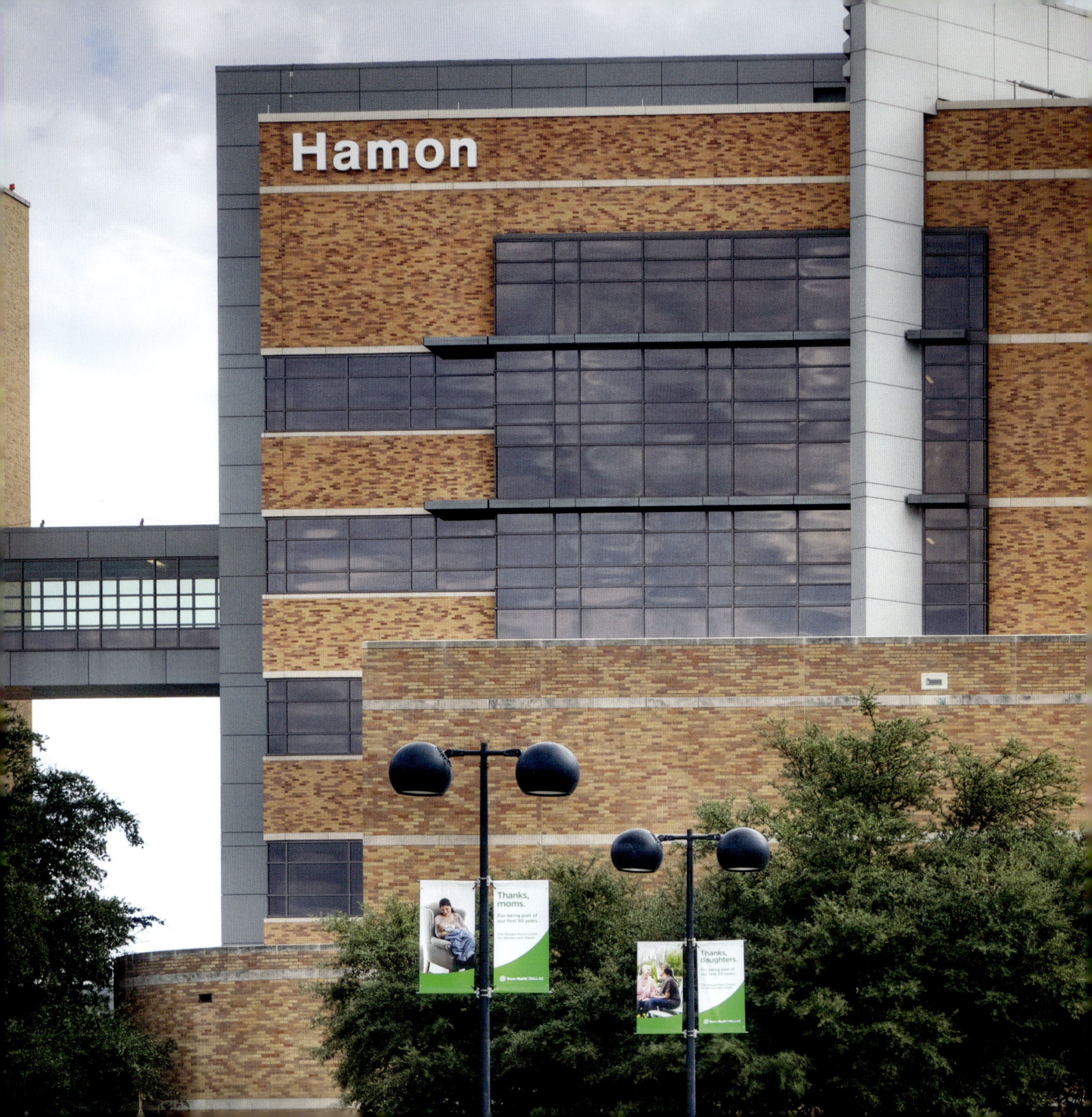
Hamon
Thanks, moms.
For being part of our first 30 years.
Thanks, daughters.

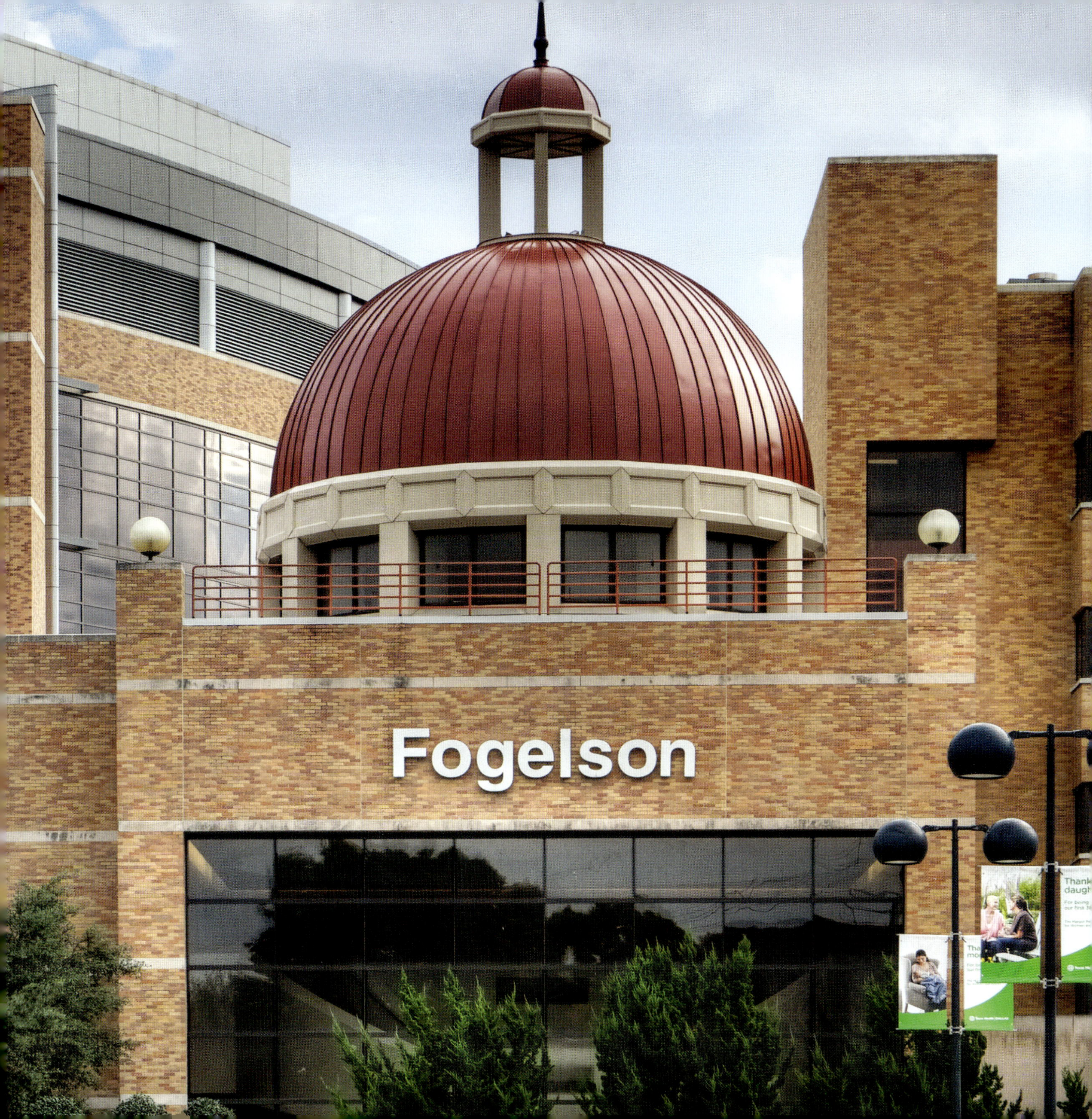
Fogelson

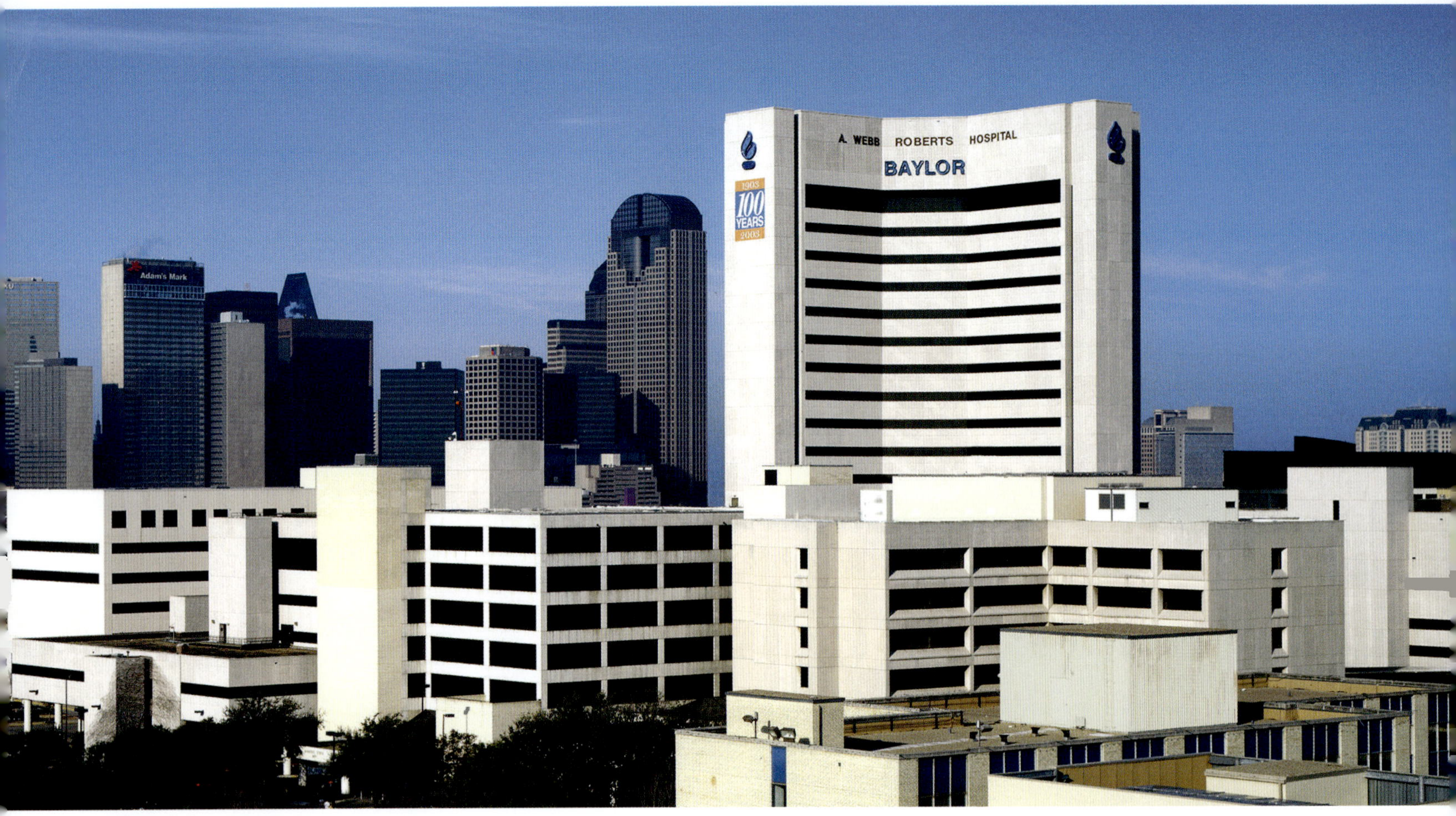

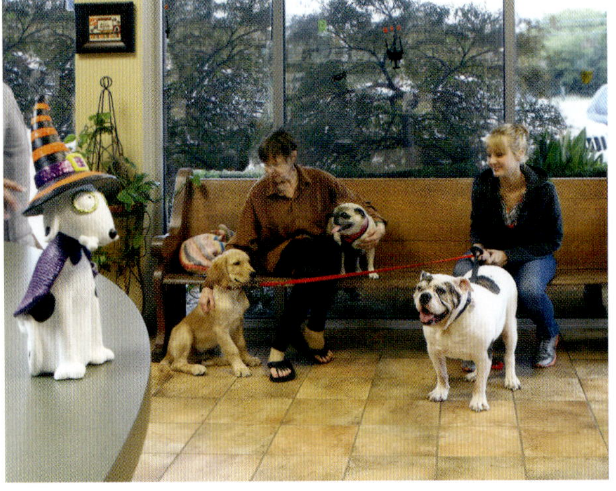

Above
Baylor Hospital, founded in 1903, is today the flagship for Baylor Scott & White Health, which includes 52 hospitals and more than 7,300 doctors.

Left
Even pets receive excellent medical treatment in Dallas. Victorian Bulldogge Gilda (foreground) is a patient at Dr. Paul Carroll's veterinary clinic.

Opposite
A colorful sign welcomes children to Texas Scottish Rite Hospital. Founded in 1921 as a hospital for children with polio, it is now known for its treatment of pediatric orthopedic conditions as well as neurological and learning disorders.

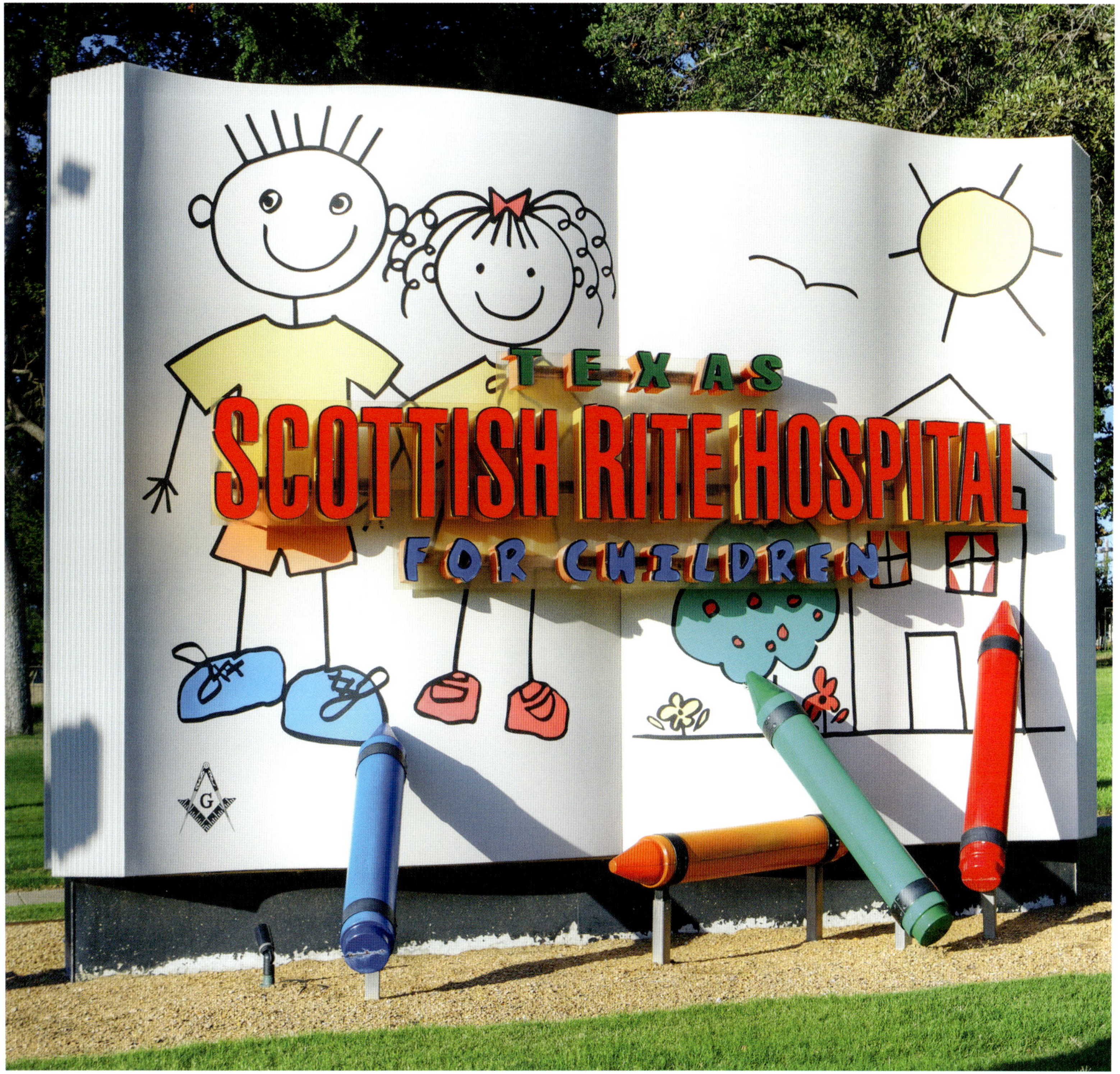
TEXAS
SCOTTISH RITE HOSPITAL
FOR CHILDREN
G

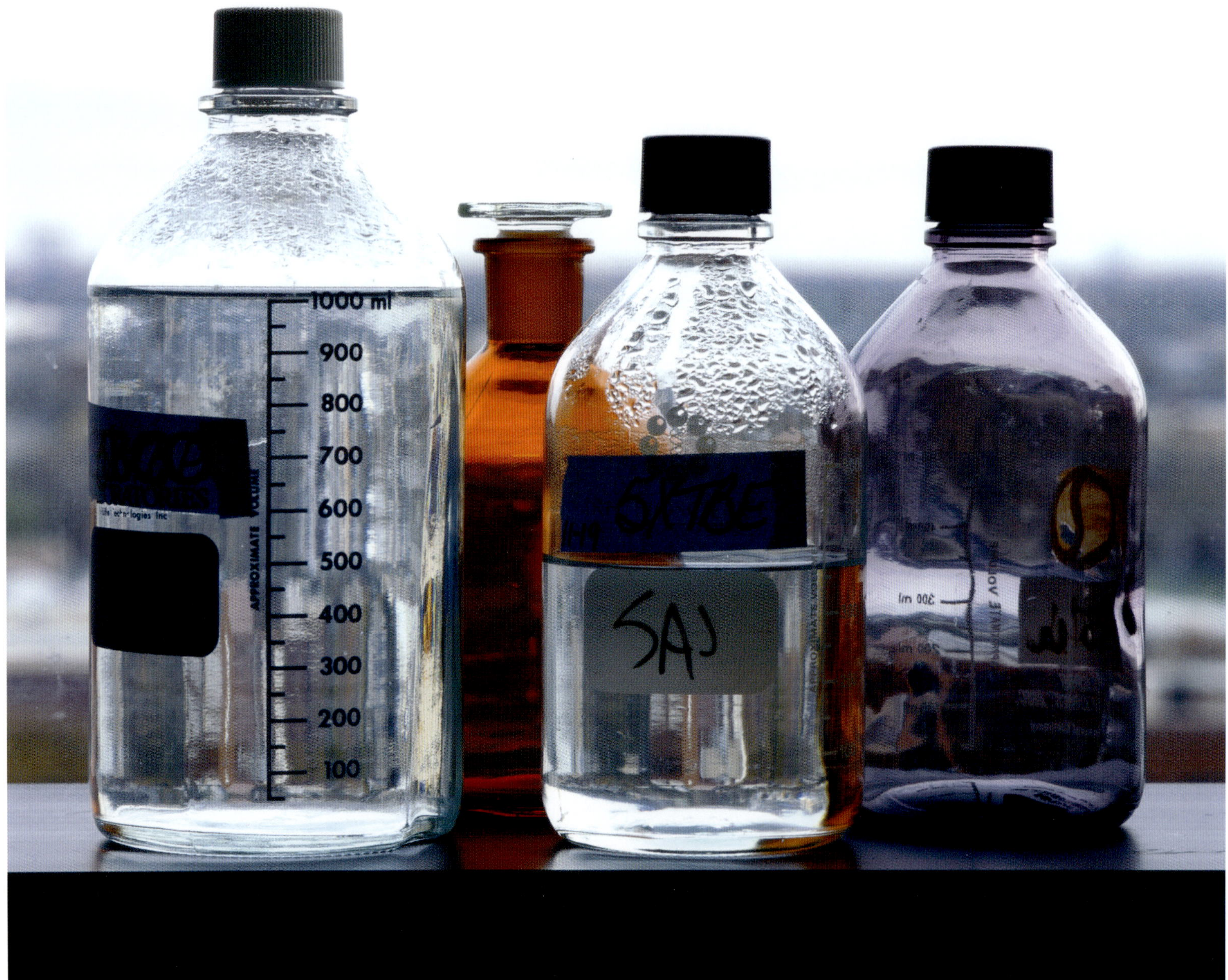
1000 ml
900
800
700
600
500
400
300
200
100
APPROXIMATE VOLUME
SAJ

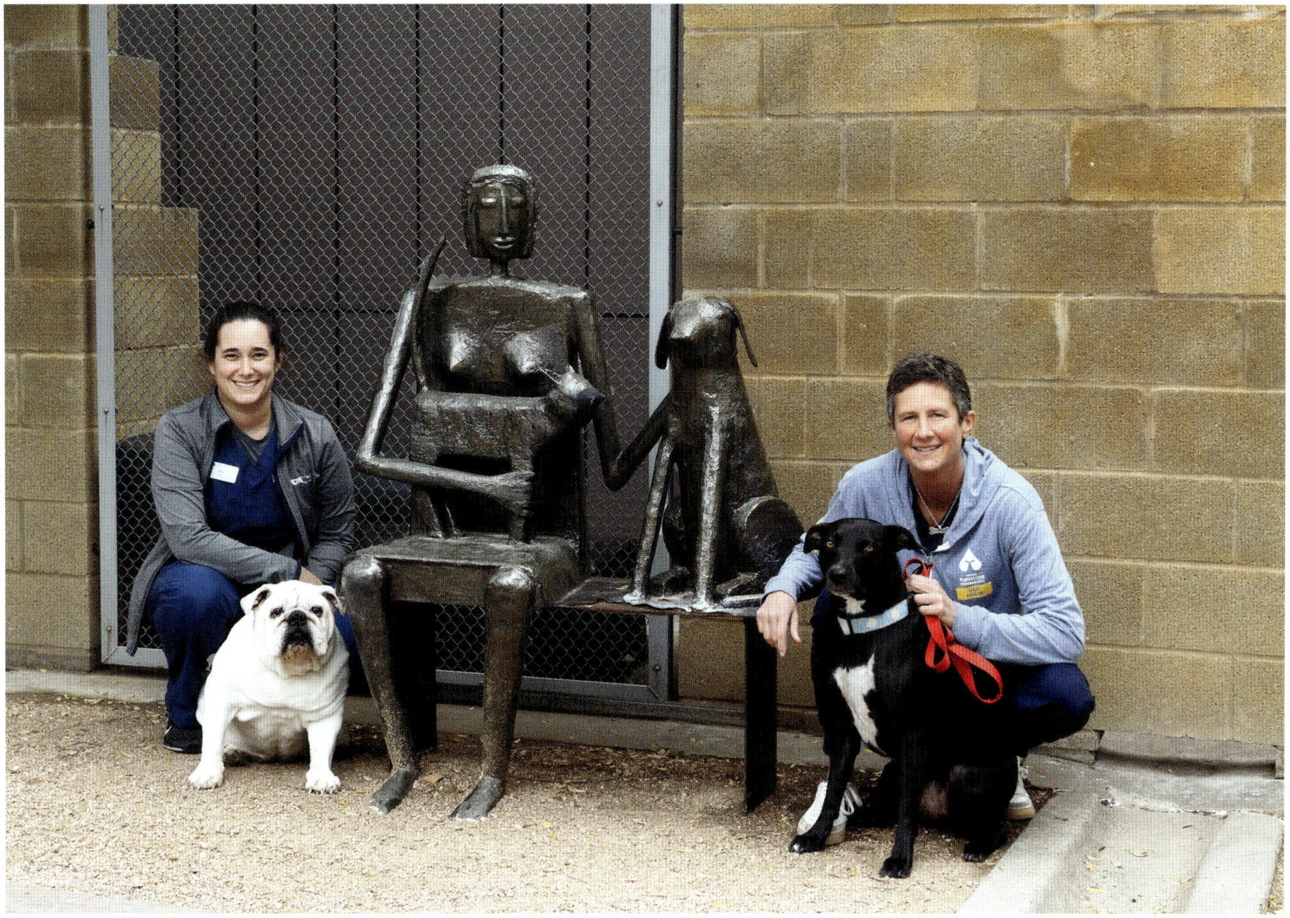

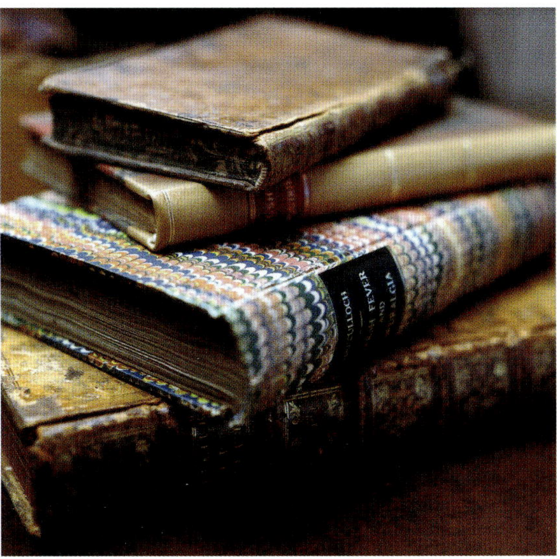

Above
Katy Trail Animal Hospital serves Dallas dogs, cats, and their people. Pictured on the left, Ellie Mae Bulldog and Veterinary Tech, Tais, and on the right is Hazel and Veterinarian Mandy Waller. The statue between them, *Woman and Her Dog*, is by artist Allen Wynn.

Left
Medical books from museum archives at UT Southwestern Medical School.

Opposite
Four back-lit bottles for medicine found in the lab at UT Southwestern.

Afterword

Nancy McCoy, FAIA, FAPT, is the founding principal of McCoy Collaborative Preservation Architecture. A seasoned preservation architect, she has national experience and recognition gained over thirty-five years of practice. Since 1997, she has practiced in Dallas, where her work includes landmarks such as the Caruth Homeplace, the Old Red County Courthouse, and Fair Park.

Carolyn Brown's photographs of Dallas's most cherished places are the product of Carolyn's knowledge of the world, which shapes her vision of Dallas and enables her to represent Dallas in her own way. A lifetime spent travelling and looking at architecture of all ages comes together with her love for her hometown to make something new out of what Dallasites take for granted every day—the places and spaces we live in. For example, from the years she spent photographing Egyptian monuments, she can see in Fair Park a similar order and form. Through her eyes, we can better appreciate the Hall of State as an offering, or temple, and as an object of reverence, representative of and a memorial to our collective history as Texans. Like many Egyptian funerary monuments, the Hall of State is made entirely of limestone, carved with hieroglyphic-like forms representing Texas fauna and flora, allowing the building to speak about its purpose. The hypostyle hall or colonnade that defines the front of the building and the geometric decoration that is common in Art Deco-style architecture make further connections to Egyptian architecture, art, and design. This book provides a similar perspective on religious structures, historic preservation, schools, parks, and other subjects. Carolyn Brown's love of architecture, composition, color, and the topic allows us to see Dallas anew in this beautifully designed book, augmented by the writings of some of Dallas's most perceptive minds.

Nancy McCoy

Epilogue

Amy Lewis Hofland is the senior director of the Crow Museum of Asian Art of the University of Texas at Dallas, a museum she has led both as a museum educator and director for the past twenty-three years. With a second location planned on the campus of the university, Amy is leading the growth of the region's Asian art museum as an inclusive place to practice intercultural dialogues and compassion.

Knowing a Place

It takes time to take it all in. The photographer knows this. She plans the journey: rehearsing the site before she arrives. She grounds herself through the steps she takes toward the subject and then: the tripod. Once she does arrive, she is fully there. She finds the light electric. She feels the air on the hairs on her face. She knows she is present. And so begins a precious, time-honored process: a witnessing of place.

The camera offers a mirror to this moment: what the photographer saw is now your moment. Your opportunity to plan the journey, to take it all in and arrive fully. She invites us in to all of it: joy, sorrow, rememberings, and discoveries. Each photograph is your personal invitation to be inside of her seeing.

She might have taken over one hundred images of one composition before she finds the one she chooses. The journey to bring this place to you continues long after the light falls, the camera bags are packed and unpacked. Then, once the one is chosen, she sits with time: hours of editing and the loving process of bringing the full experience to you as fully as she possibly can. And when it's all finished, the pages are published and it sits here in your place. She knows this place; she chose fully. And she's fallen in love all over again. And she knows

She is an artist.

Amy Lewis Hofland